W9-AVQ-455

THE
INVISIBLE
EDGE

THE INVISIBLE EDGE

TAKING YOUR STRATEGY
TO THE NEXT LEVEL
USING INTELLECTUAL PROPERTY

MARK BLAXILL AND RALPH ECKARDT

PORTFOLIO

PORTFOLIO
Published by the Penguin Group
Penguin Group (USA) Inc., 375 Hudson Street, New York, New York 10014, U.S.A. • Penguin Group (Canada), 90 Eglinton Avenue East, Suite 700, Toronto, Ontario, Canada M4P 2Y3 (a division of Pearson Penguin Canada Inc.) • Penguin Books Ltd, 80 Strand, London WC2R 0RL, England • Penguin Ireland, 25 St. Stephen's Green, Dublin 2, Ireland (a division of Penguin Books Ltd) • Penguin Books Australia Ltd, 250 Camberwell Road, Camberwell, Victoria 3124, Australia (a division of Pearson Australia Group Pty Ltd) • Penguin Books India Pvt Ltd, 11 Community Centre, Panchsheel Park, New Delhi – 110 017, India • Penguin Group (NZ), 67 Apollo Drive, Rosedale, North Shore 0632, New Zealand (a division of Pearson New Zealand Ltd) • Penguin Books (South Africa) (Pty) Ltd, 24 Sturdee Avenue, Rosebank, Johannesburg 2196, South Africa

Penguin Books Ltd, Registered Offices: 80 Strand, London WC2R 0RL, England

First published in 2009 by Portfolio, a member of Penguin Group (USA) Inc.

10 9 8 7 6 5 4 3 2 1

Excerpt from "Money for Nothing," words and music by Mark Knopfler and Sting. © 1985 Straitjacket Songs Ltd. and G. M. Sumner. All rights for Straitjacket Songs Ltd. administered in the U.S. and Canada by Almo Music Corp. (ASCAP). Used by permission. Copyright © 1985 Chariscourt Ltd. and G. M. Sumner. G. M. Sumner administered by EMI Music Publishing Ltd. International copyright secured. All rights reserved.

Excerpt from "Jerry Maguire." © 1996 TriStar Pictures, Inc. All rights reserved. Courtesy of Columbia Pictures.

Excerpts from "The Matrix." Courtesy of Warner Bros., Inc. and the Wachowski Brothers. Copyright Warner Bros., Inc.

"World Is Spiky" charts used by permission of Tim Gulden.

"The Scorpion and the Frog" used by permission of Aesop's Fables Online Collection.

LIBRARY OF CONGRESS CATALOGING-IN-PUBLICATION DATA
Blaxill, Mark.
   The invisible edge : taking your strategy to the next level using intellectual property / by Mark Blaxill and Ralph Eckardt.
      p. cm.
   Includes bibliographical references and index.
   ISBN 978-1-59184-237-8
   1. Intellectual capital. 2. Intellectual property. 3. New products. 4. Strategic planning. I. Eckardt, Ralph. II. Title.
HD53.B568 2009
658.5'03—dc22   2008036661

Printed in the United States of America
Designed by Chris Welch

CONTENTS

SECTION II

COMPETITIVE STRATEGY FOR THE COMPANY OF IDEAS

SECTION III

IMPLICATIONS FOR NATIONS, MARKETS, AND STRATEGISTS

FOREWORD

The Invisible Edge is the right book at the right time. The flattening of the world, the increased competitiveness, and the growth of distributed innovation make understanding and using intellectual property a must in today's business world. To see the timeliness of this subject you need look no further than the daily debates and discussions in the current news cycles. Companies are taking sides in what is turning out to be a modern passion play around patent reform in the United States. And no other book I have read offers the depth, detail, and historical perspective on why the world needs and benefits from a properly functioning IP system.

I have known and worked with Mark and Ralph since 2002. It was Mark who finally convinced me to move over to The Boston Consulting Group (BCG) to help him and Ralph set up the worldwide IP strategy practice there. What made my decision to work with them easy was seeing their disciplined data-driven approach to business strategy up close and understanding how the world of IP could benefit from this methodology. Our years together at BCG helped all of us gain a greater perspective on how IP developed, how it drives the U.S. economy and others, and how firms can use IP strategies to create that elusive sustainable competitive edge.

Now, with this book, you can gain the IP insight that most corporations and nations are lacking. Mark and Ralph explain how an IP strategy, a golf ball, and Tiger Woods all fit into the same sentence. They explore the power of creating and utilizing advantaged innovation networks, like those that have made Toyota the powerhouse it is in automotive technology. They delve into the current debate raging on Capitol Hill that begs many questions. Does the U.S. want an innovation economy or one controlled by established market players? Are there too many patents or too few, based on the number of knowledge workers in the economy today? And the authors provide a list of must-dos for the IP strategist who wants to win by design.

The final section of the book is a must-read for all IP policy makers worldwide. If I had my way, this book would be required reading by all the members of Congress and their staffers. As in the past, the future of the wealth of nations will, in part, be determined by what IP policies they make and implement, and this book will help frame these critical public dialogues.

As I have said before, I have had and continue to have the pleasure and privilege to work with the authors of this book. I have truly enjoyed going down the IP rabbit hole with them and am impressed with their analysis and the subsequent insights it generates. I hope that you have a similar experience reading *The Invisible Edge*. My best regards and enjoy.

> Kevin G. Rivette
> August 2008
> Palo Alto, California

THE
INVISIBLE
EDGE

Follow the White Rabbit

You take the blue pill and the story ends. You wake in your bed and believe whatever you want to believe. You take the red pill and you stay in Wonderland and I show you how deep the rabbit-hole goes.

—*Morpheus to Neo*, The Matrix, 1999

I t was a Cinderella story. When Mark O'Meara sank that twenty-foot putt on the eighteenth green of Augusta National in the spring of 1998, he secured his place in golf history. His improbable putt won him the Masters, a tournament he never led until the last hole, by a single stroke. The gallery at the eighteenth was so large that O'Meara's children, Shaun and Michelle, couldn't see the final putt. But they quickly learned the result as the crowd around them erupted in cheers and a friend turned to them and screamed, "You won! You won!"

Nearby in Butler Cabin, O'Meara's close friend Tiger Woods reportedly went "ape spit with happiness" as he watched the final shot on TV. This was a victory that nearly everyone could enjoy. O'Meara is well liked on the PGA Tour, and at age forty-one, he was the oldest first-time Masters winner ever. His surprising victory put an end to a fifty-eight-championship losing streak, and he set a record for persistence by winning the tournament on his fifteenth attempt, the most appearances ever before winning the green jacket.

Prior to the 1998 Masters, O'Meara's golf career had been good, but not spectacular. After winning the U.S. Amateur in 1979, he had played through years of rank-and-file anonymity, and despite winning fourteen PGA tournaments up to that point in his career, he had never won a major. In fact, he had failed to qualify or make the cut in well over half the majors during that span. But the 1998 Masters turned out to be no fluke as, just three months later, he won a second major, the British Open, this time in a four-hole playoff over Brian Watts. (Woods missed the playoff by a stroke.) This second major trophy came a bit easier for O'Meara: it took him only fourteen tries at the British Open before he hoisted the Claret Jug.

During his magical 1998 season, O'Meara racked up two more wins, as well as a fourth place at another major, the PGA Championship. At season's end, it came as no surprise when he was named the PGA Player of the Year. In fact, O'Meara was one of only two players to interrupt Tiger Wood's run of consecutive PGA Player of the Year awards that started in 1997 and is still going (the other was Vijay Singh in 2004). Most golfers at age forty-one are beginning to wind down their PGA careers and counting the years until they become eligible to play on the Senior Circuit, but for Mark O'Meara, 1998 was far and away the best year of his career.

The fact that O'Meara's remarkable run came at the expense of Woods, one of the most dominant and recognizable athletes in sports, only highlights the improbability of his victories. The two were close friends at the time and remain so today, despite an age difference of eighteen years. And although both men are fierce competitors, it's hard to find many other similarities between this oddest of couples. With his youth and muscular physique, Woods defines the modern golfer-athlete. O'Meara on the other hand looked in 1998 like a typical forty-one-year-old father of two: he stands a shade under six feet tall, weighs in at about 200 pounds, and endorses Rogaine.

Their golf games are markedly different as well. In the late 1990s, Tiger was known primarily as a big hitter, consistently driving the ball 300 yards or more off the tee. O'Meara, on the other hand, had always been short off the tee, but he excelled in the short game, particularly with the putter. And yet, as he approached the twilight of his career, O'Meara began to consistently outplay the best golfers in the world, including Woods. How on earth did he do it?

As it turns out, Mark O'Meara had a secret weapon: his golf ball.

From the mid-1980s through the early 1990s, Mark O'Meara was a very good golfer, so good that he maintained a World Golf Ranking in the "tens and twenties" for nearly a decade. But beginning in 1993, his game began to decline. O'Meara finished the 1992 season ranked as the twelfth best golfer in the world, but for the next several years he didn't win a single tournament and increasingly fell on the wrong side of the cut line, failing to qualify for weekend play. As a result, his World Ranking dropped precipitously until 1995 when he fell out of the top 100 for the first time in his career. O'Meara was looking for an answer, and in 1996 he found it—a new kind of golf ball, one with a solid core.

For almost a century, nearly all professional golfers used wound-core golf balls. The typical wound ball had a liquid-filled center, wrapped with a thick layer of rubber bands (actually polyisoprene thread). The cover was made of a soft, non-elastic rubber called balata. The wound ball played by professionals was soft enough that it gave the golfer a good "feel" for the ball and would spin enough to hold the greens. When you see a professional golfer stop his ball on the green, or make it back up toward the hole, that's the kind of control that the "balata" ball enabled. The ability to control the golf ball played to the strengths of guys like O'Meara, but there was a trade-off—the softness of the ball, which gave it its feel, also limited its distance.

The solid-core ball was a different story entirely. First developed in the 1980s, the solid ball was designed to generate extra distance. The balls relied on a hard cover and core, which, in industry parlance, made for less "deformation" when struck at high speed. That meant that the ball retained its shape at impact, thereby ensuring that more energy was used to propel the ball farther down the fairway. Unfortunately, all this extra distance came at the cost of control. The hard solid-core balls lacked feel, and didn't spin enough to enable the control around the greens. For the light-hitting weekend player, the solid ball allowed them to impress their friends with the length of their drives. The lack of feel didn't matter much because they couldn't control the ball anyway. As a result, the solid-core ball was for amateurs only. When it came to a choice between distance and control, the professional always chose control. As the old saying in the pro golf world goes, "Drive for show, putt for dough."

In the early 1990s, Bridgestone, who had been manufacturing golf balls since 1935, began to try out some new technology that they hoped would break the compromise between distance and control. By experimenting with new high-tech materials and novel ball construction, Bridgestone was pushing the envelope of what a golf ball could do. They were looking for the "holy grail" of golf ball design—a ball that would give a golfer distance off the tee, and control around the greens.

As an early development partner, Bridgestone turned to a Zimbabwean golfer named Nick Price to see how its new solid-core ball—the Precept EV Extra Spin—would play on the PGA Tour. As it turns out, it was a match made in golfing heaven. Like O'Meara, Price was also an older golfer who, armed with a new secret weapon, found unexpected success in the twilight of his career. While

O'Meara holds the record for the most attempts before winning the Masters, Price toiled even longer before he finally won the British Open in 1994, earning the coveted Claret Jug in his sixteenth start at the age of thirty-seven. He went on to win a consecutive major, the PGA Championship, a mere month later, again playing the round with a Precept EV Extra Spin.

Despite Price's success with its two-layer, solid-core ball, or perhaps because of it, Bridgestone didn't stop to rest on its laurels. Instead, the company continued its push to redefine what a golf ball could do. And it was from those research efforts that the company developed a critical breakthrough, a multilayer design that combined a soft core, a harder intermediate layer, and a soft, yet durable cover made from a new urethane elastomer to replace the balata. This new design proved to be the winning combination—its unusual construction made it perform like two balls in one. When struck at high speed with a driver, the hard middle layer kept it from deforming and provided great distance off the tee. When struck more slowly using say, a 9 iron or sand wedge, its soft cover and core gave it the feel and control that the professional golfer craved. It was a simple yet profound invention made possible by new materials and high-tech machinery for injection molding that enabled key new innovations like the seamless cover.

Around the same time, Spalding, an afterthought in the U.S. golf world who owned the Top-Flite brand, also began to invest in similar multicore technology. And it was a Top-Flite three-part, solid-core ball (fittingly called the Strata) that Mark O'Meara used to secure his two major victories. The rest of the industry, including Titleist, the 800-pound gorilla of the golf ball world, however, remained either oblivious or ignorant of the breakthrough technology that had begun to change the game of golf forever.

When Mark O'Meara began to use the solid-core ball in 1996, his ranking soared and, by the end of the year, he was ranked tenth in the world. O'Meara had found a ball that enabled him to compete with the bigger hitters on tour. While he would never be able to match their length, the new ball improved both his distance and his accuracy. By the end of 1996, O'Meara was ranked second in the world for hitting "greens in regulation," a measure of how proficiently a golfer gets from tee to green. For the next few years, O'Meara had a competitive advantage over the other players on tour, and in 1998, it all came together and translated into the most successful season of his career.

The professional golf tour, as you can imagine, is filled with intense competitors who are always looking for an edge, whether it's the latest putter or the hot new swing doctor. Price and O'Meara found a surprisingly powerful edge in the form of a high-technology ball. But the real sea change in the game happened when O'Meara introduced the new ball technology to his buddy Tiger. When Woods began to use the new three-layer solid-core ball, it propelled his already great game to an unprecedented level of dominance.

On the first of June 2000 at a Nike Golf sales meeting, Tiger Woods officially announced that he would no longer play a Titleist ball: he was switching to the brand-new Nike Tour Accuracy ball (a product that carried the iconic Nike brand, but unbeknownst to those present, was actually manufactured by Bridgestone). Two weeks later, he put the ball in play at the U.S. Open, scorching the course with a record total of twelve under par; meanwhile, not a single one of the world's other best golfers broke par. His resulting margin of victory—fifteen strokes—set a record for all major tournaments, a feat that led *Sports Illustrated* to dub this coming-out party as "the greatest performance in golf history."

But Woods didn't stop there, as he embarked on one of the most dominant streaks the sport had ever seen by winning the next three majors in a row. No one in modern golfing history has won the Grand Slam of Golf by winning the Masters, the U.S. Open, the British Open, and the PGA Championship in the same calendar year. Woods, though, became the first to win those four tournaments *consecutively*, an achievement the sports press has since dubbed the "Tiger Slam." And he did all this in dominant fashion. After his U.S. Open victory, he won the British Open at nineteen under par, the PGA at eighteen under, and the Masters at sixteen under. Despite being one of the younger golfers on the tour, based on skill he was truly a man playing among boys, in part because of the superiority of his golf balls. While Woods always had more than enough distance on his shots, he now had pinpoint accuracy in his arsenal as well.

Suddenly the golf world took notice: everyone wanted the new ball. As the Strata advertising campaign suggested, players wanted to "Switch and Lower Your Scores." The problem was that most professional golfers were unable to switch balls. You see, in professional golf, virtually every tour player signs an endorsement contract with one of the equipment makers. Under these contracts, players earn a regular stipend, but are required to play the equipment provided by their sponsor. The problem was that the largest player in the industry by far was Titleist, and they didn't have a multilayer solid-core ball to offer.

At the time, Titleist had endorsement contracts with more than 60 percent of the players on the PGA Tour. That meant that most golfers couldn't switch—even if they wanted to (and they really wanted to). In fact, there are reports that Phil Mickelson, one of the top players in the world, threatened to terminate his contract with Titleist if it didn't produce a golf ball that could compete with the new solid-core balls. They had already lost Tiger Woods to Nike. Was this the beginning of a player revolt?

Titleist obviously had a real problem on its hands. Its key competitors had developed a paradigm-changing technology, and they didn't have it. For many observers, though, it wasn't a great surprise that Titleist had been late to the game. As the industry's dominant player, they were less interested in revolutionary breakthroughs. Instead, they preferred to simply bide their time and wait for a technology to gain momentum before deploying their considerable resources behind the winning technology. Then, by supplying its large stable of professional endorsers with its balls, amateurs looking to emulate these pros would soon follow. "As a market leader it strategically waited until it had assessed whether solid-core technology was a fad or a legitimate innovation." Titleist CEO Wally Uihlein was quoted in *Golf Week* as saying, "Multi-cover technology is intriguing, no question about it. We'll be looking at it to see if it brings to the market any added value where the value previously did not exist." An arms race was on, and the industry's biggest player was losing badly before they knew that the race had even started.

And so, once it was clear that triple-layer, solid core was the horse to back, the 800-pound gorilla employed a tried-and-true industry leader strategy: Titleist stole the ball.

To be more precise, it stole the design for its own new high-tech ball: the Pro V1, which was introduced in late 2000. Just as industry titans had done for centuries, Titleist had waited for the market to show it the way and then it simply adopted (some would say pirated) the industry's "best practice." With the insights from the other solid-core balls in mind, Titleist created their own multilayer design. Unfortunately for Titleist, their designers were either unwilling or unable to avoid using the technology developed by their competitors. And in the end, this would turn out to be a costly mistake.

Within just a few months of the "Tiger Slam," the entire complexion of the game changed. Titleist introduced its new multilayer ball, which they dubbed the Pro V1. In the very first tournament that the Pro V1 was available, forty-seven professional golfers, more than half of those Titleist had under contract, switched to the new ball. "I've never seen such a swift, massive switch," said Frank Thomas, former technical director of the U.S. Golf Association. "Wound had been sacrosanct on tour for so long, and then in a matter of weeks it became hard to find a wound ball on tour." With these new balls, anyone could drive longer without giving up accuracy on the fairway or their touch and feel around the green.

Soon, average driving distances soared across the board—as did greens hit within regulation. While advances in club technology helped bring up the average driving distance by about five yards between 1997 and 2000, average drives on the tour leaped up fifteen more yards between 2000 and 2003. And as you might expect, the benefits of this golfing boom extended beyond the links, boosting the sales and profits of the innovative companies who championed these new high-tech balls. Both Bridgestone and Spalding emerged as major players in the golfing supply world, and Nike, with an assist from Bridgestone's technology and helped in no small part by the success of its celebrity endorser, Woods, saw its market share climb from nothing to some 8 percent almost overnight.

But nobody benefited more than Titleist. After deploying its unmatched marketing clout and distribution strength, it wasn't long before Titleist's new Pro V1, which sold for about $4 apiece, became the most successful ball in the history of golf. It captured nearly half the professional market within the first year, and grew from zero to 21 percent of the *entire golf ball industry* in just three years, reportedly earning the company more than $200 million a year in sales. Titleist, in fact, has sold more than $1.5 billion worth of Pro V1s since the ball's debut in 2000. With the Titleist marketing clout and distribution strength, none of the innovators could keep up. Pro V1 was a market share (not to mention profit) juggernaut. As the CEO of Acushnet (Titleist's parent company) said, "The Pro V1 saved the company." Well at least that's the way it looked at the time.

The rub for Titleist, though, was that they forgot a basic rule of competition. This battle wasn't going to be won by who owned the distribution channels or even who had the largest marketing budget. The spoils, in this case, would go to whoever owned the intellectual property, the IP, behind these newfangled golf balls. And that, of course, wasn't Titleist. Once Bridgestone and Callaway Golf (the company best known for its Big Bertha drivers, which had purchased Top-Flite out of bankruptcy in 2003) took a few balls apart and figured out what Titleist had done, they decided to play the game in a different way: they would use their intellectual property to take a bite out of Titleist's profits. Ultimately, the industry behemoth would cede its advantage to a couple of minor industry players: they would lose a game that they didn't even know they were playing.

Welcome to the world of The Invisible Edge. It might take a while for your eyes to adjust, but if you stick with us, you'll begin to see the world of business competition in a different way.

Journey into an Unseen World

In the 1999 science fiction film *The Matrix*, the protagonist, a young computer hacker named Neo, is told that the world he sees is only an illusion. He is offered a choice between two pills—one blue and one red. If he takes the blue pill, he will wake up safe at home, blissfully ignorant of the real world around him. But if he chooses the red pill, he will awaken to see a radically different world unseen by all but a select few. Nothing will ever look the same again.

We, like a growing number of business executives around the world, have experienced a similar kind of awakening. For years we pursued our careers thinking that we had a pretty good handle on how business worked. We studied economics and business at prestigious schools and went on to spend several decades in consulting applying the conventional lessons about economics, general management, business competition, and competitive advantage. But over time, we felt increasingly unsatisfied. Neo's mentor, Morpheus, described this feeling as "the splinter in your mind," that unsettling sensation that the prevailing theories of competition didn't explain enough of what we were seeing in the real world.

Looking back, both of us can remember glimmers of insight along the way. But like most executives, we chose to set these fleeting thoughts aside and get on with the business of the day. Eventually however, the discomfort became too difficult to ignore—we took the red pill, and decided to commit ourselves to learning more. Once we made that choice, we discovered a whole new world of business that we had never seen and, even more valuable, we found a new way of seeing the old world we thought we knew.

In a way, this book is a kind of "red pill" for you, an invitation to go on a journey with us—a guided tour of the modern, global, innovation economy seen in a new way. Our only requirement for the tour is that you agree to put on a new lens and divert your attention for a while, at least, from the things you have been taught to notice and let us help you to see more clearly the things you have been trained to ignore. We're pretty sure you'll enjoy the ride.

Before we begin however, let us tell you a bit about our own journey. We both received MBAs from leading business schools (Harvard and MIT) and then found our way to one of the world's top strategy consulting firms, The Boston Consulting Group (BCG). Over more than four decades of combined professional-services work, we served dozens of clients around the world, in numerous industries, and at every step in the value chain. As strategists, it was our job to help our clients find an edge—to achieve "sustainable competitive advantage" in the terms of the consulting trade. Along with our many colleagues, we did good work and delivered real value for our clients. We helped them operate efficiently, drive out costs, and improve their market share, and in many cases, they increased profits and raised their stock prices. But despite our best efforts and a lot of hard work, we rarely (if ever) showed them how to gain a truly *sustainable* edge.

We know we're not alone. Indeed it seems to us that the vast majority of corporate initiatives designed to improve competitiveness are really designed to implement "best practices." In other words, senior management in most companies works extremely hard just to *maintain* their position. Most of this work has become "table stakes"—the minimum requirement for entry into a globally competitive marketplace. You don't implement these best practices to gain advantage—you do it to survive. It's no wonder so many executives burn out.

Worse, we felt a greater sense of discomfort that grew beyond our frustration over this seemingly endless treadmill. When we looked not just within but *across* the industries that we knew, we were always puzzled to observe that the best-run companies (often those who pursued these improvement initiatives most effectively) were rarely the most profitable. Sometimes, the opposite was true.

Time and again, we have had the opportunity to work with industrial companies that are incredibly well run, where the management team is smart and hardworking, and where the company is as efficient and effective as any we have ever seen. And yet, despite all their efforts, they are barely able to eke out enough profit to cover their cost of capital on a consistent basis. On the other hand, we've also worked in industries like pharmaceuticals that are filled with companies where money flows like a river, as evidenced by the manicured campuses, marble entryways, and fine-art decorations that surround the executive suite. The luxurious Las Vegas sales meetings featuring concerts by A-list rock stars that are standard fare for these pharmaceutical companies would embarrass (and likely end the career of) the CEOs of our industrial clients. Some companies show an incredible lack of discipline, and yet they seem to have the ability to print money.

This was the splinter in our minds—the unexplained wrinkle in the fabric of business. Working harder and smarter didn't necessarily lead to advantage; and diligently following all of the conventional management theories didn't provide a competitive edge either. If the truth were told, we suspect that most senior managers would admit privately that they have given up the search for competitive advantage. Rather, they expend their energy on things they know how to do: operational efficiency, cost cutting, and ruthless execution.

Then, starting in 1999, we were given a unique opportunity. That's when BCG's CEO asked one of us to lead the firm's Strategy Practice Initiative (SPI) and, in his words, "draw from our client practice but . . . view it through a different lens . . . to strike off in bold directions we might not otherwise pursue, and to produce a unique sort of integration and innovative thinking." Looking back, this was a critical turning point for us both, because it gave us the luxury of reflection. In our many years of client service, the thing we lacked most was the opportunity to step back—time to think deeply and analyze what was happening in our business and the businesses of our clients.

On the theory that new strategic insights would emerge in novel situations, we started down the path of investigating never-before-seen competitive situations: developments like the open-source software movement, the genomics revolution, mobile commerce, abundant bandwidth, and cutting-edge social networks (the precursors to Web 2.0) among others. With our teams, we had the rare opportunity to dive deep and think hard. From these investigations, a common thread emerged—every one of these novel managerial situations contained some kind of intellectual property (IP) issue. Whether it was the patenting of genes, competing technology standards, software patents, or the General Public License, each situation we investigated was strongly influenced by important IP issues.

So in short order, we decided to focus on IP itself and commissioned an effort to understand its strategic and managerial implications. That's when we came across the work of Kevin Rivette. In his influential book *Rembrandts in the Attic*, Kevin described the strange new world of IP, one that most business executives, including us, had mostly ignored. But rather than treating IP as a technical or legal issue, Kevin talked about it from a business perspective. He described how companies' decisions about IP determined whether they would win or lose, and he even claimed that IP was a "key source of . . . competitive advantage."

In hindsight it seems obvious—intellectual property is the indispensable but unheralded key to understanding businesses, markets, and economies in the modern era. Through extended conversations with Kevin (who we later recruited to BCG) and our own exploration, we came to believe that IP is rapidly becoming the central foundation of businesses and markets, the most precious resource in the world, and the most important source of newly minted wealth.

Once we adjusted our lens to account for IP, deals that once made no sense suddenly appeared logical. We found that we could now explain some of these old mysteries, like why so many well-run companies fail to generate profits while others, less well run, succeed despite themselves. The insight we came upon was both simple and profound—the key to competitive advantage is to *own* the distinctive parts of your business that create value. And the only way to truly *own* your distinction is through intellectual property.

As we dug deeper, we discovered that IP plays the central role in both the creation and apportionment of value. With the right IP, companies can command premium prices, increase market share, sustain lower costs, and even generate income directly. Without it, their products (and services) lack differentiation, and they can only compete on price. Businesses that have no IP are, by definition, "commodity" businesses that, no matter how well run, lack any sustainable edge, and are destined to limp along on razor-thin margins, subject to the vagaries of supply and demand.

As we began to apply these lessons with our clients, we learned another very important lesson—IP is invisible. And just as we once were, most managers are unable see how IP impacts their business. It's not their fault really—they can't see because they've been trained not to see.

The theories of "defunct economists" and the business school nostrums that enslave our thinking were developed to describe a world whose relevance is fast disappearing. Those of us who have been trained at the elite business schools and apprenticed in leading companies have been fitted with a lens of conventional wisdom through which we see the world. This conventional lens focuses our attention on some aspects of the world, but makes it nearly impossible to see others; it fixes our eyes on labor and capital—on tangible inputs like natural resources, equipment, and factories. But the importance of these so-called real assets in the modern economy is declining. Our world is primarily a world of information and innovation, not of industry and manufacturing. Intangible assets, the most important in the modern economy, are essentially invisible—they don't show up on corporate balance sheets and economists don't include them in the national accounts. Until very recently, in fact, economists and accountants didn't even have the tools to measure the most important inputs into the world economy, or the most valuable outputs that a business produces.

As a result, most managers have abdicated responsibility for the management of their company's most important assets. Since they haven't been trained to see or manage IP, they generally defer to the lawyers and technologists to take care of it. That's not right. Senior managers need to take charge of the situation, but how can they do it without jumping headfirst into problems they aren't competent to manage? Truth be told, most of them lack the knowledge and tools to effectively manage this source of invisible advantage.

As practicing strategists, we saw an opportunity here to help bridge the gap between IP and strategy. We also realized that we would need to develop new tools, methodologies, and frameworks to make it more practical for senior executives to manage IP. Working alongside Kevin, who pioneered the field of patent data analysis and visualization and who served as our earliest guide, we began experimenting with tools that we hoped would help us (and our clients) visualize this new world we had entered.

We knew that we needed to develop new ways to help managers make sense of all of the new information we discovered. That's when our most important eureka moment occurred. We knew from Kevin's work that the information embedded in patents makes it possible to define new competitive landscapes. This treasure trove of public data contains largely untapped information about companies, technologies, inventors, and investments. We realized that the relationships between patents (citations, semantic relationships, coassignments, etc.) define the networks that drive the modern economy. With some hard work we thought we might be able to find new ways to map them—and we did, turning that idea into an invention, a visualization engine of our own (patent pending of course). By mapping the links between technologies, their owners, and their inventors, we devised a new set of tools to guide managers in their formulation of IP strategy. The end result is that, like Neo, we can now see what was previously invisible.

Armed with these new insights and new tools, the product of a decade-long investigation, we're prepared to take you on a guided tour of what we've found. We'll show you some of the things we've seen in new ways, and together we can see how far this rabbit hole goes.

Fitting You with a New Lens

While we can't help but acknowledge that there is a hot debate over IP—namely whether the rights of IP owners should be maintained or weakened—our book isn't intended as a rebuttal to IP's detractors. Rather, given the system of intellectual property rights that exists around the world today, our goal is to give business executives some insight into how to use IP to gain a strategic edge on their competitors. What we ask of you, the reader, is to take the red pill along with us; let us show you this wonderfully complex world that you might not know even existed. And to do that, we should define our terms.

That said, we're business guys, not attorneys. And as a matter of principle, we try to avoid using abstract legal language whenever we can. That means we're not going to waste your time with long-winded definitions of what a patent is or what the legal precedent behind trademark enforcement might be. There are plenty of other sources we can recommend that tackle the legal details of IP in great detail.

For our purposes, we want to make it clear that intellectual property is just that: property, albeit property that you can't necessarily hold or touch. The thing to remember about IP is that it celebrates creativity and inventiveness, whether that's expressed by penning the great American novel or by gluing together the world's first integrated circuit. Without a property right attached to it, the design for, say, a new portable music player couldn't be controlled by its inventor, regardless of the time or expense they invested in that design. Anyone who wanted to could come along and copy it. As you can imagine, very few people would invest in complex innovation projects (think books, movies, art, software, a drug, a new cell phone, etc.) if others could simply copy the idea at will. To solve this problem, governments grant property rights in creative works, and together these rights are known as intellectual property rights.

Although they're all considered intellectual property, different kinds of rights protect different kinds of creative work. Here's a quick listing of the most important invisible assets that make up the world of IP:

- Trade secrets. The sort of thing you used to keep in the corporate safe. It's property in the sense that stealing it is a felony. But if your competitor figures out your secrets on their own, you'll lose any advantage you might have held.
- Trademarks. People talk about brands as if they're a kind of magical thing. And certainly there is a lot that goes into building a brand. But the only bit of hard property that defines a brand is a trademark. And as long as you pay your registration fees, it's an asset you can own forever.
- Copyrights. Copyright protects the written output of artists and authors and, as a result, has been the lifeblood of the creative arts for a long time. Recently, the definition of authorship has been expanded to include other creative works like software code, sound recordings, and architectural designs. The term of these rights has been getting lengthened, and now extends as long as a century for some categories of expression.
- Patents for invention. This last form of IP provides an alternative to the corporate safe. In order to encourage openness and progress in technology, some governments long ago made the leap to grant inventors of new technologies

the exclusive right to practice their inventions, as long as their insights were useful, novel, and not obvious. Unlike some of the other IP rights, patents aren't forever. In general their life is limited to twenty years from the date that you apply for the patent.

That's enough to get us started—we'll give you more detail as we go along.

The Road Ahead

Before we begin, here's a quick preview of the road ahead. The first section of the book includes four chapters in which we lay the foundations for thinking about IP. We describe how IP drives economic growth, how it is linked to corporate profits, and how it is becoming the core around which the modern corporation is built, and we introduce a new tool to help us see the invisible world of IP.

In the opening chapter, we offer some big-picture perspective in arguing that intellectual property, and the innovation that leads to its creation, have become the most profoundly important and valuable engines of value and wealth across the globe today. Building on the economic and historical perspectives offered in the first chapter, chapter 2 takes a deeper look at how IP is rapidly becoming the most important source of businesses' sustainable competitive advantage. We find that companies with the strongest IP position, like those in the semiconductor, software, or pharmaceutical industries, generate the highest economic returns. To put it another way, "innovation without protection is philanthropy."

In our third chapter, we take a look at how a few leading companies have recognized that IP is the primary source of competitive advantage and are beginning to redefine their companies to focus almost exclusively on the creation and monetization of IP. For these trailblazing companies, innovation is their core competency, and IP is their product. Their examples reveal a trend that is literally changing the definition of the modern corporation.

In chapter 4 we introduce network visualization techniques that will help you to see the previously invisible world of IP. We will show you how to apply a *zoom lens* that will enable you to assess the strength of your IP portfolios within a broad industry context. Such a lens enables business strategists to examine the nodes, links, and clusters of IP networks and to evaluate the strengths and vulnerabilities of each company's IP position. It also allows you to zoom up and down to different levels of analysis, from networks of companies to specific technology domains to inventor teams and ultimately to individual IP assets.

The second section of our book is about corporate strategy. In the three chapters of this section, we describe the three fundamental strategies for competing in the unseen economy: Control, Collaborate, and Simplify.

In the fifth chapter, we tackle the strategy of *Control* and explore two methods for achieving it: exclusion and centrality. In the era of Thomas Edison and Alexander Graham Bell, it was common for companies to own all of the IP they needed to deliver their end products and services and exclude others. Some still do.

We then take the discussion to the next level and discuss strategies involving *Collaboration*. Chapter 6 explores the IP collaboration models pioneered by companies like Toyota and examines their underpinnings—in business systems designed to maximize value creation and effectively distribute benefits among collaboration partners, all while aligning interests and minimizing conflicts.

Collaborative networks, however, are no panacea: they tend to be complex in ways that raise costs and magnify risks. In chapter 7 we look at how companies can reduce this complexity through strategies of *Simplification*. In this chapter we show that choices about product architecture and collaborative standard setting have become the most strategic decisions that companies face. Getting them right depends on finding the right balance between exercising proprietary rights and voluntary sharing.

In the book's final section, we zoom out to see how IP is changing the face of economic competition between countries, and we zoom in to see that IP assets are becoming tradable commodities, and that an entirely new asset class is beginning to emerge.

As Chinese Premier Wen Jiabao has said on many occasions, "The competition of the future world is a competition for Intellectual Property Rights." In chapter 8 we take a look at the economic competition between nations and learn how IP plays a central role. The winners in the new global competition will be those who learn how best to create and utilize IP.

Chapter 9 focuses on the evolving markets for IP assets. As IP becomes increasingly separated from physical business assets, speculators are rushing into the marketplace and new companies are being formed to facilitate IP transactions. As these assets become increasingly tradable, we predict that great fortunes will be made by investors who are smart enough to understand their value and are able to apply them in their highest-value use.

Our final chapter presents an action agenda for businesses leaders and boards, summarizing key points made throughout the book and using a case study built around one of today's and perhaps tomorrow's hottest companies: Facebook. Using our new lens to guide us, we'll use the Facebook story to outline the next steps that you as a strategist can take regarding your own company. We'll lay out an action agenda for today's IP-based business that will help you apply these lessons to your own business as you compete in the unseen economy.

The Nineteenth Hole

Before we begin our journey together, it's worth taking a last look at how the competition over multilayer golf balls played out. You will recall that two companies, Bridgestone and Spalding (Spalding has since been acquired by Callaway), were simultaneously working to develop multilayer solid-core balls. Both companies made valuable contributions to the technology, and both ultimately needed access to the technology developed by the other. After long, sometimes contentious negotiations, the two companies agreed to cross-license their technology, and both companies have seen a dramatic increase in their market share.

Things have not gone so smoothly for Acushnet/Titleist. Although Titleist was able to use its brand (an important form of intellectual property) and its marketing clout to retain its market share, the profit picture is not as rosy. Titleist was caught with its innovation pants down and decided to use technology that it didn't own. The two innovators quickly discovered this fact and began negotiations in an attempt to get compensation for the use of their inventions. As all industry incumbents do when caught short by upstart competitors, Titleist has complained bitterly. By refusing to pay for the innovations that they used, they left the innovators no choice but to go to court to enforce their property.

The first of those cases, *Bridgestone v. Acushnet*, has settled. While both companies are tight-lipped about the settlement they reached in October 2007, two and a half years after the lawsuit began, we do know that Titleist settled with Bridgestone and agreed to pay Bridgestone a licensing fee for *every* Pro V1 or other multilayer golf ball it sells that is based on Bridgestone's technology. The settlement also included a payment for damages—essentially a catch-up payment on past royalties—which some industry pundits have pegged around $150 million. This may represent as much as 15 percent of Titleist's Pro V1 sales and a much higher percentage of its profits: a clear knockout blow by the underdog.

The settlement demonstrates the strength of Bridgestone's IP position, but it also shows how IP can level the playing field. With IP in hand, innovators are rewarded at the expense of old-style channel monopolists. Titleist erred in trying to steal away the design for the Pro V1; now it has to make Bridgestone a royalty payment for every ball it sells moving forward. In a sense, every time Titleist puts a sleeve of golf balls in one box to ship to a customer, it puts a few dollars in another box to send to Bridgestone. Interestingly, Callaway, in its lawsuit, has requested an injunction to stop Titleist from selling the Pro V1 ball at all. At the time our book went to press, this issue had yet to be resolved. The more likely outcome is that Titleist will reach a settlement with Callaway and will end up paying two technology partners whenever they sell a ball. If they end up reaching a settlement similar to the one they signed with Bridgestone, Titleist could be paying nearly a third of its sales to its technology suppliers.

The competition between Titleist and Bridgestone is a classic example of companies competing with two different forms of IP. Titleist owns a powerful brand that it has built up through marketing and multimillion-dollar endorsement contracts with professional golfers. Bridgestone, on the other hand, is not widely known as a sports or golf equipment company (one of its strategies was to forge a partnership with Nike to combine Bridgestone's patents with Nike's trademarks), but it has technology expertise in specialized materials that can make a world of difference in how golf balls perform. As a practical matter, these two companies have also become partners. Titleist uses its brand to sell Bridgestone's technology, and the proceeds are split between the two based on the value of their contributions. The element at the center of this competition is, of course, IP.

In the end, everyone wins: Titleist retains its position as market leader, Bridgestone is rewarded for its innovation, and golfers, everyone from weekend hackers to Tiger Woods, benefit from a high-technology breakthrough. The story also gives us our first window into the future of competition. In the game of golf today, every PGA professional is looking for an edge that will allow them to compete with Tiger Woods. In the competitive game of business, the advantage goes to companies who know how to compete using intellectual property. Join us as we show you how you can gain the invisible edge.

DISCOVERING THE UNSEEN ECONOMY

CHAPTER 1

Fueling the Fire

HOW INVISIBLE INVESTMENTS DRIVE ECONOMIC GROWTH

> We are like dwarfs sitting on the shoulders of giants. We see more, and
> things that are more distant, than they did, not because our sight is
> superior or because we are taller than they, but because they raise us
> up, and by their great stature add to ours.
>
> —*Bernard of Chartres, 1130 BCE**

O
ne of the greatest inventions in the history of the world almost didn't happen because the inventor was preoccupied with other matters.

In the summer of 1773, James Watt wasn't working on the project that
would later make him famous when some devastating news reached him.
Instead, he had been far away from his home and workshop, camped out in the
Scottish Highlands for months working as a surveyor. He was employed on one
of the great engineering projects of the day, the Caledonian Canal, and his job
was to lay out the canal's ideal path, in a course that ran along one of the world's
great geological faults, the Great Glen of Scotland—through the stomping
grounds of the Loch Ness monster—by connecting a series of natural waterways
with thirty miles of canals. Even before the news of his personal tragedy arrived
in a letter, Watt was already miserable, in part due to the weather in northern
Scotland where, even in the summer, the temperature never gets much above

*Quoted by John of Salisbury in *Metalogicon*, 1159; translation from Latin provided by Dr. Joseph
N. Yoon at Aerospaceweb.org. For original Latin text from *Metalogicon*, see also Robert K. Merton, *On
the Shoulders of Giants: A Shandean Postscript, the Post-Italianate Edition* (Chicago: University of Chicago Press, 1991), 40.

sixty degrees and gale-force winds are common. Struggling to stay dry and to retain basic amenities, he wrote to a friend that "an incessant rain kept me for three days as wet as water could make me. I could scarcely preserve my journal book."

That's when things took a decided turn for the worse: Watt's wife, Margaret, was dead. When Watt left his family to survey the Caledonian Canal, Margaret had been expecting their third child. And now the letter he held in his shivering hands informed him that neither his wife nor their expected baby had survived the birth.

As he held the letter, he was overcome with grief and guilt. He had left Margaret three months earlier for the relative stability of a surveying job. He had been forced to take up the job to support his growing family and to pay off fifteen years' worth of debts he had accumulated while pursuing his real passion.

Watt's dream? To build a steam engine unlike any the world had ever seen.

While he had made considerable progress in his pursuit (he had managed to cobble together a working, though flawed, prototype), it had come at a steep price. Not only had he accumulated debts that, in today's dollars, exceeded $2 million, his ongoing work had also contributed to the financial collapse of his friend and investor, John Roebuck. It was because Roebuck was forced into bankruptcy, in fact, that Watt had been forced to abandon his workshop to take on a steady job that would allow him to provide for his family. Now, at thirty-seven, alone but with two motherless children to support, he must have been tempted to give up his dream once and for all. And he very well might have, putting off the dawn of the Industrial Revolution for another generation or more, if not for a single piece of paper: his patent.

> *Of all things in life, nothing is more foolish than inventing.*
> —James Watt

Inventions, especially extraordinary breakthroughs like the steam engine, don't just appear out of thin air, of course: they result from mixing one part inspiration with many more parts of sweat and sacrifice. Inventions, though, are not created equal—those precious few that transform civilizations can, in fact, require more than their fair share of sacrifice to bring them to fruition. What often separates an inventor's success from failure in such endeavors is simply an incentive to keep pushing forward. And so it was for the steam engine's creator, James Watt.

Born in 1736 in the seaport town of Greenock, Scotland, Watt proved to be a curious tinkerer from an early age. The grandson of a mathematics teacher and the son of a shipwright and instrument maker, he had shown an early aptitude for tweaking and enhancing devices and machinery. He had also long been fascinated by steam: as a boy, he once drew the ire of an aunt who scolded him for playing with the hot vapor rising from her teapot. In 1758, Watt left Scotland for London to pursue an apprenticeship as an instrument maker. When he realized that his skills surpassed many of his peers, however, the young Watt proved he was as impertinent as he was intelligent.

Unwilling to wait the seven years required by the London Clockmaker's Guild, Watt returned to Scotland a year later intent on starting his own business. When he found his path blocked yet again, this time by the Glasgow Guild of Hammermen, Watt accepted an offer from a group of professors at the University of Glasgow to set up a small shop within the university.

It was in his university shop that the now twenty-three-year-old Watt, with encouragement from his friend, a professor named John Robison, began dabbling with steam power. The idea of using superheated water as a power source was an ancient one. Steam engines were first conceived by an Egyptian named Hero who lived in Alexandria around 150 BCE. But there had been few breakthroughs in the centuries since. Watt's first effort, a design for a steam-powered carriage, was also, in fact, a total failure. Nevertheless the seeds were sown. Watt soon immersed himself in learning everything he could about this troublesome technology. And, it turned out, the university could provide a rather unique lab rat of sorts for Watt to continue his studies on: a working model of a Newcomen steam engine.

Named after its builder, the blacksmith Thomas Newcomen (1664–1729), and based on a concept developed in 1698 by Thomas Savery (1650–1715), who called his patented design "The Miner's Friend," the Newcomen engine was among the first steam mechanisms ever built since Hero's time and was used early in the eighteenth century to solve one of the most basic, and critical, coal-mining problems: pumping out underground water. Early coal miners in England relied on "bell pits" to follow seams of coal deep underground. The deeper the miners dug, the more the mines filled up with water. For centuries, miners had tried everything from horse-powered pumps to small armies of children armed with buckets in failed efforts to keep tunnels dry.

It wasn't until 1712 that Savery and Newcomen's partnership delivered the world's first big breakthrough in deep-mine plumbing. By Watt's time, dozens of Newcomen engines were chugging away all over Great Britain. The machine itself, however, was completely unreliable. Not only did it constantly break down, it required prohibitive amounts of fuel to keep it running. The machines consumed so much coal, in fact, that miners often struggled to extract enough of the ore to make their whole operation profitable. Newcomen's steam engine had been around for a half century, and despite the best efforts of Savery and Newcomen and others, its performance remained virtually unimproved. But then James Watt took up the problem.

Watt went looking for the university's Newcomen, and learned that, unsurprisingly, the engine was broken and had been sent away to London for repair. (It took two years before the engine made its way back to Glasgow.) Meanwhile, Watt fell into the company of some of the university's leading scientists, including Dr. Joseph Black, a chemistry professor who quickly became Watt's friend and mentor. Black was a pioneer in the science of steam and encouraged Watt to undertake a lengthy and systematic investigation of the Newcomen's design, analyzing its strengths, its weaknesses, and most important, its energy efficiency. Working on his own time, and financing his experiments himself (the Newcomen was, if nothing else, a prodigious consumer of coal), Watt taught himself a great deal about the mechanics of using steam for power. And along the way, he made an important discovery: he learned why the Newcomen engine design consumed so much fuel.

When steam is condensed into water it creates an enormous reduction in volume, called a "phase shift," that can be exploited mechanically. While this principle of thermodynamics had been known for centuries, a practical steam engine was first described by Savery in his patent filing of 1698, something Newcomen built upon with his own invention. The Newcomen engine was a single-piston design. The operator first filled up a cylinder with steam, and then injected cold water into the cylinder to condense the steam into water, thereby creating a vacuum in the cylinder. The pressure in the outside atmosphere would depress the piston, and the resulting mechanical action powered a pump.

Savery and Newcomen, however, had left a major part of the problem unsolved. In their design, the cooling and refilling cycles all took place in one cylinder, resulting in huge amounts of energy wasted when the cylinder was reheated. By Watt's calculations, this energy loss amounted to something like 80 percent of the total energy consumed in operating the Newcomen. In other words, if he could figure out a way to keep the cylinder perpetually heated, he could improve the machine's efficiency by a factor of four.

Why had no one ever figured this out before? Watt's insight that so much steam energy was wasted came from his discovery of the phase shift involving energy storage when steam converts to water. Because steam stores six times more energy per pound than boiling water, large amounts of energy loss (or *latent heat*) can be concealed in the loss of relatively small volumes of water. Before Watt, no one appreciated how much heat energy was lost as hot water leaked out of a Newcomen engine. (The principle of latent heat was a scientific discovery of major importance during the time that was credited to Watt's mentor Professor Black, yet it appears that Watt himself may have discovered it independently, although a few years later.) The real losses were six times higher than the energy in the hot water that trickled out of the engine. Watt realized that he could eliminate this waste of latent heat by reducing the loss of steam in a cold cylinder. As he later wrote in his patent filing, "To make a perfect steam engine, it was necessary that the cylinder should be always as hot as the steam which entered it."

But how could he keep the cylinder hot and still condense the steam to produce the necessary vacuum? Watt had been pondering this question for a while. As he was strolling through the Glasgow green one Sunday afternoon in May 1765, the solution hit him all at once. In one of the most famous eureka moments in human history, Watt theorized that what he needed was another component, a separate condenser, that he could cool separately from the cylinder used to generate the steam. "As steam was an elastic body, it would rush into a vacuum, and if a communication were made between the cylinder and an exhausted vessel it [the steam] would rush into it [the vessel], and might there be condensed without cooling the cylinder."

It had taken Watt four years to reach his breakthrough, and as he threw himself into developing a prototype of his separate condenser, he found himself desperately short of cash. Not only did building the prototype promise to be an expensive endeavor, he now had a wife, Margaret (they had been married the year before), to care for and support. To try and make ends meet, he shelved his work on the engine to take on the first of many surveying assignments. Two years later, however, Watt, hounded by his debtors, turned to Black for help. Black took the opportunity to introduce Watt to John Roebuck, a wealthy ironworks owner and mine operator. Roebuck, it turned out, was having quite a few problems with his Newcomen, and when he heard about Watt's breakthrough he was intrigued. He quickly struck a deal with Watt that was, perhaps, the first of its kind anywhere in the world.

The deal was this: in return for both paying off Watt's personal debts and funding the development of a test engine using a separate condenser, Roebuck would receive two-thirds of the value of Watt's patent in return.

While patents had existed in England since 1624, they were still far from common. Savery's 1698 patent, for example, was No. 356. By 1767, as Watts and

Roebuck struck their deal, fewer than 900 patents had been granted since Parliament passed the Statute of Monopolies, which established the limited monopoly power of patents 143 years earlier. As such, there were few, if any, established precedents for the enforcement of these early patents. But things were changing fast. A number of encouraging legal developments had taken place prior to Watt's application for a patent; specifically, jurisdiction over patent law had shifted from the King's Privy Council to the common law courts, a move that made business decisions more predictable by shifting the defense of patents away from the whims of royalty. It was on the foundation of this new modern system that Watt and Roebuck built their partnership. And about two years later in January 1769, Watt's patent—No. 913—was finally granted.

Just as Watt began to build up a new head of steam, however, things began to fall apart again. In particular, the flagship project of his partnership with Roebuck, a new, "working scale" engine for one of Roebuck's mines in central Scotland at Kinneil, was proving difficult to keep operational as the engine continued to flunk every major trial run. And while there were many problems to solve, one issue in particular, the internal surface of the main cylinder, proved most nettlesome. Roebuck couldn't find a supplier who could cast such a large cylinder with the internal integrity and smoothness that Watt's design required.

Then in 1773, after four years of work, the partnership between Watt and Roebuck hit its final roadblock: without a working engine, Roebuck's mining operations, which had been struggling with losses for some time, were quite literally drowning in both water and red ink. Roebuck could simply no longer afford to fund Watt's work. Watt, for his part, turned to Black, his mentor, for a loan to cover his patent registration fees while he fell back on surveying, yet again, for the means to support his growing family. Turning his back on Roebuck, and shelving the work on his engine, wounded Watt deeply. "My heart bleeds for his situation, and I can do nothing to help him," he would write. "I stuck by him until I have much hurt myself; I can do so no longer; my family calls for my care to provide for them."

And so Watt, seated atop a dark and damp mountaintop a few months later, letter in hand, faced his reckoning. With the collapse of his partnership and the death of his wife, it seemed certain that his dream of building a steam engine was dead as well. What more could he do but soldier on with his surveying work? Didn't he owe his children that much? Little did he know that the fate of the modern industrial world rested on his decision.

Fortunately for Watt, and even more fortunately for the rest of us, hope soon emerged in the guise of Matthew Boulton, a manufacturer from Birmingham. Boulton had first met Watt some six years prior and had kept tabs on the young inventor. Lured by the potential of Patent No. 913, Boulton stepped in with an easy remedy for Watt's quandary: Boulton bought out Roebuck's share of the patent and made further funds available so that Watt could continue his work. Watt's days as a surveyor were finally done.

Watt and Boulton were a match made in heaven. Not only did the two get along famously, but Boulton also happened to own one of the largest and most sophisticated machine shops in the world. And through his connections, he was able to locate a supplier capable of producing a cylinder that matched Watt's specifications. Solving this critical problem reinvigorated Watt and gave the project new momentum. Just a few months later, in March 1776, Watt conducted his first successful trial. It had been fifteen years since Watt took up the problem, and eleven years since his eureka moment, but his years of research, tinkering, and sacrifice were finally beginning to pay off.

Boulton also made a contribution that, in hindsight, might have been his most valuable to the cause. In 1775, a year before Watt completed the trial, Boulton recognized that more than half of Patent No. 913's fourteen-year term had passed and he had yet to sell a single engine. Boulton then successfully tapped into the political support he would need to extend the expiration date of the patent until 1800. That extra breathing room meant all the difference in enabling Boulton to build up full-scale production capacity for Watt's new and improved engine. As production ramped up over the next two decades, with Watt ever improving the "horsepower" of his engines, some 325 steam engines were driving the factories and mines around Great Britain and its colonies.

The new technology was indeed revolutionary. That was, of course, because Watt's engine was no ordinary invention. To be sure, it had delivered on its promise as a miner's friend. If nothing else, it created a demand for coal (to feed the hungry engines) that would grow beyond anyone's wildest dreams. More important, however, steam had finally freed mankind from the restrictions of muscle, wind, and water power, the three traditional energy sources that had fueled man's work for millennia. With steam power at their command, factory owners could place their facilities closer to their customers, to the sources of their raw materials, and to their workforce in the cities—in other words, literally wherever they could realize the greatest efficiency in production. And the uses for this new power were limited only by one's imagination: engines were soon put to work around the world for grinding wheat into flour, shaping logs into lumber, pumping water to cities, and quite literally, coining money. Back in Britain, where it all began, more than a third of the earliest steam engines were used to power textile mills, which gave British cotton makers the competitive advantage they needed to build the world's premier export-driven economy—and an empire along with it.

And the benefits of steam weren't limited to just factories: it soon revolution-ized the transportation of men and materials. Between 1799 and 1808, Richard Trevithick, once an apprentice to Watt's main assistant, invented the first work-ing locomotive based on a carriage powered by the world's first high-pressure steam engine. Then in 1825, George Stephenson, who spent most of his early career operating Newcomen and Watt engines in coal mines, invented the con-cept of the railroad, using iron rails to guide steam-powered locomotives over long distances. Meanwhile, in 1802 William Symington used a Boulton and Watt engine to power a ship called the *Charlotte Dundas* on a twenty-mile voyage along one of Watt's surveying projects, the Forth and Clyde canal. A year later an Amer-ican named Robert Fulton who was traveling in Europe learned of the success of Symington's "first practical steamboat," and ordered his own Boulton and Watt engine. The breakthrough steamboat design that followed recast the commercial shipping business first in the United States, then in the world.

This rapid sequence of follow-up innovation, from railroads to steam ships, soon sparked a period of rapid globalization. With travel times cut dramatically (and shipping fees along with them), an entirely new far-reaching trade network emerged that connected points across the globe. The ensuing spike in productiv-ity led to an increase in per capita income growth the likes of which the world had never seen. This sharp rise in global prosperity would, in fact, form the foun-dation for what Friedrich Engels first termed the Industrial Revolution.

So what about Watt?

As the progenitor of this transformation of the global economy, James Watt left behind a significant legacy. In cultural terms, the central concepts and lan-guage of energy consumption, most notably the units of measure horsepower and watt, hark back to him. In historical terms, his bust sits in a place of honor among the kings and nobles at Westminster Abbey while his biography has been written and rewritten more than thirty times since François Arago penned *His-torical Eloge of James Watt* in 1839.

On a personal level, Watt eventually remarried, never stopped tinkering (he would later offer improvements to the telescope and oil lamp among other inven-tions), and passed away at the ripe old age of eighty-three as an extremely wealthy man, thanks to the commercial success of his invention, his patents, and his partnership with Matthew Boulton.

And yet, it all might not have come to pass if not for Patent No. 913. For one, the patent served as a lure for investors like Roebuck and Boulton; without it, they never would have risked investing in Watt's work if they couldn't be assured of receiving some form of capital in return. With established property rights, an entrepreneur like Boulton was then free to ship as many engines as he could manufacture wherever he found a willing buyer. Perhaps most important, though, after the patent appeared in publication, it created a way for fellow inventors to build upon Watt's breakthrough, or, more boldly, an incentive to try and improve upon it. In other words, it was because the invention had been disclosed in the form of a patent that other inventors could learn from atop Watt's shoulders. One could argue that it was Patent No. 913, perhaps more than Watt himself, that created the chain reaction that would subsequently ignite the Industrial Revolution and transform the planet.

The Measure of Our Ignorance

The steam engine is just a case study. But it's also more than the story of a single heroic inventor. It's a narrative that helps connect the messy realities of business with the theoretical foundations of the so-called dismal science, one that determines the policy framework within which the modern-day Watts, Roebucks, and Boultons must work. Economics has long struggled with the questions of economic growth: What is it? How long can it continue at a given rate? And what drives it forward in such an uneven way?

It probably wouldn't be too much of a stretch to say that, if you're reading this book from a developed economy, you owe at least some of your current standard of living to James Watt and his fabulous machine. We are so used to the idea of economic growth today that we simply take it for granted. For most of mankind's history on earth, though, the standard of living grew so slowly that there was no perceptible difference between the lifestyles of children and their parents, grandparents, or even great-grandparents. In fact, the improvement in average output per person (GDP) between the time of Christ and the time of James Watt—a growth of about $170 over eighty-five generations—is now accomplished just about every two years. Looked at another way, the amount of value produced per person when Watt was born was about 40 percent higher than when Jesus was born. In our day that same percentage change in output has occurred in just the past thirty years—a single generation.

This radical change in productive output since the Industrial Revolution has meant an extraordinary improvement in the way we all live. Apart from having plentiful food, central plumbing, heated homes, rapid transportation, numerous changes of clothes, a multitude of entertainment options, and lots of cool stuff, the biggest changes have come in the quality of our health and the length of our lives. At the beginning of the nineteenth century, about one in three children died before the age of five. Life expectancy for those who made it through childhood was about thirty-five years. Thomas Hobbes, the seventeenth-century English philosopher, captured it well when he described life as "solitary, poor, nasty, brutish, and short."

Beginning in about 1800, however, the world economy, without warning, began to grow. Within a single generation, the standard of living of children was markedly better than that of their parents (see Figure 1). This new phenomenon of growth obviously piqued the interest of early economists. This was more than simply an academic curiosity. If economists could discover the source of growth, and understand how to sustain it, they might be able to relegate the Hobbesian lifestyle to the dustbin of history.

When these economists looked at the question of growth, it was obvious that the amount of output of each member of the labor force had greatly increased. But how had this happened? The most obvious explanation was that the average worker in the industrial economy had much more physical capital at their disposal than those who came before. This increase in the availability of manufacturing, industrial, and agricultural equipment was viewed as the most likely source of growth, and it is the reason that we have come to call our present economic system "capitalism."

On the other side of the debate was Karl Marx, who observed in his famous economic treatise *Das Kapital* that "accumulated labour which serves as a means of new production is capital." For Marx, the main driver of value creation is the fact that "the worker not only replaces what he consumes but gives to accumulated labour [capital] a greater value than it previously possessed." As a result, Marx believed that the credit for economic growth is entirely due to labor; growth simply required sufficient time to accumulate enough of it.

Faced with this debate, economists of the time lacked the data to determine the relative contributions of labor and capital in economic growth, and they had no way to determine what impact other economic inputs might have in the growth equation. It wasn't until the late 1950s that a small group of economists were able to gather up a battery of new economic statistics about the gross national product (GNP), capital investment, and labor hours, to break out the importance of different economic resources.

FIGURE 1   World GDP Per Capita, 1000–2001 (in 1990 international dollars)

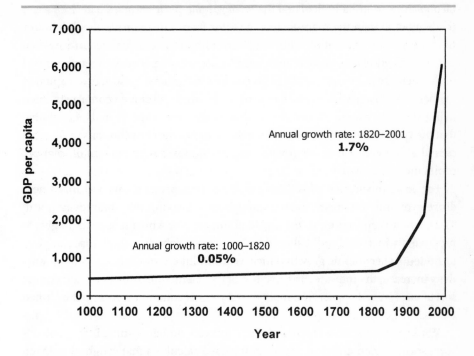

Source: Angus Maddison, *Historical Statistics for the World Economy*.

What they discovered was one of the most surprising results in the history of economics. In an analysis that he first published in 1957, Robert Solow calculated that less than 13 percent of economic growth could be explained by changes in what were assumed to be the two most important economic inputs: labor and capital. But this extraordinary finding begged another question: if growth doesn't come from increases in labor and capital, where does it come from? Solow's explanation, which earned him a Nobel Prize in 1987, was that roughly seven-eighths of economic growth per worker came from what he called simply "technical change," meaning that just a fraction of growth was driven by increases in the stock of physical capital.

In Solow's 1957 paper, he constructed a *technical change index* (he labeled this index simply "A") that showed an increase of 1.5 percent per year between 1909 and 1949, which he compared to 1.8 percent per year for his output measure (in this case, GNP per labor hour) for the overall economy. Other economists had been reaching similar conclusions about technical change. A few years earlier, Jacob Schmookler had calculated that an *aggregate efficiency index* had risen at 1.4 percent per year in the manufacturing sector from 1869 to 1928 (he didn't do a GNP per person calculation), whereas Moses Abramovitz calculated in 1956 that the *productivity of resources* had increased by 1.7 percent per year, explaining most of the increase in overall output (he measured *net* national product per capita) of 1.9 percent between 1869 and 1953. In other words all three economists, each using slightly different measures in slightly different time periods, concluded that the contribution of "technical change" dwarfed the contributions of physical capital to per capita income growth, accounting for 80–90 percent of total per capita income growth.

For economists used to believing that investments in plants and machinery drove economic progress, these findings were shocking. As Abramovitz put it, "This result is surprising in the lopsided importance which it appears to give to productivity increase, and it should be, in a sense, sobering, if not discouraging, to students of economic growth. Since we know little about the causes of productivity increase, the indicated importance of this element may be taken to be some sort of *measure of our ignorance* about the causes of economic growth in the United States."

While Schmookler and Abramovitz delivered similar results, it was Solow's sophisticated mathematical approach (he used calculus!) that caught the imagination of his fellow economists. Solow's novel approach combined new data sources with clever modeling techniques, and it delivered provocative results. This made the search for sources of growth one of the hottest fields in economics. Many minds rose up to take up Abramovitz's challenge to push back the shadows of our ignorance and shed more light on the puzzle of growth.

The first task was to choose a name for Solow's mysterious new variable. Schmookler called it "aggregate efficiency," Abramovitz chose "resource productivity," and Solow defined it as "cumulative technical change." The name that caught on with economists, at least for a while, was simply "the residual," an apt choice given that it represented quite literally everything that was left over beyond any increases in capital and labor inputs. This name seemed disturbingly unscientific to some, however, so new contenders seemed to arrive each and every year. By the late 1960s, economists had adopted the forbidding term "total factor productivity" (TFP) and surprisingly (for noneconomists) it stuck.

The real quest, of course, was not to just name this variable, but to describe what exactly it was. An interesting debate soon emerged—and defined a new branch of economics now known as "growth accounting"—that has continued for decades. Much of the debate was framed by the context of the world economy at that time, a period of so-called stagflation and limits to growth. This, of course, presented a paradox to the researchers: if the economy was getting smarter, why was growth slowing?

By the 1980s, the solution to the TFP paradox, often called "neoclassical growth theory," remained elusive. All that anyone could agree upon was that the economy was increasingly reliant on, as Schmookler pointed out, "intellectual capital" rather than physical capital. With the hunt threatening to become further mired in abstruse methods and debates, a young economist named Paul Romer introduced a needed breakthrough.

In an argument first circulated in 1986 and refined in a 1990 paper, Romer advanced three basic premises: First, he embraced Solow (his model used the same symbol "A" to describe the technology index) by reaffirming the importance of technological change as a driver of economic growth. He also offered a concise definition for what "technological change" meant; quite simply it was any improvement in the instructions for mixing together the raw materials that resulted in economic growth. Second, he borrowed from Schmookler in arguing that technological change didn't arrive magically from outside of an economy. Rather than arrive *exogenously*, like a baby via a stork, technological change was the result of "intentional actions taken by people who respond to market incentives." That meant that technology is *endogenous*—a direct product of market forces.

While debunking the stork theory of technological change was an important finding, it was Romer's third premise that proved to be his most profound contribution, one that might very well earn him a Nobel Prize someday. Romer determined that an economy's *mixing instructions* behave differently than every other kind of economic resource. "Once the cost of creating a new set of instructions has been incurred, the instructions can be used over and over again at no additional cost," Romer wrote. The critical phrase "no additional cost" transformed the debate and sparked a transition from neoclassical growth theory to what became known as *new growth theory*. In the neoclassical school of economics, all market outcomes are driven by the alignment of marginal costs and marginal benefits (anyone who has ever drawn an intersecting supply-and-demand curve is repeating the core lesson of neoclassical economics). In presenting his new school of thought, Romer had challenged this core neoclassical model saying that, with what most people now call either *intellectual capital* or *intangible assets*, all those bets were off.

Simply put, the marginal costs of intangible assets are zero.

As one could imagine, this theory rocked the establishment. Aside from its intuitive appeal, Romer's premise also had huge mathematical implications. Since models driven by intangible assets worked differently from the neoclassical models, growth economists no longer had to feel guilty about the residual. Intellectual capital, as an input to the economy, was unique. Even better, since the providers of the economy's mixing instructions—the worlds of science, technology, and business innovation—were no longer delivered by storks, Romer had opened up a whole new realm of theories for economists to explore.

While economists thrive on this kind of rigorous analysis, simpler, more intuitive explanations often suffice for the rest of us. And the idea that these generations of economists have labored to prove is really very simple, and very sensible: growth, and therefore prosperity, results from our ability to produce more valuable outputs out of the same inputs. This bit of economic alchemy is possible because inventive minds are constantly developing new and better product designs, more efficient processes for extracting and processing materials, and higher-quality, less-labor-intensive manufacturing methods. Once an improvement has been discovered, that new "recipe" can spread around the world at lightning speed and at virtually zero cost.

As a result, this accumulation of countless great ideas over hundreds of years has enabled us to produce much more, much better, and much more cheaply. It is striking to note that the portion of the labor force engaged in agriculture in the United States (and similarly in Europe) has declined from 70 percent in 1800 to less than 2 percent today. Stated differently, two nineteenth-century farmers working year round would struggle to produce enough food to keep three people fed; two modern farmers, on the other hand, can easily produce enough to feed one hundred people. That extraordinary productivity increase is the result of a long series of innovations that has increased agricultural productivity by thirty-five-fold.

The same kind of process has also occurred in manufacturing. A Model T Ford from 1907, for example, weighs about the same (because it uses roughly the same material inputs) and takes about the same labor-hours to produce as a 2007 BMW-Mini. So what's the difference between a Model T and a Mini? About one hundred years of innovation. And that's where economic growth comes from.

And yet as simple as the concept may be, we are still only just beginning to discover how to measure and control economic growth. One of the latest findings from the ongoing work in the growth accounting field is that economists have been undervaluing the importance of intellectual capital investments to the economy as a whole.

In 2006 three government economists, Carol Corrado, Charles Hulten, and Dan Sichel (CH&S here for short), wrote an analysis that they developed based on a simple premise: What if we accounted for investments in intellectual capital (CH&S called these *intangible* investments) in the same way we account for investments in physical capital? How might this change our view of the performance of the U.S. economy? A great deal, it turns out.

- In a world where everyone thinks that the U.S. savings rate has gone negative, CH&S calculated that we actually save and invest a lot more than we think: to the tune of about a trillion dollars more. That trillion dollars amounts to roughly 10 percent of the entire U.S. economy, most of which we count as consumption today. Looked at in another way, the economy invests equal amounts in intangible assets as it does physical capital.
- CH&S also found that businesses are considerably more profitable than they report and businesses, in fact, account for most of the economy's savings. The difference between reported profit and actual profit is simply investments in intangible assets. As CH&S explain, if investments in physical capital don't get subtracted from current profits and are recorded as an asset that is depreciated over time, then there is little reason to treat intangible asset investments any differently. If you treat intangible expenditure as an asset purchase that will be written off over time rather than as an expense, then true corporate profits and economy-wide savings rates will generally be higher.
- CH&S also found that accounting for intangible assets as Solow's and Romer's "A" makes sources of growth modeling a lot less mysterious. The single most important measurable contributor to economic growth, they found, was their intangible investment measure (although TFP stayed high). And, just as important, it was continuing to grow in importance.

While all the breakthrough theories posited by Romer's new growth theory have roiled the academic establishment, businesses continue to scratch their heads over what it all means to them. In other words, in an economy dominated by intangible assets and the mysterious A, how do businesses make their money?

It's a profound question and one that is very difficult to address directly, because economists are deeply conflicted about the business implications of A. They don't know how to justify its value—should the price be zero, since that's the marginal cost, and if not, then what basis can there be for determining a "fair price"? And if the price is going to be higher than zero, which it must be in order to compensate the creators of intangible assets, then how should the rights of the providers of A be protected? The practical answer, one that has emerged through a kind of historical accident, is the legal system of intellectual property protection: patents, copyright, and trademarks. And the protection of intellectual property requires the regular granting of something that economists despise.

Monopolies.

Intellectual property represents small monopolies, to be sure, that at least most of the time are limited in both duration and scope. These monopolies also reveal a fascinating disconnect between business strategy and economics. While every businessman knows that he wants as much monopoly power as he can get, every economist knows that monopolies are negative things that should be kept from businesses. The strange thing is that intellectual property monopolies are all around us. We give marketers exclusive rights to their trademarked brands for as long as they pay their fees. Authors receive exclusive rights to their copyrighted creations for one hundred years. Technologists, in fact, get short shrift since they are given only a twenty-year exclusion on their patents.

These kinds of intellectual property monopolies actually drive economists nuts. They can't defend them, but they don't know how to attack them either. As a leading economist and expert on the patent system, Fritz Machlup, once wrote:

> If we did not have a patent system, it would be irresponsible, on the basis of our present knowledge of its economic consequences, to recommend instituting one. But since we have had a patent system for a long time, it would be irresponsible, on the basis of our present knowledge, to recommend abolishing it.

In other words, even for economists who are taught to condemn any form of market power, it's just about impossible to mount an attack on the engine that drives most economic growth.

Invention Incentives Drive Economic Growth

One of our clients, the chief executive officer of a consumer goods company, once described his principal challenge as the managing of the growth rate of his company. "Our growth is simply a function of how much new work we get done in a year," he told us. "If we increased our growth rate in a year to ten percent from just five percent, that means we were more productive. We got twice as much work done in that year."

Innovation works on a similar premise. The more incentive that creative people have to invent, and to disclose their inventions to the world in a patent filing, the more new businesses can emerge to use those new technologies. And since the rate of innovation is tied to the rate of economic growth, more innovation means more growth.

For most of human history, however, there were few, if any, incentives to innovate. And, no surprise, innovations were few and far between. One economic historian claims that "the list of significant mechanical inventions prior to 1700 is a short one: The windmill, the waterwheel, and the printing press." That slow pace of innovation was also reflected in income levels: as we have shown, income per person hardly changed from the time of Christ up until the Industrial Revolution. (There were, however, isolated oases of technical advancement and relative economic prosperity in the great city civilizations, Egypt, Greece, Rome, and China.)

As mankind moved into the Dark Ages, much of what passed for technical knowledge veered into the realm of the mystical. The rise of powerful imperial and religious institutions tended to promote resistance to new ideas, and often led to active suppression. In China, the Analects of Confucius placed the idea of invention firmly out of the realm of spiritually acceptable activity: "The Master [Confucius] said, 'I transmit rather than create. I believe in and love the ancients.'" In Athens, Plato argued for a nation of servile followers, and that every man "should teach his soul, by long habit, never to dream of acting independently, and to become utterly incapable of it." For many years, traditions of technical knowledge either emphasized the mystical nature of their craft, as in alchemy, or kept the knowledge rigidly contained, as in the guild system. For anyone who wanted to invent something new, or change the status quo, the world was, for the most part, actively hostile.

These forces changed, but only slowly. Isaac Newton, the great physicist, reportedly once said, "If I have seen farther, it is by standing on the shoulders of giants." The quote, though, was not Newton's. It came originally from Bernard of Chartres, a French philosopher from the twelfth century, who sought to rehabilitate the act of innovation by taking care to pay proper respect to those innovators who came before him. "We are like dwarfs, sitting on the shoulders of giants," said Bernard. From Bernard's vantage point, the contribution of the innovator might be modest, but at least he could see farther than his predecessors. The change in attitude from Bernard's time in the Middle Ages to Isaac Newton in the Renaissance is the hinge on which the door of prosperity turns. Bernard gives virtually all of the credit to the ancients, and suggests that we (the sitting dwarves) can add but little to the wisdom they have passed down. On the other hand,

Newton pays his fealty to those who came before, but is not shy about the fact that because he stands tall, he can see farther.

The revival of a tradition of innovation in Europe helped contribute to faster growth there compared with the rest of the world. Still invention remained a rare and economically risky activity. But as the cultural environment changed around the time of the Italian Renaissance, the beginnings of an intellectual property–based economy began to emerge as well. We can now document a series of associations in time and place between the rise in inventive activity on the one hand and the rise of systems providing intellectual property protections on the other

The first truly modern "patent for invention" went to Filippo Brunelleschi in 1421. Brunelleschi was the Florentine architect who built the spectacular cathedral Santa Maria del Fiore. The cathedral's dome, often called Brunelleschi's dome, was an engineering marvel and Brunelleschi was forced to devise numerous mechanical inventions to make its construction possible. He sought and successfully obtained a patent for what he hoped might be a more broadly useful shipping concept, since he was looking for ways to bring in marble slabs from long distances and believed others might want to steal his idea. The patent term lasted only three years and the ship, one he named the *Sea Monster*, sank into the Arno River with its white-marble cargo on its maiden voyage. Brunelleschi was able to recover from this disaster financially, but historians estimate his losses may have amounted to as much as ten times his annual salary.

While the concept of patenting was not embraced in Florence beyond Brunelleschi's first foray, it was taken up shortly thereafter in nearby cities. In the years following Brunelleschi's *Sea Monster* fiasco, the practice of patent granting spread to the Republic of Venice and, as the practice gained acceptance there, the Venetian Senate enacted the world's first formal patent law, which they passed in 1474 (a law for copyrights, which emerged from a power struggle between authors and printers over rights to published works, in which copyrights for authors replaced printers' patents, followed in 1517). The statute provides a rationale for patent protection that holds up fairly well even today:

1474, March 19

We have among us men of great genius, apt to invent and discover ingenious devices; and in view of the grandeur and virtue of our city, more such men come to us every day from divers parts. Now if provision were made for the works and devices discovered by such persons, so that others who see them could not build them and take the inventor's honor away, more men would

then apply their genius, would discover, and would build devices of great
utility and benefit to our commonwealth.

In Venice at the time, the rise of patents for invention had much to do with
the city's special role as trading center of the Mediterranean economy. Unusual
for a city of its time, the Republic of Venice took an open view of immigration
and of outside talent. Consequently, the restrictive power of guilds held less sway
over Venetian politics than in other cities. Monopoly rights were often granted
to talented artisans who were newcomers to the city in order to protect them
from attacks by established guilds. The more these artisans could differentiate
their technology from common guild practices, the easier it was to justify their
monopoly privileges. In this context, the Venetian patent system was a direct
outgrowth of an essentially pro-competitive policy.

As the center of global trade and commerce began to shift to the Atlantic coast
of Europe during the Age of Discovery, Venetian artisans, especially glassmakers,
began to leave Venice for greener pastures throughout Europe. They took both
their technology and their knowledge of the Venetian patent system with them.
Venice's glassmaking technology had long been viewed as a critical source of
competitive advantage and so local glassmakers were tightly organized into a
guild, effectively secluded for centuries on the island of Murano and strictly for-
bidden (some were executed by poison when they tried) from traveling outside
the city. In 1550, however, as economic conditions deteriorated for the glassmakers, for the first time guild members were allowed to emigrate. And although
they had never applied for patents while in Venice, these emigrating Venetian
glassmakers started asking for patents as they settled farther west: in England,
France, Holland, and Belgium. The earliest recorded patents for invention in
England (to Antonio Guidotti 1537), France (to Theses Mutio in 1551), and Belgium (to Bernard Swertz in 1537 and someone named Cornachini in 1541) were
all glassmaking patents.

This continuing thread of intellectual property protection and economic innovation takes us back to where we started: James Watt's steam engine patents
and the Industrial Revolution in England. Although the City of Venice deserves
credit for the first patent and copyright laws, the rise of the first national patent
system clearly took place in England. Similar institutions nearly emerged in
France and Belgium, but the French model collapsed during the French Revolution and Belgium's patent institutions never made much progress either, due to
economic conflicts with Holland. In no other place in the world, and for the first

time in human history, an experimental test of a full national patent system was conducted in England starting in 1624.

The initial results were not all that dramatic. Patents remained relatively rare following the Statute of Monopolies in 1624: excepting one small boomlet around the 1690s, patent counts showed little growth for over a century, averaging about six per year. But during that time, the English courts and Parliamentary bodies found ways to iron out a large number of details in the governance of the patent system: how much scrutiny would a patent application require (not much, the English adopted a pretty laissez-faire attitude); how much disclosure of the invention's specifications would be needed (quite a lot; the English made it clear that full disclosure of the invention's function was the social quid pro quo for a patent monopoly); and how would the adjudication of disputes be administered (responsibility was shifted from the royal Privy Council to the more predictable common law courts)? By the time James Watt applied for his patent in 1768, the patent system had become a more widely recognized institution in the British economy. Watt and Roebuck certainly took major financial risks based on their presumption of meaningful patent protection.

In Figure 1, we noted how the sharp rise of economic growth in England was a direct consequence of the Industrial Revolution. This is well known. But Figure 2 shows that the adoption of the patent system directly preceded and almost certainly fueled the explosion of technology investments that sparked the Industrial Revolution. There is little about this period that is not controversial among economic historians, but one recent author has remarked, "The temptation to seize on the patent statistics as an indicator of inventive activity remains largely because the graph does exactly what our 'common sense' tells us it should do. It shows a marked upward trend from the third quarter of the eighteenth century."

Another way to say that is, of course, that intellectual property protection provides the critical incentive to invest in intangible assets. And investments in intangible assets drive economic growth. So it's no accident that the world's most spectacular breakthrough in economic growth took place immediately following the creation of the world's first full-scale intellectual property system.

And as the experiment continued, the institutions of intellectual property continued to show positive results. Like the migration of Venetian laws with Venetian glassmakers, the British patent system migrated to the American colonies, where they were first adopted at a state level. After the American Revolution, the Founding Fathers, many of them scientists and inventors themselves, enshrined intellectual property rights in Article 1, Section 8 of the Constitution of the United States, the first country ever to do so and one of the few that provides such prior-

FIGURE 2   English Patents Enrolled, 1660–1800 (ten-year trailing average)

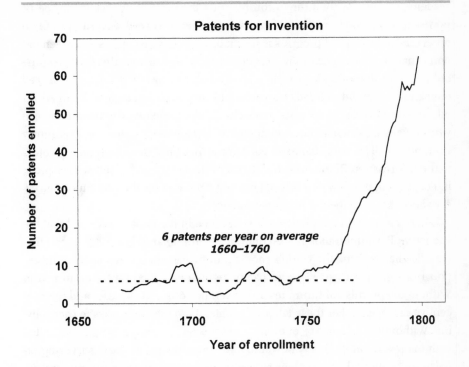

Source: Christine MacLeod, *Inventing the Industrial Revolution: The English Patent System, 1660–1800.*

ity to intellectual property to this day. Benjamin Franklin was famous for his experiments in electricity. Thomas Jefferson, himself no fan of monopolies, was
the new country's first patent examiner. Years later, Abraham Lincoln, who began
his career as a patent lawyer, even earned a patent for himself (for a method to
buoy vessels over shoals). Lincoln famously praised the institution of patent laws
when, in a speech, he said,

> These began in England in 1624; and, in this country, with the adoption of
> our constitution. Before then, any man might instantly use what another
> had invented; so that the inventor had no special advantage from his own
> invention. The patent system changed this; secured to the inventor, for a
> limited time, the exclusive use of his invention; and thereby added *the fuel
> of interest to the fire of genius* [emphasis added], in the discovery and produc-
> tion of new and useful things.

If you listen to sociological determinists, economic historians, and the many academics who take the time to comment on the topic of intellectual property, however, you would think that IP was, at best, a necessary evil. According to these observers technological progress is inevitable. Specific inventions and inventors don't matter. More specifically, academics have argued that the steam engine didn't matter to economic growth (it sped up growth by about a month, claimed one) and neither did railroads (canals would have been just as good, claimed another). Usually these academics make claims like these many years after people who actually experienced the technological developments were alive. A century from now we'll probably have someone argue that computers didn't mean much to the Information Revolution, and they'll come up with some statistics to prove it. For, as Robert Solow wisecracked in 1987, "You can see the Computer Age everywhere except in the productivity statistics."

There's a reason invention was first honored in the Renaissance and that the Industrial Revolution took hold economically in England. There's a reason that America has become the world's most innovative economy. It's because invention is an economic activity and patent rights encourage inventors to invest. Without the promise of future reward, inventors' economics suffer and their incentive disappears. For these talented people, there are other ways to earn a living. Without Patent No. 913, or even the prospect of any property right associated with his invention, James Watt would have spent his prime years surveying canals. And without the technological revolution that Watt's steam engine sparked, those canals would probably have been economically useful for many years longer. They would have had no railroads to compete with.

CHAPTER 2

Monopoly Money

HOW INTELLECTUAL PROPERTY DRIVES BUSINESS PROFITS

> "But who is to give the prizes?" quite a chorus of voices asked.
> "Why, *she*, of course," said the Dodo, pointing to Alice with one
> finger; and the whole party at once crowded round her, calling out in a
> confused way, "Prizes! Prizes!"
> —*Lewis Carroll*, Alice's Adventures in Wonderland,
> "A Caucus Race and a Long Tale," 1865

> That ain't working, that's the way you do it
> Get your money for nothing get your chicks for free
> —*Mark Knopfler, Dire Straits, "Money for Nothing," 1985*

I t's hard to manage something if you're afraid to talk about it, but the truth is that most business leaders won't talk about the profit power of their IP unless their lawyer happens to be in the room with them. Why? Simple: most monopolies are illegal and the pursuit of them is a criminal activity. Even if you want to discuss ways to improve your business profitability by flexing your firm's market power, you'd better be careful how you handle the discussion. Not only do you need to have your lawyer on hand, you also need to make sure you don't write anything down.

When it comes to intellectual property monopolies, this caution creates unfortunate disconnects for business executives in the boardroom in a manner not unlike what economists face in the classroom. We showed in the previous chapter how economists claim to study economic growth, yet are reluctant to acknowledge the central role of intellectual property rights. In a similar fashion, the creation, protection, and effective deployment of valuable intellectual property drives business profits, yet business executives outside of a few select industries rarely grant intellectual property the priority it deserves.

It's time to bring intellectual property strategy out of the shadows. More to the point, we submit that any business strategy not built around intellectual property is no strategy at all. Why? Well, without intellectual property protection a business can have no sustainable advantage over its competitors. Without sustainable competitive advantage, the odds of developing and sustaining outstanding profit performance plummet. Without an expectation of outstanding profit performance, businesses have little incentive to invest in innovation. Without innovation, the opportunity for growth vanishes. And without growth opportunities, the potential for wealth creation and generating high returns for shareholders disappears. Just about any way you look at it, a modern business needs to place intellectual property strategy close to the center of any strategic plan. Anything less amounts to negligence.

After years of experience in the strategy development process, we have become convinced that intellectual property protection is the missing ingredient in most executives' strategy toolkit. They don't talk about it much, they don't think about it enough, and they don't know how to manage it very well—and as a result their business performance suffers.

But the evidence is clear if you take a hard look at business performance: the highest business returns go to intellectual property–based businesses and that outstanding profit performance results directly from the limited market power that valuable intellectual property provides. Indeed, these profit results are well deserved, for it is the companies who innovate rapidly and compete aggressively that profit the most. Yet as we know, when competitors smell profits they come running, so without some form of protection, those competitors will quickly copy the innovations and drive the profits (for both the innovator and themselves) down to nothing.

For example, in 2001 a no-holds-barred slugfest broke out in boardrooms, courtrooms, and the business press over ownership rights to some of the most profitable technology in the world. In one corner stood Intel, the undisputed king of the semiconductor sector, whose market dominance and extraordinary profitability had earned it the nickname Chipzilla. In the opposite corner stood the challenger: TechSearch, a relatively unknown and unprofitable company that apparently offered no products or services whatsoever, which had sued Intel for infringing its patent, U.S. Patent No. 5,574,927. TechSearch would eventually lose the bout, a TKO handed down by a federal appeals court judge in May 2002, but not before earning its place in history as the first of its kind: the so-called patent troll.

The story of Chipzilla versus the Troll has been rehashed many times, especially as similar disputes have made recent headlines (see NTP versus RIM over the BlackBerry). Most retellings identify a villain, either by fingering Intel as a predatory 800-pound gorilla, or, more commonly, by calling out TechSearch as a bane of capitalism (and a boon to attorneys everywhere).

The simple truth is that both these versions are wrong: they're legal and public relations tactics that try to paint good hard-nosed business competition as a morality play. Rather, this is a tale of two companies that used the power of IP to shape their respective business strategies. In the discussion that follows, we focus in on the novel ways that companies like Intel use IP to achieve market power while, at the same time, we shed light on the ways that corporate weaklings like TechSearch can use IP to make the giants sweat.

Whoever Owns the IP Owns the Profits

One of the best places to find the signs of the key role that IP plays in generating corporate profits is by looking into the various marketplaces for capital assets. These markets provide important evidence on both how much money companies are investing in IP as well as the kinds of returns they are realizing on those investments.

When it comes to the spending side of the equation, it should come as no surprise that businesses invest greater resources in developing those assets that deliver the best returns. Using this criterion, U.S. businesses have clearly demonstrated an appetite for intangible assets by opening up their checkbooks. Measuring spending on intangible assets, however, is tricky business. It can depend, for example, on your definition of what an intellectual asset is. However, for those who have done the hard accounting work to figure out how to track it, people like Carol Corrado and her colleagues in the growth accounting field, the results show that intangible investments leave clearly marked tracks.

In the last several decades, businesses have been increasing their spending on new intellectual capital investments at a rapid rate, research by Corrado and others shows. Conservative estimates say that annual intellectual capital investments have grown exponentially to more than $1 trillion in the United States, up from less than $20 billion annually in the 1950s. On a percentage basis, intellectual assets investments have tripled their share of GNP while investments in physical capital have remained relatively flat. This shift from the physical to the intangible is reflected in the massive resources businesses have poured into software development, new product innovations in industries ranging from motion pictures to pharmaceuticals, brand development and proprietary skill, and knowledge investments. Figure 3 demonstrates how the shares of

FIGURE 3   U.S. Investment in Tangibles and Intangibles

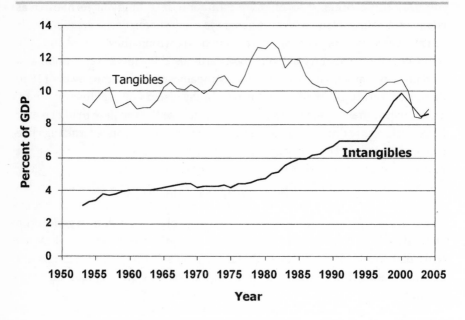

Source: Leonard Nakamura, Federal Reserve Bank of Philadelphia.

investment in physical and intellectual assets have changed over the last fifty years.

When a business invests in a fixed capital asset, no one is confused by the notion that the investing business not only owns those assets but also expects a return on its investment. Yet as U.S. intellectual asset investments as a whole have grown to the point that they likely exceed physical investments, a general tendency has arisen both within and outside companies to confuse the economic concept of *intellectual asset investment* with the more diffuse notion of *knowledge creation.* From the standpoint of society as a whole, on the spending side at least, these two ideas overlap. In other words, as companies invest in intellectual assets, they are generating benefits for society as a whole in the form of new knowledge. From a strictly business standpoint, however, the only logical reason to invest in an intellectual asset is if there is a clearly beneficial *outcome*—such as ownership rights and higher profit expectations—that results from the spending. The rub for businesses, of course, is that, the act of creating knowledge, although undoubtedly beneficial for society, won't improve business performance unless it can be protected in ways that create a competitive advantage. Without such protection, any knowledge created will simply leak out and provide educational benefits to competitors, suppliers, and customers with no lasting proprietary benefit to the company creating it. In this sense, using the phrase "knowledge creation" to describe an investment decision confuses the issues facing managers by conflating inputs and outputs, education and knowledge, and effort with results.

Simply put, when businesses invest in intellectual *assets* they need to protect the fruits of their investment in the form of intellectual *property*. Only with the appropriation of ownership rights, and not the creation of the asset itself, does an investment provide competitive advantage. Such appropriation can take a number of forms, including brand investments that are protected by a trademark, internal projects that are protected as trade secrets, written works and software programs that are protected by copyrights, and investments in designs and technology that are protected by patents. And when we see spending on these kinds of investments rising, as shown in Figure 3, even if all we're doing is measuring the *inputs* to business activity, that's one signal that the executives making those investment decisions have a reasonable expectation of seeing strong returns on them. In fact, that expectation can be extremely influential in coaxing entrepreneurs to take some risks in trying to gather some of those profits for themselves.

Intel is no exception.

The Lure of the Chase

In 1965, Gordon Moore, then the Director of R&D at Fairchild Semiconductor Division of the Fairchild Camera and Instrument Company, wrote an article for the journal *Electronics* titled "Cramming More Components onto Integrated Circuits." His short essay included the prediction that has since been popularized as Moore's Law: the forecast that computing power will double every eighteen months. Ignoring the fact that Moore was fuzzy about the timing (his predictions ranged from twelve to twenty-four months), the accuracy of his estimate was truly prophetic. And the underlying technical phenomenon he described and led has driven the most critical spurt of technological progress since the Industrial Revolution. Appropriately enough, we now acknowledge that Moore's Law is the engine that drives the Information Revolution.

The integrated circuit is a remarkable invention. If the steam engine drove the Industrial Revolution by freeing man's economic activities from the constraints of muscle, water, and wind power, then the integrated circuit has driven the Information Revolution in similar ways by freeing the economy from the calculation and memory constraints of the human brain. The inventions involved contributions from several teams of engineers who combined several advances into a unified concept: the idea that multiple transistors could be connected without wires between components by etching the connections on a piece of silicon. After discovering the tremendous potential for engineers to cram an ever increasing number of transistors onto a piece of silicon, Moore left Fairchild Camera and Instruments in 1968 to start his own company. He called it Intel, short for Integrated Electronics.

Following in the footsteps of Moore's Law, the semiconductor industry (the term semiconductors slides off the tongue a bit easier than integrated circuits) has become a hotbed of inventive activity. While Moore predicted back in 1965 that he and his colleagues could keep up their inventive pace "for at least 10 years," his challenge sparked a huge race for technical solutions unlike any the world had seen before. As technology has continued to evolve at an astonishing pace—chips that used to contain 20 transistors now pack more than 200 million onto the same real estate—the effort has attracted some of the best minds in the world, consumed hundreds of billions of dollars of research investments, and generated hundreds of thousands of patents along the way. Given the value of some of these inventions, we shouldn't be surprised that the semiconductor industry—led by Intel, Texas Instruments, and other titans—has also been a hotbed of innovation in patent strategies, strategies that have helped generate enormous value for the companies involved.

While we can acknowledge the difficult nature of accurately measuring how much firms like Intel invest in their intellectual assets, measuring the *outcomes* of those IP investments can be even more problematic. Still, investments in IP are really not that different from any other capital project: like any investment, expenditures on intellectual property involve spending money today to increase profits tomorrow. And there is ample evidence that businesses today are investing more money in generating intellectual property than ever before. However, the question remains: what kinds of profits are those investments generating?

Stock markets around the world, for one, provide an important function of assessing the future profit potential of all publicly traded companies. One way to evaluate the return on intellectual property at a high level is to compare the value of businesses as a whole relative to the value of their physical capital holdings. The bigger the difference between these two numbers, then, the more valuable the intellectual property component of a business has become. One method of representing this ratio is by comparing the market value of a company (the value of its stock plus its borrowings) with the "book value" of its physical assets in reported financial statements. Financial analysts call this the market-to-book ratio.

And over the last fifty years, the overall value of this ratio among publicly traded American firms has risen strongly. A recent study by Ned Davis Research showed that the ratio of intellectual capital to total market capitalization of U.S. companies grew from about 17 percent of company value in 1975 to 80 percent in 2005. While far from a definitive measure, this study does indeed show that investors today value companies for more than just their physical or financial assets: the real gems are in the intellectual property.

With this insight in mind, a cluster of recent academic studies have also looked at the relationship between a company's market-to-book value and its intellectual property, with a specific focus on R&D and patents. By examining stock markets in the United States, Europe, and Japan, these studies all find a clear connection: the more intellectual property a company holds, the higher its market valuation. Three main findings from these studies stand out. First, they find that patent-generating R&D investments consistently work well in explaining stock prices. This finding has been among the most reliable results, one that is also popular among academics; after all, they happen to be in the research business themselves. The problem with R&D, however, is that it's yet another measure of money spent, not value created.

The second finding gets more interesting. For the same dollar spent on R&D activity, the companies that generate a higher yield of patent output increase their market value above and beyond the typical level of patenting from R&D. This result has been more controversial (not surprising perhaps given academic discomfort with patenting in general) and has gotten stronger in recent years. There is an important problem here, however. Even though there is a loose connection between patent *counts* and shareholder value, the connection is relatively weak. Most patents, of course, have relatively little value while valuable patents create value only in their larger technological and business context. The patents that create the most bang for the buck, on the other hand, are those that are well positioned in a valuable technology area such as ink-jet printing or DNA analysis. Without the patent, therefore, the opportunity for competitive advantage would disappear. Just as the decision to spend a dollar on R&D doesn't guarantee a benefit, therefore, the receipt of a patent by itself is not a guarantee of higher profits. Still, most of these studies show a clear effect: that companies prosper when they successfully run the patent office gauntlet and generate more patent bang for their R&D buck.

The patents that really generate the biggest payoff in the marketplace, however, are the *important* ones—the ones that protect the technologies that generate large benefits to users and serve as the foundation for future technology investments for companies of all kinds. In the way that Watt's steam engine directly stimulated decades of inventive activity, important patents, therefore, are those that are frequently cited by others, spark unanticipated inventions, and by their reputation, boost investors' expectations of future profits. Not surprisingly, then, the third, and most notable, finding from these studies is that patent citations are emerging as the most powerful value marker of all. One recent study estimated that a single U.S. patent citation is associated with a valuation that is higher by $1 million.

The fact that these academic studies all focus on the stock market in attempts to measure the shadow value of intellectual property has both pros and cons. The chief virtue of using the market is that, given the volume of publicly available data, these studies use evidence that is highly interesting to both executives and investors. Stock markets also give us fairly accurate insight into how investors expect future profits to play out. At the same time, as we all know, the stock market can be an awfully mysterious and volatile index on which to base empirical research. That fact suggests that there might be other more direct and, admittedly, more subjective ways to analyze the impact of IP on industries, strategies, and competitive performance.

We have found that one of the best alternatives to using the stock market to explore the relationship between intellectual property and profits is instead to examine *profit pools* by industry segment. We can then observe how intellectual property more directly affects *current* profits by observing how different parts of an industry (what some call the value chain) rely on IP. Typically, what we find is that the largest, most stable profit pools came from business models that emphasize strong IP strategies. At the industry level, this relationship is most notable in pharmaceuticals, which ranks as one of the industries most strongly driven by patented products, and where the top 10 drug companies in 2002 generated more profits ($36 billion) than the other 490 companies in the Fortune 500 put together ($34 billion). Not to be outdone, IP-oriented industries like software, semiconductors, medical devices, and communications equipment also rank highly, with leading companies in these industries typically generating pretax profit margins in the range of 20–35 percent.

Even high margins, however, can understate the current profitability of such businesses. Digging deeper into the Intel example, for instance, we find that in 2007 it earned revenues of $38 billion, with a pretax profit margin of 21 percent (an off year compared to the 31 percent in 2005), profit levels that placed it among the elite earners of the Fortune 500. When it comes to measuring the true earnings power of a business, however, many investment analysts like to focus on the total cash flow margin of a company. This ratio subtracts out all the noncash charges that companies subtract from profit margins to account for the depreciation of their factories and equipment investments. Intel makes large investments in physical capital, around $4 billion to $7 billion annually (semiconductor foundries don't come cheap), and writes those investments off at a rate of well over $4 billion per year. If, following the common practice of investment analysts, you add back Intel's depreciation charges to its pretax profit, its cash flow margin rises to 33 percent.

With margins like these, it is easy to see why Intel has been such a darling of the markets over the past decade. But Intel's investments in foundries and semiconductor manufacturing equipment aren't the only types of investments it makes. Intel also invests massive amounts in R&D and intellectual property development. In 2007, for example, in addition to its investments in physical capital, Intel invested close to $6 billion in R&D above and beyond its expenditures in physical capital, more than 15 percent of its total revenues, and received more than 1,500 patents along the way. But what if we played a little accounting trick: what would happen if you accounted for Intel's intellectual assets the same as you did its physical assets for cash flow purposes? (There is no good reason not to treat them identically.) The result: Intel's cash flow margin rises to nearly half of its revenues. Not a bad year at the office.

When we apply these same calculations to other industries, we get the same predictably impressive results. The profit rates of the pharmaceutical business in particular also provide us with the most dramatic evidence of the value of intellectual property at ground level. Prescription drug products provide the perfect controlled experiment for the profitability of a product with and without a patent because, with great regularity, companies with patent-protected drugs get the opportunity to watch exactly what happens to their profits as their patents expire. Examples abound, and while they vary a bit in the speed of profit loss, the effect could not be clearer: when a drug is protected by a patent, the drug maker has the power to keep prices high; when the patent expires, that power disappears and price levels plummet as generic drug brands enter the market.

For example, when Eli Lilly's legendary antidepressant Prozac went off patent in 2001, the company's share of new prescriptions dropped by an extraordinary 73 percent within two weeks as generic alternatives flooded the market. A year later, the average price for fluoxetine-based products (fluoxetine is the active ingredient in Prozac) supplied by the generic competition had fallen by 85 percent. To say that this onslaught of generic competition against its flagship product was damaging to Eli Lilly is an understatement: it has taken nearly five years for the company to reverse its rapidly sliding profitability.

IP: The Last Legal Monopoly

Ever since the "trustbusters" put an end to industrial monopolies, there remains only one other legal method for a business to attain a monopoly: IP. The right to exclude others from making, selling, or using such property that comes with patents, copyrights, and trademarks provides a highly specific and limited form of monopoly rights for a company that, in turn, provides a measure of market power. But how do successful companies generate this market power? The short answer: through innovation and intellectual property.

While the evidence is clear that extraordinary profits flow to IP-based businesses, most managers have difficulty understanding how the legal rights associated with patents, copyrights, brands, and trade secrets lead to profits.

If we put aside the legalese and use plain business language, the power of IP is pretty simple. There are three components that determine a company's profits: sales volume, the selling price, and the cost of production—and IP is the main driver of all three. Let's take a look at each one in turn.

Why do customers buy your kind of product instead of using their money for something else? Why do they buy your product instead of your competitor's? The simple answer is that customers choose to buy your product over alternatives because they perceive yours to be the best way they can spend their money. It may offer better features, better design, better quality, or better price. Companies spend a lot of time and money trying to make better products and to convince customers that their products are better. But all of that effort can be wasted, and turn a profitable business into a commodity business, if the competition can instantly copy your new product or feature or co-opt your brand. In a world of reverse engineering and rapid sourcing, the only thing that keeps that from happening is intellectual property. IP gives you the ability to produce unique products with unique features and to create a brand that associates those innovations with your company and its products.

This of course begs the question: what is it that makes my product uniquely valuable to my customer that my competitors can't replicate? The answer defines your "ownable distinction." If your distinction is strong, and valuable to customers, your sales and market share will be high. Otherwise, you're just selling commodities.

Ownable distinction doesn't just drive market share, it also drives selling price. All else being equal, customers would rather pay a lower price. So if you want to be able to charge a higher price, then "all else" better not be equal. Differentiated products capture premium prices. The only reason that unique products and features stay unique is because of patents. A smart company can also create value in their brand by associating their unique products and features with their company. Brands, and the "brand premium" that companies capture through higher prices, are protected by trademarks, small symbols like the Nike "swoosh," a simple flourish that can turn a $4 cotton visor into a $16 fashion statement.

There are, though, a lot of industries like most basic-materials companies that really struggle to differentiate their products. These "commodity industries" find it very difficult (or more likely impossible) to command premium prices. Without some way to differentiate their products, they lack the opportunity for branding, leaving them only one way to compete: on price. Even within industries that have lots of product differentiation, like consumer electronics, once a technology or feature is widespread the product becomes just another commodity.

The final driver of profits is cost. Companies who can produce more for less have lower production costs. Higher productivity can come from a number of sources. One of them is scale. For decades, companies have competed on scale to drive down their costs and allow them to make higher profits (through higher margins) or to lower price to capture more market share. In the business consulting world, this approach translated into the classic scale strategy that was expressed as "add capacity, cut price, gain share." While scale continues to be an important driver of cost, it has become less important as a source of profits. As the size of the market has increased through globalization and growth, and technology has made it possible to manufacture efficiently in smaller volumes, more companies in each industry are able to achieve an efficient scale. If everybody in your industry has scale, you need to have it to even get in the game.

Another important way to reduce cost is to improve productivity through better manufacturing processes. Companies invest a lot of money and effort to improve their production methods to eliminate excess materials, labor, and overhead. Whenever a company is able to achieve lower cost due to manufacturing innovations, and it can keep its competitors from discovering or adopting its methods (think trade secrets and patents), it can achieve a sustainably lower cost position. Once that happens, companies can choose higher margins (same price, lower cost), or they can cut price and take market share. In either case, it is IP that makes this kind of innovation possible.

The bottom line is that without IP, there's very little bottom line left.

Ironically, most CEOs, even in those IP-centric industries like pharmaceuticals and high tech, fail to grasp the real source of their profits. Instead, they abdicate the responsibility of managing their company's most important and advantage-creating assets to specialized functional experts. These leaders rely on this technical and legal expertise to keep them out of trouble and, hopefully, provide some advantage. In other words, these leaders spend their time moving the deck chairs around their corporate cruise ship without understanding what actually keeps them afloat.

Market power, of course, is a sensitive legal subject. Yet outside of the fantasy world of academic research, in which "perfect competition" reigns in the absence of market power, the exercise of power in business negotiations between buyers and sellers is a simple part of everyday business life. From a regulatory standpoint, the decision to intervene in everyday business competition to impose limits on market power requires regulators to both conceive and apply what are inevitably subjective standards for what constitutes *unreasonable* power.

Over the last century or so, as courts and regulators have worked hard to reconcile the tension between the institutions of *antitrust law,* which prohibit the pursuit of market power, and the intellectual property laws, which allow it, this balance has shifted around a bit. And indeed, for much of the twentieth century, when the two regimes faced off, the antitrust side often won out. More recently, however, the pendulum has swung away from a concern over market power in any form toward a more practical posture (regulators call it the *rule of reason*) that recognizes in most cases that the value of promoting innovation outweighs the cost of allowing modest market power. In 1995, the U.S. Department of Justice and the Federal Trade Commission affirmed that they "do not presume that intellectual property creates market power in the antitrust context." Recent court decisions have defended the exercise of intellectual property rights and raised the bar for what constitutes unreasonable market power.

This is good news for innovative businesses. Greater support for intellectual property rights adds a new dimension to a strategy that can help businesses achieve their main purpose: innovating to serve customers more effectively and making money in the process. And taking a more reasonable approach to questions of market power removes constraints on strategy development that have made the entire strategic planning process increasingly valueless. After all, how can a strategist develop meaningful insights on business direction when the best way to pursue the main goal of strategy—generating a sustainable competitive advantage—is not discussable?

Strategists generally agree that, within the constraints of the law, the goal of strategy is achieving market power. Perhaps the best-known articulation of this argument comes in Harvard Business School Professor Michael Porter's classic book *Competitive Strategy.* In a framework that every MBA graduate over the last two decades has learned, Porter set forth a market power–oriented construct in which he defined what made an industry attractive. Porter's framework famously identified *five forces* that influence a company's market power and drive industry profitability: supplier power, buyer power, barriers to entry, availability of substitutes, and direct competitive rivalry.

Interestingly, nowhere in *Competitive Strategy* (and infrequently in subsequent books) does Porter mention the subject of intellectual property or its individual components, such as brands, copyright, and patents. Nevertheless, the power of exclusion that IP provides dovetails closely with Porter's model. IP provides sustainable market power for businesses against customers and suppliers; they limit opportunities for competitive entry and imitation; and they put constraints on certain aspects of competitive rivalry, most directly the competition for existing products based on current technology. Porter was exactly right. The attractiveness of a company's position depends on its strength relative to the other players in its ecosystem. As we described above, IP is increasingly the most important source of that power, and as a result, the most important source of profits. To see these powers of exclusion in action, we turn again to Intel for an illustration.

The Rise of Chipzilla

By 1978, after plugging away for ten years, Intel reached a critical turning point when IBM chose Intel's 8088 (and later its cousin, the higher-powered 8086) microprocessor as the engine for its upcoming personal computer (the now ubiquitous PC). In a single decision, IBM made Intel the standard for an entire industry. Intel, for its part, seized the opportunity to make its founder's law a mass-market reality.

By 1985, with the IBM PC now firmly established as the industry standard, Intel moved to consolidate its position in the microprocessor market: in a single stroke Intel stopped licensing its IP (chip designs) to its competitors, which made it impossible for them to produce x86 chips. Such competitive licensing was a common practice in many industries and provided customers with a "second source" for sensitive components, like microprocessors. With their unprecedented bid for dominance, however, Intel turned the tables on the traditional customer-supplier power relationship and chose to make itself the only second-source option, constructing multiple semiconductor foundries for its third-generation PC microprocessor line, the 80386 family. In the words of the trade, Intel went "single source" and, for a time, took an effective monopoly position in the PC microprocessor market.

Intel's move was wildly successful and secured its leading position in the PC market like never before. Left in Intel's wake, the rest of the microprocessor manufacturers had to regroup. Facing extinction, they needed to find a way to make their way back into the mainstream part of the market. As a first step, many of these competitors focused on product innovation, hoping to contest Intel's monopoly by making large improvements in performance.

As the PC market hit its stride in the early 1990s, a few chinks began to appear in Intel's armor: the competition had been busy. Intel management was particularly concerned about the competitive threat posed by integrated circuit designs based on RISC technology (RISC stands for Reduced Instruction Set Computing). RISC architectures were becoming potent alternatives to Intel's CISC designs (C for complex). Product families like IBM's POWER chips, Sun Microsystems' SPARC chips, and Digital Equipment's ALPHA line incorporated simpler routines for processing instructions, a design innovation that brought with it a promise of pushing the pace of Moore's Law faster than Intel's designs could keep pace with.

With integrated circuits moving from an age where transistors per chip numbered in the thousands to chips with millions of transistors, the difficulty of moving a large volume of electrical signals through all these circuits had become a much larger challenge than reducing the size of the circuits themselves. Blocked by Intel's IP from competing in the x86 market, Intel's competitors were now looking to stage a comeback by introducing RISC technology capable of beating Intel's products with faster and higher-performing designs. It also meant these competitors, on the basis of their faster chips, had begun making rapid inroads in other computing applications like handheld video games, high-performance workstations, and high-end servers.

While other companies were forced to chase new unproven markets, Intel maintained its dominance of the PC chip market. Since most computers at that time operated solely on the Intel standard, users were extremely reluctant to change out platforms. That meant that if RISC-based competitors wanted to take on Intel in the PC market, they had to figure out a way to make chips that worked with Intel systems. This is called emulation. Any competitor up for this challenge, however, found that they would have a hard row to hoe: Intel, of course, withheld any licenses or technology guidance that would help a competitor find a way to make a RISC computer operate seamlessly with the Intel CISC standard. In other words, Intel used its IP to create some significant barriers of entry in the PC market, one it continues to dominate even today.

Some Monopolies Can Promote Competition

In what may at first appear to be a contradiction, while Intel's use of its intellectual property rights secured its market power—by lifting its profitability and by limiting the short-term ability of its competition to introduce new products and technology—Intel simultaneously *promoted* competition in future products and technologies. How is that possible, you might ask? While Intel first used its IP to effectively force its competitors out of the PC market in the 1980s, those competitors had the incentive to go out and develop superior technology, the RISC chip, or face going out of business altogether. And while Intel was able to keep its competitors offering RISC chips at bay for a while, it knew it had a battle on its hands. What this shows us is that with the protection of patents, inventors can use their market power to challenge established players with substantial market power in other areas, power that would otherwise make any conventional business plan for a high-tech start-up unthinkable. Why else would Sun invest in developing its SPARC chip unless it thought it could use its own IP to combat Intel's market position? As a result, intellectual property management dramatically expands the options available to the practicing strategist. And it is in the relatively unfettered marketplace for future features and benefits that we find some of the hardest-fought competitive battles of the day, often pitting small companies against far more powerful rivals. All too often it is IP that allows these small companies to compete, and win, in the face of such competition.

In today's economy, many large product and channel businesses (like Intel) have accrued amazing levels of market power having little to do with intellectual property and in the process have become the modern-day equivalent of medieval guilds: they can set the terms of entry for anyone wanting to enter into their particular line of business. This was true for glassmakers in Venice in the fifteenth century and it's true today. Just try to enter the consumer goods business in America on a large scale without selling to Walmart or the home improvement business without selling to Home Depot. And try developing a new software business without making it Windows compatible. If Walmart, Home Depot, or Microsoft decides they want to lower your price, choose your competitor, or even enter your business, they can pretty much do whatever they want in the absence of some form of countervailing power.

With intellectual property protection, however, the balance of power can shift substantially. If you've developed technology that gives your product features that consumers value and no one else can imitate, you have what some have called an "ownable distinction." You can safely invest in building your brand reputation by coupling a proprietary trademark with those distinct features you have patented without fear of a competitor following in your footsteps. If Walmart wants to attract customers who are interested in those features you have patented without paying you for either the product or the technology, therefore, you have the legal means available to limit Walmart's options. To look at it another way, if you've developed a technology for use in your own products that your competitors need to emulate, either you can choose to keep the technology entirely to yourself or you can license it out for a price, a price that gives your own product a built-in cost advantage and makes it harder for your competitors to engage in a price war since they're already starting out with higher costs.

Of course, you can also simply choose not to make the product at all. The benefits of licensing a valuable technology without actually practicing the invention frequently outweigh the risks of all the investments required to bring an entire product to market. In this case, you can choose to treat your patent as a tradable asset by either selling it to others who might be able to put it to better use or licensing it to others who can use the technology in their own products (more on this in chapter 3).

Although the notion of using intellectual property for the purpose of differentiating your own product or licensing the rights to competitors faces little opposition, the idea that IP's greatest value may be as a tradable asset has generated a huge amount of controversy. In a sense, the reaction has an emotional component: when innovators capture profits without making tangible products, people somehow think they're making "money for nothing." In another sense, the controversy over companies that choose to focus solely on their patent holdings, earning themselves the legal label *nonpracticing entities,* reveals a deeper conflict: namely, what happens when the most powerful product players don't always win the race to provide technology solutions? In the industry most strongly associated with driving the Information Revolution, however, these controversies have been unfolding in a series of intense strategic battles that have much to teach us about the unique and powerful economics that underlie intellectual property.

The Rise of the Troll

Where did the moniker patent troll come from anyway? The controversy over patent monopolies has been heating up in recent years, in large measure by the outrage focused on this new specter of business bogeyman. Turns out that it was an Intel patent attorney named Peter Detkin who coined the term in 2001. In an interview with legal reporter Brenda Sandburg regarding a lawsuit Intel was engaged in, Detkin took the opportunity to derogatively describe TechSearch, the small and unknown company that was suing Intel, as *a patent troll*. The phrase piqued Sandburg's interest and she began her feature with what she opined was a "fairy tale . . . on a patent system run amok."

> In the sleepy village of Santa Clara, there lived a very wealthy but very fright-
> ened giant named Intel. Intel was plagued by a fearsome band of evil trolls—
> patent trolls, to be exact—who wanted a glittering pot of gold in exchange for
> doing absolutely nothing. And they were very powerful because they said they
> owned the patent on some of the magic Intel used to become very rich.

Since Sandburg devoted only a few sentences to the actual patent conflict, her piece wound up serving as a fairly effective bit of publicity for Intel. The truth is, she missed out on the chance to tell an interesting entrepreneurial story that sheds light on how IP can be used to disrupt market power.

The story begins back in 1998, when TechSearch purchased the patent that formed the basis for Sandburg's troll story out of the bankruptcy proceedings of a little company called International Meta Systems (IMS). IMS had never commer-cialized a product successfully, although they had shipped some prototype systems. For about a dozen years, however, they had attracted a considerable amount of tal-ent and money while attempting to achieve a significant innovation in the semi-conductor sector. In short, IMS had searched for what some considered to be the holy grail of the industry: a way to get RISC chips to talk to Intel systems.

After a series of false starts, IMS had nearly broken into the big time in 1995 when they were hired by SGS-Thomson, Europe's largest semiconductor manu-facturer, to help them break into the lucrative U.S. market for computer chips, then dominated by Intel. Companies like SGS-Thomson badly wanted to find a way into Intel's x86 market. For SGS Thomson, the deal with IMS represented one of several bets they were placing at the time, but for IMS it was time to bet the company.

With their contract from SGS-Thomson in hand, IMS moved aggressively to ramp up its R&D efforts and management ranks. They opened a new design center in Austin, Texas, and hired thirty new employees. They raised $13 million from venture capital firms to fund their new chip project. They then recruited a new president, an experienced technology manager named Lee Hoevel, who had formerly been head of R&D and chief technology officer at NCR.

IMS soon developed a valuable portfolio of intellectual property, including a library of copyrighted integrated circuit designs, but the most notable investment was a patent filing. In March of 1994, IMS filed what would soon become the most infamous patent in the world; and in November 1996 that patent, U.S. Patent No. 5,574,927 (the 927 patent), was granted. Its title read: "RISC Architecture Computer Configured for Emulation of the Instruction Set of a Target Computer."

Then, just as IMS's fortunes seemed ready to soar, everything fell apart. Intel continued to make it as difficult as possible for competitors to make compatible products. While a few companies succeeded in bringing Intel-compatible chips to market, SGS-Thomson ran into technical difficulties and decided to cut its losses and exit the business. That meant, just one year after landing their contract, IMS was left out in the cold without a contract and no cash flow. So when a last desperate bid for new funding fell through, the board began preparations to shut the company down for good, and Hoevel turned to the task of orchestrating an orderly bankruptcy. As part of the liquidation process, he sold off the 927 patent to a small Illinois company that was about to make headlines. That company was, of course, TechSearch.

Hoevel and TechSearch agreed to a deal in January 1998. According to the deal's terms, IMS may have received as little as $10,000 in cash from TechSearch. But the cash wasn't the point. Rather, it was the opportunity to collect future royalties from TechSearch as it sought out licensing fees from other companies that were using emulation techniques like those described in the IMS patent. Under the terms of that agreement, TechSearch was free to enforce the patent in any way it chose. In short order, TechSearch decided to swing for the fences, using its new asset as an impressive bat: in June 1998, TechSearch filed a patent infringement lawsuit against Intel.

With the lawsuit filed, Intel, not surprisingly, wasted little time in fighting back. What is somewhat surprising, though, is the fierceness with which Intel launched its counterattack. It is revealing perhaps that, despite Intel's lawyers' efforts to have the suit thrown out, the company took the patent so seriously.

If we dig a little, we find there was an interesting question hidden in this issue of emulation. On one hand, emulation techniques were a way for x86 clones, Intel competitors like AMD and IMS, to achieve interoperability with the Intel standard. But what if emulation wasn't just for clones? In a technical sense, what happened when Intel wanted to upgrade its old chips and keep the new architecture compatible with the architectures running in their installed base? How would Intel be able to move seamlessly from the 80486 generation to its upcoming Pentium chip line? In a sense, these upgraded chip designs were a lot like the other RISC competitors: they incorporated all kinds of new features and capabilities, while allowing programs and files developed on the earlier chips to run on the newer chips at the same time. Since Intel's installed user base remained its largest advantage over its competitors, maintaining backward compatibility between its new and old designs was critical. It also presented a significant technology challenge, arguably one of the main obstacles to keeping up the pace on Moore's Law.

And it wasn't as if Intel didn't know about the 927 patent: Intel had actually approached IMS back in 1995 to see if they could provide a solution to their backward-compatibility dilemma. Intel was hoping IMS might help them incorporate some of the benefits of RISC technology without having to give up their CISC customers. And it was this precise argument over the similarity between backward compatibility and emulation that the TechSearch lawyers seized on, calling the 927 patent "the most significant design breakthrough since Von Neumann's" (the James Watt of computing, John Von Neumann first had the idea of separating a computer's memory from its processing unit).

So when TechSearch sued for patent infringement, Intel didn't merely oppose the claim; they mobilized for war. They attacked TechSearch just about every way they possibly could:

- Intel countersued TechSearch, arguing that the 927 patent was invalid. They even enlisted the IMS engineer, Lee Scantlin, who invented the emulation methods, to testify that his patent wasn't really a valid invention after all. Intel's claim, however, didn't get very far. Not only had they validated the patent's claims by initiating discussions with IMS over it, the 927 patent itself had already been cited by other engineers in 140 other patent filings, including in 11 filed by Intel itself.
- Intel tried to buy the patent surreptitiously. In October 1998, just a few months after TechSearch filed suit, a Cayman Islands company named Maelen approached the IMS creditor committee and challenged the sale of the 927 patent to TechSearch. As it turned out, Maelen was a shell company controlled by Intel. The bankruptcy judge objected and the story found its way into the *Wall Street Journal*. Needless to say, this sneak attack didn't go very far either.
- Embarrassed by the Maelen fiasco, Intel accused TechSearch of being a "patent extortionist." This accusation was also published in the *Wall Street Journal*. TechSearch responded that they weren't "extorting anyone, but merely exercising [their] constitutional right to enforce a patent." They also sued Intel for libel.

- Recognizing that accusing opponents of a felony might not be very helpful in patent court, the Intel defense team decided to shift tactics. That's when Peter Detkin, Intel's assistant general counsel at the time, came up with something more creative. In his conversation with Sandberg, Detkin came up with the clever idea of calling TechSearch a troll. Sandberg, as we learned earlier, loved the idea and the term caught fire. All of a sudden, Intel had reclaimed the moral high ground.

- Intel's final claim was that they simply weren't infringing on the patent at all, despite a concession that their Pentium chips used a number of RISC techniques. The judge who reviewed the case, however, decided that Intel's method of achieving backward compatibility in their own chips was *not* emulating their earlier designs in the specific way described in the 927 patent. As a result, he ruled in Intel's favor. The verdict was later upheld in May 2002 after an appeal by TechSearch to the Federal Appeals Court.

After all the drama and intrigue, Intel won the fight on a technicality. They didn't earn the nickname Chipzilla for nothing.

The lasting legacy of the TechSearch struggle, though, had little to do with Intel's legal victory. Even if they had won the infringement suit, TechSearch would certainly have reached a settlement that Intel could afford. Intel has previously settled several large patent infringement suits over the years, with companies like Digital Equipment, Intergraph, and MicroUnity, each for hundred of millions of dollars. The main legacy was the term patent troll, conceived in the heat of battle as a way to save face after a public relations fiasco. And although IMS and TechSearch have passed into obscurity, the label lives on.

Patent troll. It's an evocative term. Like the character from the fairy tale about Billy Goat Gruff, it suggests an ugly little creature who hides out underneath a bridge that he doesn't own and springs out unexpectedly, threatening to eat innocent passersby. It channels a kind of moral outrage, the idea that the troll is making money without actually doing anything of value. But as the TechSearch example shows, the real question over trolls is whether or not the company that invents valuable technology has a right to realize the value of their asset when their original business aspirations fail. IMS spent years investing in attempts to solve problems in semiconductor technology like emulation. When, after investing more than $20 million, their business plan eventually failed, the fact that they moved to sell off their most marketable asset was not only their right, it was their fiduciary obligation. Indeed, the only dispute surrounding the 927 patent more heated than the Intel litigation was the shareholder litigation that arose over the way in which the IMS board performed its duty. For several years, disgruntled shareholders could become members of the "IMS Legal Defense Fund," a group that existed mainly to accuse Lee Hoevel of letting TechSearch buy the patent for too little!

If Lee Scantlin had invented a technique that Intel used to solve a critical problem of backward compatibility, why wouldn't that be valuable? If Intel knew about the technology and tried to use it without compensating IMS, why shouldn't they be compelled to pay? If IMS chose to sell off their patent in a bankruptcy proceeding, why wouldn't they sell it to a buyer who would find the licensing opportunity an attractive one? And if TechSearch chose to seek a windfall by strong-arming Intel in ways that IMS had been reluctant to do, how was this any less anticompetitive than Intel's earlier move to "single source" the 80386 chip models? From a business standpoint, the critical question is not whether TechSearch had a right to monetize a patent that they were able to buy at fire sale prices. Rather, the question was simple: did Intel use the 927 emulation technology? Two courts decided that they didn't. So they didn't have to pay TechSearch a nickel.

In September 2002, a little over a year after her story "Trolling for Dollars" appeared, Brenda Sandburg noted an interesting postscript to the story of Chipzilla and the Troll. Peter Detkin had a new job. "A top lawyer at Intel Corp. is leaving the fold," wrote Sandburg. Where was he going? To Intellectual Ventures, what some observers have called a "patent troll on steroids."

And now that he's joined Intellectual Ventures, what does Detkin have to say about patent trolls? In a recent magazine interview, in which the interviewer defined a troll as "a person or business that doesn't produce a product or service, but instead makes money from licensing and patent assertion primarily," Detkin responded.

> My concern is that the term has now been used so broadly as to mean any plaintiff you don't like. Look at the definition you just used. Under that definition the University of California is a troll, Intel's a troll—and since I was at Intel at the time, Lord knows I wasn't trying to call myself a troll. But Intel routinely asserts patents—that it bought, that it's not practicing— against others, looking for money. IBM would be a troll. Thomas Edison would be a troll.

In this case, where you stand on the issue probably depends on where you sit.

A Different Kind of Economics

If we want to solve technical problems rapidly, society must provide incentives that would not exist without government intervention. Few would dispute that Moore's Law has become a spectacular force of economic and technical change. But this law is not like a law of nature, it's more like a forecast of the rate at which semiconductor engineers will be able to keep up an unusually rapid race of technical progress. The force that keeps Moore's Law going is the force of competition, with engineers racing to solve problems before others come up with the same or better solutions sooner. Some of the engineers pushing the pace on Moore's Law work for Intel, which has been a powerful source of new solutions and rapid progress. But a large number of those engineers work outside of Intel and their work helps to keep Intel running fast. They have an obvious incentive to keep working on these critical problems—issues like backward compatibility and emulation between RISC and CISC chips—because if they do they may get wealthy.

Unlike large companies that have established products and channels to market them through, small companies like IMS don't have the resources or financial flexibility to challenge competitors the size of Intel head-on. But with talented engineers, investor support, and a network of partners, IMS had a chance to make a competitive difference, either directly with a product like the Meta 6000 or indirectly by solving an important problem and licensing the solution to the company that is in the best position to profit from the innovation.

These companies don't need to spend years building redundant products, factories, or sales forces. All they have to do is *win the race* to solve a *critical technical problem*. If they do—meaning they solve the problem first and the problem ends up being a valuable problem to solve—they can end up with an asset of substantial value. Sometimes they can make the asset valuable within their original business plan. Other times, the business plan fails and the return to investors comes when the original owners sell the rights to the asset to someone else. And sometimes, the asset has more value potential in the hands of a company like Tech-Search if they can demonstrate both the priority of the original inventor in devising the solution and the unauthorized use of the invention by others.

The Intel-versus-TechSearch saga points out a number of the notable features of an intellectual property asset like a patent. The patent was an output of a sustained, multiyear product development process involving millions of dollars. Investors, partners, and competitors all showed serious interest in the technology at different times and for different reasons. And the question of the importance of the invention was a tricky and challenging one to answer: potential licensors and licensees all behaved as if it were a reasonable question to pose. In the end, the answer required the intervention of the courts to decide on the outcome, not a surprising situation when the stakes were so high and the solutions so potentially valuable.

More broadly, when considering how businesses deal with questions of intellectual property management, one comes away struck by how little the normal rules of strategy and management apply. Intellectual property differs in fundamental ways from other kinds of economic resources, in much the same way that the continuously variable signals of analog electronics differ from the bits and bytes of digital computers. Most economic resources are well described using the smooth supply-and-demand curves of neoclassical economics, where competitive differences occur at the margin: it is here that small percentage differences often make the difference between competitive success and failure. The economics of intellectual property couldn't be any more different. They are digital and asymmetrical. Intellectual assets can cost millions to create, yet cost virtually nothing to replicate. As property, they can carry enormous value during their term of protection, yet turn completely valueless when their period of protection expires. And, especially in the case of patents, the problems they solve can be incredibly hard to figure out, or even to describe as a problem to begin with, before the inventor develops the solution. Once the solution is shared, though, the answers can seem obvious in hindsight and represented as trivial or obvious.

In addition to these "digital" qualities of intellectual property, there are other factors that shape the unique economics of a piece of intellectual property. First, intellectual property varies enormously in value, with most of the protection provided amounting to little. Indeed the vast majority doesn't have much value at all. The small subset of intellectual assets that attract the most attention represents a small fraction of the total assets created. Second, the value of technology is largely determined by the nature of its interconnection to other related assets and thus can only be valued in a relational context. The more important the assets, the more likely others will want to connect to them. And because this web of connections can take many unexpected directions, the conceptual boundaries of a piece of protected technology can resist familiar categories like industry, product, or process type. Third, with patents in particular, the granting of the right to exclude others for a specified term requires disclosure of the invention. So the act of obtaining the right provides an invitation for others to compete for ways to obtain the benefits of the claimed invention: by working around it, improving on it, finding ways to render it invalid, and even to use it without notifying its owner. Finally, since the act of innovation can be embedded within copyrighted software or encapsulated within a firm's trademarked reputation, intellectual property assets are often overlapping and complementary.

Expensive to create; costless to copy. Temporary. Confusing ex ante; obvious ex post. Worthless more often than not. Completely relational. An invitation to compete. Self-reinforcing. All of these attributes contribute to making intellectual property so unusual and so difficult to manage.

To top it all off, there's an active and critically important debate (one that's going on more in the classroom but being ignored in the boardroom) over whether or not our current IP system is actually necessary (or even actively harmful) in the modern economy. So it's worth stepping back for a moment to ask what kind of results society is getting from its intellectual property system.

As recently as 1984, the proceedings from a National Bureau of Economic Research (NBER) conference on "R&D, patents, and productivity" reported concerns over "a worldwide decline in patenting" that some of the experts there felt was implicated in the "longer term total factor productivity growth slowdown which may have started in the late 1960s." Barely two decades later, some of these same conference participants declared a new concern: the "marked increase in patenting" that began in the mid-1980s. One of them has taken to declaring a new crisis in this patent resurgence, arguing that the rise in U.S. patent counts is a problem that needs to be solved.

We've done a wide range of analyses of U.S. patent data, including the trends for issued patents since the patent system began here in 1791. And it's true that we have witnessed a large absolute increase in patent counts over the last twenty-five years. But if we might reasonably expect the absolute number of patents to be tied to economic activity in some rough sense, we would expect patents to grow as the economy grew. Indeed, we might expect patents to increase as our economy became more technologically advanced. So instead of focusing on the absolute numbers, rather it's the relative count of patents, relative to the inputs or to past levels, that really matters.

In Figure 4 we have laid out on a ratio scale a graph showing granted U.S. patents since 1791. Clearly we have seen healthy patent growth in recent years, about 4.4 percent annually between 1980 and 2004. But this growth has come on the heels of the much longer period of stagnation that had the NBER economists worried in 1984. For the entire first half of the twentieth century, patent growth was basically flat, at well under 0.7 percent per year, a situation that sparked the concern over the limits to growth of our innovation economy. In addition, our overall propensity to patent, measured as the amount of patents relative to the overall workforce, actually declined dramatically from World War I onward. As Figures 5 and 6 (pages 68 and 69)

FIGURE 4   U.S. Patents Granted, 1790–2007

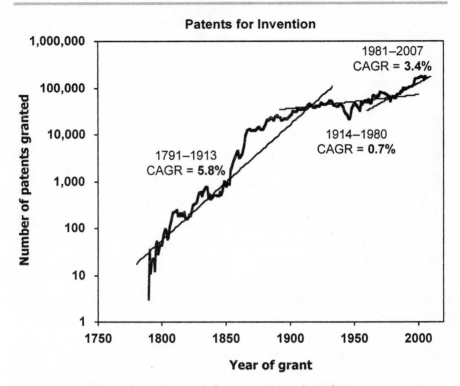

Patents for Invention

Source: USPTO; author analysis. CAGR stands for compound annual growth rate.

show, the ratio of patents per million workers (or thousand knowledge workers) in the United States fell throughout most of the twentieth century. And the uptick in the last few years represents only a modest recovery.

Perhaps the most striking trend in Figure 4 is not the recent recovery in patent growth, but rather the sustained high growth rates in American patenting all through the nineteenth century. As we've seen, the Industrial Revolution saw the longest sustained period of patent growth in human history. From 1791 to 1913, U.S. patent awards grew at an annual rate of nearly 6 percent per year, an amazing growth to sustain for over a century. And while we might take comfort in the renewed innovative trend, undoubtedly fueled by the Information Revolution and the innovation areas such as biotechnology that information technology has enabled, it seems to us a bit early to declare a new crisis of too much patenting. Arguably, the rise in innovation that began in the United States during the mid-1980s has helped fuel the sustained growth in GDP and productivity that began

FIGURE 5   U.S. Patents Granted per Worker, 1919–2006

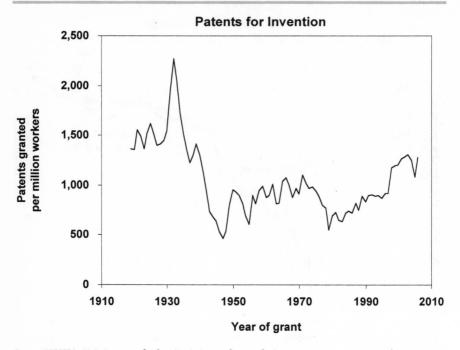

Source: USPTO; U.S. Bureau of Labor Statistics; author analysis.

shortly after. In addition, none of this renewed propensity to patent comes in a vacuum; the rapid rise of U.S. patenting has come alongside similar patent explosions in other parts of the world, such as Japan, Korea, and China, all of them bidding to be world leaders in innovation.

The innovation race of the eighteenth and nineteenth centuries may have been kicked off by James Watt, but he was only the beginning of a long and distinguished line of technologists, many of whom achieved far greater personal wealth. Thomas Edison was a famously prolific patent producer. The Wright brothers fought hard and long to defend their patent rights against their contemporaries in the emergent aerospace industry. Alexander Graham Bell won the patent race for the telephone, delivering his patent application to the U.S. Patent Office literally hours before his rival in the field, Elisha Gray, filed similar patent applications of his own. If the outcome had been different, we might have all grown up making phone calls on the "Gray System."

The Information Revolution may seem as inevitable as the Industrial Revolution in hindsight, but we should not forget that many of the companies that are

FIGURE 6   U.S. Patents Granted per Knowledge Worker, 1860–2000

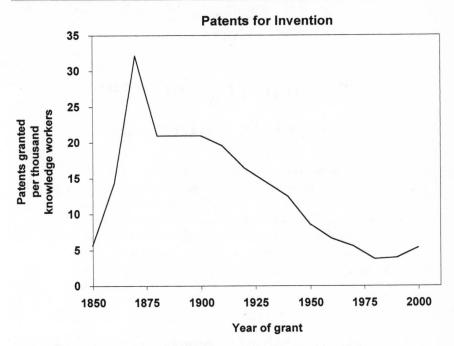

Patents for Invention

Source: USPTO; U.S. Bureau of Labor Statistics; author analysis.

leading the Information Revolution have been built around intellectual property strategies. Before he sold his first operating system, Bill Gates used a deliberate strategy of selling packaged software rather than sharing the original source code in building Microsoft. Gates rejected the prevailing practice of giving software away for free in order to sell hardware or, even worse in Gates's view, allowing fellow hackers to "steal their software." In a competition more focused on patents than on copyright protection, Gordon Moore brought the microprocessor to the world first by defining the terms of an innovation contest with Moore's Law and then by bringing the leading-edge inventors in the field together in his new company Intel to find ways to win that race.

The great rivalries and businesses of the world have been built around the race to define and to solve critical problems. To the winner go the spoils. And as long as we have strong intellectual property rules, those spoils can be worth enough to encourage the innovators to train hard and run fast. As for the rest of us, it has generally been a good thing to have a race.

CHAPTER 3

The Company You Keep

UNLEASHING THE COMPANY OF IDEAS

> Here and there, it is true, we find islands of conscious power in this ocean of unconscious cooperation, like lumps of butter coagulating in a pail of butter milk. The factory system itself, while it involves endless specialization of the work of ordinary men, involves also deliberate co-ordination of their diverse activities by the capitalist employer; and the head of a single big business today exercises a width and intensity of industrial rule which a Tudor monarch might have sighed for in vain.
>
> —*D. H. Robertson*, The Control of Industry, *1928**

I f we can agree that intellectual property ownership is a powerful driver of business profits, then it begs an intriguing question: why would a business bother with owning or managing any other kind of asset? After all, who wouldn't embrace a business model whose goal is to maximize profit potential by focusing only on those activities that result in the highest returns? In other words, why wouldn't every business bind its activities as closely as possible to intellectual property and *only* intellectual property? In the language of stock trading, this would mean steering businesses in the direction of becoming an "IP pure play."

This term, however, often leads to some confusion about what a sustainable IP pure-play company actually looks like. Wall Street and the media that cover it are prone to describing so-called patent trolls like TechSearch as examples of these IP pure plays, when, in fact, they are two entirely different breeds of companies. If we use Detkin's definition as our guide, trolls are a highly specialized

---

*Most commonly cited via reference to Ronald H. Coase, "The Nature of the Firm," *Economica* 4, no. 16 (1937): 386–405. Coase provides the main surviving citation of Robertson's statement, which captures the spirit of Coase's argument so well it is now often attributed to Coase.

species that rely heavily on opportunity and speculation rather than on, say, building any kind of organization capable of securing reliable returns or promoting innovation. Think about the TechSearch business model again for a moment. *Its entire business strategy was built around a single patent.* Even if Lee Scantlin's inventions did provide a useful solution for Intel's Pentium development problems, expecting that a single document could best Intel, one of the world's most prolific patent machines, in a high-stakes showdown was a long shot at best. And most of Silicon Valley, particularly Intel, knew it. Otherwise, rivals would have been beating down Lee Hoevel's door to secure rights to the 927 patent. The lesson learned is that while TechSearch was indeed built solely around an IP strategy, it fell far short of delivering on any kind of long-range business model. At best, narrow models like theirs should be seen as mere liquidation strategies for failed ventures looking for ways to monetize their assets in a bankruptcy.

TechSearch, however, isn't the only small company that has attempted to make some money on the backs of one or two patents; several similar companies, in fact, have even managed some success along the way. Rates Technology (RTI), based in New York, built a modest licensing stream based on two patents it acquired in the VoIP (Voice over Internet Protocol) business. Asure Software (formerly called Forgent Networks) located in Austin, Texas, generated more than $30 million annually in settlements and licensing revenue between 2004 and 2006 on the strength of a single patent covering the ubiquitous JPEG digital image format. And Ampex, based in Redwood City, California, the inventor of the first commercial video recorder and holder of several hundred patents, avoided bankruptcy in 2004 by licensing a single patent on digital image compression technology. While these companies have defended themselves from critics who accuse them of troll-like activity (RTI has sued or threatened Google, Cisco, and Lucent Technologies among others), their near total dependence on licensing just one or two patents makes them close relatives of Detkin's primordial species of troll.

The company that has been featured, and criticized, most prominently for its aggressive use of IP, however, is NTP, the media's patent-troll poster child. NTP is, of course, the company that kept millions of BlackBerry users (and even the U.S. government) on the edge of their seats, wondering whether a judge's decision would shut down their handheld wireless e-mail devices. As the instigator in the fight with Research in Motion (RIM), maker of the BlackBerry, NTP is also the company cited most often by journalists and academics to describe the ills of the U.S. patent system. By asserting that it had invented the technology on which the BlackBerry operates, NTP could hardly have made more enemies than if it had sued the baker of the first apple pie.

Most of the stories written about NTP, however, overlook the company's interesting and innovative history. Like TechSearch, NTP was formed as the holding company for the patents of a failed start-up, in this case a company called Telefind based in Coral Gables, Florida. Founded in 1986 as an entry into the paging business, Telefind's founders successfully filed twenty-three patents between October 1987 and September 1989 based on their advances in the technology for transmitting wireless messages. By 1990, Telefind's paging network was operating in 150 cities and had begun sending a rudimentary form of e-mail to its customers' beepers. They had also begun work on plans to allow laptop computers to upload those e-mails from their blossoming paging network, which, we now know, brought them to brink of implementing the world's first wireless e-mail system.

Telefind's rapid progress didn't go unnoticed either, as AT&T came calling in 1991. Sensing a big break, Telefind invested heavily in revamping its paging system to make it compatible with AT&T's network. The decision to bet all the company's chips on the potential partnership soon proved a mistake, though, as AT&T went in a different direction, partnering with a competing pager provider instead. Later that same year, cash poor and facing bankruptcy, Telefind finally went under. In the liquidation process, one of the company's founders and its lead engineer, Thomas J. Campana Jr., came away with ownership rights to Telefind's patents. In 1992, Campana teamed up with Don Stout, a friend and patent lawyer, to cofound New Technologies Products, or NTP for short.

One of the most overlooked aspects of NTP's story is that Campana did not just sit back and rest on his accomplishments building Telefind's patent portfolio. Rather, always the engineer, he continued to push forward, now focused even more directly on developing wireless e-mail technology, receiving dozens of new patents along the way.

RIM, for its part, got its start in 1984 as a supplier of industrial automation tools to clients like General Motors. Three years later, the company made its first foray into the pager business as a consultant to a subsidiary of Rogers Communications, a paging system operator based in Canada. It was through its work with Rogers that RIM began to develop some expertise in the wireless business, but it wasn't until they formed a partnership with Ericsson, the Scandinavian handset maker, in 1991 that RIM began making a name for itself in the emerging field of wireless e-mail. The company filed its first patent in 1993 and launched

their now ubiquitous and widely praised BlackBerry product line in 1999. In the
years since, RIM's rate of patent filing has exploded, leading to a massive portfolio that now lists some 250 patents. But more important, and again, often overlooked, is that when RIM launched the BlackBerry it was already playing catch-up
to Campana and NTP.

Campana, who died of cancer in 2004, was a pioneer in the field of pager and
wireless e-mail technology. In his combined time at Telefind and NTP, between
1989 and 2003, he received some fifty separate patents. Perhaps more impres-
sively, Campana's patents have been cited more than 500 times by the likes of
major corporations like AT&T, Motorola, Sony, and Intel.

The surprise, to some perhaps, is the name of the company that cites Campana's work the most as prior art on its own patents. No, not Motorola, AT&T, or
Intel. The answer: RIM, whose own patents cite Campana's work twice as frequently as Motorola.

Given this fact, it would seem fairly obvious to journalists and academics alike
that NTP had sufficient grounds for filing a lawsuit against RIM in 2001 for patent infringement. Yet this is where the story gets slightly off track. As the bout
between RIM and NTP heated up to make front-page news, RIM borrowed a page
from Detkin's playbook by labeling NTP, quite disingenuously it would seem,
a patent troll, a destructive company that hid "under bridges they didn't build
themselves."*

Given Campana's track record of innovation, and RIM's own acknowledgment
of his advances, this sort of label hardly seems accurate let alone appropriate.
While RIM certainly felt threatened by the lawsuits levied by NTP, and hence the
need to fight back, it seems they were resolved to bringing the fight into the public domain and, eventually, into the courtroom.

NTP, for its part, exhibited a willingness to settle out of court for a license fee
at every stage of the conflict. They notified RIM of their concerns over patent infringement in January 2000 (less than a year after RIM introduced their Black-
Berry in February 1999) and offered them a license. RIM never responded. In
late 2002, still early on in the legal dispute, a judge ordered RIM to pay NTP a
$54 million settlement along with an ongoing 8.55 percent license (which would
have worked out to about a $180 million liability up to that point). RIM declined
the offer and appealed the verdict. Then in late 2004, the Court of Appeals for

*This line is a direct quote from a RIM legal brief in its case against NTP. "BlackBerryBlues" by
Kim Isaac Eisler, *Washingtonian Magazine*, September 2005.

the Federal Circuit upheld the lower court verdict. Still, NTP was willing to settle, though its price had risen to $450 million to be paid in a single a lump-sum settlement.

Following the Court of Appeals decision, many thought a deal based on this lump-sum payment was imminent. RIM, however, still stuck to its guns in its negotiations with NTP. They continued to pursue a reexamination of NTP's patents and insisted on making the settlement deal conditional on a "money back guarantee" based on the outcome of the reexamination (an unusually aggressive demand). Negotiations broke off yet again. It wasn't until 2006, six years after NTP's first offer to license, and under the threat of a nationwide shutdown, that RIM finally agreed to pay NTP $612 million to save the BlackBerry.

All of this begs the question: was NTP negotiating in bad faith by demanding an exorbitant price from RIM or was it other way around? In answering that question, it might be helpful to consider that the lower court jury needed a mere three hours to find in NTP's favor on its infringement complaints while the lower court judge described the contest as "not a close case."

Even so, was NTP the predator and RIM the prey? Certainly, by developing its own intellectual property and not manufacturing its own products, NTP had a strong negotiating position: they needed nothing at all from RIM. Viewed in that light, perhaps NTP was predatory to some degree, particularly because they, like RIM, refused to back down. But to accuse NTP of acting like a *troll* seems far-fetched. NTP had a large portfolio of technology to bring to the hunt, an ongoing program of innovation, and a widely cited set of claims that commanded respect from many companies. If you were to classify NTP, and companies like it, as a predatory species, there is a more natural fit with a different kind of animal.

A shark.

Consider the metaphor for a bit. Like sharks, which must constantly swim and feed to survive, the most successful IP pure plays are companies that continuously innovate. They are self-sustaining engines of new ideas, valuable inventions, and successful technologies. Companies like TechSearch, on the other hand, are more like scavengers, trolling the landscape for undervalued patents that provide solutions to critical problems. The problem with such scavengers, of course, is that they're not sustainable without a constant supply of low-hanging fruit to take advantage of. Case in point: after TechSearch took its shot at Intel, and failed, the company quickly turned away from the semiconductor business.

Sharks and IP pure plays don't wait for their sustenance: they actively seek it out. They have no choice. And since IP pure plays like NTP don't actually make and deliver a product, they cut down on their exposure to threats from competitors by eliminating their reliance on the technology of others. Because these kinds of companies lack predators of their own, as a species feared by all they lie at the top of the corporate food chain: a position that most business executives would kill for. But a position high on the food chain doesn't mean that a shark can afford to live a sedentary life. Sharks are large, active animals and need to consume a lot of calories to survive. Similarly, investing in innovation over a long period of time is an expensive proposition. So, like a shark, a sustainable IP pure play has to keep swimming all the time.

It is no surprise, then, that businesses based on pure IP models evoke strong emotions from among more than just their prey. Some, like Peter Detkin, struggled with the idea initially. But after recognizing an opportunity within the threat, Detkin launched a shark of his own: Intellectual Ventures, a patent company that also finances ongoing innovation that received some $350 million in start-up funding from A-list technology companies like Microsoft, Intel, Sony, Nokia, and Apple.

There are numerous pundits who raise theoretical objections to the idea of IP pure plays. You really aren't a company unless you make a product, they say. Or, innovation can occur only when a business is somehow "close to the customer," they say, so only by invoicing customers can you qualify as an innovator. To be sure, customer intimacy can provide one basis for valuable innovation, as we'll see in later chapters. The advent of a new kind of economics, however, has given us a new lens to challenge these old intuitions and change traditional views about what it means to be an innovator.

These changes have, in fact, been brewing for years. Perhaps the earliest example is Texas Instruments (TI), the company that started the semiconductor business alongside Intel. TI faced a crisis in the early 1980s as Japanese competitors began attacking their position in the semiconductor memory business. By 1985, the Japanese had driven industry giants like Intel, Motorola, and National Semiconductor completely out of the memory chip market, leaving TI as the lone major American producer in the market. After examining the competitive landscape they faced, TI recognized that while the Japanese enjoyed the advantages of low-cost financing, efficient manufacturing processes, and highly favorable (at the time) exchange rates, they remained vulnerable when it came to their technology. The Japanese, TI learned, relied on patent licenses from their American competitors to manufacture their own chips. So, bucking a long-standing trend of complacency and cooperation in the industry, TI decided to go on an intellectual property offensive. The license rates for semiconductor patents had always been set quite low, less than 1 percent of sales. But with many of its licensing deals nearing the end of their five-year terms, TI made a bold move. The company raised its license price tenfold and, simultaneously, filed suit against a group of eight Japanese companies, a list that included Hitachi, Sharp, and Matsushita, along with the major Korean manufacturer Samsung.

TI's shark attack was swift, unexpected, and decisive.

Realizing that they had no legal standing, the Asian manufacturers quickly agreed to TI's terms. And the results were impressive. TI earned over $1 billion in licensing revenue between 1986 and 1990. In 1992, the last year TI reported its license revenue separately, the company generated more than $520 million in licensing fees, which accounted for some 71 percent of the company's entire pretax operating income. While TI continued to manufacture its own semiconductors, this dramatic shift in strategy made it clear to the semiconductor industry as a whole that IP *on its own* could be a huge contributor to a company's success. It is no surprise that in the years following the shift in TI's strategy, the semiconductor industry has become an important focal point for some of the most important IP strategy innovation around.

IP pure plays aren't just information technology companies either. Biotech, for one, is a hotbed for IP pure plays. Although most traditional pharmaceutical companies are heavily involved in manufacturing, the large network of small, innovative, and efficient biotechnology companies typically focus all of their efforts on research and development. A Boston Consulting Group study conducted in 2004 estimated that while these biotechnology companies account for less than 5 percent of the total amount spent on the industry's R&D, biotech companies like Millennium Pharmaceuticals, Chiron, and Genentech had generated fully *two-thirds* of the worldwide clinical pipeline for new drugs.

IP pure plays have evolved even in the glamorous world of fashion and apparel, where innovators like Nike are built entirely around their intellectual property. Nike, for example, boasts a diverse IP portfolio that includes trademarks on its brands, copyrights that protect its designs and "trade dress," as well as a slew of patents for innovations such as its Shox insole support. Like most of the leading footwear companies, Nike has long since abandoned manufacturing its products. Like NTP, they have instead framed their company around their most profitable activities: design and development.

Redefining the Company

From time to time, new technologies emerge that do more than simply enable new products or reduce the cost of making existing products. Some inventions actually change the economics of business in such a powerful way that they profoundly affect the way that economic activity is organized; they quite literally change the structure of the *company*. There are so many assumptions and associations that ride along with references to this thing called a "company" (or, alternatively, a *corporation* or a *firm*) that we run the risk of assuming too much, or worse, ignoring the significance of important changes in what the word means in real life.

Steam power, for example, did more than just revolutionize manufacturing. Controlling the delivery of energy to the point of production made it possible to rethink how businesses were organized: it allowed entrepreneurs to place different dividing lines between firms and, more important, it blurred the lines that existed between firms and their external marketplaces. Prior to the advent of the steam engine, most people had a fixed picture of what a company looked like. But with the advent of the Industrial Revolution, that picture changed abruptly. Companies grew larger, worked across a wider geographic range, and adopted a new range of support activities—finance, payroll, accounting, sales, and distribution—that continue to define what a "big company" does until this day. Several companies born and modeled in the heart of the Industrial Revolution, like Siemens (1847), Colt Manufacturing (1847), Singer (1851), and General Electric (1878), still survive as household names.

But the company that embodied the definition of a big company best, perhaps, was Ford Motor Company. While Ford made the automobile available to the masses, it also showed the world how to manufacture on a mammoth scale through its River Rouge complex, perhaps the most famous example of a large, self-sufficient manufacturing facility. Built in Dearborn, Michigan, between 1917 and 1925, the Rouge, as it was well known, long symbolized Henry Ford's vision of efficiency in manufacturing. At its peak, the complex was nearly two miles long and three-quarters of a mile wide, employed more than 100,000 workers, and served as the hub of a far-flung logistical network that connected fleets of ships and rail cars.

Ford's vision of housing everything he needed to manufacture cars under one roof also led to some unexpected innovations. Ford was friends with the prolific inventor Thomas Edison and the two believed (mistakenly as it turned out) in the superiority of direct current (DC) for electricity generation. While Edison's DC power had many advantages over its rival, alternating current (AC), it did have a significant flaw: the farther the power traveled, the more energy got wasted. That meant that the economics of DC electricity made sense only for those who could build the generator close to the where the demand for the power was greatest. So Ford resolved to make in-house electricity generation part of his master plan for the Rouge.

At the heart of the Rouge complex stood Powerhouse No. 1, a gargantuan fortress spiked with eight towering smokestacks that covered more than six acres and stretched 300 feet into the air—and three stories underground. Originally equipped with 27,000 direct current motors, seven massive Babcock and Wilcox boilers, two General Electric steam turbines, and a control room that looked like it could be the cockpit out of a Flash Gordon movie, the power plant provided a wide range of energy services for the Rouge complex. In effect, Powerhouse No. 1 was designed to power the operations of a small city.

When Ford first laid the plans for his plant in early 1900, more than half of the electricity generated in the United States came from private installations like Powerhouse No. 1. By the time it was built, however, the Rouge model was no longer on the leading edge, as the country had shifted over to independent utility suppliers to get their electricity. And when Ford died, shortly after the end of World War II, the Rouge was widely criticized as a strategic mistake. Alfred Sloan's more decentralized vision for General Motors was seen by the Whiz Kids who took on postwar management of Ford as the model for the future. Meanwhile, the Rouge chugged on.

Years later, on January 29, 1999, Henry Ford's great-grandson Bill Ford, who had taken over the helm of Ford Motor Co. as chairman, prepared an announcement: the company would revitalize the Rouge, modernize it, and make it a model of environmental responsibility. In preparation for the big announcement, maintenance crews were preparing to shut down one of the plant's seven boilers for its annual maintenance. Part of that shutdown protocol included closing off two aging, manual valves that controlled the flow through several of the plant's natural-gas lines. Several hours later, the control room crew noticed a dangerous spike on their gas monitor. "Someone left the valve open!" the supervisor reportedly yelled. Moments later, a gigantic explosion ripped through Powerhouse No. 1, killing six of the workers inside.

The explosion was a tragic postscript to the long history of industrial-age vertical integration—a compelling illustration of the kind of destructive forces that can build up inside companies when they are designed to do too much.

If mechanical power was the force of change for companies born during the industrial age, it has been information technology that now alters the shape of corporations in the information age. Yet our view of what a company should look like often lags behind the possibilities offered by the Information Revolution.

When we hear the word *company*, what do we think of? Companies make products in factories, distribute them through warehouses, and sell them through a sales force or retail stores, we say. Companies ship boxes to customers with physical product inside and, in return, the customer pays the company thirty or sixty days after receiving an invoice—a payment process administered, of course, by the company's finance department. We know, of course, that some companies "deliver" services instead of products. But no matter what a company sells, it needs to employ a lot of people, from secretaries and accountants to systems analysts and experts in supply chain management. And to handle the benefit programs and payroll for all those employees, the company needs a full-fledged human resource department. It all might sound a bit silly when you say it out loud, but too often these industrial-era biases color the way we think and act.

But if we can understand why the advent of mechanical power brought all of a company's function under one roof, why is it so difficult to acknowledge that the free flow of information, which has virtually eliminated the need for what we still call "paperwork," has changed what it means to *be* a company? Just as the steam engine made production more mobile by allowing manufacturers to locate their "mills" away from the waterfalls, information technology now allows business executives to eliminate the paper in the work while also moving the clerical activity away from the source of the transaction. Although on an individual basis most of these transactions cost pennies apiece, processing large volumes of them often yields large economies of scale. As a result, companies increasingly look toward third-party firms to take on the functions that they no longer have the expertise or volume to tackle. This dismantling of a company's traditional functions has created a whole new species of companies that operate under the umbrella term of "business process outsourcing," or BPO.

The advent of BPO means that one company's overhead is another company's gold. As a result, an entire new industry has sprung up to cost-effectively tackle what used to be considered a company's most mundane tasks. Payroll companies like ADP and Paychex, for example, have automated the age-old job of the paymaster by building highly automated and proprietary software "engines" and, along the way, have emerged as some of the most profitable companies in the world. Similarly, benefits-processing companies like Hewitt have emerged to automate the transactions associated with health and retirement benefits. In fact, BPO specialists have begun to emerge in just about every industry. Small banks outsource large chunks of their back-office operations to BPO companies like Fiserv, First Data, and Bisys. Even large corporations, the remnants of our industrial-age legacy, have increasingly handed off their data-processing operations to firms like IBM, Accenture, and EDS.

In the past, most companies that rejected the benefits of BPO mistakenly assumed that it wouldn't be worth their time and effort. It has been the advent of globalization, and access to lower-cost labor forces, that continues to change people's minds. The dramatically lower costs of, say, a call center staffed by an Indian workforce or goods manufactured in China have increasingly opened business executives' minds toward the possibilities of BPO.

Interestingly, BPO companies tend to work more easily with smaller companies. ADP's typical payroll client has about one hundred employees and Fiserv tends to serve community banks with an average of about $200 million in assets. One reason for this is that larger companies find it more expensive to rip out existing processes or the "enterprise resource planning" (ERP) platforms that the firm previously invested millions of dollars installing.

Globalization, however, can change the cost equation for these big companies, too. Most large multinational companies have spread their footprint beyond any one specific geographic location. Rather than outsource their call center, a large company might just build its own Indian facility. This practice is called *offshoring*. Many larger companies have even begun to develop hybrid operations that *combine* outsourcing with offshoring. They can make things in China, handle customer inquiries from a call center in Iowa (using employees with familiar accents), manage billing in India where the hourly costs are cheapest, and ship products to customers literally anywhere in the world with UPS or FedEx.

The combined effect of globalization and BPO—in both its offshored and outsourced versions—means that what used to be routine corporate processes are now rapidly finding their way out the front door. The jobs have been moving as fast as the BPO operators can organize themselves. Indian outsourcers like Wipro and Infosys have been growing as quickly as they can add employees (and in an odd sort of outsourcing recursion they are increasingly turning to their own offshored operations in Eastern European nations to meet the demand) while the Indian BPO operations of Accenture and IBM, who each added some 10,000 employees between 2000 and 2005, are growing even faster.

This continuing evolution of the corporate landscape then begs a critical question: Why do we have companies at all? Why not let free markets do all the work, with all of the major business processes floating around, as D. H. Robertson once said, as free agents in an "ocean of unconscious cooperation"? If we define companies as bundles of processes, or "islands of conscious power" as Robertson called them, what then constitutes the shorelines of these islands?

The economist Ronald Coase provided some of the most influential answers to these questions back in 1937, in what has since become known as Coase's Law. Coase argued that "a firm will tend to expand until the costs of organizing an extra transaction within the firm become equal to the costs of carrying out the same transaction in an exchange on the open market or the costs of organizing in another firm." While Coase's Law has recently become popular as a tool to explain the advent of outsourcing and globalization (he won the Nobel Prize in Economics in 1991), he was actually trying to explain why, in his time, companies were growing as big as they were. Writing in the heyday of factories like the River Rouge, Coase noted that inventions that bring factors of production closer (like the steam engine, the telephone, and the telegraph, and improvements in managerial techniques) all tended to make the firm *larger* by making it cheaper to put a wide range of activities under the same roof. Coase's Law, in other words, helped to explain why the sizes of companies, both then and now, tend to ebb and flow over time depending on their transactions costs.

If you combine Moore's Law with Coase's Law, then everything we thought we knew about what the structure of a company should look like goes out the window. What we are left with is a new breed of company, one that looks dramatically different from those of Ford's River Rouge era.

Consider, for example, a story about the Procter & Gamble Co., the giant consumer products company in Cincinnati, Ohio. A confidential memo began circulating around P&G's corporate headquarters in 2001 that reflected a radical concept. In the future, the memo argued, the successful operation of P&G's sprawling global operations wouldn't require 100,000 plus employees. Instead, the company could operate with a core group of closer to just 25,000 people. Everything left over could be bought in the form of BPO services from the outside, the memo's author argued.

The memo spread like wildfire throughout the company. Old-timers were appalled at the whole idea and, as CEO A. G. Lafley ruefully acknowledged, "it terrified our organization." At the same time, though, it electrified others. A couple of years after the memo first leaked, IBM's CEO, Sam Palmisano, met up with his client Lafley. Over lunch, Lafley asked Palmisano the same question posed by the now infamous memo: how many employees did P&G really need? When Palmisano, perhaps embarrassed, declined to make a guess Lafley bailed him out: how about just 25 percent? That's when Palmisano saw the future: he smelled a massive opportunity for IBM to expand its services business into the BPO space, something it has aggressively pushed into over the past several years.

P&G has done a fair amount of outsourcing over the last few years—including areas like facilities management, human resources, and information technology—but it has come nowhere close to reducing its payroll by 75 percent. Still, revenue has gone up by about 40 percent since 2000 while employee count has stayed flat. That means that as the company has continued to focus in on its core activities, employee productivity has soared.

Lafley's now legendary question to Palmisano raises a fascinating set of possibilities. What if you really could jettison 75 percent of the conventional activities of a corporation, leaving everyone left to focus solely on innovation, its most profitable task? What would a company like this look like, and how would you ever get there from here?

Qualcomm's Choice

When we think of inventors, most of us would conjure images of middle-aged men in white lab coats mixing concoctions in a beaker, or modern-day James Watts, tinkering with their contraptions in a workshop. Few of us, though, and for good reason, equate inventors with glamorous movie stars. But it was the Austrian film beauty, Hedy Lamarr, who poured the foundation for one of the key inventions of the wireless revolution—and inadvertently sowed the seeds for what would later become one of the world's most profitable companies, Qualcomm.

But long before telephones, let alone *mobile* phones, were household staples, people still looked up to the stars for inspiration. And few stars were more iconic in Hollywood than Lamarr, who was born in Austria Hedy Kiesler Marky. The headliner of more than thirty films in as many years (as well as six marriages), she was a risk taker who reportedly won roles because of her beauty rather than her acting skill. Her most prominent film role came in *Samson and Delilah* (1949), in which she starred as Delilah opposite Victor Mature's Samson, though her true claim to fame may be that she was the first actress to appear nude in a mainstream commercial film, the 1933 romantic drama *Ecstasy*.

Yet Lamarr's brainpower may have even exceeded her beauty. As she once noted, "Films have a certain place in a certain time period. Technology is forever."

And aptly enough, if Lamarr's Hollywood star has begun to fade, her legacy as an inventor—the mother of the wireless revolution—shines brighter than ever.

In the early 1920s, however, Lamarr was still in Austria, unhappily married to a wealthy Austrian arms manufacturer with Nazi ties. Unlike most of her female peers, she had little use for Viennese society and the other perks of an upper-class marriage. She was instead fascinated by a different subject altogether: the radio control of torpedoes.

When her husband and his colleagues in the arms industry sat down to talk business, Lamarr angled in whenever she could. Eager to oblige the legendary beauty, they kept her abreast of the latest in military technology. Lamarr became fascinated by one subject in particular: the difficulty in directing torpedoes to their targets. Naval warfare was in a state of flux at the time. While self-propelled torpedoes had proven to be an exceedingly deadly weapon, their effectiveness had been greatly reduced with the advent of radio-jamming technology. Fleets escorted by "torpedo-boat destroyers" (later just destroyers) that could jam the frequency on which a torpedo was being guided could avoid submarine attacks since the radio-jamming escort ship could easily knock the torpedo off target.

On the eve of World War II, Lamarr fled Austria for the United States. And even as she began her career as a Hollywood starlet, she spent her spare time working on ways to help her adopted country's navy sink more Nazi ships.

The reason ships could jam radio-controlled torpedoes so easily, Lamarr discovered, was because the torpedoes were guided by radio signals that were sent over a single frequency; all an evading ship had to do was find the signal controlling the torpedo and drown it out with extra noise. Lamarr's idea was to divide up the radio control signal, spreading it out across many different frequencies, and then make the signal "hop" across the frequencies based on a predetermined code. The torpedo and the mother ship would each have a copy of this code that would help them synchronize their signals as they accessed them on multiple channels. While Lamarr received a patent for her solution, which we now call "code division multiple access," or CDMA, back in 1942, it has since become the basis for the technology that continues to drive mobile telecommunications all over the world. (Unfortunately for Lamarr, her breakthrough was so far ahead of its time that the military declared it top secret—the title of her patent was literally "Secret Communication System"—for most of its commercial life; as a result, she never received a dime for her invention.)

The first of what we now call cell phones were a lot like mobile radio stations—or torpedoes; every connected call grabbed a specific bit of radio spectrum until the call was complete. This straightforward approach, which was based on analog technology, was called "frequency division multiple access" (FDMA). The problem with FDMA, as you can imagine, was that as more and more people placed calls with their phones, they quickly ate up all the available channels. As a result, early cell phone users were often out of luck when they wanted to phone home, particularly during peak hours or holidays.

With the advent of digital technology and second-generation (2G) phones in the 1980s, carriers learned to carve up each call into digital packets and each frequency into small time slots, an approach called "time division multiple access," or TDMA, which then allowed more than one phone call to share the same frequency band.

As mobile phone use continued to skyrocket, however, even TDMA soon reached its limits. There was simply too much volume in both calls and information to pass through the available spectrum. Enter the ideas behind Lamarr's patent (which was now in the public domain). By using code division, a carrier could divide up a phone call into separate digital packets and, rather than send them on a single channel like before, hop them across different frequencies to take advantage of any openings in the entire "spread spectrum" and reassemble the message again based on the predetermined code.

The company that adapted Lamarr's idea, and thus eliminated busy signals on Mother's Day around the world, was Qualcomm. Irwin Jacobs, a communications engineer and former MIT professor, founded the San Diego–based company in 1985. A year later Jacobs and his engineering team began by building upon Lamarr's approach to code division, adapting it from torpedoes to cell phones. A year after that the team filed their first patent, which, in time, has become one of the most highly cited technical documents in history, serving as a core reference for more than 850 subsequent patents.

Jacobs and his team proved to be visionary technologists and their inventions, based on Lamarr's original concept, have changed the world of mobile communications. But Qualcomm accomplished far more than a simple technical solution. Over the decade that followed the filing of their first CDMA invention, Qualcomm waged a relentless and ultimately successful campaign, in which the company invested in an ongoing program of invention that yielded hundreds of improvements to CDMA technology to make their vision of CDMA cell phones a commercial reality. In 1989 they persuaded PacTel, the dominant phone carrier in California, to collaborate with them in setting up a trial system in their home city of San Diego. Following the success of that trial they arranged demos around the world, from New York City to Seoul, Korea. They endured brutal criticism (one Stanford engineering professor claimed that Qualcomm's CDMA model violated the laws of physics) and intense opposition from European TDMA proponents. "They are absolutely hated in Europe, because they are not part of the regional club and because they are so gutsy and so American," said one industry analyst. At crucial points, they even appeared to have lost the standards battle, because a critical industry association declared TDMA the American standard in 1992 (a decision that was promptly overturned as TDMA suppliers fell behind on some of their commitments).

Despite its success in the lab and the field, though, Jacobs and Qualcomm struggled to build a traditional company out of their revolutionary technology. In fact, the company seemed more adept at spending or losing money than it was at making it. For one, companies like Motorola and Ericsson, recognizing that they risked losing control of both technology leadership and negotiating power, escalated the fight by challenging the validity of Qualcomm's CDMA patent portfolio in the courts—which resulted in expensive legal battles that stretched for years.

Qualcomm also struggled to line up enough vendors to keep up the supply of CDMA handsets. That led Jacobs to partner up with Sony in 1994 to manufacture handsets under a new brand, Qualcomm Personal Electronics (QPE). While the decision to launch QPE helped ensure a steady supply of cell phones, it was also slowly bleeding the company to death: QPE lost an average of nearly $100 million a year between 1997 and 1999.

In 1999, however, the company reached a key inflection point: in a deal that included the purchase of Qualcomm's wireless infrastructure division, rival Ericsson finally agreed to pay Qualcomm a substantial license fee for rights to their technology. With a licensing deal with Motorola already in hand, that meant that Qualcomm had divested an unprofitable manufacturing business while finally putting the most serious threats to CDMA patent portfolio behind it. But the company still faced a looming problem: its handset manufacturing arm continued to lose money at an alarming pace. Wall Street, in turn, continued to punish the company's stock price even as it rewarded competitors like Nokia. That's when Jacobs and his management team asked themselves a pivotal question: do we really need to make any products to be a profitable company?

The answer they arrived at, one that might have sent shivers down the spines of business school professors everywhere, was no. And they didn't wait long to act on that decision. Just a few months after the deal with Ericsson, and right before the Christmas holidays, Qualcomm sold its interest in QPE to Kyocera, a Japanese manufacturer. So after all the New Year's revelries had died down,

Qualcomm rang in the new millennium as a very different company. As Jacobs framed it, "We'll do the innovative part and let others do the manufacturing."

No longer weighed down, or distracted, by its unprofitable attempts at infrastructure and handset manufacturing, Qualcomm could now focus solely on its most valuable asset: its patents. That meant striking licensing deals for its extensive patent portfolio, which, along with sales of its CDMA chip designs, soon accounted for 90 percent of the firm's sales, some $3 billion worth at the time. Profits, not surprisingly, also exploded, with cash flow margins rising to nearly 40 percent of sales. And as the company successfully shifted into what could be described as the ultimate example of an IP pure play, Wall Street rewarded it. Qualcomm's stock price, which had long languished below $4 a share, had begun moving up and reached $20 a share by the beginning of 2000. But then, helped by their divestiture of QPE and some irrational exuberance on the part of investors, the stock price continued to climb, reaching $80 a share by the end of the year—a spectacular 2,600 percent rise in little over a year.

Qualcomm's decision to focus entirely on its IP not only helped the company weather the dot-com bust more than most telecom companies, particularly those heavy in manufacturing, it has also enabled the company to expand on and strengthen its patent portfolio, both in the United States and around the world. (Qualcomm's portfolio stands at more than 7,000 patents and counting.) And unlike TechSearch, which went to battle with one highly contentious patent, Qualcomm goes to market with a large portfolio of high-quality patents that have become the foundation for the future of wireless telecommunications.

Qualcomm's patents, for example, are already at the core of the next generation of wireless technology, called 3G (third-generation). While Qualcomm has developed its own standard for this technology called CDMA 2000, many of its rivals, particularly those in Europe, back a competing standard called Wideband CDMA. What makes the story interesting, though, is that Qualcomm's existing patents form the core of both technologies, meaning that whatever standard is adopted, Qualcomm will be in a position to profit.

This is not the behavior of a troll, is it? Certainly, you never hear anyone on Wall Street referring to Qualcomm as such. Why? Perhaps the company is being awarded for its aggressive behavior rather than being punished because of it. In other words, investors love a shark.

Measuring the Impact of Innovation

By any measure, Qualcomm's focus on the creation, management, and licensing of their innovation assets as the core of their business activity has been a success. The company has received numerous patents resulting from the large number of inventions in their core CDMA technology area. But more important than the absolute number of these patents (actually each invention produces a "family" of patent applications all over the world) is the high quality of these patents: high quality in the sense that anyone who wants to deploy CDMA techniques has to make use of their inventions and also in the sense that technology developers in the field generally credit Qualcomm's inventions in their own patent filings as part of their requirement to credit those who have developed prior art.

Because so much money is at stake, the consideration and distribution of credit has become an increasingly high-stakes game. As a result, Qualcomm has found themselves the target of others who want to deploy CDMA technology while also limiting Qualcomm's share of the total technology pie. This contest for credit has spawned a bit of a PR war around wireless patents. All of the industry players realize that if they can make a legitimate claim for maximizing their own role in the returns to the technology, while minimizing the role of others, the payoff will be huge.

This is especially true for the companies that built their wireless businesses around TDMA technology, the obsolete second-generation (2G) standard still used around the world. Companies that bet their business on TDMA have been forced to convert to CDMA, the Qualcomm technology, in order to participate in the third generation (3G) of data-enabled devices. As these companies entered the 3G game, though, they have tried to work around the 3G standard (CDMA 2000) set by Qualcomm by developing their own standard, which has become known as "wideband CDMA" (or WCDMA). But, as the name implies, the WCDMA standard is clearly based on CDMA technology. And because the TDMA players like Nokia and Ericsson would prefer not to pay Qualcomm any additional licensing fees related to CDMA, the question of how much credit to give Qualcomm in the 3G market has become increasingly controversial.

This controversy reached new heights after a paper, sponsored by the European manufacturers, was published in 2005. The paper's authors, David Goodman and Robert Myers, counted the number of patents that the industry players have "declared essential" to the WCDMA standard. They then assessed those patents, offering a technical judgment as to whether or not they were "actually essential" to the standard's core. When Goodman and Myers counted the patents declared essential for the WCDMA standard, they found that 38 percent of those patents were owned by Qualcomm; but after their cursory technology analysis, only 19 percent of those patents that they judged to be essential belonged to Qualcomm. While these determinations were not legally binding, they did serve a blow to Qualcomm's efforts to collect its licensing fees from its European rivals using this new standard.

While Goodman and Myers's approach does have some surface appeal, it is, in fact, a flawed analysis. For one, it is clear that their analysis of the technology was far more subjective than objective. Judging technical contributions can be devilishly difficult when many inventors collaborate to produce the insights that make a technology system work. More important, Goodman and Myers's analysis entirely missed the issue of patent citations, one of the most reliable (and quantifiable) markers of a patent's influence on subsequent technology. By that measure, Qualcomm's patent portfolio is one of the most valuable technology portfolios in the world.

In Table 1, we show a simple analysis of the patent portfolios of the top six contributors to the 3G standard for WCDMA. We analyzed those top portfolios based not only on the number of patents companies *declared* essential for the WCDMA standard, but also on the degree to which *other inventors judged* those patents to be important based on citation frequency.

Using this new lens, we now see that not only does Qualcomm have a large number of patents, they also have the most important patents. Out of nearly 2,000 patents "declared essential" to the WCDMA standard, Qualcomm's portfolio of patents received 48 percent of the total citations received by other inventing companies, three times the number of citations received by Ericsson, the next most frequently cited company. Nokia, the leading European handset manufacturer, received only 3 percent of the total citations. The paradox, of course, is that even though the Europeans developed WCDMA to try and circumvent Qualcomm, they ended up leaning on their competitor's technology more than ever.

Citations dynamics can therefore be used to support an assessment based on technical merit rather than by market power or regulatory influence. The established players certainly appreciate the importance of getting patent protection in WCDMA. Indeed, as insiders in the WCDMA standards-setting process, Nokia and Ericsson had a chance to beef up their patent counts as soon as they could see where the technology was going. Technology analysts who watch the 3G world have said that since industry insiders could and did pad their patent numbers furiously as the standard was finalized, the importance of patent counts can be overstated. But the legal discipline of the patent application process, and the

TABLE 1 Declared Essential WCDMA Patent Families and Their Citations

Company	Essential WCDMA Patents (%)		Citations by All Other Patents (%)		Citations by Other Essential Patents (%)	
Qualcomm	383	(19%)	15,484	(38.5%)	1,147	(48%)
Ericsson	278	(14)	5,194	(13)	183	(8)
Nokia	244	(12)	2,046	(5.5)	73	(3)
Motorola	215	(11)	4,441	(11)	262	(11)
Interdigital	57	(3)	2,241	(5.5)	130	(5)
Philips	44	(2)	1,246	(3)	113	(5)
All other	764	(39)	9,546	(24)	478	(20)
Total	1,985	(100)	40,198	(100)	2,386	(100)

Source: The ETSI IPR Database; author analysis.

statutory requirement to cite prior art, provides an important and objective measure of the technology competition. By this measure, Qualcomm is the clear winner in the contest for credit in the WCDMA race.

UPDATE: On August 23, 2008, as we were preparing to go to press, Nokia
and Qualcomm reached a settlement of all patent litigation between them worldwide, including the antitrust action pending in Europe. Although the financial
details of the settlement were not announced, Nokia has agreed to license Qualcomm's patents for fifteen years, give Qualcomm a license to Nokia's patent portfolio, and transfer a number of patents that it had "declared essential" related to
past, present, and future wireless standards. The settlement essentially secures
Qualcomm's position at the center of the wireless technology world for the next
fifteen years. In the two days after the announcement (a period in which the S&P
500 Index fell by 1 percent), Qualcomm's stock rose more than 20 percent and
Nokia's stock rose about 5 percent, an increase in combined market value of more
than $20 billion.

Unleashing the Power of Intellectual Property

When business executives design a company, they tend to work on simple no-
tions of mathematics: they subtract low-value activities while keeping and adding
high-value activities wherever you can find them. When it comes to innovation

activities, however, simple business math doesn't apply anymore. There is actually a conflict—a divide-by-zero error you might say—when a company tries to sell and manufacture products and reinforce its IP at the same time. Managers that expend energies on things outside of innovative technical activity can actually make the whole worth of their company less than the sum of its parts. Far less.

IP, in other words, can be far more valuable when it stands alone from the other, more traditional activities of a product business. To demonstrate this somewhat counterintuitive point, consider Figure 7, which shows a four-box matrix that illustrates some of the negotiating dynamics companies face when it comes to their IP: the horizontal axis reflects a firm's strength in IP, while the vertical axis presents a firm's market share or sales power. To further simplify things, the chart has four quadrants, which means that a company can have one of two positions—either strong or weak—on either of the two dimensions.

The lower right quadrant reflects the new breed of firm represented by the company of ideas: the *shark*. Qualcomm is a shark, for example, because it made a strategic choice to stop subsidizing its weak product positions in handset manufacturing and infrastructure, subsequently choosing to focus on its strong IP instead. A shark, by its very nature, is focused on a single purpose, innovation, which means that it doesn't need to assemble IP rights to make an entire product. Sharks like Qualcomm also hunt alone, which means they don't have to depend on the handset and infrastructure inventions of other companies to keep swimming. Instead, they keep their IP free to license to all manufacturers, who, despite owning some of their own IP, are weighed down because they also make products. Qualcomm's competitors, like Nokia, Samsung, and Ericsson, need access to Qualcomm's technology to sell their own branded handsets, yet at the same time, Qualcomm doesn't need to reciprocate. This edge gives Qualcomm far greater negotiating power when they sit down across the table from the other handset players. Actually, the negotiation is simple: Qualcomm names the price for accessing their technology. If the other companies balk: negotiation over.

This plays out directly in the economics of mobile phones, for example. A typical 3G phone using WCDMA sells for about $200. For a company like Samsung to put together a fully functioning unit, they need to assemble a number of physical components: a processing chip, an antenna, a battery, a keyboard, the plastic housing, a screen display, and some internal circuitry. The total cost to manufacture these components is a secret, but let's say for now that it comes to around $150, not including the large capital investments needed for the necessary factories and machinery. It's when we dig into the accounting behind the

FIGURE 7   The IP/Product Matrix

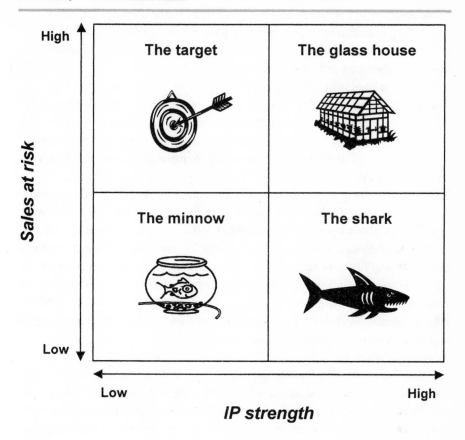

component costs, though, that things get interesting. Samsung actually owns some of the inventions behind a handset's technology, so they don't pay anything for those. As far as using the technology that they didn't invent, though, which includes much of Qualcomm's groundbreaking CDMA work, they need to pay for licenses from other companies. And that can get expensive in a hurry: using the licensing rates available at press time, the sum of all these fees comes to as much as $50 per handset. This leaves Samsung with only a few bucks per handset to reinvest in R&D. (Nokia, by contrast, which owns a far larger share of the IP that goes into a WCDMA handset, pays only a fraction of what Samsung pays, roughly $15 according to published royalty rate estimates.)

Qualcomm, on the other hand, receives about $10 for every handset Samsung sells—as well as a similar check from each of Samsung's competitors. Since Qualcomm doesn't need to build the physical capacity to build handsets themselves, they can reinvest a portion of that $10 profit in adding new features or solving the next generation of user problems. This is the kind of arithmetic that shows the advantage of being a shark.

The shark label is one we apply with respect: these companies are highly fit and often relentless models of commercial innovation. Though they typically begin their innovation investments from a commercial starting point, they also frequently begin from more research-focused roots. Consider the growing commercial success of universities, which has been jump-started by a shift in U.S. government policy.

Whereas the sum of U.S. industry spent about $200 billion in R&D in 2004, U.S. universities and colleges conducted more than $40 billion in research. And, because only about 5 percent of those R&D dollars were subsidized by industry, institutions (based on new regulations governing government-funded research) have started to file their own patents on their innovation. While it's hard to be any more focused on research than a university, an increasing number of universities have aggressively entered what is now commonly known as the "technology transfer" business. This is academic speak for the commercial licensing of patents granted to university professors, which has become a big business for these universities.

Columbia University, for example, earns $160 million annually on its patent licensing while MIT and Stanford, which have been in the licensing business for decades, generate between $50 million and $60 million per year from their patents. Research universities all over the world, in fact, have been expanding their roles in the licensing business, becoming ever-larger players in the commercial landscape. Quite simply, these universities are evolving into what we call *scholastic sharks*.

In contrast to the shark's position, consider the upper left quadrant of Figure 7. Here we find many emerging-market companies, such as those that use manufacturing cost advantages to rapidly build market share with their products. Since these companies are often newcomers to areas with established technology, meaning they have little IP of their own, they have no choice but to compete on cost. Because they aren't weighed down with R&D or marketing budgets, these companies can become formidable competitors because they can keep their costs low. When it comes to licensing technology to manufacture higher-end products from IP-rich competitors, however, they bring little to the negotiating table. As a result, these emerging companies have two choices: either they can pay licensing fees to companies like Qualcomm, or even more integrated competitors like Nokia, or, on the other hand, they can make products for a company that has already assembled its IP rights and compete on a contract manufacturing basis instead.

The upper left quadrant is called the *target* position because it contains plenty of manufacturing and product activity, but a lack of IP strength, exemplified by high-technology companies in emerging markets. Much of the Japanese economy was built on companies like these (more on this in chapter 8), including the semiconductor companies first targeted by TI in the late 1980s. Among today's targets are Korean handset manufacturers who have found themselves paying large license fees to Qualcomm, Nokia, and other handset innovators. In China, the entire DVD industry was decimated as companies like Philips, Sony, and even LG, the Korean technology company, took action to prevent Walmart from illegally importing DVD players. As opposed to sharks, targets have a weak position in an IP negotiation and, despite their low-cost operations, can find themselves highly vulnerable. If the shark is a predator, the target is prey.

The shark and the target hold the unbalanced positions in Figure 7. Historically, though, most large companies have sought to grow in a more balanced way: seeking to hold large patent positions while generating substantial market share at the same time. Companies in this position typically deploy their IP merely as a supporting asset for their manufacturing and selling activities. When they avoid entanglement with the technology of others, these companies can find themselves in an extremely attractive competitive position. It is a much more frequent case, though, that such companies lack complete technological autonomy. Not only does this tend to limit their market share, it also means that they need their competitor's IP to make their own products. Because so many companies, particularly large, established players, have bundled their IP with other activities like manufacturing over time, they generally all find themselves facing off against each other in similar positions.

That's why the upper right quadrant in Figure 7 is called the *glass house* position, because companies that live in glass houses shouldn't throw stones. Just as in the Cold War, when the nuclear arsenals of the United States and the USSR forced a stalemate around mutually assured destruction, companies are forced to trade favors through cross-licensing to make any progress whatsoever. Companies effectively say to each other, "You can use my technology if I can use yours; and I won't attack you if you don't attack me."

Most of us would be surprised how much of the world's economy is built on this form of barter trade, particularly because these kinds of transactions are massively inefficient. These hidden cross-licensing networks are pervasive though, and while these situations often provide a comfortable equilibrium for the established players, they also create many problems. Valuable property, for one, gets taxed to subsidize noncompetitive assets; bundles of inefficient activity then remain stuck together because the barter trade prevents the liquidity that reveals higher and better uses. Companies with a traditional mind-set also frequently destroy the value of their IP assets by subsidizing their less-competitive manufacturing and product businesses as they avoid explicit licensing. While some companies, like Qualcomm and TI (to a lesser extent), evolved from glass houses to sharks, most companies remain stuck in the glass house position: visible and vulnerable.

Newer and smaller-market businesses, those that have yet to establish a track record of innovation, actually have more options in how they evolve. These companies sit in the lower left quadrant in Figure 7, in what we call the *minnow* position. Even though minnows may have modest product sales and a developing new-technology portfolio, they can choose their path as they move along each axis.

In the past, entrepreneurs were taught to bundle products and technologies together and grow like companies have always grown, along the balanced path. In some cases, when the value chain that delivers the innovation is closely tied to the innovation itself, this growth path may, in fact, be the only one available. Frequently though, this full business model results in huge overheads and activities that are beyond the company's core skills. In other cases, especially in emerging economies, companies have raced to build product volume, usually through some kind of contract manufacturing relationship. Entering these races without any homegrown innovation, though, usually leaves the emerging company on a path to becoming a target. Many of these companies are not even aware that they have a choice, but it may well be the most important strategic decision they ever make.

The most interesting minnow stories, like those of IMS and NTP, have most often been associated with the company's obituary. But as Qualcomm and some others have shown, companies can succeed—and evolve into sharks—when they focus on innovation.

The New Company of Ideas

The idea that companies might actually be able to make a business out of innovation was, until recently, an alien concept for economists. For a long time, most economists assumed that technological progress came from outside the economy, from scholars and scientists, and washed over the economy as a kind of beneficial rain. In the jargon of the trade, that meant technological progress was *exogenous,* meaning that markets didn't affect innovation.

The truth is that this nice bright line between research (which is something that intellectuals did in universities) and product development (which happened exclusively inside large corporations) didn't make much sense in a world where the "residual" contributed the lion's share of economic progress. This important idea finally began to dawn on a few maverick economists shortly after World War II. Some of them started to realize that innovation is a distinct and at least partially separable field of economic activity: one with different economic drivers. These mavericks pointed out the novel thought that the conscious choice to invest in the development of intellectual assets, to create valuable property from that investment, and then to generate revenue and profit from the value that the innovation contained was something that happened "inside" the economy; innovation, in other words, was *endogenous* to companies and influenced directly by markets.

The first man to really understand this concept was a Minnesota economist named Jacob (or Jack) Schmookler, perhaps the most underappreciated economist of the twentieth century, particularly for his efforts to advance the thinking behind the economics of innovation. Although he didn't receive a Nobel Prize for his work, Schmookler was among the first to develop concrete measurements of the contribution of technology to economic growth. (Remember that Robert Solow, who did receive a Nobel for his equations, used a lot more math than his predecessor.) Schmookler was the first economist to use the U.S. Patent Office filings as a data resource for measuring inventive activity. Schmookler also appears to be the first modern economist to use the term "intellectual capital" in a coherent economic framework.* Other economists spoke of the "knowledge economy," or of the importance of technical change, but Schmookler's 1966 book *Invention and Economic Growth* developed a full framework for the marketplace for ideas that holds up well today.

Before Schmookler, most analysts of invention came from sociology departments and took pains to point out the fact that innovation was a social process: technology proceeded in a gradual and cumulative process, no single inventor

---

*Nassau William Senior provides the first known mention of the phrase "intellectual capital" in his treatise *Political Economy* (London: Richard Griffin and Company, 1854). But it was part of an extended discussion that had little to do with innovation and hardly anyone noticed.

was more important than any other, and every invention that mattered would simply emerge when the time was ripe. Schmookler, though, demonstrated that most innovations come from the demand for technology solutions, not the mere supply of new ideas. In other words, businesses put money behind inventions when they see an opportunity in the market and not because new knowledge suddenly makes new inventions technically feasible. He also described with precision the economic events that were necessary in order for an invention to reach the market: it had to be technically feasible; the inventor or inventors had to acquire the necessary knowledge to make the invention while, at the same time, recognizing the critical problem that their invention solved; the inventor(s) then had to make a specific decision to invest the time and resources to make the invention happen; the inventor(s) needed to develop the insight (the eureka moment) on how to solve the problem and produce the invention; and last but not least, the inventor(s) had to reduce the invention to an operable form. And Schmookler also saw that the final product that emerged from this "invention production line" was, at least some of the time, a patent.

Schmookler did a terrific job in describing the basics of the innovation economy, but after passing away suddenly at the age of forty-five in 1967, he wasn't able to take his insights all the way to their logical conclusions. His agenda was left unfinished until Paul Romer's work on *endogenous growth theory* in the mid-1980s. Romer was aware of Schmookler, cited his work, and also identified critical things that Schmookler missed. Schmookler, writing a decade before Moore's Law was published, simply assumed that innovation was bundled with the other activities of the traditional industrial firm. Romer, writing a decade after Moore's Law had become a mantra, recognized that the economics of innovation opened the door to an entirely different way of looking at business.

In short, in a world where Moore's Law has put into play the constraints of Coase's Law, everything has changed. In this new world, the Information Revolution does more than simply facilitate outsourcing within developed economies and provide the distribution pipe for the massive integration of the global economy. It makes possible an entirely new kind of company, one that is highly focused on innovation and only innovation. It allows an expansion of our traditional model of invention, moving beyond just the individual inventor laboring in his or her workshop. It also allows us to move past the traditional company in the form of a vertically integrated research and manufacturing corporation. Now innovation teams—funded by venture capital, focused on technical vision, and protected from large product firms and channel owners by their ownership rights in technology and brands—have emerged as the essential core of the modern business enterprise.

This new enterprise doesn't look like the River Rouge. The assets with the most value come in tiny little pieces full of legal and economic uncertainty. Their value is revealed when many other inventions cite them, but those inventions compete with the original inventions and solve new problems. They don't last forever nor do they assure position. But they can be worth a lot, and just might be worth even more if you narrow the economic focus of your firm's activities and avoid investing in too much non-innovation-related activity around them. In short, the company of ideas has been born.

Unlike today's Ford Motor Company, the company of ideas looks a lot more like Qualcomm, which has jettisoned the low-value-added activities in its business to focus on the core source of its competitive advantage. In a world where Schmookler's innovation production line has become the largest source of shareholder value, companies like Qualcomm are revealing new possibilities for organizing the modern company. Faced with these possibilities, the strategic challenge for a CEO like A. G. Lafley is not determining the number of employees that P&G needs; rather, it is deciding *what is the company you keep?*

As we have seen, the strategic core of the modern company is not merely centered on its innovation; it is also protected by its intellectual property. Under the right circumstances and with sufficient protection, companies can eliminate other peripheral functions and focus exclusively on this core. This is new territory for business leaders, and it presents a set of strategic options that were once unthinkable. If the corporation as we knew it, then, is being "blown to bits," as one of our former colleagues once wrote, what does that mean for the future of running such a business? What is a CEO to do?

CHAPTER 4

Advantaged Innovation Networks

TURNING COMPLEXITY INTO A COMPETITIVE EDGE

Smart(employees) = log(employees)
Most of the smartest people work for someone else
Innovation will occur elsewhere
—*Joy's Law, in three successive versions**

O n June 8, 2000, a surprising piece of information crossed the news wires: Durk Jager, chief executive of Procter & Gamble, was "retiring" just seventeen months after he had taken the position. Replacing him was Alan Lafley, who, despite a twenty-three-year stint with the company, was someone most outsiders had never even heard of. The announcement made more than just its employees wonder what exactly was going on over at P&G.

For Jager, though, the writing had been on the wall for weeks; the decision to step down was made for him. P&G's board of directors had recently convened an emergency meeting after a second consecutive quarter of disappointing earnings. The company's stock price was in a free fall, dropping from $118 per share in January to the mid-$50s by early June that year. The venerable consumer goods company, an icon of stability and a Dow Jones index stock since 1932, had lost

---

*Named for Bill Joy, cofounder of Sun Microsystems. The first version is based on a report by former Sun employee James W. Thompson (see http://www.smallworks.com/archives/00000368 .htm), who was at Sun from 1988 to 1992. The second and third have emerged as popular forms based on a speech by Joy in Silicon Valley in 1990, first cited by George Gilder in "The Coming Software Shift," *Forbes ASAP*, August 28, 1995.

some $75 billion in market value in a matter of *weeks*. So in a move unprecedented in P&G's proud history, the board asked their CEO to step aside.

But how did Jager's reign unravel so quickly? A rarity in an era that rewards job-hopping, he had spent his entire thirty-year career working at P&G. He had even served as a member of the board for eleven years—six in his role as the company's president and chief operating officer. And by all accounts, his aggressiveness and leadership earned him respect within the company as well as on Wall Street. Built like a linebacker, he often seemed larger than life to those who worked with him.

Prior to earning the promotion to CEO, Jager, a native of the Netherlands, had built a stellar track record as a global manager. Fluent in seven languages, he successfully moved through assignments in Europe and Japan, where he earned a reputation as someone with a penchant for stepping on toes in the name of results. During a six-year stint in Japan that began in 1981, for example, Jager led a profitable turnaround by tailoring products to Japanese consumers and by forcing out large numbers of sales managers at a time when lifetime employment was still the norm in most large Japanese businesses.

By 1990, following his successful stint in Asia, Jager earned a promotion to P&G's headquarters in Cincinnati where he became a protégé of Ed Artzt, then CEO of P&G, a man once nicknamed "The Prince of Darkness." And although Jager occasionally took pains to lighten his image by separating himself from the unpopular Artzt, he remained a self-professed tough guy nevertheless. Jager was reportedly fond of wrapping up meetings by saying, "Let's break some kneecaps." Yet Jager also possessed an extremely agile mind that led coworkers to describe him as "scarily smart" and "a genius."

When Jager took the reins as CEO in 1998, he turned up the pressure for change, much as he had done in tackling his prior assignments. His grand plan, as he made it clear, was to make P&G a "much, much tougher competitor." In his annual shareholder letters, he stressed concepts like "organizing for speed," "faster, bigger innovation," and "accelerating growth." The pace of business had changed, he would say, and P&G needed to pick up its pace as well: "We can and must do better," he argued. The company, in other words, needed to start breaking more kneecaps.

But just seventeen months later, P&G's board, faced with a plummeting stock price, made the switch to Lafley, who, along with impeccable managerial credentials, came across as friendly and engaging. Like a sports team that fires its hard-nosed coach in favor of a more subdued "player's coach," P&G's board had, in essence, chosen Jager's opposite. And Lafley quickly went to work on damage control. He pledged to put on the brakes, blaming P&G's poor earnings results on his predecessor's overly aggressive efforts at change. As such, he urged investors to be patient. "In hindsight, it's clear we changed too much, too fast," Lafley said at the time. "The transition that we expected to take about a year to complete is clearly going to take a year longer."

Early pundits, though, particularly the business press, were skeptical. *Business-Week* warned that "warm and fuzzy won't save Procter & Gamble." A writer at *Fortune* wrote that Lafley, unlike his predecessor, didn't have that celebrity CEO personality to lead a turnaround. "He looks like a college professor—fresh scrubbed, a bit nerdy," the article went on to say. "He's not someone who wows a crowd," and "he doesn't have much dazzle or flair."

These skeptics, though, severely underestimated Lafley's managerial skills.

Over the next six years, P&G, under Lafley's leadership, returned to Wall Street's good graces. By 2004, P&G had even earned a return to the top of *Fortune* magazine's Most Admired Companies list after a five-year absence and, by the end of 2005, the stock price had finally recovered the many billions in value that had been lost during the first half of 2000 prior to Jager's departure. The upward trend continued through 2007. Lafley, in turn, earned praise far and wide as a management visionary. But what was the secret ingredient behind Lafley's success that Jager somehow missed? In many ways, it was the contrast in how each man approached innovation, not just their personalities, that made all the difference.

A Different Approach

When he served as CEO of P&G, Jager made it clear that he was betting the future of the company on its research and development capabilities, and he put all his considerable weight behind efforts to beef up and speed up the company's product development capabilities. He even named himself the chair of the company's Innovation Leadership Team to ensure that he could keep his eye on promising product ideas that others might not recognize. And along with his emphasis on churning out new products, Jager also drove the company hard to accelerate its internal processes. He wanted faster new-product development times, streamlined manufacturing, more centralized and larger-scale administrative services, and a stepped-up volume of patent applications.

After his dismissal, though, Jager was criticized for driving all these changes too far, too fast. One critic blamed his failure on trying to change P&G from a

Ford to a Ferrari. But looking more closely at what he actually did reveals more clearly what the drawbacks of his tough-guy strategy really were—and how they contributed to the missed opportunities that he left behind for Lafley to capital-ize on.

For instance, even as he forced cutbacks throughout the rest of the company's operations, Jager always made sure to dole out plenty of goodies to his technical teams. He raised R&D spending by 50 percent in five years, which boosted the rate of R&D investment from less than 3 percent of total revenue in 1995 to nearly 5 percent by 2000. In Jager's mind, increased spending on R&D was the single most vital factor for P&G's future success. "Connections create breakthroughs," he wrote in his 1999 shareholder letter. "Last year, for example, we were granted more U.S. patents than any of our competitors. We hold over 25,000 patents worldwide, and this technology base is paying off."

Jager also pushed his management team to set aggressive or "stretch" targets in a wide range of managerial routines like sales forecasting, management com-pensation plans, and financial budgeting. Yet Jager did little to change the basic conditions that surrounded the operations he asked his managers to speed up. Instead of changing the basic architecture of the enterprise, Jager was asking the same people working in the same way to do more, faster. And while sales did increase, so did costs, which quickly dragged down the company's profits.

In the end, despite Jager's deep (and by all accounts sincere) affection for how the process of innovation worked inside the company, it was his profound mis-understanding of how that process really worked that contributed to his downfall. And the irony was that Jager missed the strategic importance of a message he preached himself: that P&G's rise as a consumer products giant happened more by chasing opportunity than by pushing it.

Lafley, on the other hand, didn't share Jager's enthusiasm for internally fo-cused research and self-contained new-product development. Upon taking over the CEO role, Lafley promptly cut back spending on R&D by $300 million (from $1.9 billion in 2000 to $1.6 billion in 2002), which in turn pushed down R&D as a percentage of revenue back to its pre-Jager level. Lafley decided that his big-gest near-term profit growth opportunity was not rolling the dice on new break-through innovations; rather, it was focusing on—and celebrating—P&G's top "billion-dollar brands," the short list of product families that had the strongest market and technology positions. Put another way, Lafley decided his best short-term bet was not launching an endless search for the next Febreze, but in simply selling more Tide.

Lafley wasn't proposing to give up on innovation; instead he wanted to find a better way to embrace it. Rather than spending more money, in the hopes that more investment would yield higher returns, Lafley looked for ways to open up collaboration between his research group and the outside world. P&G had historically been a proud and private company, convinced that, by virtue of its smarts and deep well of innovations, it could outpace the competition. Yet as Jager strained the limits of P&G's internal talent in a frenzied search for breakthrough innovations, Lafley saw a greater opportunity to find innovation outside the company, opening up P&G's research activities to external collaborators.

At the same time, Lafley pushed to stimulate external licensing of the company's key brands, where he effectively opened up the P&G patent portfolio to all comers, including direct competitors. Today *every* patent in the P&G portfolio is available for license to *any* outsider beginning five years after its issue date, or three years after its introduction to the market, whichever comes first.

At first resisted by traditional insiders, this new open licensing policy has had unexpected competitive benefits for P&G product developers, who are pushing themselves ever harder as they watch the three- and five-year timers tick. As one profile of this new P&G policy noted, "When you open your intellectual-property portfolio to others, it forces you to make faster decisions about the kind of technology you want to keep for your own products. Plus, it encourages you to compete with yourself to make new discoveries faster in order to exceed the inventions you've already made available to others."

Like any good consumer products company, P&G branded its licensing program, and because of its success it has evolved into a billion-dollar brand in its own right. Eschewing the traditional term *research and development*, P&G was instead advocating an alternative approach called Connect and Develop, a brand that meant new technology could come from anywhere and P&G technology could be sold anywhere. Jager's River Rouge–style approach to product development— where R&D dollars went in the front of the factory and new billion-dollar brands came rolling out the back—was quickly transformed into a vital innovation network, teeming with transactions and embracing commercial opportunities whenever and wherever they presented themselves.

The results, as you may have guessed, have been dramatic: R&D productivity is up by more than 50 percent; the success rate of new products has more than doubled; and in the five years since Connect and Develop began, more than one hundred new products have been launched that incorporated key technology resources from outside the company. Back in 2001, when Lafley took charge, less than 20 percent of P&G's "ideas, products, and technologies" came from outside the company. By 2006, that proportion had risen to 35 percent and Lafley has set an overall target of 50 percent for the future. Innovative indeed.

The Network Lens

To see the business world the way Lafley does requires a shift in your lens or field of vision. Consider how the world looks when you combine two effects: on one hand, a movement away from the fully integrated River Rouge approach to one with many more highly focused components of activity working in a more specialized set of tasks; on the other hand, a pervasive growth of new exchanges between those smaller units, exchanges that—as we can see with P&G's development activities—can emerge at many points in the process, from scouting out and in-licensing leading-edge technologies to help transform an aging skin care brand (Olay Regenerist), to launching mutually profitable collaborations with niche competitors (Crest Spin Brush), to monetizing internal P&G technology by out-licensing to a competitor better positioned to exploit the technology commercially (Sunny Delight). When business activity is decomposed into lots of specialized components connected by lots of unpredictable exchanges, there is only one way to think about the resulting landscape: it's a network.

In a network, there is much less of a role for the traditional command-and-control CEO, that feudal monarch on an "island of conscious power." Tough guys have trouble in a network. Their simple theories of top-down "transformation" and military-style "execution" tend to break down in the face of the unexpected. Uncertainty and misdirection confuse them; complexity and connection constrain them. Let's-break-some-kneecaps managers like Jager can find themselves in hot water when the world won't submit to their strong wills and straight-lined plans.

Jager hasn't been the only tough-guy CEO to fail in recent years of course: cost-slashing Jacques Nasser of Ford was fired from Ford in 2001; "Chainsaw Al" Dunlap was forced out of Sunbeam in late 1998; and memorable scandals consumed "visionaries" like Jeff Skilling at Enron who, before resigning in disgrace in 2001, preached that his company didn't need any assets, and Bernie Ebbers at WorldCom who, before resigning in 2002, tried to buy up an entire global telephone network solely on credit.

Not only does this idea that companies thrive after they embrace decentralization help shed light on our outdated notion of the Superhero CEO, it also provides opportunities to adopt new strategies—strategies that embrace a world of specialization, connection, and complexity. Network-based strategies require a different mind-set, one that views competition in a different way. Using market share doesn't help in judging competitive position. Assessing the operational effectiveness of stylized value chains doesn't help either, since network relationships are suppressed in the simplistic linear representations of process flows managers typically use when they think of their business model as a "chain" of sequential activities. In a network, competitive dynamics are *relational,* and to view this effectively, you need a lens that can account for more than just the individual participants and their attributes, but also the connections between them. For example, your lens needs to show you who is at the center of the activity, or who is close to whom. Your lens should also enable you to answer questions like, how many degrees of separation lie between key rivals? Who controls the critical bridges that make them influential in brokering deals? And, like P&G's newly flexible technologists racing the three- and five-year patent licensing clocks, how are the patterns of connection changing over time?

The changes that Lafley implemented at P&G provide a clear example of how, through the conscious management of connections, a company can reap advantages from an innovation network. It was only when the company shelved Jager's notion of isolated and integrated product development, and adopted its Connect and Develop model instead, that P&G was able to unleash a whole new set of network-based opportunities, many of which have already yielded concrete benefits.

The one major departure from tradition on P&G's part, of course, has been its willingness to source new invention ideas from outsiders. This gives P&G a chance to find a way around the limitations of Joy's Law. Named for Bill Joy, a founder of Sun Microsystems, Joy's Law states (in one of several formulations) that "no matter who you are, most of the bright people don't work for you." So rather than trying to secure a monopoly on smart inventors, P&G began to work with as many smart people outside the company as it could. "For every P&G researcher, there were 200 scientists or engineers elsewhere who were just as good," two of P&G's senior R&D managers claimed. "That meant there was a total of perhaps 1.5 million people whose talents we could potentially use."

One example of how this inside-out collaboration can work dates back to 2003 and the successful launch of the "Mr. Clean Magic Eraser" line. The technology for the eraser, a foamlike pad that helps remove stains on everything from kitchen sinks to carpets, was originally developed by BASF, the German chemical giant, for soundproofing and insulation. It was actually a Japanese company called LEC that originally chopped the foam into hand-size cleaning pads, and it was in an Osaka, Japan, grocery store that P&G managers first came across the product. Those managers then posted a description of the pad on the company's "eureka catalog" network and enlisted the support of market researchers in Cincinnati to help determine its commercial value. Within a year, the product launched in Europe and, as of 2006, the product line had beaten its initial sales projections by a factor of two.

P&G demonstrated that Connect and Develop works outside-in as well, as it offered up its own technology to anyone outside the company who was willing to license it. Licensing the company's top brands, though, was, at first, a difficult pill for tradition-minded product managers to swallow. After all, why would you give your competitors access to precious technical advances that cost years and millions of dollars to develop? In a world without antitrust laws, P&G would prefer 100 percent market share, but realistically P&G knew it could never achieve a monopoly position for many of its products. So what do you lose when your competitors begin selling your technology for you? Nothing; in fact, you have everything to gain. As the head of P&G's licensing efforts argued, "If your competitors are paying you to use your technology, then you have a leg up on them because they're writing you checks." When P&G licenses technology to its competitors, it generates revenue every time its competitor sells a product. Not only that, but it locks in a spread between its product cost and its competitor's, which reduces its vulnerability to price attacks in the product category while ensuring that P&G's margins are higher than its competitors. Now, that's a smart way to leverage your intellectual property.

An example of where P&G used licensing to its benefit was in finding a new home for some of the innovative technology that came out of its beverage business. While the company had long supported a roster of well-known food and beverage brands like Folger's coffee and Pringles potato chips, it had also been steadily pruning back its line by selling off others like Crisco, Hawaiian Punch, and Duncan Hines. The company had sold off another beverage brand, Sunny Delight, but had retained ownership of the nutritional formula behind the fruity drink that made it easier for the human body to absorb calcium from a liquid. Rather than developing another product around that formula, or worse, just shelving it, P&G turned it into a profit stream by licensing it to Tropicana, the orange juice king, instead.

As P&G's story shows us, the language of networks and complexity has begun seeping into regular business discourse in all kinds of unexpected ways. This vocabulary has become pervasive, in part because of the rise of the networking technology that weaves together the World Wide Web, but it has also evolved to describe more than just Internet routers. For instance, most people now routinely describe their own social interactions as "networking." You also can't read a business story these days without running into a host of other network-related terms like ecosystems, value nets, and swarming.

Networks have begun to penetrate the business world in other ways as well. Online social networking communities are all the rage these days, most notably Facebook and MySpace. Sites like LinkedIn and Ryze have evolved to extend the social networking idea to business connections. There is even an emerging consulting trade where companies and organizations ask for help in leveraging their internal social networks.

Yet while many business executives would say that they have warmed to the power of networks, few have actually tried to adapt their own business strategies using network theory. One reason for this, of course, is because networks can look complicated. Indeed, network diagrams can serve as a kind of Rorschach test in gauging an executive's comfort level with a network lens. Some lean in, drawn by the detailed rendering of some business landscape with an expression that says, "Hmm, that looks interesting." Others recoil, intimidated by the jumble of circles and lines, and clearly think to themselves, or even exclaim out loud, "What is this gobbledygook?"

With a little interpretation help though, a network's complexity can be boiled down to its three most basic elements: *nodes*, the agents acting in the network; *links*, the connections between nodes; and *clusters*, the lumpy patterns of connection that develop as a network grows. Looked at in a different way, nodes can represent companies, technologies, people, teams, or assets (like patents) while links can represent alliances, collaborations, or supply relationships; or in the case of patents and scientific literature, they can represent coauthorship or citation relationships. When you use these definitions, and then look at the resulting connection patterns between groups of companies or technologies—whether they are spread out evenly or lumped in clusters, highly centralized around a single hub or floating about without a clear center—you can develop a clear picture of a competitive landscape.

The big stumbling block in using this kind of analysis in a business context is that network dynamics usually work at multiple levels, while most network diagrams—usually static and two-dimensional—work at only one. To make network strategy concepts truly useful, you can't get trapped at just one level, you need to be able to move up and down—from people to companies to industries and back down again—with the ability to change your perspective from each vantage point.

In other words, you need the ability to zoom.

Zooming

Most of us have been introduced to the concept of zooming by using Web sites like MapQuest to get customized driving directions or, more dramatically, by using the satellite images supplied by Google Earth to view the world in color, zooming in to view cities (nodes) and roads (links) and then seamlessly zooming up to see the beauty and contours of our planet's oceans and continents. Zoom in again to a city like New York, and you can view the Empire State Building from the side or zoom out again and fly across the continents to check in on landmarks like Mount St. Helens, the Swiss Alps, or Ayers Rock. At any point in your virtual journey, you can choose the elevation level that gives you the perspective that interests you the most. And it is often by viewing something from many different angles that you get the clearest picture of what the territory really looks like.

This ability to zoom through multiple levels with speed and agility is by no means limited to mapping software. The challenge of moving up and mastering different skill levels is the basic idea underlying the design of many modern video games (if you don't know this, ask your kids, or grandkids!). And in the popular movie trilogy *The Matrix*, when Neo chooses to swallow the red pill over the blue one, he begins an epic journey that takes him through numerous levels of consciousness and involves acts of zooming that would make Superman envious on a successful quest to save humanity (but sadly, not the girl).

The notion of zooming, though, isn't just a modern construct or limited to online games and tools. In Dante's *Inferno*, for instance, there are nine circles of hell, and in science, there are entire schools of thought dedicated to zooming. In biology, the organicist school emphasizes the need to apply different rules depending on whether you're inspecting a molecule, a cell, a piece of tissue, a larger organ system, an organism, or an ecosystem. And the field of fractal geometry in physics is dedicated to observing geometric objects at different scales of magnification and characterizing the degree of "self-similarity" at different levels. The notion of zooming, like the language of networks, has certainly secured its place in the popular zeitgeist.

One of the best applications for zooming, aptly enough, is in viewing a network's nodes, links, and clusters. You can start with a single node, then zoom out a bit to observe all of the connections to that original node and, if you then zoom out even farther, you begin to see the lumpy clusters that define the structure of the network. And by adding some simple attribute data, you can impose order on groups of nodes and assign them to discrete clusters. Then after zooming out once again, you can reorient your view of these clusters, reframing them as nodes at a higher level, where you can analyze the links that exist between these clusters. With different kinds of information, of course, you can take your zoom in the opposite direction—zooming deeply into the components that make up the original node.

While this all might sound interesting, you might be wondering what all this zooming has to do with analyzing business strategy. Consider that a business, like a network, competes at many different levels. Sales representatives compete for customer orders, for example, while recruiting departments compete for talent. Software programmers compete to write better code and marketers compete for catchier slogans. And everywhere there is competition, there is a need for strategy. Competitive strategies operate, therefore, at every level of the enterprise.

And the notion of competing at multiple levels is particularly true when it comes to a company's intellectual property. Let's take patents as an example. Patents are often treated as individual items, just a bunch of stand-alone text on a pile of paper. Patents, though, rarely result from an isolated moment of inspiration. They typically emerge from an extended period of investment and invention. The claims made by any single patent are often the end result of a long stream of inventive activity, the sum of which is more of a unit than any single document. And as experienced inventors know, most patents fall within a larger patent family. Large patents are often broken down into smaller ones called divisionals and continuations and they are often filed in multiple countries.

Given the power of this new lens, we can zoom out and see companies not as collections of business units, but as portfolios of patents. Zoom in and we can view technology portfolios composed of individual patents, but if you zoom out again you see that patent families really help you see the innovation path more clearly than the individual documents. Zoom in closer and you can see that patent portfolios represent the work created by inventor teams that grow and branch out over time. And at the most minute level, we can zoom in on the collection of claims, the lengthy list of dependent claims as well as the core set of independent claims that define the invention.

And by zooming, we can see better all the contours and irregularities of the

IP landscape. Patents are abandoned or sold. Companies change hands and their portfolios move along with them (or not). Research programs heat up and die off. New fields emerge using old technology and overlooked technologies branch off in unexpected directions. This entire web of invention, though, is connected through the tissue of citations, collaboration, and coauthorship. Every individual patent is also a component in a larger matrix of related technology and citations. Those business strategists who can visualize this terrain, and zoom through it more rapidly than their rivals, will have access to a tool of considerable strategic value that could mean the difference between a company's success and its collapse.

Some of the most spectacular strategic mistakes in the history of the business world, in fact, involved brilliant moves at one level of the IP landscape that failed to consider the strategic repercussions those moves would have at another level. As we'll see in chapter 7, the IBM PC was both late to market and offered an inferior user experience compared to its competitor, an Apple computer. Yet IBM's product soon became the industry standard in spite of its shortcomings because, unlike Apple, it didn't seek to control every aspect of its PC. At the same time, IBM failed to recognize that simply creating the product architecture and assembling the final product would not give it a sustainable competitive advantage. The company gave away the critical component positions in the PC, like the operating system and the central processor, to Microsoft and Intel. As a result, most of us now work on "Wintel" computers rather than IBM-branded PCs.

Nokia, which pioneered mobile telephony, is another cautionary tale as the company attempts to wriggle free from or at least reduce the license fees it is forced to pay its rival, Qualcomm. On one level it is obvious that driving down the costs of their handset's "bill of materials" makes sense for the company's bottom line. But if we look at Nokia's strategy from a higher level, does it really make sense for the company to push for a lower value for wireless patents, especially when Nokia itself has one of the top patent portfolios in the world? If Nokia succeeds in lowering the value of the IP in the wireless industry, the company risks undermining its competitive advantage and turning its handsets into a commodity category, one that is vulnerable to dozens of new competitors from China, Korea, India, and Southeast Asia who will swarm the market once the barriers to entry are reduced.

Without zooming tools at hand, information often becomes trapped in bottlenecks throughout a company. That, in turn, gives certain gatekeepers the ability to clamp down on that information for their own personal gain within the company's power and political structure. For example, we recently met with the management team of a cutting-edge German biotechnology company to discuss IP strategy. The executive in charge of the firm's intellectual property also served as the head of the R&D and legal functions. Sensing a threat from our presence, he had assembled a group of his legal and scientific staff to join him in defending what he considered an intrusion into his domain. "All of this strategy talk sounds good," he told us. "But when we do a major deal, we have to review every last page of every scientific paper and patent. My people need to read full text." While this executive's legal and scientific acolytes seated around the table all nodded dutifully, some of the nontechnical staff rolled their eyes. None of them, however, opened their mouths to contradict this somewhat outlandish claim. After all, reviewing the full text for every patent in this firm's portfolio would mean carefully reading some 50,000 pages of dense technical prose. At stake, of course, was not the best interests of the company; rather, it was the illusion of control that this chief priest of the sacred texts needed to convey instead.

Competitive Advantage in a Network

Michael Porter once defined strategy as the pursuit of actions that provide a sustainable advantage relative to competitors. While this helpful definition of strategy continues to hold true, we are still left to define how competitive advantage should be analyzed today. Back in the 1970s, for example, strategic analysis meant product analysis. In those days, strategic-planning departments and consultants would collect data on unit prices and costs and then break down each element in order to quantify what the differences were between competitors and what drove those differences. Since strategy was driven by products, you could discover the keys to winning by measuring relative market share and by drawing scale or experience curves.

A decade later, with much of Western industry reeling from the threat of Japanese competition, the focus turned to operational effectiveness. Since strategy was now process driven, strategic analysis meant drawing process flowcharts. In this environment, whoever delivered lower cost of quality, better customer satisfaction, or faster delivery times gained the upper hand. That meant a change in tools was needed; in this era that meant a switch from cost curves to flow diagrams, which became widely used to model the relative speed and quality of the competition's processes.

Today the nature of competitive advantage has shifted yet again. Rather than products or processes, we are now left to decipher the power of the network. To help us do this, we can look to several recent major works written about networks, each of which tends to focus on a particular dynamic of networks that helps us to discover where competitive advantage in a network comes from. In *The Tipping Point*, for instance, Malcolm Gladwell argued that an epidemic (whether of syphilis or the hottest new brand of sneakers) reaches a wide population by passing a "tipping point," the moment when a certain type of person—he calls them either connectors or mavens—becomes actively involved in spreading it. Gladwell's connectors are characterized by having an unusually high number of personal connections through which they can spread the seeds of the epidemic. An entire school of network theory has emerged around this idea. In fact, in many kinds of networks, it is actually just a small number of nodes in the network that attract an unusually high share of the total links (the network equivalent of the 80/20 rule, which says that 20 percent of a network's nodes are responsible for 80 percent of its traffic). Given this rule, Gladwell's advice is that if you can persuade the mavens that you have a cool product, you can then generate a fashion trend just by enabling these connectors to do your word-of-mouth marketing for you. Marketers have since coined the term "buzz marketing" to capture this very same idea and consumer goods companies now employ their own versions of connectors to help hype their products.

Dr. Stanley Milgram, another theorist who has sought to unravel the riddles of connectors, performed his own experiment in 1967 to see how personal networks function. Milgram gave 296 "starters"—100 Nebraska stockbrokers, 100 Bostonians, and 96 random Nebraskans—a document and asked each of the participants to mail the piece of paper to friends, family, and acquaintances who could help forward the document on its final "target," a stockbroker based in Boston. Of the sixty-four documents that eventually reached the final destination, the average mail "chain" required six steps to reach the target. Milgram's article was titled "The Small-World Problem" and his finding—that people are separated in a network by an average of "six degrees"—has become shorthand for the potential of collaboration in a network: you're only six degrees away from any insight in the world, if you can find the right path.

A third group of theorists, many of them associated with New Mexico's Santa Fe Institute, have focused their research on the properties of what they call *complex adaptive systems*. Looked at in this way, networks become self-organizing under the influence of individual nodes (or "agents" in their parlance) that, operating on simple rules, can produce elegant, efficient, and highly organized results with little or no conscious leadership. One of the researchers' favorite metaphors is an insect swarm, and they describe how *swarm intelligence* can create elegant and complex architectures that rely on no form of hierarchy whatsoever. This subversive notion—that bosses may, in fact, be unnecessary—has sparked a great deal of research into how to employ the power of these complex adaptive systems in the workplace, particularly in areas like route planning, logistics, and simulation modeling.

While each of these approaches tackles an important aspect of network theory, the models still struggle to deliver any true insight into competitive advantage. Gladwell, for instance, does a wonderful job describing epidemic theory, but he does a better job of finding real stories about sexually transmitted disease than he does in finding real businesses that set strategies based on connectors and mavens. The small-world theorists, on the other hand, have helped perfect the structures of social networks in order to speed introductions across a network, but these ideas have worked better with teenagers than businesses. As for the complexity theorists, their enthusiasm for the natural beauty of emergent phenomena has simply tended to shroud their abstract concepts of leaderless strategies in mystery.

But by definition, business strategy is not an emergent phenomenon. It involves conscious choices by leaders to commit resources. So in order to make the network lens viable, practicing strategists have long needed more practical tools.

Fortunately, a diverse set of observers have succeeded where others have failed and have managed to make these key themes—unequal connection, small worlds, discovering order amid complexity—-more practical. Some of these are scientists writing for popular audiences; other scientists have simply captured the public imagination with a creative insight. A few observant journalists have crystallized some key business insights, and some business leaders, like Bill Joy, have formalized key thoughts themselves.

A popular book that successfully boils down the elements of a network into something more practical for business strategists comes from Michael Lewis, the author who is best known for sports books like *Moneyball* and *Blindside*. Lewis, though, also has a keen eye for the world of business and his book *The New New Thing*, which was published in 2000, follows the exploits of Jim Clark, the well-known Silicon Valley entrepreneur. Lewis shadowed Clark for months, in part because Clark bore the distinction of being the first man in history to found three billion-dollar ventures from the ground up: Silicon Graphics (the workstation company that brought 3-D graphic animation to Hollywood), Netscape (the original Internet browser, which was purchased in 1998 by AOL), and Healtheon (an Internet-based health information company that merged with WebMD in 1999).

At one point in the book, Lewis recounts Clark's meeting with a group of Morgan Stanley investment bankers where he pitched the original strategy for Healtheon. In the meeting Clark drew a simple network diagram, informally known as the "Chart of Many Bubbles," that depicted the U.S. health care system as a set of eleven nodes—hospitals, health plans, patients, doctors, pharmacies, employers, and so on—with Healtheon at the very center of it all. One of the investment bankers then asked Clark a question: "How would all the companies in the little bubbles feel about a Silicon Valley upstart organizing them into a Chart of Many Bubbles and moving into the middle?" As one of Clark's subordinates stepped up with a "long and happy answer" to the banker's question, one that elaborated on the virtues of eliminating waste and creating partnerships, Lewis dismissed this as merely the easy-listening version of the strategy, "a smokescreen" for Clark's real strategy. "We want to empower the doctors and the patients and get all the other assholes out of the way," Clark told Lewis with a laugh. "Except for us. One asshole in the middle."

Vulgarity aside, there is a certain clarity in Clark's strategic vision. Holding down "the middle" of a complex network can be a position of competitive advantage. Network theorists have long recognized the value of what they call *centrality* and have developed ways to measure it. Other businesses have had similar intentions, including Microsoft who found their way into the middle of an important architecture—the IBM PC—as did Intel. P&G is trying to position itself in the middle of an active exchange market for consumer goods innovation. And in a different way, so has Linus Torvalds, the Finnish software developer who led the development of the kernel of the operating system derived from his name: Linux. (We'll come back to Linux later.)

The network theorist who has most clearly formalized Jim Clark's intuitive and colorfully phrased insight is the sociologist Ron Burt, a professor of sociology and strategy at the University of Chicago. In his book *Structural Holes*, Burt explains that position in a network is defined by the competition for relationships. And any set of relationships that connect two parts of a network that are not already connected provides advantage and profit to the competitor in the middle of what Burt calls "a structural hole." Burt argues that "players with networks rich in structural holes . . . enjoy high rates of return on investments. These players know about, take part in, and exercise control over more rewarding opportunities. Competitive advantage is a matter of access to holes."

In an innovation economy, gaining a position in the middle of the innovation network, therefore, is one of the most effective and critical ways to achieve competitive advantage, though, to be fair, it is easier said than done. The peculiar thing about networks is that they have a way of rapidly adapting in a way that neutralizes powerful central players. When Bill Joy formulated his somewhat whimsical law, he was actually making a serious point. Even though some in the computer industry were quick to assign invincibility and omnipotence to Microsoft because of its central position in the world of PC software, Joy argued that growth in an innovation network constrains even the most powerful players. The larger a network becomes, the more likely it is that talented innovators will look to leave the central player, which, in turn, makes it less likely that any single node can remain in the middle of everything for very long. The natural desire for autonomy in seeking new solutions will lead new players to pursue their creative impulses "elsewhere," as Joy so eloquently put it.

When talent and innovation are broadly distributed, therefore, network advantage can be found in more ways that just holding down the middle. Finding ways to connect a diverse group of active but not individually dominant players can also lead to advantage. The open-source software movement, which has been widely praised for its network innovation, poses perhaps the greatest challenge to Microsoft's dominance in the packaged software industry. Open-source software communities like Linux—so named because they openly publish their source code, in contrast to the more traditional models of software development used by Microsoft and others where code is kept as a trade secret—have attracted massive numbers of independent programmers to collaborate on large-scale software projects that rival, and often outdistance, Microsoft's products. Successful projects like Linux, Apache (a competitor to Microsoft's IIS Web server), Mozilla (reborn from Clark's once defunct Netscape Internet browser), and Open Office (Sun Microsystems' response to Microsoft's ubiquitous desktop suite) have proven that by increasing connections, and adopting a strategy based on an expanding network, even the most powerful hub position can be overcome.

Just as central positions are limited in their competitive dominance, though, so are large-scale networks. Networks are expensive to build and maintain since every connection requires resources to remain active. As a network grows larger, the increased weight of its connections has a tendency to produce noise, waste, and inflexibility, both inside large bureaucracies and in complex collaborations like an open-source project. What Ronald Coase called transactions costs are the Achilles' heel of these collaborative approaches to managing innovation. Since transactions costs reduce the competitive performance of an overly complex network, there is yet another way to achieve a network-based advantage: *simplicity*, in the form of clear rules, negotiated standards, or elegant new designs.

This is why some of the most important competitive battles of our time are being fought in the esoteric realm of technical standards bodies over seemingly arcane issues of technology. The average nontechnical executive's mind blurs when considering these increasingly important standards and the bodies that determine them, with a bewildering phalanx of acronyms that sounds like a foreign language of its own: ETSI versus TIA, WAPI, or 802.11; Blu-ray and Bluetooth; 3GPP versus 3GPP2; JPEG and MPEG; ATSC or DVBC; DHWG and IGRS; RFID with EPC, and so on. The list goes on and is seemingly endless. What these battles really involve, though, is the struggle over how to take complex webs of interdependent technologies and simplify the underlying architectures and rules that give them coherence. In other words, competitive advantage goes to whoever owns the standard and even the smallest change in the rules can the spell the difference between profits and losses for all the other players in the game.

Gaining IP Advantage

Ron Burt wrote about network-based competition this way: "Competition is an intense, intimate, transitory, invisible relationship created between players by their visible relations with others. It is being cheek by jowl with respect to the passing environment that makes the [players] competitors." In such an intense, intimate form of competition, the most critical asset that competitors bring to an innovation game—the difference maker that changes the rules—is their intellectual property. Strategists, in other words, need to think about how to use their IP to gain competitive advantage in a network of relationships.

Unlike other forms of property, IP assets lack clear property lines and every bit of intellectual property you can own comes with connections to other valuable innovations. These ownership rights are also constantly changing; they are embedded in a dynamic technology context, one in which new advances and new inventions are constantly added. And one of the best ways to observe this context is by observing the legal property lines provided by patent citations, the references to the "prior art" on which the patented inventions builds and over which the patent can claim no ownership rights. Patent citations are important because they make the relationships among technologies, and the related property rights, explicit. Patent citations also illuminate the boundaries between what one company's invention is, and what belongs to prior inventors. Using this lens to provide context, innovation landscapes become simple networks of patent citations.

A few analysts have taken the first tentative steps toward building an analytical discipline around these patent citation networks. Joel Podolny, a sociologist and business school professor, for instance, sketched out some early patent citation networks in his discussions of "technology niches" and "focal inventions" in the semiconductor industry. Podolny, however, eventually steered his research toward social networks, which left the power of visualizing these patent networks untapped. Commercial firms like CHI Research (now IPQ) have developed patent quality measures using citation data, but like the citation academics have not used network models to take their findings to the next level.

It's not hard to understand why. Looking at a patent network can quickly become overwhelming, particularly if the technology landscape is complex. As you move beyond the simple networks that Podolny first drew, you quickly run into the problems of scale. While a network of about a dozen nodes can yield useful insights, technology fields that involve hundreds or even thousands of patents quickly outstrip the capabilities of conventional visualization techniques. There simply isn't enough paper or enough room to view the landscape in context.

That's where zooming comes in. Zooming enables you to look beyond networks of individual patents to the network of companies that own the patents. At the same time, you can view groups of patents within those companies or the individual inventors who are central to an innovation network, like Campana's work at Telefind and NTP. You can also follow the leads set by standards organizations as they will often label and publish lists of patents as "essential IP" for a specific standard.

When the number of patent documents in a technology area gets too large, the most useful way of visualizing patent networks is by looking at networks of patent portfolios, a zoom level that allows you to see the positions of the competitors. Take Qualcomm's CDMA technology as an example. Their seminal 1986 CDMA patent, Patent No. 4,901,307, is one of the ten most highly cited patents in the history of the U.S. Patent Office (based on our analysis with PatentCafe). With 850 citations, that document sits squarely in the middle of the wireless telephony patent network. But Qualcomm didn't stop inventing in 1986; they continued to invest in a large portfolio of patents in the CDMA area, investments that have given them a powerful advantage over their competitors. Table 1 (on page 89) contrasts Qualcomm's patent portfolio with its key competitors'.

Figure 8, on the other hand, shows the same set of patents in a network diagram made up of the all the major patent portfolios in the European (ETSI)
WCDMA standard. Each bubble represents a company's portfolio of patents
while each link is the sum of citation connections between the patents in one
company's portfolio related to the patents filed by another company. While Qualcomm did not participate in developing the WCDMA standard (their influence
was most direct in the U.S. CDMA2000 standard) the company continues to
assert that its patents are central to the WCDMA standard. In moving to third-
generation (3G) wireless technology, the old TDMA vendors found they needed
to use code division technology as they moved to a higher bandwidth. As a result,
they have been forced to rely a great deal on Qualcomm's CDMA technology, a
claim backed up by the large number of citation links into the Qualcomm patent
portfolio.

FIGURE 8   Assignee Citation Network of ETSI Patents

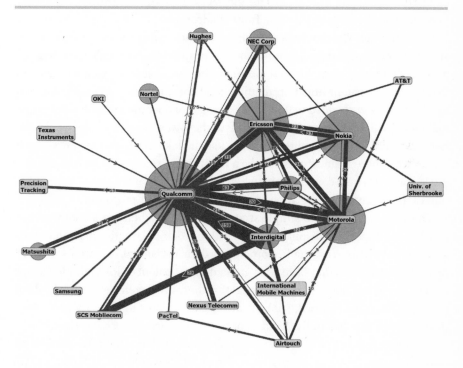

Source: The ETSI IPR Database; author analysis.

Qualcomm's patents, as the network diagram shows, are by far the most central, and their portfolio is cited more frequently than any other company's portfolio, including Ericsson, Motorola, Nokia, Philips, Samsung, NEC, Hughes, Nortel, and Texas Instruments. The leading GSM/TDMA manufacturers, Ericsson, Nokia, and Motorola, form a small club of their own, comprising the highly connected cluster in the upper right, in which even Motorola's influential patent portfolio is secondary when it comes to the centrality of Qualcomm's position.

When viewed this way, it's easier to understand the strength of Qualcomm's competitive position in the 3G technology world. Without the need to rely on other companies' patents (remember that Nokia, Ericsson, and Motorola all make handsets), and with a large portfolio of highly influential patents, Qualcomm gets more than a visual advantage in a network map—they possess a commanding strength when it comes to the negotiating power they can bring to the table when the validity and relevance of any of their patents is called into question. When it comes to negotiating royalty rates for the WCDMA standard, you wouldn't want to be on the other side of the table from Qualcomm.

Why? Because Qualcomm's portfolio of patents stands a better chance of surviving any challenge than the portfolio of a company that has just a few isolated patents. "Full-text" guys, like our German biotechnology manager, will tell you that success in patent litigation requires total command of every technical and semantic issue embedded in thousands of pages of documents, and to the extent that these disputes revolve around details at the lowest zoom level, he would certainly be right. Tough disputes, though, usually take place in a territory much higher up, where negotiators can take a much more reasonable view of the disputed content. There comes a point when the strategic issue becomes less a question of fine textual interpretation and more a question of probabilities.

This all comes down to simple strategic calculus. Whenever a patent owner faces an infringement dispute, the strength of their negotiating position originates from two sources: the importance of their individual inventions and the breadth of the claims they have been granted by the patent office. Although a first read of any patent document may reveal that there are dozens, even hundreds of specific inventions claimed, sophisticated readers know that the meat of most patent documents lies in the handful of what are called *independent claims*.

While every patent has at least one independent claim, the total number of claims can vary greatly. The most extensive of NTP's wireless e-mail patents, for example, has only fifteen independent claims. Any company involved in a legal defense around infringement understands that any individual claim might be overturned with an aggressive attack. Assume for the moment that the probability of a successful attack on each independent claim is 98 percent. While those are good odds to bet on, they still relate at best to a single patent. As you add new patents, and the number of independent claims rises, the odds of winning quickly begin to ebb away.

Why is this? Think for a moment about the odds of a successful defense against every relevant claim, *even if the odds of winning every individual dispute are 98 percent*. For a patent portfolio with ten independent claims, the odds of winning slips to 0.98^{10}—still more than 80 percent. With twenty claims, the odds of winning against every claim go down to 0.98^{20}, or 67 percent. If you extend this to fifty relevant claims, about the size of a serious patent portfolio, the odds of winning fall below 40 percent. For patent portfolios that are strongly related by citations—for example, RIM's frequent citation of NTP's patents or Ericsson's frequent citation of Qualcomm's patents—the strategic arithmetic we're describing can provide a very real advantage, or disadvantage.

We can see the advantage of having multiple claims at play with NTP's successful suit against RIM over the BlackBerry. (For a refresher, see the full story in chapter 3.) Recall that Thomas Campana had accumulated nearly fifty relevant patents related to wireless e-mail and pager technology between his work at Telefind and NTP that were listed on RIM's own patents. Three of these patent applications in particular, all filed in May of 1991, ultimately yielded eight different granted patents relating to wireless e-mail technology that relate most closely to RIM's BlackBerry technology. Five of these eight provided the guts of the RIM case, with some 1,600 total claims and more than 50 separate independent claims between them. Try as RIM might—and make no mistake, RIM fought the infringement charges tooth and nail and even succeeded in getting the Patent Office to reconsider the scope of the NTP claims—it couldn't overcome NTP's extensive claim portfolio.

By contrast, the single patent IMS brought to bear against Intel in its dispute over the backward compatibility of its Pentium processors (see the full story in chapter 2) was far less effective. As good as Scantlin's inventions for IMS might have been, and as close as his inventions were to the techniques Intel was using in its Pentium designs, the single IMS patent had only three independent claims. All Intel had to do to win the case was prove that their technology didn't do *exactly* what those three claims described, certainly one situation that demanded a detailed reading of every word of the full patent text. Intel's victory was assured as soon as it convinced the judge that it had used a slightly different approach than the one detailed in the patent's claims.

FIGURE 9   The Network Strategy Cycle: Three Basic Strategies,
            Their Limits, and Forcing Economics

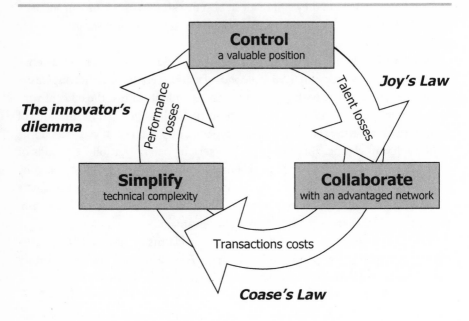

Control, Collaborate, Simplify

In such a complex competitive landscape, IP strategies require the development of relational advantages. And for the creative strategist, there are many options to consider in this networked world, and each path can lead to a different type of strategy. In the diagram in Figure 9, we have outlined the three principal IP strategies: Control, Collaborate, and Simplify. These strategy options echo the three attributes of a basic network—nodes, links, and clusters—and comprise a cycle: one where opportunity leads to success, success confronts its limits, and limits create new opportunities. The discussion of these dynamics provides the basic structure for the next three chapters.

COMPETITIVE STRATEGY
FOR THE
COMPANY OF IDEAS

CHAPTER 5

Control

INNOVATION WITHOUT PROTECTION IS PHILANTHROPY

Happy families are all alike; every unhappy family is unhappy in its own way.

—*Leo Tolstoy*, Anna Karenina*

T here's something missing in the stories we tell ourselves about business success. Most of the examples and case studies we read are tales of perfect businesses (happy families) that have neat, compact narratives leading from challenge to redemption. These stories are often romantic tales of struggle and conquest, where a charismatic leader transforms a bad business into a good one. Not surprisingly, these tales are often told in autobiographical format, where a triumphant (and often) retired CEO looks back on his success and describes how he managed "straight from the gut" or imbued his company with "the discipline of getting things done." (One business writer we know labels this genre CEO porn: *Maxim* for business leaders.)

We also find a variety of "whodunits" and "howdunits" on our newsstands and bookstores where an insightful strategist stumbles upon an unhappy customer group with unmet needs. These stories, while more cerebral than the CEO superhero yarns, all tend to have the same plot: A strategist successfully conjures up a creative new business design to profitably meet the needs of these unhappy

*Based on the widely used translation by Constance Clara Garnett, 1901. Tolstoy's 1877 novel is available at Project Gutenberg at www.gutenberg.org/etext/1399.

customers. The beautiful new design involves constructing a new value chain, one that supports a new economics of price, cost, and value. Then, after persuading a financier to support the plan, the new concept catches on and grows like wildfire, the stock takes off, and the main characters get rich. Everyone lives happily ever after.

While these stories make for compelling classroom lessons, and even some entertaining performance art at consulting conferences, they are, of course, woefully incomplete. The perfect business story is a rare beast, found perhaps only in Hollywood and on white boards, while the brash and bullheaded leader, as we saw in chapter 4, is largely a myth. Things often go wrong in business— particularly as small businesses try to become big businesses—and to find out why, you'll need to follow more than just a few characters and simple plot lines.

One character most of these stories leave out, of course, is IP. The problem, though, is that when IP is part of the plot, its role is often oversimplified as well. When people think about an IP story, they usually assume it's just a tale where one company excludes its competitors from a key market, keeps its prices and margins high, and commands unusually high market share for a long period of time. While this aspect can indeed be part of the narrative, the complexities of business tell us that it can really tell only part of the story. Like with any good read, a strategist can't easily predict what they might find on the next page.

The key narrative element in any IP story begins with a company *owning* some kind of intangible asset. To the maximum extent possible, a company needs to own the assets that provide it with a distinction in the marketplace. Those assets can range from a collection of claims in a patent, to an entire patent portfolio, or even to the functional workings of a key component in a complex design. In other words, some of the most effective and profitable companies find ways to own and control positions that have a lot of competitive value. Indeed, some of the world's most celebrated business strategies are control strategies: Microsoft's operating systems, General Electric's original lightbulbs, and more recently developed medical imaging equipment and Hewlett-Packard's ink-jet printer cartridges. The problem is, professors and journalists have turned what should be "howdunits" featuring IP into simplistic "whodunits" starring the nerdy Bill Gates, Jack Welch the tough guy, and the up-from-the-garage duo of Bill Hewlett and Dave Packard. The popular versions of these stories love the brand but ignore the trademark. They love the innovation but ignore the inventor. Most notably, they suffer from the salesperson's conceit: every invention is created from whole cloth by a single heroic character.

If we were to retell stories like these, only adding the character of IP to the plot, we begin to see these supposed heroes in a new, more complicated light. Bill Gates, for example, made his most important strategy decision well before the IBM PC and its breakthrough DOS product. Just a few months after starting up his fledgling microcomputer software business, in which he planned to sell a version of the BASIC programming language for the first Altair microcomputer, Gates actually sparked an intellectual property innovation in the computer business. In his now legendary "letter to hobbyists," Gates challenged the widespread practice among hobbyists (today we would call them "hackers") of copying proprietary software code. His letter argued: "The feedback we have gotten from the hundreds of people who say they are using BASIC has all been positive. Two surprising things are apparent, however: (1) Most of these 'users' never bought BASIC (less than 10% of all Altair owners have bought BASIC), and (2) The amount of royalties we have received from sales to hobbyists makes the time spent on Altair BASIC worth less than $2 an hour. Why is this? As the majority of hobbyists must be aware, most of you steal your software. Hardware must be paid for, but software is something to share. Who cares if the people who worked on it get paid?" As the world's wealthiest man today, it's now obvious that Gates found a way to get paid more than $2 an hour: in the process of pioneering the practice of charging for pure intellectual property, Gates effectively launched the modern software industry.

Microsoft's most successful and enduring industrial-age counterpart is General Electric (GE), the company that quite literally electrified the world. GE was launched by Thomas Edison, who, like Gates, owed his personal wealth as much to his novel approach to protecting his intellectual property as to his technological achievements. Edison is a named inventor on 1,093 U.S. patents, the output of a career of innovation that over six decades spanned technologies like the electric lightbulb, cement manufacturing, and the phonograph. Edison's productivity level, like Gates's success, was actually the result of a historically significant strategic innovation; his success in patenting was driven more by his organized approach to innovation and his productive team of engineers than by his personal genius as an inventor. In his laboratories at Menlo Park and Orange, New Jersey, Edison pioneered the model of the dedicated corporate *innovation factory*: with R&D expenditures going in one end and inventions and patents coming out the other. For well over a century (starting in the nineteenth and continuing into the twenty-first), Edison's team held the record as the single most prolific inventor group in the history of the USPTO.

Nucor, the onetime upstart to national steel-producing stalwarts like U.S.

Steel, redefined steel making and pioneered the mini-mill. After beginning with steel bars, the company moved upstream into the sheet steel business in the early 1990s. For a while, they were one of the "perfect business stories most favored by academics and business writers. Then something happened. As the steel business turned tough due to Asian competition, competitors copied their mini-mill model. To confound their problems, Nucor failed to patent its innovative thin-slab rolling system, which further eroded its edge. While sales continued to grow, profit stagnated: in 2003, the company earned less than half of what it had ten years earlier, and profit per ton dropped from $40 to under $20 for three years running. After hitting bottom, though, Nucor turned things around—but it wasn't because their CEO came riding in on a white horse. Rather, it was by renewing the firm's commitment to innovation, and this time, creating a powerful patent portfolio. After launching joint ventures in strip casting in 2006, Nucor's profit per ton soared to nearly $130 and their stock price went up from the mid-$20s in 2005 to over $60 per share by the middle of 2008.

Today Hewlett-Packard is a sprawling conglomerate cobbled together from the acquisitions of Compaq and DEC, best known for the inventive spirit of its founding owners and more recently for the Machiavellian maneuverings of its board of directors. For many years, though, well over half of HP's profits have come from its printing business, namely its ink and toner supplies. HP has built a patent estate of more than 4,000 patents related to ink, toner, and cartridges, and it has vigorously defended its IP position. The company, for example, has long encouraged customers to return their used ink cartridges to dry up the supply to refillers like RhinoTek that love to exploit the HP brand and resell used cartridges as new. The company has also had to confront retailers like Walgreen, who they have challenged for importing ink cartridges based on HP technology from Chinese copycats like Ninestar. As a result, HP is able to sell barely differentiated commodities like ink and toner in patent-protected cartridges that gives them margins that would make a software company envious.

Many people mistakenly attribute Hewlett-Packard's success to its "blades and razors" business model: they believe that the company has profited by essentially giving away its printers so that it can make money on ink. But if the journalists and business school case writers invariably miss the central role of IP protection in the story, they do the same thing when writing about the original "blades and razors" business—Gillette. Despite the popular mythology, theirs isn't a story about business models and marketing. Rather, it's a story about invention and intellectual property, a story with different characters and a different plot than most outsiders have ever heard.

Gillette Razors and Blades

On March 11, 2004, eleven weighty patent applications hit the United States Patent Office. They came from a group of inventors at the Boston-based Gillette blades and razors group and heralded the launch of the company's latest men's shaving systems: the Fusion and Fusion Power razors. Eighteen months later, on September 15, 2005, the day after Gillette "unveiled" the new product to the marketing and advertising world in what one wag described as "metrosexual nirvana," most of these applications were made public. Any visitor to the USPTO's Web site could read hundreds of pages of detailed technical specifications telling them everything they could ever want to know about the inventions embodied in Gillette's latest shaving system. The most prominent lead inventors on the patent filings were three young engineers: Charles Worrick, who patented the "shaving system," including the razor and blade design; Evan Pennell, who focused on the individual blades or "cutting members"; and Vincent Walker, who led the development of the pivoting blade unit and shaving cartridge.

One of the eleven applications filed at the patent office that day also included the name of an old Gillette hand: Bob Trotta. Even as he was getting ready for retirement, Trotta, a thirty-year veteran of the company, found himself on the cutting edge of Gillette technology one more time. He had teamed up with the group of three younger engineers on a patent application for a "blade unit" assembly that included a trimming blade on the rear edge of the blade unit. This trimming blade is one of the signature features—and arguably the most valuable—of the Fusion shaving system, a fitting swan song for an inventor who has contributed more to the male shaving experience than any other single individual in the world.

Trotta, who has now retired and lives outside of Boston on the road to Cape Cod, headed up the blades and razors technology group at Gillette for many years and stands among the company's most prolific inventors. His patents span several generations of shaving technology, from the Sensor to the Mach 3 and, of course, to the Fusion. Trotta is an engaging and curious man, an engineer's engineer, whose mind overflows with ideas and insights. And although he is tight-lipped about the details of Gillette's technology management and IP strategy, he expounds with infectious enthusiasm on a wide range of subjects: from the science of skin and hair to the necessary qualities of a great engineering talent, and even to the methods he believes the Egyptians really used to build the pyramids. Not surprisingly, Trotta also likes to hold forth on the importance of patented technology, which, he says, Gillette was built on. The company was founded by

King C. Gillette, who started the business with a patent on a safety razor with disposable blades. Trotta will tell you, though, that William Nickerson, the technologist who developed the machines that made mass production of the safety razor possible, was just as critical to the company's early success. "Gillette was a great salesman who had the original concept," says Trotta. "But without Nickerson's engineering skill, you would never have heard of the company."

Trotta is also a big advocate of coupling engineering know-how with acute observation skills. He points out that shaving in the real world is something very different from a controlled lab experiment and that it's critical to observe real consumers working with innovative product concepts in the course of regular daily life. Not surprisingly, Gillette's commitment to such observation is legendary and any story about the company's blades and razors business inevitably begins with a trip to the South Boston shaving lab.

> The company's version of the holy grail is to create the perfect shaving experience that will hold customers forever. To that end, every day, a rotating panel of Gillette employees goes to a shaving test lab in the South Boston plant, where they denude their faces, armpits or legs—the men in cubicles equipped with bathroom mirrors, the women in rooms equipped with showers, baths and sinks—and rate the experience on closeness, comfort and the like. Sometimes they use Gillette products, sometimes a competitor's. They don't know which; the researchers tabulating and tweaking the results certainly do, and they feed the data back to the designers.

Accounts like these often focus on how Gillette employees, by using new products, literally get "closer to the customer experience." These stories then invariably turn to other aspects of the blades and razors business: such as the advertising campaign, Gillette's wide global distribution, or even the notion that as every new product is launched, the next-generation product is already in the plans. Then, at least until P&G took over Gillette in 2005, the stories usually closed with some commentary about the financial performance of the company, pinned to the latest trends in Gillette's stock.

And to be clear, Gillette's razors consistently drove the company's profits. Company insiders referred to the blades and razors business as "the bank," even going so far as to suggest that Gillette's razor business is more profitable than printing money. (It costs the U.S. Mint about 4¢ to produce a dollar bill, which, in fact, gives the Mint a slightly lower profit margin than Gillette earns on its razors.) The central character in this parable of near perfect profit performance is the role of the captive consumer: the notion that once someone has purchased or been given the razor, they'll keep buying the blades. It's a business school case study in a nutshell: give away the razor, own the consumer, and mint your own money by selling packs of high-margin blades.

But if you stop to think for a moment, the notion of a captive consumer is simply not a very compelling way to explain the enduring success the Gillette's shaving business. Buying a new razor costs only a few dollars; getting a new one is not really an obstacle for the typical buyer. All of us have the opportunity to purchase a similar razor offered by a competitor—or even pick up a cheap disposable version—any time we walk into a grocery or drug store.

Indeed, Gillette has many competitors all over the world, all of them willing to sell an inexpensive razor and blade combination. Some of these competitors have also invested a great deal in shaving technology over time, particularly Schick, which also owns the Wilkinson Sword brand. What makes Gillette's success remarkable, then, is less the role of captive customers and more its ability to sustain its competitive performance advantage. As one commentator noted, "The [world's] most popular product is also its best: Gillette is simultaneously the Porsche and the General Motors of shaving." In other words, the success of the blades and razor business is not a result of customer *laziness;* rather, it's a result of customer *restlessness.* Enough men (and women) are eager to improve their shaving experience, and they find that Gillette's technology reliably produces the best-quality shave.

Think about it. How many other product areas do you know where customers actually complain when a company introduces an improved product by saying, "My experience is already good enough, why did you bother making it better?" The first Fusion models, with their extra blades, even stirred up some ridicule, including several clever Internet spoofs. The most common reaction, though, has been great enthusiasm over the improvement that extra blade brings to the shaving experience. At the time of the printing of this book, in fact, sales were booming and the Fusion shaving system had just become the newest billion-dollar P&G brand, the fastest ever to reach that milestone.

Why is it that, given that most observers appreciate the value of technology, so many business analysts miss the reason that Gillette is able to generate a sustainable competitive advantage in performance? Few journalists and business school professors who cover or profile Gillette ever talk about their IP strategy. And if they do, the discussion mostly centers on courtroom events rather than their management methods. Turns out, though, that Gillette likes it that way. That's why, when you talk to someone like Bob Trotta, he's willing to discuss almost anything about shaving—except how Gillette has managed its patents. Gillette's success with its blades and razors business is a simple story of superior technology *and* its protection. It's a story that begins with a relatively small group of creative engineers, people like Trotta, Worrick, Walker, Pennell, and a few dozen others who do the majority of the R&D work. This group then measures its progress and success not by the number of patents they generate but on the effectiveness of their scientific observations, commercial judgment, and strong patent protection of identifiable consumer benefits. These inventors have been developing Gillette's technology base and patent portfolio for decades and, as a result, Gillette has left their competitors in the dust: their share of the global blades and razors market has grown to more than 70 percent.

Figure 10 depicts Gillette's razors and blades R&D program over time. While the display shows the career patent output of more than fifty of Gillette's most prolific shaving inventors, a few in particular are worth noting. Francis Dorion, for example, invented the first two-blade razor back in the 1960s, the Trac II, for which he later received a patent in 1971. Michael Gray, an industrial designer, has been designing men's razor handles for Gillette for more than thirty years, receiving sixty-four U.S. patents along the way. All but two of these, though, are "design patents," patents filed to protect the distinctive look and feel of the Gillette razors rather than their function. Jill Shurtleff is Gray's counterpart on the female shaving side; she was the industrial designer behind the distinctive Sensor for Women and the Venus razor handle designs. A recent group of engineers—Charles Worrick (who supervised the overall Fusion shaving system and also worked on the Mach 3), Evan Pennell, and Vincent Walker—have all been in the center of developing Gillette's latest product, the Fusion shaving system. Pennell—who worked to make the spacing of the five "cutting members" of the Fusion—was also the main link to the Fusion Power team, led by Uwe Schaaf.

The central character in the recent history of Gillette's blades and razors business, though, has been Bob Trotta. Trotta holds more utility patents (patents for invention) than any other Gillette engineer; his personal portfolio of patents is more highly cited than any other engineer's patents; and his work spans the range of product introductions from the mid-1970s all the way through to the Fusion. In fact, if you trace Trotta's sequence of inventions, you end up with a guided tour of the entire modern history of Gillette shaving technology. Beginning in 1976, as a recent graduate of the University of Massachusetts (Amherst) school of engineering, he invented the pivoting head for the Atra razor and then added the lubricating strip that marked the rollout of the Atra Plus in 1985. He later supervised the design of the Sensor shaving system (playing a role similar to

FIGURE 10   Gillette's Community of Shaving Invention

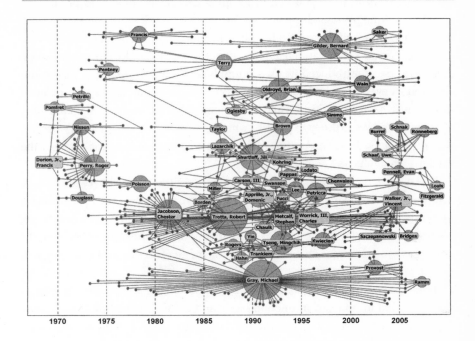

| 1970 | 1975 | 1980 | 1985 | 1990 | 1995 | 2000 | 2005 |

Worrick's on the Fusion system) and eventually led the way on a surge of patents filed in the fall of 1990, patents that accompanied the launch of the Sensor that same year.

One of these, a patent on an "oscillating razor," was never introduced in the Sensor. Trotta argues that the reason Gillette delayed introducing a powered model until the Mach 3 was both because it was too expensive and because the marketing experts didn't think it gave consumers enough bang for their buck. It also made little sense for Gillette to compete on the oscillating feature, Trotta says, because "power is not protectable." If you take the time to look at the early patents for power feature, you quickly realize he's got a point. Schick actually filed for a patent on their version of vibrating razor technology ten months before Trotta filed his own oscillating razor patent. Interestingly enough, Schick executives seem to have made the same marketing calculation as Gillette since they too waited to introduce a power feature. (When Gillette later introduced the Mach 3 Power line in 2004, however, Schick quickly followed them to market with the Quattro Power in 2005.)

By the mid-1990s, Trotta was heading up development of the Mach 3. Unlike the power feature, Gillette developed a great deal of technology to protect the Mach 3's unique multiblade design, as the dense network of inventors, centered around team leader Bernard Gilder, filing patents in this period demonstrates.

Schick, on the other hand, needed to up its ante in the premium-razor stakes. And, in 2003, it introduced its own multiblade design: the Quattro. But before the product even launched, Gillette filed suit, charging that Schick's four-bladed design infringed on critical Gillette technology, specifically U.S. Patent No. 6,212,777 (known as the '777 patent), which covered the blade geometry used in the three-bladed Mach 3. As a result, the most contentious patent battle of the modern era of shaving soon erupted.

The dispute boiled down to a question of whether the '777 patent covered blade arrangements involving multiple-blade configurations in general or, specifically, just three-blade arrangements. It was a close case, with momentum seesawing back and forth, as lawyers on both sides battled over the meaning of the patent's key phrase: "a safety razor blade unit *comprising* a guard, a cap, and a *group of first, second, and third* blades" (emphasis added).

In January 2005, Gillette lost the first round when the Massachusetts District Court refused to issue an injunction blocking further Quattro sales. The Court of Appeals for the Federal Circuit then reversed parts of the District Court judge's ruling and, in April, sent the case back to the District Court along with an interpretation of the word *comprising* that was far more favorable to Gillette. Gillette, in fact, soon found itself on the brink of victory when, in December, the District Court judge sent the case to trial. If Gillette had won the case, Schick could have been forced to pull the Quattro off the shelves, destroy its entire existing inventory, pay damages on past sales, and redesign their razor in a way that didn't infringe Gillette's patents. This would have forced Schick to further degrade the quality of their razor that, according to many shavers at least, was already inferior to Gillette's.

We will never know what the outcome of that trial would have been, however. After P&G acquired Gillette later that same year, the case was settled in February 2006, and as with many important IP agreements, the terms were not disclosed. If P&G received royalties in this settlement from Schick, perhaps they realized that the application of their Connect and Develop strategy in blades and razors gave them the opportunity to approach the business more like a shark and earn royalties on the Quattro. Only insiders know for sure.

The choice to settle may also have reflected P&G's confidence in their ability

FIGURE 11   U.S. Patents and Patent Applications Protecting the Gillette Fusion

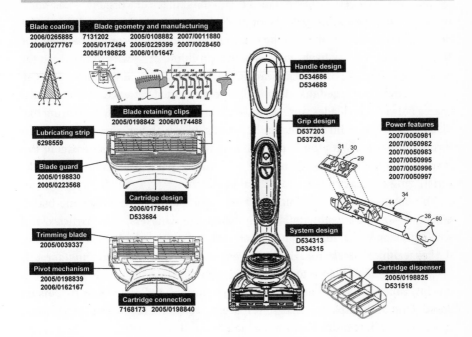

to control the next generation of shaving technology with their Fusion patents. Launched in January 2006, the Fusion shaving system took decades of experience in building a technology foundation, and protecting it through intellectual property, to the next level. From the timing of patent disclosures to the blanket of IP that surrounds virtually every feature of the product line, the Fusion razor reflects the fruits of a finely tuned IP management system.

Figure 11 shows how a blanket of more than thirty new U.S. patents protects the inventions that are embedded in the Fusion and Fusion Power razors. These patents cover a wide range of novel methods—everything from a technique for crimping the blade steel that enables the production of more closely spaced blades to the design for Trotta's trimmer blade—and credit a wide group of inventors from around the globe, a list that includes team members from the Shaving Headquarters in South Boston, to the R&D center in Reading, England, to the Braun research facility in Kronberg, Germany (where the Fusion Power team worked). Perhaps the most important technology, however, covers the way the blades glide across a shaver's face to produce the elusive benefits of "closeness and comfort." The '777 patent on the Mach 3 showed how blade *exposure*—the angle at which successive blades engage with the skin to cut whiskers—was worth fighting over. The Fusion patents, on the other hand, emphasize a different aspect of blade geometry: the spacing between the blades. The spacing between the Mach 3 blades was relatively wide—about 1.5 millimeters—which was about the same as most of the other blade cartridges on the market at that time. But Gillette researchers learned that their consumers reported better comfort when the spaces between the blades were narrower than 1.5 millimeters. By narrowing that distance, the blades hit whiskers rather than skin, which has a tendency to bulge through the gaps. With the Fusion, Gillette reduced the interblade spacing to a mere 1.1 millimeters to help keep the skin surface flatter and, as a result, make the shaving experience more comfortable.

The downside to a more narrow blade spacing, though, is that the blades quickly become clogged with shaving debris (cut whiskers, skin particles, and shaving soap), which makes it harder to wash out the debris after each stroke. So the key technical breakthrough on the Fusion became its ability to *simultaneously* keep the five blades close together while also allowing the debris to rinse out quickly. Gillette has even developed a "wash-through index" to measure rinsing speed. One of their patent filings even seeks protection for these ideas of blade spacing below 1.25 millimeters and a high "wash-through index." A whole series of inventions make these advances possible and Gillette has worked hard to exclude its competitors from delivering closeness and comfort features that come anywhere close to the innovations underlying the Fusion shaving experience. Figure 11 highlights the patents that relate most directly to this control strategy.

Close on the heels of their improved blade assembly, Gillette introduced yet another advancement in razor design: the Fusion Power razor. The company, though, has moved into the power market gingerly; Gillette, in fact, offers substantial discounts to customers who use the manual razors. Since a powered razor is expensive, cost clearly becomes an issue. And despite Trotta's claims that "power is not protectable"—which was certainly the case with the Mach 3, given Schick's IP position—Gillette now appears more confident that they have stronger IP legs to stand on when it comes to the design for the Fusion Power. Figure 11 shows six patents (with a dozen independent claims) that surround the Fusion Power system, which also offers a meaningful advance in terms of vibration control over the Mach 3. Interestingly, a number of power patents protect features that have not yet been implemented, suggesting that Gillette has laid the IP groundwork for new advanced power features that we may see sometime down the road.

Wherever Gillette, or for that matter Schick, chooses to make its next bet on new shaving products, you can be sure that Schick and Gillette engineers are watching each other's patent disclosures like a hawk. After all, everyone in the real blades and razors business knows that's how the battle is won or lost. Indeed, the fact that Gillette has been winning the blades and razors technology battles for so long is what has made its shaving business so profitable, not the urban legend that lazy customers won't switch razors. More specifically, Gillette's ability to create and defend a blanket of protection surrounding its shaving innovations, thereby controlling critical technologies—such as new blade exposure angles, tighter blade spacing, and better debris wash-through—allow Gillette to sustain its *competitive edge* in delivering the "closeness and comfort" promise that defines its brand identity. For those of us who begin our days shaving with "the best a man can get," we may not know how much we owe to Bob Trotta, but the *invisible edge* that he and his colleagues have built over the years is what makes it possible for Gillette to print money while delivering us a terrific shaving experience, one that is quite literally at the *cutting edge*.

The Exclusionary Basics of Competitive IP Management

The best intellectual property managers, like those at Gillette, are very protective of their methods for managing the IP process. For companies that invest heavily in innovation, the effective management of the modern-day version of Edison's original *innovation factory* has become one of the few management tasks that can actually contribute to competitive advantage. In a sense, this takes us back to the basics of invention as an economic activity that Jacob Schmookler defined back in 1966. Schmookler noted that invention, like a physical factory, was driven by market demand. As a factory, invention most closely resembles a highly customized job shop, made up of diverse activity centers and a project-driven tempo. Any given project can follow a different path and go through different steps. In its simplest terms, though, successful IP development means running a unique kind of factory, one that uses really expensive talent to produce wildly unpredictable outputs. While these innovation factories can be tough to manage, they can also provide some of the most attractive investment returns any business can ever find.

If you run your innovation factory well, your business can develop valuable differentiation and raise the odds of attaining the holy grail of strategy: a sustainable competitive advantage. If you outsource the innovation factory completely, you risk losing your distinction and will inevitably end up in a commodity business. Indeed, one could almost define the common business phrase "a commodity business" as a business with little to no intellectual capital. Just as important, if you do invest in innovation, but fail to activate the part of the factory that focuses on appropriating that innovation and *excluding your competition* from copying your ideas, you won't *own your distinction* either. Even if you've come up with the greatest invention or business idea in the world, all you will have accomplished is to gift-wrap your investments for your competition and customers.

In short, innovation without protection is philanthropy.

Excluding competitors from copying your differentiation is not a simple process however. Some of the world's best business innovations have, in fact, been copied aggressively, leaving the original inventors behind with little to show for their amazing new idea. IBM, for example, developed the PC but didn't find a way to protect their position. They soon found themselves surrounded by suppliers like Intel and Microsoft, as well as direct competitors like Dell and Compaq. As a result, they sold their PC operation to a Chinese manufacturer, Lenovo, and they're now out of the business altogether. We'll talk about this in more detail in chapter 7. Nucor was widely celebrated for pioneering the mini-mill for structural steel and steel bars and grew rapidly, but competitors like CMC and Chaparral flooded in and kept their profits flat for a decade.

But IP protection extends beyond just high-tech machines and manufacturing. Starbucks clearly revolutionized the daily experience of coffee drinking and, as a result, their brand has become synonymous with premium coffee drinks. But their success simply attracted copycats: Dunkin' Donuts is now pushing its new lattes aggressively; McDonald's, which one Starbucks executive criticized as "selling hot, brown liquid masquerading as coffee," has added premium coffee and baristas to their outlets (and even bested Starbucks in a recent *Consumer Reports* taste test); and other premium coffee stores like Peet's and Caribou Coffee have been growing every bit as fast as Starbucks in recent years.

In much of our discussion so far, we have focused almost exclusively on patents. While patents are among the most visible and valuable forms of intellectual property, they are by no means the only mechanism you can use to protect intangible investments. In owning and protecting intellectual assets, it's important to note that there are more options than patent to keep a sustainable edge over the competition. Successful executives manage IP with a wide range of tools and find ways to combine numerous protection techniques: each has its own dynamics, yet each can reinforce the value of the others. The best-managed IP factories do more than simply assemble all these techniques in one place; they also combine their management of a portfolio of IP formats in an integrated way.

1. **Trade secrets.** The practice of protecting inventions by keeping them closely held as a trade secret has, relative to patenting, been losing favor over recent years. That is not to say, though, that these secrets are unimportant. When we think of trade secrets, though, we usually think of things like Coca-Cola's "secret formula," the recipe for the famous carbonated soft drink. What most of us don't recognize, however, is that the recipe has been public for years, at least certain versions of it. The secret was widely exposed when it appeared in print in an "unauthorized history of the great American soft drink and the company that makes it." In contrast to trade secrets like these (that aren't really secret), there are numerous companies that retain trade secrets of great business value. Consider, for example, the growing focus on developing tools and systems built around corporate knowledge management, which has become the modern face of trade secret management. Capital One, for instance, has invested in a proprietary database that captures the results of their credit card trials, which, in turn, helps them to fine-tune future credit card promotions. The company now regards the information gleaned from that database to be one of their major sources of competitive advantage. Toyota Motor Company too has instituted a discipline of capturing the results of process improvement experiments in their A3 reports, so called because they report on the findings of production experiments and indicated actions in a format that fits on one page of A3-size paper. We'll talk much more about Toyota in chapter 6.

When you zoom down inside a company of any size, its private collection of trade secrets comprises a body of work that resembles the larger world of publicly disclosed intellectual property, only in microcosm. Indeed, the entire field of corporate knowledge management is essentially the management of these private document collections and their associated innovator networks. Proprietary repositories of internal publications and analyses, which are increasingly being managed electronically with structured databases, are similar to the U.S. patent database. Because companies can exclude competitors from access to these repositories (while allowing employee access via indexing systems that allow convenient search and retrieval), trade secrets are developing new value. Any individual idea may be hard to protect this way, but the entire corpus is not; as a result, it is emerging as a powerful source of competitive advantage.

2. **Copyrights.** One reason that selling packaged software makes for such a good business is the difficulty of reverse-engineering the packaged (aka "compiled" in a set of binary 1s and 0s) program, which makes the original source code one of the few cases in which traditional modalities of "secret code" still work pretty well. The legal rights of software are even more effectively protected by copyright: even if a competitor is wily enough to get a copy of the source code, it's illegal for them to use it commercially. Since Moore's Law has helped launch a steep downward trend in the price of computer hardware, Bill Gates's most significant innovation showed the world that the most sustainable price point in computing was where the marginal cost was also the lowest: the software.

When Nathan Myhrvold, the former chief technology officer at Microsoft (and the man who recruited Peter Detkin from Intel to Intellectual Ventures), recently testified before the U.S. Congress, he offered up an interesting perspective on the power of copyright protection in building the software business model:

> When I first entered the software industry in 1984, the very idea of basing a business on software was novel. At the time, there was only one publicly-traded software company. Virtually all software programmers worked for hardware companies. Software was considered a radical and unproven thing as the foundation for a business model. I know that seems bizarre from our vantage point today, but it really was the case . . . an additional reason they were skeptical was the fear that people wouldn't respect copyright. This was a very real concern, and in the early days of the software industry there was widespread theft of software. The software industry mounted a two-pronged campaign. First, it educated people that this was wrong; popularizing the notion that misappropriation of software was "piracy." The industry made the argument that piracy was bad and buying software was good because it would lead to more features and better software. Second, it mounted a very aggressive litigation program to go after people that violated software copyrights.

Myhrvold's testimony gives us some insight into the importance of copyright protection in the world of software, but other huge industries like publishing, music, and movies also live or die today based on the strength of copyright protection. The challenges in managing copyrights, though, are a good deal different from those posed by other IP forms. Because copyrights offer relatively long-term protection—U.S. copyright terms last a century or more and require no application—managing copyrights used to mean that you focused almost exclusively on preventing piracy. Things have changed in other ways since those early days of software described by Myhrvold. The number of copyright enforcement issues that managers now confront has grown to include challenges like peer-to-peer music file-sharing networks like Napster, Kazaa, and Gnutella, as well as the rampant copying and resale of movies and software in China. Publishers of all kinds have struggled to enforce their copyrights, while, at the same time, figuring out how to enable greater access to their unique digital content.

But just as technology creates new problems, it also provides solutions. The rise of electronic media has invoked a new wave of technologies to help manage digital rights as well as new ways to deliver content to consumers. As for the file-sharing competition, despite a public debate that tends to center on the ideological issues of information sharing, as the obstacles to piracy have risen (later-generation file-sharing networks have had to introduce more anonymity and encryption provisions to avoid being shut down) both the costs of illegal downloads and the benefits of legal distribution have become more evident. So as the cost of piracy has gone up, legitimate content publishers have learned that consumers will happily spend 99¢ for a song via iTunes or Bearshare. With reasonable copyright safeguards in place, therefore, publishers can now build audiences who simply want to buy content at a reasonable price and put together their own listening, reading, or viewing experience.

3. **Trademarks and brands.** Piracy tends to dominate discussions about trademarks as well, particularly because brand pirates often trade counterfeit Fendi bags in the same flea markets that offer illegal copies of the latest movies that are still running in theaters. Trademarks actually engender less controversy than other forms of IP, perhaps because even the most fervent ideologues have little trouble conceding the right to exclude others from stealing your identity, corporations included.

In the most minimal sense, trademark enforcement protects companies from free riders, competitors who would benefit from marketing and advertising expenditures that they themselves didn't make. Those who think of this form of piracy as a harmless street corner business, though, might be surprised to learn that trademark piracy is actually a multibillion-dollar business run by multinational criminal enterprises. Most of this contraband traffic is exported from Asia, but the federal agencies responsible for policing this illegal traffic emphasize that it matters less *where* the piracy originates from and more about *who* the pirates are. Governments around the world, therefore, rely on businesses to help them identify pirates that they can target through law enforcement activities.

Trademarks, however, do more than merely protect marketing expenditures; they are another way for a business to reap rewards from an ongoing stream of valuable invention. The world's most valuable brands protect commercial reputations built from years of delivering on a promise of consistently superior innovation. Gillette is "the best a man can get" not just because their commercials tell you so, but because the company offers a promise of an unbeatable grooming experience to which most men willingly attest. Other top brands do the same. In addition to their patent prowess, Intel, for example, encourages consumers to rely on their lengthy track record of innovation by buying computers with "Intel Inside." General Electric highlights their long tradition of invention with their marketing slogan, "Imagination at Work." Samsung, a relatively new entrant among the world's top twenty brands, strikes a similar theme in their corporate tag line: "Imagine the Possibilities." Perhaps no single branding slogan captures the way that companies link their reputation for innovation into their brand like HP's simple yet powerful branding message "Invent."

4. **Design patents.** Somewhere between trademarks and new technologies lies a business realm that is often underappreciated: the world of industrial design. For some reason, product designs continue to be undervalued by most firms. Consider the iconic appearance of Apple's iPod (see opposite). In fact, three separate design patents cover the look of this ubiquitous product. Similarly, Gillette's distinctive men's and women's razor handles are also covered by dozens of design patents.

Compared to traditional patents, design patents are both less expensive to acquire and to get approved; you don't need to go through the same tedious review process required for a patent. The fourteen-year protection period they provide, though, is shorter than either a utility patent (twenty years from filing date) or a trademark (unlimited). Yet design patents can be quite effective in protecting products and innovation investment that may fall short of a new functional invention. They are also often part of a portfolio of protection that is developed by companies that are assembling features, functions, and an innovative design in support of a branded product. An interesting side note is that, in addition to its design patents, Apple has also filed a trademark for a slightly more simplified image than the one shown on page 141.

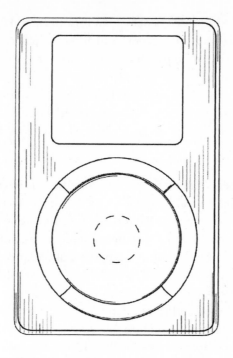

Source: U.S. D469109.

5. **Utility patents.** Generally referred to as "patents for invention," these assets are often the most challenging IP asset to build and manage. They are also often the most valuable. The downside of utility patents is that they are expensive to pursue, time-consuming to obtain, costly to defend, and often controversial. Each one is a serious project all by itself; individual patents often involve dozens of claims, and sometimes hundreds of pages of text, all of which must go through a demanding review process with the Patent Office that typically involves substantial negotiation. This negotiation takes the form of an iterative process of "office actions" and "responses," a sort of tug-of-war in which the Patent Office, on one side, tries to make sure each claim is specific, clear, and limited while the inventors, on the other, try to maximize the scope and value of their invention. The process involves a great deal of technical detail and subject matter expertise; it's not unlike the process of trying to get a scientific paper or article published in a major journal.

From a managerial standpoint, however, this investment is anything but an academic activity. Patent applications consume considerable time and energy from the most talented people in an organization. Each application requires legal advice and consultation, which means paying fees to expensive law firms and filing fees to patent offices, which for a global application can average $50,000 or more per filing. More important, the construction of patent claims involves a host of strategic choices: any individual invention can be positioned narrowly or broadly, in the direction of one strategic objective or another, and perhaps most difficult of all, needs to effectively anticipate other future inventions.

Because the process of filing for patent applications is so complex, it has become one of the most critical functions in an innovation factory. Like other repeatable processes, the activities that produce inventions and patent filings can be broken down into discrete sets of component processes, processes that can be mapped, measured, and managed with modern tools. In 2001 Ford Motor Company, a major patent holder, decided to work together with British American Tobacco, a major trademark holder, to develop some highly automated tools for managing their invention and IP creation processes. The software spinout that resulted has become a start-up venture called Anaqua, a Boston-based software company that helps companies manage their IP assets by providing the equivalent of an "enterprise resource planning" (ERP) tool for innovation processes. Today Anaqua can count other sophisticated IP-economy companies like Microsoft and Kimberly-Clark as flagship customers.

In a similar way, IBM has almost accidentally backed into the IP ERP business because it was forced to maintain services and support for its own innovation software tools to buyers of former IBM subsidiaries like Lenovo and Hitachi. It wouldn't be a stretch to think that tools like those offered by Anaqua and IBM could very well end up becoming the SAPs of the IP economy.

Sophisticated IP managers do more than just manage the basics; they also find creative ways to couple their management of technology protection with an overall approach to product life cycle management. Here again, the blades and razors business provides an early example. In the summer of 1921, just a few months before King Gillette's original safety razor patent was due to expire, the Gillette Safety Razor Company announced a "New, Improved" razor and blade line. They lowered the price for the original model, which had remained $5 for years, to $1. The company then introduced the new (and patent-protected) version at the previous $5 price level. This clever pricing strategy introduced a product-line management practice that Gillette has followed successfully for nearly a century: give price-conscious customers a chance to save money with older technology while at the same time encouraging those looking for the best shave to trade up to the newest, and higher-priced, technology.

This kind of life cycle pricing has become one of the main ways to mark the business progress of successful innovations over time. Pharmaceutical companies work hard to upgrade their best products, transferring premium-brand positions to new, patented versions from off-patent molecules. The most notable success in this area has been AstraZeneca's successful shift of its "purple pill" brand positions: Prilosec (the original) became Nexium ("today's purple pill"). But retaining premium-pricing positions requires meaningful improvements in product performance, an element most drug developers have struggled with.

As a whole, companies have many tools available for protecting their innovations and excluding competitors from their distinctive positions in the marketplace. Sometimes the need is just for a single tool, where the crisp execution of the associated protection processes is the key to success. Other circumstances may dictate that these tools interact and reinforce one another, which requires skillful coordination across multiple functions like marketing, legal, R&D, and manufacturing. With the financial stakes set so high, and, due to expensive resources and multiple moving parts, IP decisions frequently rise above the tactical level and into the corner office. Inevitably, IP development requires making strategic choices that involve the CEO.

Aligning Protection Priorities with Business Goals

Although some members of the IP priesthoods would like "lay managers" to believe that their resource allocation issues bear no resemblance to the more conventional business-planning routines, the investment choices made around IP investments are, in fact, no less strategic than investments in physical assets and they are often more important to the future success of the corporation. Decisions about IP demand the *informed* involvement of senior business managers (although in practice this rarely happens), an involvement that often requires getting into some, at least initially, intimidating detail. Any good executive knows that there are times when zooming in on key business details can be essential to business success. Strategic management of IP development is no different and involves more than a group of lawyers deciding on claims language; IP investments involve substantial bets on what will be valuable in your business. In order to generate a high return on expensive intangible investments, IP development needs to be closely aligned with strategic business goals.

Since competition motivates your rivals to do everything you do and more, the key benefit in developing IP is the ability to exclude your competitors from doing the things that matter most to your business. Depending on what your business is and where you're trying to go, protection priorities can vary a great deal. Businesses that fail to exercise their exclusion rights do so at their peril because IP gives a property owner an exclusive right to commercialize the assets created, either through traditional product sales or as a product in its own right.

For a consumer-driven business, the most valuable exclusion right is the one that excludes competitors from deploying features similar to those that most clearly define its own brand image in the marketplace. In other words, IP can help you *own your brand*. At a bare minimum, this means the right to exclude them from using your trademarks, your "trade dress" (the distinctive styles and colors in which your product is packaged and your messaging is communicated), as well as your distinctive product designs. A more valuable benefit, though, is the right to exclude competitors from delivering those benefits that give your product its critical edge, like the "closeness and comfort" of a Gillette blade unit or the satisfying thwack delivered by a Callaway Golf Big Bertha "sound-enhanced composite golf club head," which is protected by U.S. Patent No. 6,406,378.

Alternatively, some manufacturers want to exclude competitors from selling complementary components that might slot into their proprietary designs. This kind of exclusion allows you to *own your customer's solution*. Some of Gillette's Fusion patents, for example, cover the precise way in which Fusion cartridges click into place on a Fusion razor, which prevents third-party cartridge makers from selling knockoff cartridges. Similarly, Hewlett-Packard (HP) has developed an extensive portfolio of ink patents that distinguish its ink-jet cartridges from its competitors in the ink refiller industry. HP also employs their own internal crew of chemists to conduct chemical footprint analyses of competitor inks to make sure they're not using HP patented chemistries. One of the HP chemists who conduct the testing recently commented, "It's like the corporate version of *CSI*."

Many businesses, most notably those that sell basic materials like steel, paper, and cement, tend to rely on operational advantages to build competitive advantage. For most of these basic-materials businesses, though, companies in the industry can achieve very little sustainable advantage when equipment suppliers own most of the IP. This trap has led to a situation in which "basic materials," "commodities," and "low profits" have become interchangeable terms in business. In commodity businesses, developing a competitive cost advantage usually requires adding new plants and new capacity faster than your competition, decisions that can quickly lead to a capacity arms race and the business equivalent of nuclear conflict: a price war. One powerful way out of this trap is to actually *own your operational edge* by controlling patents on the technologies that give you an operational advantage and exclude your competitors from adding capacity that relies on this technology. For example, Nucor, after seeing the entire steel industry copy its mini-mill business model (which it failed to patent), has shifted to an exclusion-based approach in its newest growth initiative. Working alongside equipment developers like Siemens and steel makers BHP Steel of Australia and IHI of Japan, Nucor entered into a joint-venture company called Castrip to commercialize a revolutionary steel-making technology. First conceived by Henry Bessemer back in 1857, the continuous casting of strip steel has been made technically possible for the first time by Castrip. As part of a partnership with a global granted and pending portfolio of more than 1,500 patent filings, Nucor has positioned itself with an ownership position in what may well turn out to be the biggest new thing in steel since, well, Nucor.

In some cases, making operational improvements to existing businesses involves adding new functions on top of an existing process as opposed to introducing revolutionary process transformations. In this situation, the new functions often include enabling existing products with new information capability, which is then attached to the existing design. Since the new functions usually fall outside the historical competence of the existing businesses, companies investing in these extensions often find that their best opportunities lie in the points of connection between the new component(s) and their old design. Businesses that can *own the interface* between old and new functionality can often obtain a valuable advantage. We found an example of this recently in some work for a transportation equipment company that was adding electronics to its basic vehicle design. When they considered how they could exclude their main competitor from copying their new design, they had expressed confidence that this competitor was way behind them in their new product efforts. Imagine their surprise, then, when we uncovered the fact that not only had their competitor begun filing patents in the same area, but that they had already filed a patent on the key *interface* (some specialized antenna capability) that we had hypothesized might be especially valuable.

Allocating resources to internal IP development is a necessary but not always sufficient way to build competitive advantage in the places it matters most. Inevitably, someone else will develop IP—an individual patent, a small portfolio, a brand position—that anticipates a problem that an individual company didn't see or wasn't working on. In rapidly changing industries, that kind of anticipation is often the norm rather than the exception. In these situations, the obvious option is to simply go out and buy or license the assets that you need, or, in other words, to *acquire your future.* In activities such as drug development, where major companies regularly buy the most promising drug candidates developed by smaller biotech companies, this kind of activity has become routine. But in any industry where internal development of every future product advance is not the answer, IP acquisition is a necessary choice. Although maligned by some critics as having used acquisition recklessly, Cisco Systems, in fact, built its leadership in the rapidly growing network equipment business largely as a result of an aggressive (but always friendly) technology and IP acquisition program, one in which it decided on its targets based on the social network of technology partners with which it had worked.

Finally, even when a business is destined for failure, the right kind of IP development can make that business a viable target for acquisition. For companies that recognize this inevitability, or for start-up companies in which investors support a business for the specific purpose of finding a strategic buyer, this kind of IP investment allows you to *own your exit path.* In the IMS story, we saw how a single patent could become a material issue in a liquidation strategy. More orderly exit strategies, though, often make better sense for much larger companies. For example, following a period of explosive growth in the Customer Relationship Management (CRM) market toward the end of the year 2000, the software company Siebel came to a realization: as competitors like SAP and Oracle added and acquired their own CRM modules, Siebel's own stand-alone CRM offering was likely to lose ground to more comprehensive offering. As a result, Siebel began to search for ways to enhance its exit value. One way they did that was to ramp up their rate of patent filings, which grew sharply in 2001 and 2002. When these patents started publishing in 2003 and 2004, they sent a signal to the marketplace that Siebel might be something more than just a fading software vendor and might even be looking for ways to transform itself into a shark with a more aggressive patent-licensing approach. As a result, when Oracle (itself an aggressive software patent applicant) agreed to buy Siebel for nearly $6 billion in late 2005, one of the assets they acquired was a sizeable and fresh portfolio of CRM patents.

From Exclusion to Centrality

By accepting the importance of setting priorities, business executives effectively concede that there are limits to their ability to exclude competitors from every idea and every innovative concept. Total exclusion requires a degree of market power that truly is monopolistic in the historic sense of the word; it presumes a complete kind of autonomy that most business executives can only dream of. Very few businesses, in fact, have reached such safely autonomous positions in their target market.

These kinds of businesses, though, can make for very happy families: they generate cash, provide healthy returns to shareholders, and can afford generous compensation for their most valuable employees. To the outside world, their loyal customers, visionary executives, and skillful marketing programs often appear to be perfect—and they frequently become the subjects of hagiographic books. These elements of happiness, though, are often an effect rather than a cause, in large part because these happy families don't have to deal with strong competition. Although Gillette competes directly with Schick and several other minor players, for example, their blades and razors business enjoys more than 70 percent market share. In terms of both talent and process, the company's top-to-bottom product line is the closest you can get to complete technical autonomy.

Interestingly, Gillette is an unusual exception to Joy's Law when it comes to attracting and retaining talent. One indicator of Gillette's uniquely autonomous position can be found in their citation patterns. Although their patents are reasonably highly cited, with more than ten cites per patent on average (Schick, on the other hand, boasts only six citations per patent), the vast majority of the citations are from their own patents—there are very few citations by companies other than Gillette. The citation rate per patent from other companies is 1.5 on average for Gillette; for Schick it's only 1.7. If you haven't got a chance to get close to the state of the art in shaving, why would anyone bother to invest in patents that bear on Gillette's (or Schick's for that matter) prior art?

Because of Gillette's active and ongoing research program, virtually no one else in the world besides Schick bothers to invest in the science and advanced engineering of shaving. Consequently, most of the top shaving technology talent in the world works for Gillette, many of whom spend their entire careers with the company—with a little help from a flexible approach to management. The employees working for the company's research group based in Reading, England, for instance, which pursued projects to advance the science of skin and hair, were motivated to remain with the company for their entire careers (it also helped that a relatively large set of senior managers were unusually well compensated). Science and engineering activities were also accorded high status within the company, which created an atmosphere that encouraged the top engineering talent to stay. One of the best examples of this was Alfred Zeien, Gillette's CEO from 1991 through 1999, who originally began his career as an engineer. Zeien proved that engineers could build a good life working for the company. This environment stands in contrast to the more fashionable "war for talent" atmosphere: one in which managers aggressively force out loyal talent to bring in younger and lower-cost workers, workers who know virtually nothing about the company's intellectual assets, rather than recognizing the value of a more experienced employee's knowledge of the company's technology. Obviously the more that companies opt for this latter method, the more difficulty they'll face in overcoming Joy's Law over the long haul.

Even if a business can defy Joy's Law by remaining autonomous on talent, though, they will also face increasing limits to their exclusion ability. If outsourcing your innovation activity is the fastest path to commodity hell, then managers who attempt to manage a modern innovation factory like Ford's old River Rouge project are sure to find themselves in a ring of their own in Dante's *Inferno*. These managers believe that they can tightly control the entire process by which raw talent and information is transformed into innovation and IP. That's not the way the innovation factory works anymore, even in the most autonomous businesses. Since the innovation process relies on knowledge, the walls of the factory can no longer protect its internal workings from the outside marketplace; instead, these walls have been transformed into membranes. At every step of the process, managers now have the option of selecting an idea from inside the factory—or purchasing one from outside. These managers also have the ability to sell their own ideas to other innovators outside the factory. The result of this transformation is that the buying and selling of intermediate (or semifinished) innovation products has exploded. In short, the factory *leaks*.

Even for the companies that choose to seal the walls around their internal innovation factory, they quickly face limits that can have nothing at all to do with talent or process. For many perfect businesses, the biggest challenge of all is the high standard they set with the crown jewels of their business: the curse of rising expectations. How does Gillette make anything else perform as well as the male safety razor business? How does Pfizer find the next Lipitor? How can any other business inside Hewlett-Packard measure up to the ink-jet printing business? No public company is autonomous in the sense that they can ignore the pressure from shareholders to answer such questions. Yet the search for these answers often produces bad decisions that force great businesses into strategic blunders.

Consider the case of Pfizer's seven "billion-dollar brands": Lipitor, Norvasc,

Zoloft, Celebrex, Viagra, Zyrtec, and Lyrica. Lipitor comes off patent in 2010 and is already struggling with the threat of generic competition. Norvasc came off patent in late 2007. Celebrex is caught up in the VIOXX problem and may present safety problems of its own. Viagra, the staple of prime-time television advertising, highlights the ethical problems that haunt the broader industry it competes in: it's an impotency drug marketed as an aphrodisiac. All of Pfizer's blockbuster drugs, in fact, are built to treat chronic conditions rather than improve underlying health. While that might be a recipe for ongoing profitability, it is also one that has helped make the industry a magnet for controversy. The extraordinary profits of major pharmaceutical companies provide strong evidence of the power of intellectual property–based businesses; at the same time, they highlight the importance of using the innovation factory to solve valuable problems. We highlighted the R&D productivity challenge facing the industry in chapter 3. Despite being a perfect business from the perspective of profitability, the major pharmaceutical companies face a curse of their own: rising expectations that have become a walking advertisement for a disruptive technology to come in and shake up the entire health care industry.

Gillette's acquisition of Duracell is a similar cautionary tale. Under pressure to extend the company's growth into new sectors, CEO Al Zeien acquired Duracell in 1996. The goal was to turn the battery business into a premium product. Even as its new high-performance batteries began to gain some traction, Gillette soon found itself embroiled in a price war with its main battery competitor, Energizer. That price war, combined with the economic downturn of 2000, resulted in a long series of poor quarters for the company. This string of adversity produced a state of near panic for Gillette's board, particularly because they were then under the strong influence of investment manager Warren Buffett. Zeien subsequently retired and the board turned to an outside "turnaround artist," Jim Kilts, in 2001, a move insiders believed was a prelude to the sale of the company. Four years later, the combination of an improving economy and Kilts's cost cutting had helped the company's stock price recover. Kilts then wasted no time in picking up the phone to call A. G. Lafley to tell him Gillette was for sale. By 2005, Gillette was a part of P&G and Kilts had personally pocketed some $150 million.

Interestingly, P&G had survived its own trap of elevated expectations under the leadership of Durk Jager. Even though P&G, like Pfizer and Gillette, had a secure base of strong power brands, the pressure resulted from the fact that their growth opportunity was less secure than their profit performance. As a result, they put profit at risk to invest in growth. For Jager, the rub was that even though he understood the problem, his attempt to push growth through internal innovation fell short because he mistakenly relied on a closed-wall River Rouge approach to innovation. Current CEO Lafley, on the other hand, has pioneered the search for a new and better way. As we discussed in chapter 4, he is working, successfully so far, to place P&G in the center of a network of advantaged innovation.

For a company operating from a position of strength, the choice to reach out to create a wider network of connections to help generate IP can be an effective way to retain a position of control even without the ability to be completely self-reliant. By creating a series of relationships that place your business as a hub in an innovation network, strategies based on *centrality* provide the means to control information, relationships, and access to opportunities, rather than a specific invention or product on their own. Many successful businesses are finding ways to balance a strong position of control with a less autonomous model. Like Jim Clark's vision for Healtheon, they choose to place themselves, one way or another, at the center of a network of activity because they have the unique ability to add value through their intellectual property. And, in fact, there are a few different ways companies can accomplish this.

The simplest way for a company to assert its centrality is by adjusting the input-output balance in the innovation factory, *shifting from make to buy.* By becoming an active and knowledgeable buyer of intermediate innovation products, a company can gain an edge over its competitors who continue to keep things inside. A growing proportion of new drug candidates for the pharmaceutical industry, for example, come from sources outside the company like biotech firms. Blockbuster drugs like Pfizer's Lipitor and GlaxoSmithKline's Paxil were externally sourced this way. With insufficient blockbusters coming through their own innovation pipeline, these large pharmaceutical companies find it necessary to trade off inside development for IP purchased on the outside. They can then add value to their purchases through their expertise in clinical trial management, sales, and marketing. Although they don't abandon their internal R&D, these companies have transformed themselves into leaky innovation factories that rely on their internal R&D activities as well as ideas from the outside.

As businesses step up their buying activity, and begin to introduce innovation concepts at a wider range of stages in the innovation factory, experienced buyers will learn that this kind of sourcing is unlike most any other purchasing activity they're used to in business. To generate more effective in-licensing opportunities for innovation, companies in industries like consumer electronics, automotive, and biotechnology have begun instituting more directed technology-sourcing activities, with the goal of *making IP scouting a core skill*. Because it focuses on creating a constant flow of new assets to replenish an existing roster of perishable assets, IP scouting resembles the kind of talent scouting we often associate with professional sports, and at least in some respects actually involves traditional talent scouting as part of the activity.

When the innovation factory requires more fully characterized solutions, but lacks the internal talent or resources to solve critical problems, some companies have taken the approach of creating new talent markets where they had never existed before. Eli Lilly, the drug manufacturer based in Indianapolis, has launched what it calls its Innocentive program: where the company posts problems to which it would like a solution along with the price it is willing to pay for that solution. In this way, Lilly stimulates an inventor pool for which it can *pay for value* in generating innovative work while acquiring the IP rights as part of the purchase.

For solutions that are already developed, there are a number of companies that have worked to increase the liquidity of the marketplace for trading technology. By *setting up a private marketplace,* companies can increase the volume of technology exchange in areas that are close to their needs, by either buying for or selling from their innovation factory. P&G, for example, has teamed up with partners like DuPont, Honeywell, and Delphion to create a technology exchange known as yet2.com, with the expressed goal of "unlocking value from their technology portfolio." P&G, one of the exchange's original sponsors, is more of a seller in this marketplace than a buyer and posts a wide range of patented technologies there. But yet2.com is a key part of P&G's Connect and Develop strategy, where the marketplace gives the company visibility into both sides of the technology trade, while giving a special boost to the shark side of their patent portfolio. We'll discuss the emerging marketplace for IP in greater detail in chapter 9.

For some companies, the most effective way to put itself at the center of an active exchange of IP is to develop a friendly hosting environment for user-generated IP. With a friendly host, users can generate content that provides rewards for themselves in terms of learning and status and the hosting company can *get content for free.* The entire multiplayer gaming industry, from Sony's Everquest to the Sims, is built on this principle. To a large extent, eBay and Yahoo have also built their businesses by making themselves attractive hosts for a wide range of market transactions and content interactions.

In all these approaches, the business goal is to create new transactions that put the company at the center of a controllable innovation network. It's important not to confuse these kinds of centrality strategies with new transactions that result from mass collaboration, or even with more complex strategies that involve product architectures in which a company's goal may be to achieve a central position in a complex network. In the kind of initiatives described above, the goal is to stimulate networks that are all heavily weighted toward the hubs. To the extent that centrality is an outcome of more complex strategy activity, these strategies can be similar to those described here, but they are more of a result rather than an action. That said, straightforward centrality strategies can help, in fact, to create a powerfully central position when they stimulate a more interactive approach within a larger innovation network.

Regardless of whether your control strategy is based on effective exclusion or on effective positioning as a central hub, the inevitable problem with any perfect business is that it invites opposition. In an ideal world, all business leaders would like to have complete control over their own destiny, and in instances like Gillette's razor business, and some of the others we've cited here, some companies on occasion actually do approach this business nirvana. But the fact is that relatively few businesses are able to completely control the innovation in their marketplace either through exclusion or by formally creating a central hub. More commonly, sustained success requires companies to collaborate, even when they'd rather not. As we will discover in the next chapter, the proper management of intellectual property is often the key to creating value through collaboration, and is certainly critical in determining who will capture that value.

CHAPTER 6

Collaborate

REALIZING THE BENEFITS OF OPEN INNOVATION

A scorpion and a frog meet on the bank of a stream and the scorpion asks the frog to carry him across on its back. The frog asks, "How do I know you won't sting me?" The scorpion says, "Because if I do, I will die too." The frog is satisfied, and they set out, but in midstream, the scorpion stings the frog. The frog feels the onset of paralysis and starts to sink, knowing they both will drown, but has just enough time to gasp "Why?"

Replies the scorpion: "It's my nature . . ."

—*A fable attributed to Aesop (620–560 BCE)**

I n recent years, the business world has begun to idealize the notion of collaboration. As the cost of business interactions has plummeted, many theorists have been seduced by a new utopian vision of innovation, one where global communities of like-minded idealists throw off the shackles of the corporate politics (or employment contracts) that bind them and share knowledge and information freely to solve tough problems through mass collaboration. These theories, in a way, shape a kind of neo-socialism for the information age. Just as industrial-age socialism criticized the ownership of capital by capitalists, these neo-socialists criticize the ownership of intellectual capital by artists and inventors. They argue that "information wants to be free" and that intellectual property

---

*www.aesopfables.com/, "Aesop's Fables: Online Collection," by John R. Long. The Greek historian Herodotus provided the first surviving report of the existence and life of Aesop, a Greek slave who collected fables—like "The Tortoise and the Hare" and "The Boy Who Cried Wolf"—that became a major part of Greek literary tradition. The fable of "The Scorpion and the Frog" is often attributed to the ancient Latin or Greek texts associated with Aesop but may, in fact, be a later addition to the Aesop's Fables corpus.

rights impose unnecessary "transactions costs" on communities of creative people. A critical foundation for this neo-socialist argument is the underlying economic assumption that the Information Revolution has changed the rules of the
game and created new conditions that permit collaborative work to flourish without the need for ownership rights.

Ideology aside, there's a practical problem with this utopian vision (as anyone
who has ever spent much time in an Internet community can tell you). Even with
the help of these new technology tools, *collaboration is hard*. This is true in online
communities and it's true in business as well. Numerous studies have shown
that, despite rapid growth in collaborative business arrangements such as joint
ventures, alliances, and partnerships, most of these arrangements fail, perhaps
as many as 70 percent.

It shouldn't come as much of a surprise, then, that most CEOs would rather
avoid cross-company collaboration. Indeed, proposing a strategy for a joint venture is often the fastest way to get yourself kicked out of a meeting in the executive conference room. And it's not just their high failure rates that make business
collaborations so unpopular at the top. Their reputation for both complexity and
conflict, for one, makes executives wary. So even if these arrangements were more
successful, we doubt they'd be more popular.

CEOs are accountable to shareholders for their own profit performance, not
to their partners, after all. Satisfying investors is hard enough even without the
added difficulty of distributing ownership, decision making, and earnings with
partners. As a result, corporate collaborations can easily frustrate even the most
statesmanlike of chief executives. That's why most companies bring strategic
activities inside the corporate tent whenever they can, to reduce the potential for
fighting over profits. Seasoned managers know well that disputes about transfer
pricing, cost allocation, and internal profit distribution can escalate even with
inside-the-company collaborations. In the automotive industry, for example, no
major auto *manufacturer* lets an independent company *distribute* its cars in its
major markets: Subaru was the last major brand with independent distributor
owners in the United States. Subaru's Japanese owners at Fuji Heavy Industries
put an end to this arrangement in 1990 to stop the squabbles over inventory,
pricing, and sales management.

There is, however, a shift taking place. It is simply not possible for a business
to control all of the strategic elements of their business in house. The days of
River Rouge are long gone. This is especially true in industries where continuous
innovation and IP ownership are important, which increasingly means all of
them. In these cases, *collaboration isn't optional; it's essential*. When different par-

ties each own critical IP, but don't have *all* the IP they need to bring a product to market, they can be forced to share proceeds with each other to escape technological gridlock. In this sense, the requirement to share IP forces collaboration, even among parties who would, all else being equal, rather go it alone. And even one-on-one collaborations likely won't be enough anymore either; the future lies in multilateral collaboration. As far back as 1866, the sewing machine industry found a solution to the overlapping patent problem when it introduced the first *patent pool.* Today collaborative IP-sharing arrangements have quietly become far more common as technology players in industries ranging from RFID to digital video have been forced into IP-based collaborations.

While most businesses typically don't jump into collaborative arrangements with enthusiasm, they often find that *collaboration can yield unexpected benefits.* By simply participating in a larger network of innovation, companies can gain access to new opportunities and markets while also learning how to orient their strategies to achieve greater success. Successful collaboration can expand the pie available for all network participants, making the collaborative whole worth more than the sum of its individual company parts. By working together, a group of companies in an innovation network can often solve a broader range of problems that drive an industry forward, especially when there are large numbers of interdependencies between the component parts of an innovative new product. One example of this is the Boeing 787, an aircraft Boeing designed using an unusually collaborative approach to working with its parts suppliers to produce what a former CEO described as "a bunch of parts flying together in close formation."

There is little doubt that, business benefits aside, the technology of collaboration has exploded over a short period of time. As anyone who has spent time in an online collaborative community can tell you, *collaboration can tap powerful new resources,* resources that can substantially change the fates and fortunes of community members. Communities that succeed in attracting the largest groups of active participants—so-called mass collaborations, like the Linux kernel development team, the Wikipedia contributor group, or the volunteers who participate in the search for extraterrestrial intelligence run by SETI—recruit their entire workforces effectively for free. The value of each individual participant's community membership exceeds the modest personal cost of his or her contribution of these services. Yet when you sum all of these contributions up, their total value can be extraordinary. And when the commercial hosts of this ever-growing list of communities like Sony's Everquest gamers, eBay's collectible traders, Yahoo's discussion groups, and Amazon.com's book reviewers leverage the difference between individual microcontributions and the cumulative value they provide, they can actually generate a large *participation premium*. This premium has enormous economic value around which the hosts can build an attractive business while also exploiting the broader commercial influence of their communities to make themselves extremely formidable competitors.

Some communities go even further by evolving into independent forces that more broadly influence rules, policies, and politics. These kinds of communities demonstrate some of the noneconomic effects of collaboration; that is, that *collaboration can generate large spillover effects*. Communities like MySpace or Yahoo Groups can support a sense of identity and affiliation while others like Wikipedia or Wiktionary can provide an ongoing repository for collections of human knowledge. Gaming communities such as Everquest or Second Life create virtual economies that provide participants with a vehicle for both entertainment and self-actualization and, like some advanced forms of collaborative software development such as Linux and other open-source software communities, they can even play a role in determining commercially valuable technical standards. (As standards development bodies, technical collaborative groups have even started to create a novel form of global governance, a subject we'll explore more deeply in the next chapter.)

Put simply, business collaboration works when multiple parties cooperate to enlarge the size of an economic pie, even as they compete with each other over who gets the biggest slice. While it can be difficult to sustain, collaboration makes economic sense when the long-term, collective benefits outweigh the possibility of going it alone, especially when IP is at stake. Making collaboration around IP work successfully, though, requires a number of things to come together at once: a degree of openness and information sharing between partners, rules for sharing benefits from pooled contributions, teaming behavior that defers short-term, individual benefits for a greater good, and the kind of commercial trust that enables transactions to happen without difficulty or delay. And, perhaps most important, it requires a system for equitably distributing the benefits accrued from the joint development of any IP assets. In other words, the new economics of information creates new opportunities for collaboration, especially around IP.

The Economics of Collaboration

Unlike the edges of corporations, which are defined by the assets they own, we typically don't think of boundaries when we think of collections of people and IP. With the rising need for new collaborative forms, though, we are also seeing a rising need for ways to structure collections of technology, either in the form of knowledge or patents or in the networks of talented people who make these collaborations successful.

As information becomes easier to share, and communities have become easier to form, such large-scale communities have become far more prevalent. Information technology has created new opportunities for mass collaboration: between individuals in a network of companies, between individuals within companies, and between mixed communities of volunteers, students, employees, and users across a wide range of organizations. Some of these large-scale communities are famously flexible and loose in terms of structure. Yet the most successful mass collaborations can only function with a clear set of rules—for membership, for decision making, for conflict resolution, for managerial discipline, and for the distribution of rewards—that allow a core set of community leaders to shepherd all the participants in a common direction.

While the new information economics haven't removed the difficulties involved in collaboration, they have radically expanded the options for doing collaborative work—between companies, across converging patent claims, and within self-organizing communities—that, in turn, open up new benefits of collaboration. From a business perspective, there are three main benefits to collaboration:

1. **Delivering complex solutions to the market.** The future of collaboration is not the traditional joint venture; it's the network. It is only by bringing together lots of complementary businesses that companies like Toyota, for example, are able to both expand their slice of the global automobile market, and also make sure its partners share in the rewards.
2. **Getting to market with complementary patents.** Going to market alone with a single patent is unlikely to achieve competitive advantage; going to market in partnership with dozens of companies holding hundreds of patents can achieve competitive advantage for a generation. When companies combine complementary IP assets into what are known as patent pools, such as the MPEG LA pool that forms the foundation for the video compression industry, look out.
3. **Energizing and tapping external innovation.** As we learned from Bill Joy, innovation usually happens outside the walls of your company. The key to stimulating innovation, therefore, is to tap forces outside the company that present dozens of solutions for each and every problem you seek an answer for. But how can we create the right incentives to accomplish this goal? One approach to solving this riddle, you may be surprised to learn, lies at the root of the so-called open-source software movement.

Old-style collaborations provided ways to capture these benefits, but typically involved a *bilateral* approach: one company negotiating an agreement with another company. New-style collaborations, by contrast, expand the number of participants involved in these arrangements and offer new options for strategy that use *multilateral* approaches. We will spend the rest of the chapter digging deeper into each of these approaches, using examples of cutting-edge companies to not just tell you how collaboration could happen, but to show you how these new-style collaborations are already happening around you.

Delivering Complex Solutions to the Market

The most common form of business collaboration happens when multiple companies work together on a solution to a customer problem that none of them can deliver on their own. Historically, these collaborations have been primarily two- or three-way partnerships. But in a world of increasing specialization and functional atomization, it is becoming more common for larger networks to emerge that connect large numbers of companies in more complex alliances.

The simplest and perhaps most common way to collaborate, though, is through a joint venture. The Sony Ericsson Mobile Communication AB, for example, is a joint venture between a consumer electronics company and a tele-communications company that makes advanced mobile phones. Nucor formed a joint venture with BHP and IHI to develop Castrip technology. Omgeo brings Thomson Financial and DTCC together to streamline paperwork in financial services. While putting together agreements like these can be complicated, once organized they don't look much different from any other conventional company. The partners collaborate in the simplest way possible: they contribute their physical assets, talent, and IP to a new stand-alone company and they extract benefits based on a simple ownership formula that determines their share of the profits.

When more than two companies are involved in a looser system that delivers a whole solution, designing a collaboration structure to help all the participants realize benefits becomes more complex. Most critically, network participants have to find ways to sustain a long-term collaboration, simultaneously negotiating prices among themselves while also working together on operations to reduce costs and improve quality. In this context, these groups are developing innovations that may not have a single creative source. For instance, a single supplier might complete a design concept for one of its customers, or that supplier might have a promising technology idea that needs customer involvement to refine and make operational. This kind of open innovation is often necessary to deliver the promise of a complex solution. But it can also fail from the get-go if the collaborators leave open critical questions of credit and ownership.

In these situations, there is a hard competitive value to commercial trust; when two parties trust each other to share the benefits of innovation, they are more likely to gain competitive advantage in industries where such opportunities are common and the distribution of credit is hard to predict in advance. Toyota is perhaps the most celebrated model of a company that has found a way to turn commercial trust into concrete competitive advantage in its supplier network. Encouraging networks of customers and suppliers to make progress together requires all the network members to leave money on the table for their partners as they agree to share information and insights in ways that put their own negotiating position at risk. Suppliers share trade secrets with their customers based on an expectation that they will share in the performance benefits of the whole network. Suppliers and customers also work together on incremental innovation without regard for where the benefits will fall and who will receive the credit. And when patented inventions or copyrighted software is involved, the privileges of ownership can be shared as well.

LESSONS FROM TOYOTA

It's hard to pick up a business book these days without reading some kind of admiring reference to the Toyota Motor Company, and for good reason. Toyota is far and away the most world's most valuable auto company, arguably the world's most successful manufacturing company, and second only to General Electric as the world's most admired company. From a management perspective, Toyota is among the most benchmarked companies in the world. For decades it has sustained a small industry of academics and consultants who have worked to articulate the lessons of what has been variously described as the Toyota Production System and The Toyota Way. Most profiles of the company emphasize the soft side of its collaborative business practices. But there is nothing soft about Toyota's competitive performance. It's no accident that their approach has been labeled "lean manufacturing." Toyota's collaborative behavior succeeds in large part because it fuels a relentless drive toward competitive fitness. Toyota's collaboration strategies are celebrated because they work, not because they're nice.

The global automotive industry is made up of a small number of assemblers (e.g., the "Big 3") along with hundreds of parts and component suppliers organized into multiple tiers. Because they control the critical decisions about purchasing and design, assemblers like Toyota tend to have most of the power in the system. On the flip side, purchased parts and components make up the vast majority of a car's value. As a result, it's virtually impossible to build a great car without an effective and competitive supplier network. In the auto industry, one of the greatest management challenges is orchestrating the delicate balance of competition and cooperation between the assembler and its suppliers. And the collaborative relationship between them is a perfect laboratory to examine alternative innovation strategies.

It's no secret that carmakers in the United States have had a contentious relationship with their suppliers for decades. These tensions have reached a boiling point recently with the advent of large-scale divestitures of carmaker parts divisions (General Motors' 1997 spin-off of Delphi Corp. and Ford Motor Company's 2000 spin-off of Visteon). But these spin-offs only ushered in a new phase in the struggle, and created the conditions for even more conflict. While the carmaker-component supplier conflict may subside from time to time, whenever an automotive executive declares a new cost-cutting initiative, such as Jacques Nasser's "Ford 2000" program or Ignacio Lopez's "Global Purchasing System" at General Motors, you can be certain that the fighting has resumed.

The source of these conflicts is actually quite simple: carmakers want to squeeze every last cent out of parts prices. And it's easy to see why: given the vast volume of purchases (General Motors buys more than $100 billion in parts from around the world every year), just a small reduction in price can have a huge and immediate effect on the bottom line. These purchasing wars are a classic zero sum game. Price reductions in components simply shift profits away from the suppliers and put them directly on the assemblers' bottom line.

From an automaker's point of view, squeezing your suppliers for price reductions seems completely rational: it makes you more profitable—at least in the short term. And if the same parts with the same quality can be purchased from multiple suppliers, then why wouldn't you force those suppliers to compete on price and purchase parts at the lowest possible price? From a strategic perspective, it's the right thing to do as long as you believe three things: (1) that supplier technology doesn't matter, (2) that it's good if suppliers' margins are kept as low as possible, and (3) that overall productivity will improve if individual suppliers have both the incentive and the ability to reduce their costs by working alone.

If, however, true competitiveness results from the opposite conditions—supplier technology and innovation matters a lot, suppliers need to sustain margins that motivate them to invest in improving their designs and processes, and the best lever in the system is collaborative efforts that improve quality and design costs out—then the carmakers' microscopic focus on parts pricing is misguided.

Suppliers who lack differentiation and compete on price alone inevitably get weary of being beaten up. So whenever the supplier has even a modicum of negotiating power based on IP, the tables can turn quite quickly. We know a CEO of one such supplier who, in the midst of a struggle to escape bankruptcy, was able to use a small patent portfolio to raise the price of its component in a development project from its original target of $2,000 (the expectation of the carmaker's engineering staff) to more than $4,000. In the short run, this exercise in negotiating power was a good outcome for this supplier, but not necessarily the best long-term result for the development project.

While such examples are few and far between, they demonstrate how the scorpion and the frog parable applies to business: in the long run, U.S. automakers who have exploited their purchasing muscle to squeeze the life out of their suppliers have found themselves struggling to stay above water. The Big 3 U.S. carmakers seem to take turns—first Chrysler, then GM, then Ford—staving off their own bankruptcies. In 2006, the three U.S. automakers lost some $27 billion before taxes combined.

Unlike its U.S. rivals, Toyota has structured a very different and more collaborative model, one that interlocks ownership interests in a network of suppliers and assemblers—what the Japanese have termed a *keiretsu*. For Toyota, taking an ownership position in their suppliers' businesses (and allowing certain suppliers to take an ownership interest in Toyota) not only helps align their financial interests directly (Toyota generates over 10 percent of its net income from its equity in its *keiretsu* partners), it strongly promotes a more open approach to innovation. Working in such a collaborative network not only increases the incentive to pursue shared interests in improved productivity, it also reduces incentives to adopt adversarial purchasing tactics, to renege on deals, and even to hide technology development.

To promote this kind of open innovation within its supplier network, Toyota uses a number of managerial mechanisms, generally taking the long view by investing in network development. This is a practice that a hard-nosed purchasing manager might criticize as "leaving money on the table." But suppliers like Denso, Aisin Seiki, Toyoda Gosei, Tokai Rika, and Aichi Steel have long formed their corporate identities through their positions as members of the "Toyota Group," an association that brings both privileges and obligations. Toyota also provides a formal structure for suppliers to form regional organizations with names like the *Kyohokai* in Japan and BAMA and GAMA (short for the Bluegrass and Golden State Automotive Manufacturers Associations respectively) in the United States. These supplier associations organize activities that include information exchanges, training programs, and social events. And although Toyota has an obvious presence in the groups, the company promotes the notion that its suppliers form relationships with each other, rather than enforcing a hub-and-spoke model where communication flows only through Toyota. Toyota also invests in its supplier network more directly, by subsidizing operational consulting activities (a service that comes without charge to suppliers) and by promoting "voluntary study groups," or *jishuken,* where noncompeting suppliers can work together to help raise quality and productivity.

The competitive superiority of Toyota's collaborative approach, one it has sustained over a long period of time, has become obvious. Toyota has improved its quality and productivity at a rapid and consistent rate for three decades, a story of lean production that most business executives know well. What most in the business world have overlooked is that Toyota's supplier network has improved its quality and productivity performance in lockstep with the improvements of Toyota itself. To put that another way, not only is the final stage of assembly getting more competitive all the time, all the components have also been getting more competitive at the same time. And while they may not necessarily be as productive as Toyota, other Japanese companies now follow similar approaches and have reaped similar benefits.

In Figure 12, we compare the results of Toyota's open-innovation strategy with that of the U.S. automotive industry. Interestingly, the U.S. assemblers improved their productivity performance rapidly beginning in the 1980s and are now nearly as productive as Toyota. The same cannot be said about U.S. suppliers however. They have shown basically no productivity improvement in nearly four decades. The reason that Toyota and other Japanese automakers continue to outpace the U.S. automakers has little to do with assembler productivity. Rather, Toyota has figured out how to help its suppliers improve their game at nearly the same rate as Toyota itself. For U.S. automakers, trying to compete with a network of stagnant suppliers is like trying to run a marathon with weights tied to your sneakers. Rather than wonder who is responsible for this failure, the far more relevant question is: how do you solve this problem? As Toyota has so clearly shown, there is only one answer: collaborate or die.

According to researchers who have conducted extensive interviews with Toyota suppliers and managers, the norms of *Kyohokai* collaboration make it clear that membership in the Toyota supplier groups involves not just a privilege of receiving ideas, but, more important, an obligation to share:

FIGURE 12   Comparing Labor Productivity Gains in U.S. and Toyota Supply Networks

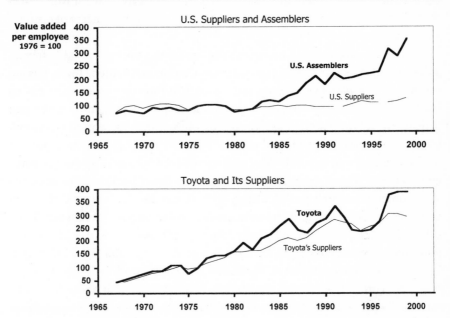

Source: Adapted from Marvin Lieberman, 1997 and 1999; *U.S. Annual Survey of Manufacturers, Analysts Guide,* Daiwa Securities Corporation; author analysis.

Production processes are simply not viewed as property and Toyota accepts that some valuable knowledge will spill over to benefit [component] competitors. Thus, any production related knowledge that Toyota or a supplier possesses (cost, quality, inventory management, etc.) is viewed as accessible to virtually any member of the network (with perhaps the exception of a direct competitor) because it is, in effect, the property of the network . . . In effect, Toyota states that "We will help you, but in return, you must agree to help the network." The rule can be stated as follows: *The price of entry into the network is a limited ability to protect proprietary production knowledge. Intellectual property rights reside at the network, rather than firm, level* [emphasis in original].

For a productivity performance like this to sustain itself over decades, this model of open innovation needs to extend far further than mere incremental changes on the plant floor—after all, the nature of the parts being built changes dramatically over time. That means the model must extend into the development of new technology as well. Toyota, of course, has built more than just a parts supplier network, or even just a simple *keiretsu* of interlocking share ownership: it has built a collaborative community of suppliers bound by shared development work, shared improvement initiatives, and shared property. In other words, Toyota has created an *innovation keiretsu,* a model for taking the concept of open innovation to another level.

As we know, however, the best collaboration intentions can easily go astray. In order to enable its innovation *keiretsu* to function smoothly, then, Toyota has developed unique ways to encourage collaboration around the most sensitive of its knowledge-creating investments and joint-development programs. If the participants in these programs lacked serious mutual ties, these high-stakes collaborations would easily break down. That's why Toyota, in managing its intellectual property, has embedded collaboration directly into its patent development process. Toyota quite literally shares its patent ownership more than any other company we've ever encountered. Over the last decade, Toyota has the highest level of patent coassignment in the automotive industry and perhaps the highest of any company of similar size. Figure 13 shows a picture of Toyota's innovation *keiretsu* alongside that of Ford (if you can even call that a *keiretsu*). It is a striking visual depiction of how differently Toyota works with its suppliers than does Ford. Toyota and its suppliers have developed a rich network of innovation coownership while Ford (as well as the other U.S. and European automakers we have looked at) has utterly failed to do so.

Perhaps the most spectacular example of Toyota's innovation prowess has been the success of the Prius, the world's first mass-marketed hybrid electrical vehicle (HEV). With increasing political and environmental pressure to find an alternative to gas-guzzling cars, the Prius, which runs on battery power half the time, has received wide acclaim—winning several "Car of the Year" awards around the world—for its innovative design, unique driving experience, and remarkable fuel efficiency. Meanwhile, due to its fifty-mile-per-gallon performance, nearly double what comparable conventional cars can boast, the U.S. Environmental Protection Agency awarded the 2007 Prius its highest rating for fuel efficiency.

Developing its breakthrough hybrid design, though, was no easy matter as Toyota practically had to reinvent the automobile in the process. In order to bring this car to market years ahead of the competition, Toyota worked in close collaboration with its key suppliers to develop critical inventions all throughout the power train. (For nearly ten years after the Prius's 1997 debut, only Honda and Nissan succeeded in bringing other HEV cars to market.) Its closest collaborator has been its battery supplier, Matsushita Electric, with which Toyota developed a deep partnership in order to create a battery design that could successfully power a mainstream car. Since Matsushita had not been a traditional member of the

FIGURE 13 Toyota's and Ford's Innovation *Keiretsu*s

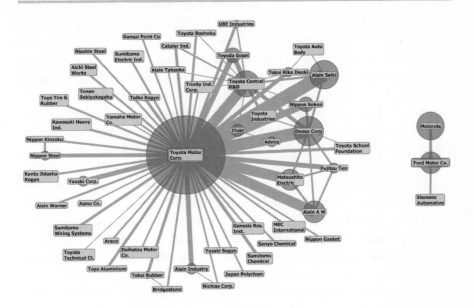

Toyota Group, the two companies formed a joint venture called Panasonic EV Energy in 1996. The two companies also developed nearly one hundred jointly owned patents covering HEV technology, one of the largest coassignment relationships in the entire Toyota supplier network.

While U.S. automakers have invested in fuel cells and European automakers have invested in diesel technologies, Toyota has beaten them both to market with the first mass-market alternative power train. Toyota is so far ahead in HEV technology that it could literally lock the other automakers out of the market using its patents. But rather than starting an IP war, Toyota has willingly licensed parts of its HEV technology to competing automakers. By collaborating with its suppliers, Toyota has built a technology lead that will ensure its profitability in the HEV market even if they don't end up making the cars. More important, they have developed an automotive innovation machine that can run much faster than their competition.

The key to this high-performance innovation machine is technology cycle time. Think for a moment about how Toyota's approach to patent development affects the innovation speed of its supplier network. Because of its open-innovation model of technology development, Toyota, unlike Ford and GM, has a more intimate knowledge of what patentable technology its key suppliers are working on because those suppliers trust that Toyota won't misuse that critical information in price negotiations. At the same time, Toyota is also more willing to share its own technology with in-network suppliers like Aisin Seiki and Denso at an earlier stage because it has confidence that its *Kyohokai* members won't abuse that information in order to get a temporary leg up in their bilateral pricing negotiations. U.S. suppliers, on the other hand, know from painful experience that the only way they can avoid pricing disasters in new products is by keeping technology development secret until it's protected. As a result, *the best technology circulates much faster* in Toyota's network than in Ford or General Motors and Toyota's patent portfolio reflects this advantage.

Our analysis shows that Toyota's citations of Denso and Aisin Seiki occur nearly a year faster than Ford's and General Motors' citations to their key suppliers, Visteon and Delphi. The same effect operates in reverse as Toyota's suppliers are able to follow on its innovation much more quickly than do Ford's and GM's. It's no wonder that Toyota and its suppliers have left the U.S. automakers in the dust.

The Toyota supplier network demonstrates one way an open-innovation strategy can work. It shows that, by taking a team approach to innovation, *it pays to be in a winning network*. At the same time, the Toyota network has accumulated powerful technology advantages on both the component and assembly side because it *respects the power of intellectual property*. Along the way, the company *avoids destructive pricing battles* that train suppliers to keep as many secrets from the carmakers as they can. In the process, *they develop strong commercial trust* and develop confidence that *the whole network will share in the benefits* of high performance. Such commercial trust is built over time by Toyota's strategic commitment to its collaboration strategy: by investing in network capability, by promoting shared ownership at multiple levels, and by taking advantage of the iterative nature of technology development to innovate faster than the competition.

Getting to Market with Complementary Patents

Although joint ventures or network arrangements like that employed by Toyota typically require IP sharing, they often bring other assets into play as well. Increasingly common these days, however, are arrangements in which IP and only IP is shared. In their simplest form, these collaborations involve basic cross-licensing agreements, where two companies with competing products and overlapping inventions grant each other the right to use each other's patents. But in a growing range of technology areas, IP owners are finding it both valuable and necessary to pool a range of inventions in a separate, stand-alone collaborative entity in order to bring their technology to market.

Cross-license deals allow two companies with parallel R&D activities and competing products to declare a kind of technology truce: "I'll let you use my patent inventions if you let me use yours." Usually these deals take the form of barter trade, where little money changes hands relative to the value of the rights exchanged. In most cases, an imbalance in patent value is either ignored or dealt with as a balancing payment. Like most barter trades, these deals promote inefficiency as both companies avoid full and open valuation of their IP. These deals are also usually bilateral, but as these cross-licenses accumulate, they result in a large (and largely invisible) network of technology-sharing agreements. These networks can have far more value than any of the hard assets a company might own. One recent example of this was the 2005 deal between IBM and Lenovo. When Lenovo bought IBM's PC business, they bought its network of cross-license agreements along with the trademarks for the ThinkPad brand and IBM's collection of PC patents. Almost overnight, Lenovo had transformed itself from a contract manufacturer with no ability to get to market without infringing thousands of patents, to a full-scale global brand with access to a wide range of technology that it didn't need to own.

Cross-license deals also allow companies to share IP and incorporate the licensed technology into their own products. In more advanced forms of collaboration, companies can place their patents into a joint-ownership pool that is managed as a licensing business and administered by a third party. Popularity of these so-called patent pools has ebbed and flowed over time, as antitrust policies have seesawed on permitting or restricting their use. When they are available, patent pools are, in fact, the best solution for clearing what has commonly been called the "patent thicket" (described below).

The rising transparency of IP transactions should be viewed generally as a good thing that promotes open innovation via market-based collaborations. As we move away from a barter economy to one composed of more visible collaborations, new forms of collaboration and new kinds of players have begun to emerge. Markets for technology have also grown in importance, as both buyers and sellers of IP are placing greater focus on getting value out of the exchange. The reemergence of patent pools provides a valuable example of how market mechanisms rise up to solve problems of complexity in the technology arena.

LESSONS FROM PATENT POOLS

Despite the fact that the video technology that MPEG LA sells penetrates households around the world, MPEG LA* is probably the biggest collaborative enterprise that few people have ever heard of.

MPEG LA describes itself as a "reseller of consolidated license portfolios," largely for digital video technology. In simpler terms, MPEG LA organizes what are commonly called *patent pools,* collaborative arrangements of multiple patent holders to license a portfolio of patents surrounding a technology area. Patent pools are considered an important way to solve a problem commonly called a *patent thicket.* These thickets can result when a technology platform consisting of many patents also has many owners, making it costly and inefficient for users to negotiate the number of licenses required to make use of the whole platform in a product. At an industry level, patent thickets can increase uncertainty and conflict in the use of a valuable new technology, effectively blocking its use.

Patent pools, though, used to be illegal. For years, antitrust regulators considered them to be little more than a cartel of technology providers who conspired to fix prices. In a purely functional sense, fixing prices is a pretty accurate description of what a patent pool does: in order to promote liquidity in technology markets, it sets a price at which technology users can license patents from technology providers. But as technology users and providers learned long ago, setting a fixed price for patented technology is one of the most efficient ways to establish a functioning market for patented innovation, and not necessarily the sign of an abusive monopolistic cartel. So when a company wants to obtain rights to use a closely connected set of patented technologies, an organized patent collaboration of multiple inventors can be a model of open innovation and a very good thing for everyone involved.

Patent pools have had a volatile history. The first pool was formed in 1856 and brought six separate manufacturers of sewing machines, including Singer, the heavyweight player of the day, together in a mechanism that would allow the companies to avoid suing each other into bankruptcy. One of the early and more notable pools formed in the aerospace industry. During World War I, a committee convened by Franklin D. Roosevelt, then assistant secretary of the Navy, recommended a patent pool as a way to settle the patent conflicts between the Wright

*In its two-part name, MPEG stands for "Moving Picture Experts Group" (which is a standards body) and LA for "Licensing Authority." MPEG, the standards body, is completely separate from MPEG LA, the licensor.

brothers and Glenn Curtiss, the two leading aerospace pioneers of the time. The
pool put all of the patents from both sets of inventors into a single entity, the
Manufacturers Aircraft Association (MAA), which subsequently set a license fee
of $200 per plane with the proceeds to be split as follows: 67.5 percent to the
Wrights, 20 percent to Curtiss, with the rest allocated to administrative costs.

While patent pool formation peaked in the 1930s, concerns over their abuse
continued to spread. In response to these abuses, in 1945 the U.S. Supreme Court
withdrew its support of patent pools, complaining that "the history of this country has perhaps never witnessed a more completely successful economic tyranny."
This shift in judicial attitudes led to a rapid decline in the number of new patent
pools formed during the 1950s, a trend that led to their disappearance from the
scene as not a single new patent pool was formed from the 1960s all the way
through the 1990s.

As patent pools fell out of favor, an alternative approach became more common. Instead of pooling their patents, large firms began to offer each other licenses to their respective patent portfolios, which in turn led to new kinds of
collaborative networks, invisible webs of agreements in which firms exchanged
"IP for IP" in privately negotiated *cross-licenses*. The rise of cross-licensing
practices shifted thicket-clearing mechanisms away from market-based, open-
innovation agreements, which offered clear royalty fees and distribution-sharing
agreements, to an approach that was less transparent both from the standpoint
of a public declaration of the agreements and from the economic standpoint of
placing a market value on the exchange. This approach, in fact, has proven popular in industries composed of a relatively small number of large players. In the
semiconductor sector, for example, companies like Intel have long embraced this
"IP for IP" model as the preferred way to do business.

But as time passed, it became clearer to the regulators who had put the brakes
on their formation that a world without patent pools led to all sorts of undesir-
able outcomes. The cross-licensing networks of large firms led to industry dynamics that some saw as clubby and anticompetitive. And as smaller firms began
to develop technology with the help of venture capital funding, they often preferred to license their own technology separately on a cash basis. As the problem
of patent thickets became more common in some rapidly developing sectors, this
rising collection of individual license deals led to a new problem called "royalty
stacking," where users were confronted with the prospect of negotiating a large
pile of license agreements, one with each individual patent holder. Faced with a
world defined by hidden webs of cross-licenses on the one hand and increased
royalty stacks on the other, regulators revisited the benefits of one-stop shopping

for patent portfolios composed of multiple owners. They realized that, although allowing patent pools could, in theory, promote cartels among companies with competing technologies, these arrangements would actually enable more frequent collaborations between companies. A collection of patent portfolios could then come together quickly to promote rapid progress.

So, by the mid-1990s, patent pools made a comeback. Under the new IP and antitrust regime called the "Rule of Reason" adopted in 1995, regulators took a fresh look at patent pools. They decided to welcome collaborative licensing structures. This quickly led to the emergence of new pools organized by companies like Philips and Thomson along with stand-alone pool developers like MPEG LA and Via Licensing. MPEG LA, in fact, pioneered the stand-alone format as the antitrust regulators' test case for the positive effect of patent pools. The MPEG 2 patent pool was created (starting with the early drafts of the MPEG 2 standard in 1993) after an exhaustive analysis of the patents revealed the core patents that were essential to making the digital video technology function. MPEG's members then recruited the pool's members from those core patents' owners, created the MPEG LA organization and, working in close collaboration with the U.S. Department of Justice, obtained the relevant legal clearance. They hammered out the terms under which patent pools were to be acceptable, using models like the MAA previously developed in the aerospace industry as templates, and set the terms to circumvent potential abusers. The group's request for antitrust clearance was approved promptly in 1997 and resulted in the MPEG 2 patent pool, the first of its kind in some four decades.

The MPEG 2 patent pool illustrates how a patent pool can support a remarkably large number of players engaged in open innovation. The patent holders in the group currently include twenty-five separate companies* from seven different countries owning more than 600 patents. And MPEG 2 was only the beginning. After setting up the model, MPEG LA continued to branch out and now manages seven active pools and several more, including digital television and digital rights management, still under development. MPEG LA is not alone in the world of patent pool hosts, however. Via Licensing, which licenses both RFID and the Dolby sound technology, operates under a model quite similar to MPEG

---

*Alcatel Lucent; British Telecommunications plc; Canon, Inc.; CIF Licensing, LLC; Columbia University; France Télécom (CNET); Fujitsu; General Instrument Corp.; GE Technology Development, Inc.; Hitachi, Ltd.; KDDI Corporation; LG Electronics Inc.; Matsushita; Mitsubishi; Nippon Telegraph and Telephone Corporation; Philips; Robert Bosch GmbH; Samsung; Sanyo Electric Co., Ltd.; Scientific-Atlanta; Sharp; Sony; Thomson Licensing; Toshiba; and Victor Company of Japan, Limited.

LA. Philips has a separate division called Intellectual Property and Standards, which manages pools for audio and video electronics, while companies like Sony and Thomson also manage similar collaborative activities.

Since MPEG LA files no public financial statements, no one except its members knows how big it really is. Nonetheless, it's interesting to speculate about just how big it might actually be. The market licensing rate for using the MPEG 2 standard is currently set at $2.50 per decoder. The devices that use these decoders include DVD players, personal computers, and set-top boxes, a set of products with worldwide sales that we conservatively estimate at more than 400 million units in 2006. When we apply the market license rate to that base of licensees, we end up with a rough revenue estimate of about $1 billion in royalties on the MPEG 2 pool alone. If you add in the revenue from the other six pools that it runs, you begin to realize that MPEG LA is a remarkable multibillion-dollar enterprise, one that brings together a staggeringly large group of innovators in a massively profitable endeavor. While that profit flow is certainly impressive all by itself, you can also consider the product sales of the video products based on MPEG technologies. From that perspective, MPEG LA's technology covers products with between $50 billion and $100 billion in annual revenues, which by comparison would rival Fortune 50 companies like IBM, Dell, and Time Warner in size and profitability.

While antitrust regulators have approved standards-based pools like MPEG2, we have not yet seen widespread formation of patent pools in the absence of a standards body. As the problem of patent thickets grows in a wide range of high-profile technologies like nanotechnology, alternative energy, and electronic medical records, we may see new business models emerging that extend the idea of IP collaboration even more broadly.

Although cross-licensing practices have been the most convenient way to exchange technology rights for small groups of competitors, patent pools have been rediscovered as an alternative model for a world with a more wide-open and competitive field of innovators. Patent pool collaborations are *opening up the markets for innovation* and introducing a new commercial trade where once barter trade reigned supreme. By *bringing the cost of technology directly into the cost of goods sold,* these pools are simultaneously extending the reach of technology markets and creating a new market discipline. As technology exchange moves out of clubs and into the open, companies are beginning to see new opportunities and new challenges. They are learning that innovation can be quantified and measured, that it is an important part of the bill of materials for almost any product, and that the issue of access to technology matters just as much—if not more—than its price. Open-innovation models like patent pools can *reduce the cost of purchasing IP* when a large group of companies are investing in technology in the same field and can *speed up the access to clusters of technology* by bundling together critical inventions, thereby clearing a patent thicket that would otherwise slow the pace of innovation.

For business strategists, choosing when and whether to participate in (or drive) these collaborative licensing programs has become a critical decision. In technology domains with lots of interdependencies, an efficient patent-pooling mechanism can speed the adoption of a new technology. In the extreme, it can make the difference between acceptance and takeoff on the one hand, or gridlock and rejection on the other. Until recently, the IP transactions that surround the production of technology products has been little more than an administrative afterthought for most managers. But sophisticated companies like Philips and Thomson have recognized the strategic importance of setting the price and choosing the terms of availability of important technologies in their industries and have staked out a central position in the management of IP exchanges. In the process, they are demonstrating that how you manage collaborative IP exchange in your business can make the difference between winning and losing.

Energizing and Tapping Collaborative Development Networks

The ease with which you can organize a community around just about any topic of interest represents an opportunity for business collaborations that would have been unthinkable just a short time ago. Although usually based around sharing the benefits of past innovation, patent pools, for example, demonstrate the practicality of multiparty joint ventures. Other more dynamic forms of open innovation, ranging from simple prize-based marketplaces to full-throttle development communities like Linux or Wikipedia, have succeeded in orchestrating large-scale collaboration to generate new content and solve new problems. Although the modern forms of mass collaboration can trace their roots back decades (if not centuries), it is clear that we are all now at the cusp of a huge explosion in these kinds of activity.

The idea of using prizes to stimulate innovation goes back a long way—at least to 1714. At that time, the English government offered a prize for the first person to devise a practical way for a ship's navigator to determine its longitude. This was no small feat—the use of star charts to determine latitude had been known for centuries, but finding a method to determine longitude while at sea proved much more difficult, and numerous ships and sailors failed to make it back to their home port as a result. It wasn't until 1773 when, much to the chagrin of the leading astronomers, a clockmaker named John Harrison claimed the reward with a solution from an entirely different field of study. Two centuries later, in 1919, Raymond Orteig, a French-born hotel owner from New York City, offered a $25,000 award for the first aviator to complete a solo flight across the Atlantic Ocean. That challenge, of course, triggered Charles Lindbergh's famous 1927 flight on the *Spirit of St. Louis*. Today, nearly a century after Lindbergh's flight, we still see prizes offered for technical progress. What is different today, however, is the use of prizes to encourage *commercial* innovation activity. Eli Lilly's Innocentive model, which we discussed in the last chapter, has emerged as a highly developed approach to using prizes to promote a specialized market for innovation. Another recent example is the Goldcorp Challenge, in which a gold-mining company gave away half a million dollars in prizes (with a $95,000 first prize) to geologists outside the company. But unlike Innocentive, which simply defines the problems it wants outside inventors to solve, Goldcorp actually offered to share some critical IP that would make the prize seekers more effective: they allowed the outside geologists to use the company's most precious information assets—previously top-secret company data on mineral deposits and seismic test results—to help them find gold deposits in their Red Lake, Ontario, mine.

Organized prize competitions such as these are an interesting but relatively limited model of open innovation. By far the largest breakthroughs in mass collaboration have come from self-organizing collaborative development communities. The most famous of these was sparked by Linus Torvalds, a Helsinki University graduate student, who used early Internet news groups to recruit programmers for a collaborative development project to develop the kernel for an operating system. Torvald's new OS, which was modeled on UNIX, was subsequently named Linux, in tribute to two of its key influences. Of similar renown, Jimmy Wales, an Internet entrepreneur who made his fortune providing "adult content" based on a "guy-oriented search engine," sponsored the first collaborative Web site based on *wiki* (a Hawaiian term that means "fast") software with the goal of developing an online encyclopedia. The result was Wikipedia, which has become a de facto standard for online information and far and away the world's most widely read encyclopedia.

Success stories like Innocentive and Wikipedia demonstrate how collaboration can serve as a platform for generating, capturing, and defending user-generated innovation from large communities of participants. The key to success is generating a substantial participation premium, essentially getting talented participants to join a development community and contribute work for no direct monetary benefit. Needless to say, building businesses around a resource model that depends on voluntary effort has its limits; for every Linux success there are cautionary tales like that of the Aibo, a failed effort by electronics giant Sony to build a collaboration community around an AI robot product in early 2006. Nevertheless, understanding the conditions under which mass collaboration communities can work is critical. Under the right circumstances, mass collaboration can play an invaluable role in business strategy as well.

LESSONS FROM LINUX

Of all the utopian socialists who contest the economic importance of intellectual property rights, Richard Stallman has developed an alternative worldview that is far and away the most consistent, clearly articulated, and fully formed. It's also the most extreme: Stallman doesn't like the concept of intellectual property very much. In fact, he has made it his life's work to foment a revolution against the emerging intellectual property regime in software. While he lives in a different era, his approach is not unlike that of Karl Marx during the Industrial Revolution: where Marx wrote the *Communist Manifesto*, Stallman has written the *GNU Manifesto*; where Marx believed capital was "surplus value" unjustly appropriated by capitalists from the toil of laborers, Stallman believes that computer software should have no owners and that programmers should be able to share the fruits of their labor freely; and like Marx, Stallman argues that what many would describe as entrepreneurial virtue is instead a bourgeois corrupting force. "Live cheaply," he recently counseled a group of students. "Don't buy a house, a car or have children. The problem is they're expensive and you have to spend all your time making money to pay for them."

Stallman's conversion to the cause of what he calls "free software" came in the early 1980s, a few years after he graduated with a physics degree from Harvard. At the time, he was working in the MIT Artificial Intelligence (AI) Lab in Cambridge, Massachusetts, and was considered one of the very best hackers in one of the world's top hotbeds for hacker talent. It was in his time at MIT that Stallman went through the most searing experience of his young life. He had taken sides against LISP, a start-up company that was attempting to commercialize the fruits of the AI Lab's programming efforts in competition with Symbolics, another commercial software company, which had been more friendly to the AI Lab's hacker culture. In its race with Symbolics to develop an AI-based operating system, LISP had hired away most of Stallman's MIT colleagues and shut down access to the AI programming work into which he had put so many hours. While

Stallman (known to fellow hackers as RMS) had not gone down easily, performing what would later be celebrated as legendary displays of hacker virtuosity, LISP eventually won and, as a result, Stallman lost everything that mattered to him most.

Stallman was so outraged by the dissolution of his AI community that he decided to start a new project, one that would be protected from the commercial intruders that had cherry-picked MIT's AI software assets and spoiled the dynamics Stallman cherished of its academic development community. LISP had taken away the free software that his developer group shared, converting the code into a proprietary asset along the way. This came as a surprise to Stallman. Not only was LISP's maneuver legal, it was, in fact, the most likely outcome of the licensing rules that governed software code. Stallman was nothing if not a skilled strategist and he knew that he needed to fight fire with fire—so he resolved to find a way to protect his next collaboration from expropriation by these same commercial interests. In consultation with a clever lawyer, he developed one of the most innovative software licenses of all time: the General Public License, or GPL.

The design for GPL gives any user the right to run code licensed under its terms for free (Stallman takes pains to point out that this right constitutes "free speech, not free beer") and to modify the program in any way they like for their own use. But this freedom came with very specific conditions, including (a) an *open-source* condition—any modifications that you distribute must include the human-readable source code (in other words, not just the compiled code); (b) a *credit for contributions* condition—the individual programmer credits for the source of the code will not be removed; and (c) a *viral license* condition—any additions or modifications of the code will fall under the terms of the GPL as well. This simple license "hack" effectively protects the code, not from unauthorized use (which was hardly a concern for Stallman, since he had no licensing revenue goals) but from unauthorized appropriations of the source code from the core developer community. Simply stated, you're free to use and modify open-source code, but whatever you do to it becomes open source itself. Brilliant!

While he was crafting the license, Stallman also began working in parallel on his new operating system. As a model for his project, he chose UNIX, the operating system developed by Ken Thompson and Dennis Ritchie at Bell Labs, because of its highly modular structure. By using the public UNIX interface standards, and simply mimicking the function of the system's modules, the architecture could serve as a template for replicating the UNIX functions without requiring reuse of its proprietary code. Indeed, Stallman named his project "GNU" after this underlying design principle, since his project would mimic

UNIX without being a copy of UNIX itself. In what passes for humor in hacker circles, GNU was a recursive acronym, standing for "GNU's Not UNIX."

Stallman declared his intent to start the GNU project in September 1983 (he issued his *GNU Manifesto* about eighteen months later) and began his work on the major GNU modules shortly thereafter. After a false start on a C compiler conversion, he successfully built some of the early GNU modules: he converted his own text editor, Emacs, to the GNU format in 1985; completed a built-from-scratch GNU C compiler in 1987; and then finished a GNU debugger in 1988. By 1990, with most of the major pieces in place, Stallman turned his attention to the toughest part of the job: the "kernel" or the heart of the operating system. Against his wishes (he wanted to name the program after his girlfriend Alix) one of his codevelopers christened this project the "HURD." The objective of the HURD development effort was to upgrade a "microkernel" called Mach by adding a collection of server processes on top. Unlike some of his earlier feats of marathon programming (Stallman once spent a stretch of three years without any living quarters beyond a cot in his MIT cubicle), the effort required would be larger than even a programming genius like Stallman could take on by himself. The kernel project would clearly require a development team.

Not surprisingly perhaps, Stallman's kernel development effort "stalled" here. Some would argue that the whole idea of upgrading the microkernel was a miscalculation. Others blame the delay on the dynamics of the team. Stallman, though brilliant, is famously rigid and uncompromising. He can be virtually impossible to work with in groups unless those working with him have completely embraced his worldview. As a result, the HURD team remained small, moved slowly, and accomplished little.

In the meantime, Linus Torvalds, a master's student sitting in his dormitory at the University of Helsinki in the spring of 1991, was working on solving a less grandiose but (eventually) similar problem. He was a frequent user of the university's mainframe computer, but logging on required Torvalds to make frequent trips across campus to one of the terminals in the central computing facility. Thinking ahead in dread to the cruel Helsinki winter, and partly because of his admitted lazy streak, Torvalds saw these trips across campus as something to be avoided at all costs. He wanted to figure out a way to access the mainframe directly from the warmth of his dormitory room. He decided he would try to write what he called a "terminal emulator" program, software that would make his new '386 PC function like a terminal access point. Before long, he realized that he had tackled a much bigger problem than he had anticipated. In order to achieve the desired function of his "terminal emulator," he had to write an operating system. Or the heart of one, at least.

A project that might have scared off a more timid soul struck Torvalds as a challenge. So he persevered, deeply immersing himself in the literature and minutiae of operating system theory. He quickly realized that if he was going to make serious progress, he was going to need help. So he reached out through the Internet in the late summer of 1991 in a famous series of e-mails to enlist others as participants in his kernel project.

> Hello netlanders, . . . Do you pine for the nice days of minix-1.1, when men were men and wrote their own device drivers? Are you without a nice project and just dying to cut your teeth on an OS you can try to modify for your needs?. . . :-) I'm doing a (free) operating system, just a hobby, won't be big and professional . . . I'd like any feedback on things people like/dislike . . . This is a program for hackers by a hacker. I've enjoyed doing it, and somebody might enjoy looking at it and even modifying it for their own needs . . . Drop me a line if you are willing to let me use your code.

Torvalds got the response he wanted, and it was rapid. Before year-end, "there actually started to be a number of people using it and doing things with it"—the first glimmers of a community of fellow hackers. By early 1992—"that's when Linux took off"—he had a functional developer team numbering in the hundreds and enough code that people he didn't even know had begun using the first "self-hosting" Linux version 0.10, which he had introduced in November 1991. By 1994, the group was confident enough in their work to release the "ready-for-prime-time" product, version 1.0. The community was growing by leaps and bounds along the way. And the spontaneous and large-scale emergence of the volunteer development group provided enough resources so that Torvalds could orchestrate the development of an operating system kernel that was not only functional, but also powerful.

And by a stroke of luck, it just happened to fill the critical hole in the GNU project. Linux was perfectly positioned to serve the role Stallman's HURD project had been designed to carry out. When combined with the other key modules of the GNU project's operating system (many of them, like the GNU C compiler and the EMACS text editor, developed by Stallman himself), Torvalds's kernel made Stallman's vision a reality. An entirely free operating system, Linux was licensed under the GPL (Torvalds somewhat reluctantly adopted Stallman's license in 1992), it was every bit as functional as UNIX, and its potential hinted that it might even pose a challenge to Microsoft's dominance in the operating system business.

Stallman and Torvalds's creation soon caught on like wildfire. Mainstream companies like IBM embraced Linux and other open-source projects like Apache (a Web-server program), in part as cheaper versions of their UNIX offerings (most of which struggled) and in part to defend themselves against Microsoft's stranglehold on the operating system market. What started as one visionary man's quixotic quest and another lazy man's summertime diversion had turned into an industrial-strength piece of software that soon had Microsoft, the world's most valuable company, shaking in its boots.

Those of us that have followed the open-source software phenomenon closely over the past decade have become intrigued by a basic question: how can a group of volunteers, operating with no formal project management discipline, and who give away their product for free, successfully compete with Microsoft, arguably the world's toughest competitor? Most management theory would predict that a project like Linux is destined to fail. Or, more boldly, *anything* like Linux could never happen to begin with, because business doesn't work like that. Organizations need revenue to survive and workers need to be paid or they won't work, the textbook would say. Any attempts at productive activity that fail to recognize these basic principles won't get very far.

But the performance of the code emerging from Linux development teams has been nothing short of spectacular. These "hackers" (as opposed to "crackers," who do the illegal stuff) have achieved extraordinary things, developing some of the fastest supercomputer clusters in the world for one. Linux operating systems drive more than half of the burgeoning market for embedded devices in a diverse range of products that includes Philips's TiVo, Ericsson's cordless Web pad, Nokia media terminals, Mercedes concept cars, and many more.

What's surprising about the open-source movement, however, are that the key perceptions most commonly attached to it—that they renounce IP for free software and that every project is an emergent collaboration made up of altruistic volunteers—are basically little more than urban legend. Upon closer examination, none of these perceptions turn out to be true.

Despite Stallman's free-software propaganda, the GPL license is actually highly restrictive and utilizes the power of copyright law *to strongly protect* the collaborative work of the Linux development community. Despite the freewheeling, rapid-fire developer culture of the kernel development network, overlaid on top of the collaborative work flow is *a clear hierarchy with decision rights over what makes it into* the code. And despite the voluntary roots of the community, the most active Linux developers nearly all make their living working for *companies that pay them to work full-time on Linux.* In short, Linux isn't completely free, it isn't completely self-organizing, and its primary contributors aren't volunteers. Instead, the success of Linux, and the open-source phenomenon more generally, are the result of several critical decisions and commitments that create an environment where this kind of mass collaboration can succeed.

Protection
In one of life's notable ironies, Richard Stallman may go down in history as one of the great IP strategists of all time. His licensing innovation, the General Public License (GPL), which is often called "copyleft," provided ironclad intellectual property protection first for his GNU project and then for the closely related Linux project. Unlike earlier "free software" projects, the protection afforded by the GPL has enabled the code base to scale without being expropriated for competing commercial purposes.

Organization
The source code for the UNIX operating system is modular and hierarchically organized. Linux code follows a similar modular structure and therefore can be developed in parallel and discrete functional pieces, for which specific group members are given key maintenance responsibilities. The maintainers of key software modules have formal responsibility and decision rights on what additions or modifications go in and what stays out. Participants debate key design decisions actively and openly, and always seek consensus. But when ties must be broken, lines of authority are clear. At the top, the buck stops clearly with Linus Torvalds, who is intensely engaged, highly respected, and highly visible both inside and outside the core developer community.

Funding
Numerous companies pay active developers to work full-time on Linux. Three of the top fourteen developers, for example, work for IBM. The cost of supporting these developers is a drop in the bucket for Big Blue, which has spent more than a $1 billion supporting Linux. For years Alan Cox, the single most active programmer, worked for Red Hat, a $400 million computer services company with $4.5 billion in market value. Red Hat's business focuses exclusively on open-source projects like Linux. Other core participants have worked for SuSe and Mandrake (companies with similar business models), Sun Microsystems (which, like IBM,

competes with Linux in its proprietary UNIX offering), and specialty semiconductor players like Transmeta and Moxi. In a sense, by funding developer time,
these companies are participating in a joint venture, a venture they hope they can
influence and learn from based on close proximity to the action, even if they have
to relinquish formal control of the process.

If the world's most successful mass collaboration has been supported by effective, if unorthodox, managerial interventions, there must be something important to learn from what has worked so well, right?

Tragically, perhaps, the creative inspiration for the world's most successful
collaborative project will not go down in history receiving much credit for the
resulting success of Linux. It was Stallman, of course, who conceived, designed,
and orchestrated the operating system that we know today as Linux. But Stallman
deeply resents that emergent branding choice and, as a result, he has mounted
a personal campaign to persuade the world to refer to Linux as GNU/Linux (pro-
nounced *GaNoo slash Linux*). Since the defining element of the program is not
its architecture, but rather its central component, the world will never call his
triumphant operating system design by the name he christened it, GNU. For it
is the Linux kernel, not the product of his failed HURD project, that stands at
the center of the product's architecture. Thus, the name Linux (and by implica-
tion the man, Torvalds) has stuck as the project's most critical hub. Without control over the central components, as so many technology pioneers have learned,
credit goes to others.

As the Linux example shows, mass collaborations have emerged as a powerful
and viable new form of open innovation even if they are often misrepresented as
a form of utopian socialism in action. Often, these mass collaborations evolve
under unique circumstances, where a confluence of visibility, general utility, and
high importance—as in encyclopedias, dictionaries, and operating systems—
combine to spark a large-scale community of contributors. Nevertheless, when
a creative architect can find ways to attract *a large community of talented contributors who donate content,* these communities become a force to be reckoned with.
Often they can produce more timely content (e.g., Wikipedia), with fewer errors
(as open-source leader Eric Raymond has said, "With enough eyeballs all bugs
are shallow"), and at larger scale (compare the 2,000 members of the Linux development group with the 200 Microsoft developers who worked on Vista) than
their more traditional competitors. Yet these communities are also more fragile
than commonly recognized; they succeed only when their sponsor(s) *develop clear
rules for sharing IP.* These rules can often cede valuable commercial rights to the
community, as in Stallman's GPL. But by tapping into the participation premium

provided by a large community, creative strategists can *find new ways to accomplish key business goals:* they can rapidly replace underperforming, proprietary technological standards, reduce the cost of developing complex infrastructure, and create new opportunities for commercial offerings that are well adapted to the needs of the community.

Limits to Collaboration

Discussions about collaboration often return to the basic concept of transactions costs we discussed back in chapter 3. In a way, the Information Revolution has reduced the cost of moving information so much that some have argued that you don't really need companies at all—the basic inputs to Coase's Law have been "blown to bits" and will be entirely replaced by large-scale collaboration. Although those kinds of prediction make great headlines, they are clearly overstating the case. For while it is true that some kinds of transactions costs are falling dramatically, and that skillfully designed collaboration can reduce some costs, experienced executives know all too well that collaboration can also *increase* transactions costs. Hamstrung by the need for consensus, business collaborations can end up making decisions based on the consideration of the wrong alternatives, collapse into destructive infighting over profit sharing, and waste valuable time by moving too slowly toward consensus solutions. In short, while collaboration may be more necessary than ever in the Information Age, it is just plain hard to do.

Mass collaboration also has a dark side that we ignore at our peril. Consensus can stifle innovation, cripple challengers, and perpetuate an economic status quo. Collaboration flourishes when companies can realize the value of commercial interdependency. But almost by definition, the most active commercial connections occur among well-established companies and ecosystems. That means that the rewards of collaboration can flow toward the larger and more established at the expense of new and unconnected players.

Our legal and antitrust system has long recognized this dark side of collaboration and has developed rules to counter it. Indeed, there are some forms of business collaboration that are just plain illegal, and rightly so. As Adam Smith famously remarked, "People of the same trade seldom meet together, even for merriment and diversion, but the conversation ends in a conspiracy against the public, or in some contrivance to raise prices." So while the laws on collaboration have shifted substantially to recognize the necessity of open innovation in a world of rapid technological change, regulators have not yet embraced the principle of collaboration completely. At the same time that video technology companies carefully prepared their case justifying the MPEG 2 standard, for example, the Department of Justice denied an application for a relatively simple patent pool for laser eye surgery patents for reasons that, at least in part, proved to be inaccurate. The climate for collaboration has improved, and it needs to, but obstacles, not all of them unwarranted, remain.

Anyone who has worked in a modern business, though, has seen some kind of collaboration failure. Critical business decisions get watered down or overly compromised in a bureaucratic committee process. Powerful entrenched interests force value-destroying compromises on their business "partners" because they have the power to make others adapt to their own selfish interests. Senior leaders sustain subsidies for a poor-performing business for longer than they should, in the spirit of a private club rather than the spirit of a competitive market.

That means that sometimes the best solution is less collaboration, not more. When collaboration demands the consideration of too many connections it can lead to an explosion in transactions costs that can kill the performance of an entire web of businesses. In order to reduce transactions costs in a complex and connected world, then, the best strategy can sometimes be something entirely different than a multilateral collaborative strategy or even a stand-alone control strategy. In the right circumstances, the best strategy of all can be to make things simpler. It is to this class of strategy that we turn next.

CHAPTER 7

Simplify

WINNING BY DESIGN

" 'Tis so," said the Duchess; "and the moral of that is—'Oh, 'tis love, 'tis love, that makes the world go round!' "

"Somebody said," Alice whispered, "that it's done by everybody minding their own business!"

—*Lewis Carroll*, Alice's Adventures in Wonderland*

ontrol and collaboration have their advantages as broad strategy approaches, but they also have limits. While hard-charging CEOs might like to control everything, for instance, it's tough for any business to do so. And as much as collaboration holds out the promise of reaping the rewards of open innovation, it's tough to make real-world business collaboration come together. This has led some writers to popularize the idea that strategy is a choice between the poles of open collaboration and cutthroat competition. There's something fundamentally unsatisfying about this linear view of strategic choice, however. If everyone competed for everything, we'd have price wars all the time; and if everyone collaborated on everything, no one would ever get anything done. If we were limited to just these two options, it would be hard to imagine any business turning a profit.

Whether they emphasize control like Gillette, or collaboration like Toyota,

---

*In a chapter called "A Survey of Capitalism" in D. H. Robertson's *The Control of Industry*, the chapter in which Robertson introduced the metaphor "islands of conscious power" that Ronald Coase later quoted in his seminal article on transactions costs, Robertson led off with this quote from Lewis Carroll.

businesses are, one way or another, confronting the problem of complexity. And complexity can kill a business. It destroys efficiency. It saps energy. It increases transactions costs. It erodes focus. It distracts attention. Complexity, though, is an inevitable outcome of the kind of economic interdependency that characterizes our modern economy. If left alone, complexity tends to run amok. While a certain amount of complexity is inevitable, there are times when runaway complexity can even shut down the growth of an entire industry. To avoid getting caught in this complexity trap, businesses need to make deliberate choices to reduce it.

But how does a business put constraints on the growth of complexity? Aside from the poles of control, in which complexity is denied, and collaboration, in which complexity is embraced, there is a third option: simplification. Simplification strategies can enable a finer parsing of the business problem, one that allows a strategist to sort out places where collaboration makes sense and where a business should compete aggressively for control and advantage. More than that, simplification strategies can take situations that appear to be "La Brea tar pits"— with powerful resources literally stuck in place with nowhere to go—and unlock the barriers to progress. But in order to make simplification strategies work, business and IP strategies need to come into close alignment with the product development process. Indeed, more than other strategic approaches, simplification strategies depend crucially on strategic interventions in the product design process. Design strategies lie at the heart of meaningful simplification, but without IP strategies to go along with them, simplification can bring great value to the user, while they also destroy value for the designer. For this reason, and many others besides, simplification strategies are rarely easy to pull off; in fact, executing a successful simplification strategy can be the hardest challenge of all.

Product designs get complex for many reasons: rising demands from customers, the constant temptation to try to "be all things to all people," technology bottlenecks that prevent some parts of an improving design from fulfilling their potential, and the natural tendency for organizations to add new features. Attempting to satisfy every customer desire in a single product design can result in bloated software with too many features (a common complaint about Microsoft Office) or, like the modern equivalent of a Swiss Army Knife, produce an overly convergent electronic device that ends up being a lousy phone, camera, PDA, and MP3 player all at the same time.

As product designs get more complex, their complexity gets echoed in the related networks of organization and ecosystem. Organization designs, for example, tend to accumulate layers and bureaucratic procedures and the associated overhead costs tend to rise. At the same time, supply and distribution networks get more complicated and the cost of goods sold rises as well.

On the other hand, great product designs are so simple they are often described as elegant. Yet our reactions to them are often restricted to the way they appear to the user, to the "front end" of the design. Some of the best product designs are elegant, on the other hand, because they simplify innovation and supply activities, the "back end" of the design that may not have anything to do with the user. Nevertheless, the best designs are efficient because they deal directly with root causes of complexity whether they face forward or backward.

Any experienced manager understands the potential benefits of simplification on both the operational and marketing sides of a business. On the operations side, simplicity saves money by reducing the number of transactions and the costs that go with them; these costs are often the hardest to see and the hardest to root out. Simplicity also saves money by increasing economies of scale in operations, allowing key activity centers to focus on their most important outputs thereby reducing the per unit cost of operations.

When it comes to marketing, a simpler product design generates value by saving customers time and irritation. Just think of the work you had to do the last time you bought a home computer or a new car, to make sure you got a good price, chose the right model, and selected the right optional features. Simple designs reduce the hassle in that work without denying you the chance to make choices that matter to you. Simplicity also reduces the risk that making one purchase (say, a new PC) won't reduce the value of a related product (say, a printer) or make it obsolete. Some kinds of simplification can also just make using the product easier and improve the customer's experience. The benefits of simplicity are pervasive and they apply to everything from warehouses and organization charts, to designs for everything from an SUV to an MP3 player. The ubiquitous iPod by Apple is a terrific example of how simplified design can make an important difference. The iPod is only one of dozens of MP3 players on the market, but its user interface is so simple and intuitive that it captured more than 80 percent of the market shortly after its launch.

At another level, every experienced strategist knows about the value of simplicity. By applying key design rules, for example, a strategist can help transform a business plagued by runaway complexity, allowing it to escape the La Brea tar pit trap. Strategists can also focus their investments on a business's supply chain and product development so that it can target customers more precisely. Strategists can decide where they need to cooperate—and where they want to compete. Over the long haul, simplicity allows greater agility in decision making, shorter decision cycles, and less time wasted in meetings. When you keep things simple, you don't wind up being average at a lot of things; you can become the best in the critical areas in which you've chosen to compete.

Product design isn't the only place where simplification matters. Business school curricula are built around innovations in management. Not surprisingly, then, the best-selling case studies are all examples of simplified design of a different kind, elegant business models. For a business school professor, the design of a Walmart or Cirque du Soleil "business model" can be every bit as elegant as a Fendi bag or an Apple iPod.

Simplification also unleashes a whole new set of options for IP strategy. In one sense, simplification provides a kind of sorting function to help managers decide where control is possible and where collaboration might work better. In another sense, simplification strategies create the occasions in which strategists actually define what their business is and what it's not. In both ways, the opportunities in simplification often create the most consequential choices any strategist faces.

If product design is the key to simplification, then managers need to develop a better grasp on how to think about it. Design is a multiscale concept that creates opportunities for intervention at many levels of zoom. Important design choices can be made at every level of aggregation, from the smallest detail of a product's architecture, to the design of the manufacturing floor, all the way to the design of the organization, and even to the design of the entire network of relationships in the business ecosystem.

Consider one of the examples we've dug into so far, the wireless telephony industry. If you focus on handsets as the product, then the components include the chips, the casing, the speakers, and so forth. Zoom in on the chips and you get to another level of design, one involving circuit layouts, wafer fabrication, and hardware versus software trade-offs. Zoom out to the wireless infrastructure and you can observe a system with completely different elements: cell phone towers, handsets, and signal technology. Depending on your zoom level, you can observe at one level the battle between Qualcomm and Nokia over licensing fees for entire handsets, at a lower level the competition between Qualcomm and Broadcom over patent infringement in mobile phone chipsets, and at the highest level the international standards wars between technology consortiums variously supporting WCDMA, CDMA2000, and even the Chinese efforts in TD-SCMA. No matter where you look, there are design issues and IP competition everywhere.

In order to get underneath the real issues involved in the interaction between design and IP, we need to introduce a weighty word, one that defines the strategic outcome of design activity: *architecture*. What is architecture? This term, too, has many definitions, but in a business context architecture is a *strategic design*. By that we mean a specification of the discrete functions that a product performs (the nodes), a protocol for how these functions interact with one another (the links), and a division of design responsibility that shapes the relations between a business and its surrounding ecosystem (the clusters).

Developing an architecture requires the designer to do several things, such as: devising a conceptual framework that sets out the *purpose* of a design; deciding on which functions are to be *included or excluded* in the architecture; organizing functional elements into groups (componentization); defining the component boundaries and connections between them (interfaces and standardized rules); and making sure that all the main components can operate smoothly together (interoperability and compatibility). A good architecture, then, sets the terms around which a few simple rules can guide high-stakes strategic choices. In effect, these strategic designs cut through the complexity of all the potential strategies and facilitate clear choices. They basically allow companies to "mind their own business."

While IP and architectural strategies often get decided separately, connecting the two is critical. A designer's options are often limited by the IP that competitors own. Even when having the "freedom to operate" is not an issue, a strategic architecture will design in elements or interfaces that can be controlled through IP. Likewise, IP strategy must be developed with architecture in mind. Often the decision about where to seek IP protection depends on the choices made by the product architect. The net effect of these interdependencies is that developing a simplification strategy is not very simple. Like any elegant product design effort, simplification strategies must seek and find elegance in the midst of complexity. In short, successful strategists must consider the *combined* effect of their design initiatives and their IP strategy. Without the other, each remains incomplete.

TALE OF TWO ARCHITECTURES
Part 1: Projects SPREAD and Chess

Most computer histories undervalue IBM's contribution to technology. These stories are usually written by outsiders, steeped in the Silicon Valley culture, who paint the history of computers as a struggle between the stodgy IBMers in blue suits versus the heroic hackers in ripped jeans and tie-dyed T-shirts. And while many breakthroughs in computing *technology* have indeed sprung from Silicon

Valley, many of the world's most critical innovations in computer *architecture* have actually come from IBM's labs in the Hudson Valley. Indeed, two IBM engineers named Fred Brooks and Gerrit Blaauw first applied the term architecture to computer hardware and software in the early 1960s. To them, architecture was more than just an abstract concept and they were followed by generations of IBM innovators who embraced the term as a guide to action: by applying the language of building design to computer design, these engineers found it possible to clarify how product design choices affected business decisions.

IBM, more than any other company, in fact, has a history of creating and promoting highly successful computer architectures. Yet successful architecture has not always led to business success. When they succeeded, as in the IBM System/360, they made IBM one of the world's most valuable companies; when they failed, as was eventually the case in IBM's PC business, their successful PC *architecture* still spawned some of the world's most valuable companies. Whatever one wants to say about IBM's corporate culture—as with any stereotype, the company's reputation for blue suits, white shirts, and conformity has some truth to it—when it comes to computer design, IBM has been among the most aggressive computer companies in the world. And on a number of notable occasions, IBM has quite literally rolled the dice and bet the company in the pursuit of simplicity.

SYSTEM/360: THE SPREAD TASK GROUP

In 1960, as computing technology was moving away from vacuum tubes, IBM was offering customers a choice of eight computers (1620, 1401, 1410, 7070, 7074, 7080, 7090, and the Stretch/7030 "supercomputer"), all based on the then state-of-the-art transistor circuit technology. Each of the eight lines targeted specific applications and customers—schools, businesses, scientists, or the government—with no common design and no shared road map for the future. Since only two pairs of machines were compatible, that meant the company was supporting six distinct technology families, which overlapped with each other in one way or another. While each of the lines also had a successor product plan in the works, no one had given much thought to the problem of product proliferation. Although most of the managers within IBM's key operating groups saw little in common between their individual struggles, a few key executives at the group level saw this unconstrained march into product and application complexity as a disaster in the making. Donald Spaulding, the chief of staff for the group executive in charge of these divisions, remarked at the time, "If we implement all this . . . we are going to wind up with chaos, even more chaos than we have today."

And make no mistake: the increasing complexity of the product line spelled big trouble for IBM and its customers. Redundant product development efforts across the eight lines raised costs everywhere in subtle ways, as customer training, sales, and service personnel training resources had to be dedicated (and duplicated) for each product. Software programs written for one machine couldn't be used on the others. Peripheral equipment for each line could serve only that line's customers and applications. Product complexity would also hit customers every time they outgrew a system and needed to move to a more powerful machine: since none of the low-end products were compatible with the high-end products, customers were forced to start from scratch with each major upgrade.

Aside from these obvious problems, there were actually some very good reasons for the complexity. By providing so many different designs, IBM could closely meet the needs of each narrowly defined customer group without forcing them to accept the inevitable trade-offs that would arise under a common platform. Since computer memory and processing power was expensive, each design team worked hard to squeeze value out of every penny of computing power and give the customer exactly what they needed, nothing more or less. In practice, however, this meant maintaining widely different platforms up and down the product line.

Inevitably, the technical tensions between markets turned into a political battle, where divisions were pitted against each other and the division managers lined up against the group executives. In 1961, the two main product groups, the General Products Division (GPD) and the Data Systems Division (DSD), reported to a single group executive named Vince Learson. GPD was based in Endicott, New York, and produced lower-performance designs for both business and scientific customers. John Haanstra, the head of GPD, was a prominent advocate of divisional autonomy and a natural opponent of a simplification effort. His division already had a product line that enjoyed unusually high volume and profits, making it "fat, dumb, and happy," according to one insider. Its business products like the transistor-based 1401/1410 models and the vacuum tube–based 650 models, each of which had broken records in the marketplace for unit volume, were particularly profitable. From Learson's perspective, major product overhauls, especially if they involved complex and risky transitions from old to new lines, would put the group's sterling profit performance at risk.

The situation at DSD, which was based in Poughkeepsie, New York, was different. With a bewildering array of incompatible products in their 7000 series (to say nothing of the fragmented customer priorities and multiple development plans), DSD's key leaders had long seen the need for product line simplification, at least when it came to the high-end products that were within the division's authority.

In 1959, a committee headed up by a young engineer named Fred Brooks issued a sweeping set of recommendations for a DSD product line rationalization. Brooks's committee made the case for a completely new DSD line, one that would still be based on transistor technology but would replace the entire 7000 series of products with a single product family that would for the first time have upward—but not downward—compatibility. In other words, customers who traded up to more expensive equipment could run programs from the cheaper equipment on their new machine, but not the other way around. The new family was to be called the 8000 series. While the 8000 series concept gained wide support from both inside and outside the division, only the approval of one constituent mattered in the end, Vice President Learson. And Learson was a skeptic. After listening to Brooks's eloquent and passionate case for the 8000 series, Learson promptly replaced the head of DSD product development, Brooks's old sponsor, with an engineering manager from GPD named Bob Evans.

Learson gave Evans the task of figuring out whether his skepticism about the 8000 series idea made sense. Learson was particularly concerned about making such a large commitment to a transistor-based line when the next generation of computing power based on integrated circuit technology was only a couple of years down the road. In addition, Don Spaulding had just issued a lengthy memo spelling out the case for a more drastic and corporate-wide simplification strategy. Before long, Evans also became convinced of the value of a simpler corporate standard, and he too became a determined opponent of the 8000 series. In his new role, he became both Brooks's boss and his debating partner. In the meantime, Brooks had emerged as the leading spokesman within IBM for the popular 8000 series plan and, as a result, the two men soon found themselves on opposing sides of a great debate.

Evans and Brooks, in fact, carried on what was by all accounts a knock-down, drag-out fight over Brooks's plan for a unified DSD product strategy through the early months of 1961. Brooks won the first round with an effective March presentation to the Corporate Management Committee. But again, Learson replaced the top DSD development manager and, in turn, the new head agreed with Evans. In May, Learson ended the fight with a clear top-down decision; he terminated the 8000 project and asked Evans to go back to the drawing board to develop an entirely new strategy.

On May 15, Evans announced the death of the 8000 project in a dramatic gathering of the entire 8000 series project team. In the words of a participant, "There was blood all over the floor." Evans, however, was magnanimous in victory. He had developed an abiding respect for his sparring partner, Brooks, who had proven himself to be a worthy opponent in corporate infighting over the prior months; Evans recognized that Brooks was, in fact, a true architectural visionary. So as Evans turned to his marching orders from Learson, his first move was to ask Brooks to lead the task force that would develop "the NPL," IBM-speak for "the new product line."

Today, as a practicing professor of computer science and a vigorous septuagenarian, Fred Brooks is living proof that merely working for IBM doesn't mean you have to be dull. A brilliant engineer, Brooks, along with Evans and a third IBM colleague, won the National Technology Medal for their work on the 360. He also wrote a well-known and witty book on software project management called *The Mythical Man-Month*. Brooks's analysis of the problem of software project management is most remembered for his wry observations on the futility of clumsy managerial intervention—"The bearing of a child takes nine months, no matter how many women are assigned. Many software tasks have this characteristic"— but Brooks wrote the book in order to share some of his hard-learned lessons from leading the 360 project. Brooks sees one of his lasting contributions as the insight about the importance of the concept of architecture in guiding the work of computer designers. His magnum opus, *Computer Architecture: Concept and Evolution*, was published in 1997 and runs more than 1,200 pages long.

But the experience that shaped his life's work almost didn't happen. Despite winning Evans's respect and receiving his exciting new assignment, Brooks wasn't able to move quickly into his new role for quite some time because the corporate indecision (and infighting) over the NPL continued for months. It wasn't until November 1961 that the seas of the stalemate parted. Learson, at Spaulding's urging, convened another committee to tackle the product simplification problem. This time Learson got all the key players involved from the start. Haanstra, Evans, Brooks, and ten others were allocated to a new effort that was dubbed the SPREAD project. At the time, SPREAD stood for *Systems Programming Research Engineering and Development,* but over time the acronym took on a different meaning, as *Spaulding's Plan to Reorganize Each and All Divisions.* This group of a dozen IBMers were, almost literally, locked in a hotel conference room near Stamford, Connecticut, and told not to return to their jobs until they had a solution to the product line complexity problem. They didn't leave that room for almost two months.

The result of the group's work—"The Final Report of the SPREAD Task Group, December 28, 1961"—has become something of a classic in industry circles. The document lays out the ground rules for one of the most revolutionary product architectures ever devised, the System/360. Named for its 360-degree market coverage, the new architecture was positioned as both a next-generation design as well as a truly general-purpose machine that could serve every market segment with integrated circuit technology. In order to do this effectively, the 360 design team had to adopt a set of architectural ground rules that would make the product lines compatible in two ways, both *upward* and *downward*. IBM's customers were, for the first time, able to upgrade to a new computer without sacrificing the data and programs developed for their old machines; they could also now add new equipment (including peripheral equipment) of any type and at any size level they chose without worrying about whether it would fit in with the rest of their computing investments. These customers could make such complex investment decisions with far greater confidence that IBM would service and support their installation as far into the future as they needed.

The "ground rules" that the SPREAD team (and later groups) developed made all of this compatibility possible. The level of technical detail the product planners had to specify was quite remarkable, but perhaps because of their hard work the standards they developed lived on. For example, the decision to set the basic unit of measure in computing, the *byte*, at eight binary digits (or bits), was made by the SPREAD team, which considered six-, seven-, and twelve-bit alternatives. This decision and the many others that emerged out of the intense discussions during the design process set the standards that define mainframe computing to this day. IBM's current flagship mainframe computer, called the zSeries, can still run programs developed for the System/360.

The pervasive compatibility that defined the 360 came at a cost, however. From the top to the bottom of the line, the architecture had to support competitive performance at memory sizes ranging from 8K to 512K (yes, that was the size of *mainframe* memory in 1964) and a "performance range factor of 50." Compatibility also came with market risk, for as the SPREAD report noted, "IBM compatibility may encourage competition to be compatible with us, in order to tap our support efforts."

Compatibility required technical breakthroughs as well. In order to make downward compatibility possible, the 360 designers came up with the idea of keeping the hardware cheap and simple by converting hardwired processor routines into software, or "microcode," and then storing these software instructions in read-only memory (ROM). This sacrificed some computing power at the high end of the line, and created some competitive vulnerability, but it was a crucial technology choice that made compatibility feasible.

Meanwhile, the internal political outcome was by no means certain. Although Haanstra was nominally the chair of the SPREAD committee, he withdrew midway through the process. And over the next few years, according to Brooks, "his dubiosity became animosity. Completely." Haanstra did everything he could to retain a separate GPD product line. It wasn't until January of 1964, in a dramatic three-day showdown (just a few months before the planned announcement of System/360!), that matters finally came to a head. After an intense argument, the 360 concept finally won the day. According to Brooks, Haanstra didn't even show up for the third day of the meeting.

Haanstra was replaced as GPD head in March; he soon left IBM for General Electric.

The System/360 was a huge financial success for IBM. Over the next five years, the company's revenues and profits doubled as their market capitalization reached historic heights. Although the relative openness of their architecture created some competitive risk, they entered the 1970s as the unquestioned leader of the information technology industry, just as the next generation of computing technology, the microprocessor, was about to change the competitive landscape yet again.

THE IBM PC: PROJECT CHESS AND THE ACORN

By the late 1970s, IBM found itself facing an even greater challenge to its leadership in the computer industry—the first truly usable microprocessor, the Intel 8080. The rise of relatively inexpensive computing power in the form of the microprocessor had brought substantial computing power within reach of the individual user. This new technology inspired many enthusiastic computer engineers to consider the possibility of doing something no one could have ever considered before—bringing computers out of the corporate data center and into the home.

Ed Roberts was one of these engineers. Roberts had been running a calculator company named Micro Instrumentation and Telemetry Systems (MITS, for short), and was the first inventor to put Intel's 8080 microprocessor in a small housing box designed for home use. He called his contraption the Altair 8800.

When a picture of Roberts's revolutionary design appeared on the cover of *Popular Electronics* magazine in January 1975 ("The Home Computer Is Here," exclaimed an accompanying editorial), he electrified the computer hobbyist world. Most notably, the magazine cover caught the attention of a young college dropout named Paul Allen as he was walking through Harvard Square. Allen, who was working with his high school friend Bill Gates, then a Harvard freshman, to get into the computer-language business, immediately saw the importance of Roberts's invention. He literally ran across campus to show Gates the magazine, exclaiming that MITS was the ideal customer to help them break into the business. They recognized that Roberts might be hungry for a stripped-down version of the BASIC programming language, originally developed at Dartmouth College and widely used in minicomputers. "So we called this guy Ed Roberts," Gates later recalled. "We said, 'We have a BASIC, do you want it?'"

Roberts may have announced a revolution in home computing but he hadn't thought much about software. In fact, he desperately needed a programming language and other software for the Altair 8800 and, as a result, he agreed to listen to the young men's pitch. Six weeks later, when Allen and Gates flew down to meet with Roberts in Albuquerque, New Mexico, they had actually put together a functioning BASIC and successfully demonstrated to Roberts that it would work on his machine. Roberts immediately hired Allen as MITS's director of software, and Gates moved with him to MITS headquarters. Together Gates and Allen developed software for Roberts's new machine, including a BASIC interpreter, a FORTRAN compiler, and a primitive "disc operating system" called MITS-DOS.

But Roberts's announcement electrified more computer enthusiasts than just Gates and Allen. The Altair 8800 inspired a host of imitators, including the Commodore PET (April 1977) and the Atari 400/800 models (December 1978). The breakthrough design, however, came from two young Californians named Steve Wozniak and Steve Jobs, and was announced in April 1977 at the West Cost Computer Fair. It was called the Apple II, and soon became a top seller.

And it wasn't just the new class of computer entrepreneurs who began to take note of this emerging product category. One of the most interested observers was Bill Lowe, an executive in IBM's Entry Level Systems (ELS) unit, based in Boca Raton, Florida. Although IBM remained focused on the corporate market with the successors of the System/360 product line, its managers recognized that their corporate customers were interested in *desktop* computers as well. In fact, in September 1975, only a few months after Roberts announced the Altair 8800, IBM introduced the IBM 5100, a portable desktop computer that could link up with the System/370 (the successor to the 360) and fit into a suitcase. While it was a move in the right direction, the 5100 unfortunately lacked the power of a real Intel-style microprocessor. As a result, it didn't sell. When he stepped into his new role overseeing these so-called entry-level systems, Lowe quickly realized that, although IBM might have some big opportunities in the desktop market, the right design for this new application probably required a sharper departure from the corporate standard than the poorly-performing 5100 line.

So Lowe and his team spent time learning about the market. He spoke to retailers who said they would love to sell an IBM PC to consumers. But these retailers cautioned Lowe that IBM would never succeed if they approached the desktop and home markets the way they approached "big iron," a nickname used to describe IBM mainframes. IBM couldn't count on their large staff of maintenance engineers to do consumer repair work. Instead, the PC would have to be based on simple, standard parts—simple enough so that retail store employees could service the PC themselves. And with designs like the Apple II, the Commodore PET, and the TRS-80 gaining marketplace momentum, Lowe worried that IBM might already be too late.

Lowe concluded that IBM was going to have to take some shortcuts if they wanted to get in on the action. As he juggled a number of possible strategy options in his head, Lowe took his emerging diagnosis of the market situation to IBM's corporate headquarters in Armonk, New York, in early July 1980. In his presentation, Lowe made the case that trying to develop a true "entry level" product while working within the normal IBM bureaucracy would take far too long. Instead, he discussed some alternatives to approaching the market, including the idea that IBM could buy Atari to enter the market quickly. The acquisition idea didn't go over well, but the overall message was received loud and clear, particularly by Frank Cary, IBM's CEO. Cary told Lowe to come back in two weeks with a crash plan to get a product to market within a year. The initiative was codenamed *Project Chess* and the new computer was christened the *Acorn*.

Lowe returned to Boca Raton and began recruiting a team of IBMers for the endeavor. Like the SPREAD Group, there were a dozen members of the team, and they started calling themselves "The Dirty Dozen." As the team began their brainstorming sessions, they quickly realized that if they were to meet their one-year target date and gain the market acceptance they hoped for at the same time, they would need to use proven technology as a foundation. Basically, they would need to devise the simplest kind of assembly possible, relying almost entirely on off-the-shelf components and on what the team called "an open architecture." The team moved quickly to reach out to some of the suppliers they'd need to enlist to provide those components, even calling suppliers before their design had received final approval. (Interestingly, one of their first calls was to Bill Gates, who was now heading up his own fledgling company, Microsoft.) The team then began interviewing Gates and other software vendors the following week.

The Project Chess team focused on the Intel 8088 as their processor of choice from the start. While the 8088 wasn't as technically advanced as some of the other options, and wasn't even the best Intel had to offer, IBM wasn't looking for the state of the art. Following their market intelligence, they merely wanted something cheap and reliable at the core of their hardware assembly. Like Roberts, they also knew they would need languages and other software. When they called Microsoft, they asked about the computer language that Allen and Gates had first developed for MITS. When they called Gates a second time, they asked him if he had an operating system, too. He referred them to another software company, Digital Research, a company that had supplied the operating system—CP/M (for Control Program/Microprocessor)—used by most of the industry to that point. When he learned that IBM's meeting with Digital Research didn't go very well, Gates stepped into the breach. Microsoft could meet the full range of IBM's software needs, Gates promised. He then quickly began looking around for any operating system he could get his hands on.

On August 8, 1980, Lowe took his plan for the Acorn back to Armonk. His presentation, which reflected the Boca Raton team's emphasis on speed, described the architecture of their emerging design. The proposed architecture is shown in Figure 14, a faithful reproduction of the original chart: font styles, layout, symbols, and all. The project team clearly described the architecture as "open," but there was one notable exception, the "IBM hardware." Unfortunately for IBM, Lowe didn't have a clear idea of what that meant. Most of what would go inside the box would be off-the-shelf electronics, as the truly proprietary hardware would eventually boil down to a single chip. At the time, though, that all seemed like a minor detail. IBM knew they needed to outsource everything to get to market on schedule and that their open-architecture design would give them a leg up in the competition to attract software developers needed to write applications for their new design. In Lowe's mind, the more open the architecture the better, an idea his bosses agreed with. Lowe's pitch, as a result, was successful and the Project Chess team got the green light to go forward.

On August 12, 1981, almost a year to the day after Lowe presented his visionary plan to his bosses in Armonk, IBM announced its new product to the world. No longer called the Acorn, it was, in an ode to minimalism, called the IBM PC. The product, due to its simplicity however, received mixed reviews from the technical

FIGURE 14 The Original Architecture Plan for the IBM PC

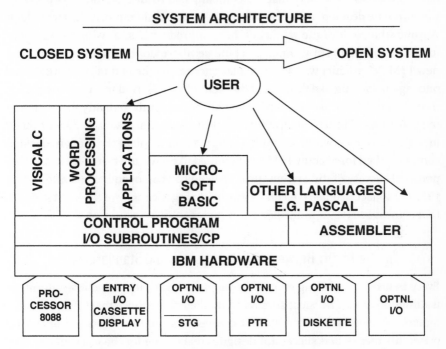

Source: *Triumph of the Nerds: An Irreverent History of the PC Industry* (New York: Ambrose Video Publishing, 1996).

press. Many complained that the IBM PC wasn't a particularly innovative design or a very powerful machine, or that it was based on outdated technology. All of which was true—but basically beside the point. The overriding concern of Lowe's team was to get a product out there before the market momentum got away from them. Most important, IBM hoped that its open architecture and sterling reputation would change the basis of competition in the industry; instead of looking at just hardware, customers would now be enticed by the broader range of software applications they could get along with their brand-new IBM box. A more open architecture would also encourage software developers to write applications for the IBM PC at a faster rate than the competition. On this point, the Project Chess team got it right. Before long, a torrent of software, including office productivity stalwarts like Lotus 1-2-3 and Microsoft Word, was developed for the new IBM architecture.

The most important thing the PC accomplished, though, was that it convinced IBM's business customers that the company had made a serious move toward the corporate desktop using the latest generation of microprocessor technology. Anyone who doubted the validity of the new product class or who was reluctant to use this newfangled technology could set those doubts aside, however. The new IBM PC product was a spectacular success. By the end of 1984, IBM was, once again, looking like the king of the technology hill. And in a way it was. Contrary to the Silicon Valley–centric view of the computer industry enshrined in most histories of the personal computer, it was really Bill Lowe's design, unveiled in that August meeting in Armonk, that set the standard for the modern desktop computer. And for a while, IBM's PC seemed like a worthy follow-up to the phenomenal success of the System/360. The choice of an open architecture for the IBM PC, in fact, seemed well on its way to joining the roster of the most successful business strategies in the history of the world.

The Trade-Off Between Differentiation and Standardization

Every first-year marketing student learns that the key to competitive advantage is differentiation. The most successful marketers are those that offer their customers value and features that their competitors can't match. Short of cutting price, this means that successful designs create value for the customer as they use the design, with features that solve problems in ways that can't be copied.

Every first-year operations student, on the other hand, learns, in a similar fashion, that the marketer's instincts for differentiation can be expensive. As a result, realistic executives force real-world designers to moderate their approach to differentiation by constraining them with sets of standards and rules. The economics of working with standardized parts, even if they're not perfect for the job, often outweigh the benefits of the customized component. As an end result, good design finds the economic sweet spot between the Model T designs ("you can have any color, as long as it's black") and a level of customization only the rich can afford. But in the middle of this tension between the chaos and customer value of differentiation, between the straitjacket and conceptual clarity of simplification, is where designers, the Fred Brookses or the Bill Lowes of the world, sit. The designer's seat is a position of surprising power. As the master of architecture, he also becomes the master of business strategy, for in a fundamental way, choosing an architecture is often the economic equivalent of choosing a strategy.

To demonstrate both the business value of simplification and what it actually means to a designer, let's turn to a visual for help. Figures 15 and 16 are before-

and-after pictures—two versions of a software product now known as Mozilla, but more recognizable in the corporate world under the name of Netscape, the original Internet browser. First introduced in 1994 by Netscape Communicator Company (another Jim Clark effort to become the "asshole in the middle"), the Netscape Navigator browser took the computer world by storm and was one of the most critical pieces that contributed to the Internet boom of the late 1990s. Indeed, it was such a central part of the emerging Internet software suite that Microsoft decided to develop its own product, Internet Explorer, to attack Netscape. They then bundled Explorer together with Windows 95, its operating system, effectively giving the browser component away for free with any Windows purchase. Not surprisingly, by 1998 Netscape's business was in deep trouble, losing market share at a rate of close to 2 percent per month. As a final Hail Mary pass, Netscape turned Navigator into an open-source project called Mozilla. But much to the surprise of the open-source proponents, who predicted that the Mozilla project would become a magnet for developers, when Netscape opened up the code base something weird happened: very few volunteers showed up. For most of the rest of 1998, there was very little progress made to the code base, and the browser's market share continued to plummet. (In the meantime, Netscape was acquired by AOL and eventually disbanded in 2003.)

Figure 15 shows why the Mozilla design failed to attract open-source developers. The software architecture was a complicated mess, a tangle of interconnected files and long-distance "function calls" that developers typically call "spaghetti code." Even those developers who might have been willing to contribute to an open-source browser project couldn't find a way to get started. The software had so many interdependencies built into it that a change in one place might ripple to literally dozens of other parts of the system. For a new developer trying to contribute to the project, there was no way to do anything without running the risk of screwing the whole thing up. Even the most skilled developers couldn't find a way to get up to speed. The Mozilla open-source project seemed destined for the same ill-fated end as Netscape Navigator, this time for entirely architectural reasons.

Into the breach stepped Brendan Eich, chief architect of the newly formed project. He realized that Mozilla needed a fundamental redesign (what software programmers call "refactoring"). So he organized a team of three developers and went to work. He took one big hunk of the code that was a repository of miscellaneous functions and broke it down into smaller pieces, separating numerous libraries of data from networking functions and other add-ons. He then changed out one major component (the "rendering engine") and replaced it with a more established component called "Gecko" (where do these guys come up with these

FIGURE 15 Simplifying Mozilla by Shifting from an Integral to a Modular Architecture: Before refactoring (April 8, 1998)

Source: Adapted from Alan MacCormack, John Rusnak, and Carliss Y. Baldwin, 2006.

names?). Eich imposed a set of standards and protocols for how files together and then developed a road map of planned additions that would improve the browser's function over time. He also incorporated a number of features designed to make it easier for outside coders to participate. And when his team was finished refactoring, the result was the vastly simpler design shown in Figure 16. What had originally failed as both a business and a collaboration had been

FIGURE 16   Simplifying Mozilla by Shifting from an Integral to a Modular Architecture:
             After refactoring (December 11, 1998)

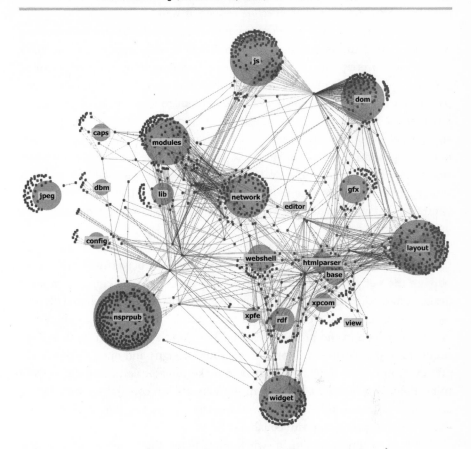

Source: Adapted from Alan MacCormack, John Rusnak, and Carliss Y. Baldwin, 2006.

transformed and revitalized. Intrigued, volunteer developers soon took notice of
Eich's work.

Over the next several years, the tide began to turn for Mozilla. The new code
base started to attract a meaningful design community. A loyal user base emerged
as market share for Internet Explorer began to peak. And as the Mozilla software
got better and better, the development community supporting it grew larger still.
In 2004, the newly branded version of Mozilla, now named Firefox, began winning design awards for "best browser." And in 2005, Internet Explorer's market
share dipped below 90 percent for the first time since 2000. By 2007, Mozilla's

Firefox global market share had grown to about 15 percent, which provides a remarkable testimony to the idea that an open-source licensing strategy will succeed only if the underlying *architecture* is open as well.

It's worth pausing for a moment to consider the word *open*. It's an appealing word, of course. And as a result, the "open" label has today been appropriated for use in many overlapping and (often) confusing applications. Openness can be used as a synonym for many desirable attributes, ranging from liquid and transparent marketplaces to publicly available content to zero royalty licensing arrangements to aggressively modular product designs. The word *open* has significance in both architecture and IP. In its architectural sense, open has come to mean *aggressively modular:* as in the "open architecture" of the refactored version of Firefox. When it comes to IP, open means *publicly available* as in "open source," or *nonproprietary* as in "open standard." As we shall see, the false assumption that open architecture and open IP must go together can lead to serious strategic blunders.

Most successful simplification strategies rely heavily on open architecture. Choosing an open over a closed architecture provides a powerful lever for simplifying the network of business interactions that support a complex product design, often called the ecosystem. The reason for this is simple: Integral designs require intense business collaboration that matches the functional interdependency embedded in the product design. They don't easily accommodate large numbers of participants. By contrast, modular designs and open architectures give everyone in the industry a chance to make valuable contributions, yet still mind their own business. Ecosystem participants are constrained only by the architectural ground rules laid out in the design and not by the social overhead that inevitably goes along with collaboration.

Rather than simply flipping a switch, making the choice between an integral or modular design usually requires selecting a position along the continuum between open and closed architectures. At one extreme are designs that are completely open; that is, the most aggressively modular structures. These extreme designs share three features: (1) they are cleanly *componentized*, with relatively few interconnections between components, (2) all the components are highly *compatible* (both upward and downward) with clear standards for the architectural family that make it possible for users to reconfigure components as they like, and (3) their functional elements are expected to be *convertible* so that they are usable in later generations (i.e., they are backward compatible) of the same architectural family.

By contrast, the most completely closed (or *integral*) designs represent the polar opposite. Instead of crisply separate components, closed architectures are made up of clusters of functions that are closely integrated and connected together at many points. Instead of being compatible with other components, closed architectures emphasize their unique attributes and make it hard or even impossible to construct interfaces with the design. And instead of convertibility over time, closed architectures typically promise little in terms of an upgrade path; closed designs tend to be far more disposable. In between the two extremes, though, lies a wide array of options.

Choosing between an open and a closed design means making a strategic choice between differentiation and standardization. Open architectures depend on clear standards to make it easier for multiple participants in a business system to contribute while working independently. Closed designs, on the other hand, can give a single design group the ability to create a much more tightly controlled, and therefore differentiated, user experience. While choosing the architectural strategy that will lead to a superior result is rarely obvious, successful simplification strategies usually require a commitment to standards of one kind or another.

One important strategic option that lies in the middle is particularly worth noting. This is the more limited form of modularity, where a relatively modular structure exists for peripheral components and applications, but also where all of these add-on modules are built around a single, and highly integrated, central component. In many industries, these central components are called *platforms* (some academics also call this architecture "bus modularity"), and successful examples of this architecture are quite common. Examples include Windows and Intel's position in the PC, Harley-Davidson's "custom Harley" motorcycles, and even track lighting. The greatest strategic value of platform architectures often results from technologies with a rapidly changing architecture that frequently add new components, one on top of the other. This pattern is commonly known as a *technology stack*. The main integral component in a technology stack has a huge amount of power both because it occupies a central position in the architecture and because it enables (and constrains) further rapid development of new modules.

The debate over whether an open or a closed strategy (or something in between) will work best is one of the longest-standing debates in business. Once you understand the competing design strategies, you can see how the debate recurs in many forms. In the early days of the mainframe, for instance, it took the shape of the struggle between IBM's Evans (the componentized and compatible System/360) and Haanstra (the closed and unique 1401 series). In the automotive industry, the same debate has raged for decades, only using a different language. The advocates of integral design in the auto business style themselves as "car guys" in the image of Lee Iacocca; they dream of designing and marketing highly distinctive vehicles like the Ford Mustang and the Chrysler minivan. At the other end of the spectrum stand the "whiz kids" from finance who pride themselves on their sophisticated financial analysis and push hard to save money by sharing components across multiple vehicle lines, even in "world cars" like the aptly named Ford Mondeo. Similarly, the open architecture of the IBM PC stood in stark contrast to the closed system of Apple's Macintosh design, which though widely recognized as having a superior user experience, was surpassed in the marketplace because of the PC's open architecture. Indeed, Steve Jobs may well be the technology world's most successful and charismatic advocate of relatively closed, integral designs (an advocacy that continues to unfold today in the form of the iPhone).

The debates between open and closed architectures often go on for years before the debaters ever account for a second dimension, the IP dimension. While both open and closed architectures can yield elegant designs that produce enormous value for their customers and partners, the value that a company can capture is critically connected, sometimes in surprising ways, to the choices they make regarding what parts of the design they actually own and can protect. Smart strategists don't assume that open architecture means open IP, but too many strategists don't even consider the IP question when setting their architecture strategies, or else they consider it too late.

TALE OF TWO ARCHITECTURES
Part 2: Control Programs, BDOS, and BIOS

The commercial life of the IBM System/360 family has continued far longer than its designers could have ever imagined. The top-selling IBM zSeries line remains 360 compatible while the 360 family has become synonymous with the category of what we all now call the "mainframe" computer. The mainframe market has continued to prosper, in spite of the desktop computer revolution, as demand for high-powered computing and networking applications continues to soar. Although IBM faces a fair amount of competition in high-end computing—from UNIX- and Linux-based operating systems, from Fujitsu and Hewlett-Packard mainframes, and from Cray and Sun supercomputers—Big Blue has retained its hold on the market for "big iron." It owes its continued competitiveness in this market almost entirely to its IP.

Although the 360's architecture was open—componentized, upward and downward compatible, and convertible through time—the basic design was protected from its very beginning. On April 6, 1964, the day before the grand announcement of the 360 line, IBM filed a patent application for a "data processing system." The invention was the collaborative effort of sixteen inventors, including the two chief hardware architects, Gene Amdahl and Gerrit Blaauw. And the end result of all their work, U.S. Patent No. 3,400,371, was a massive document; a total of 964 pages made up of 495 pages of engineering drawings and 131 claims. Not only was the document physically impressive—it bestowed some powerful protection on the visionary new design.

The compatibility features of the 360 line, though, created opportunities for focused competitors to target specific functions and develop competitive component designs of their own. As early as 1967, in fact, employees in IBM's San Jose lab started defecting to develop 360-compatible designs. In 1968 Memorex, for instance, shipped the world's first 360-compatible disk drives. They were soon followed by a large group of new participants who entered the market for providing input/output devices (storage, printers, displays), which created some unwanted competition for IBM in a high-stakes, big-revenue business. "The I/O devices could make up half the revenue of an installation," noted Brooks.

Due in large part to its open architecture, IBM also started to see competition from "clones," products with different *component technology* but that were otherwise compatible with the 360 *architecture* in every way. In fact, the chief architect of the 360, Gene Amdahl, launched the IBM 360's toughest competitor. Amdahl, who left IBM in 1970 after continued disputes over the direction of the technology, founded the Amdahl Corporation, a company that made 360-compatible mainframes, including the Amdahl 470 V6, which debuted in 1975. Amdahl's success, Brooks said, was largely due to the fact that "he was not tempted to deviate from the architecture" in any way. Other companies, most notably RCA with its Spectra 70 line, tried to introduce largely compatible products. But because they deviated from strict compatibility, and tried to sell a competing operating system, programs developed for their competing lines were only partly interchangeable with the 360. By contrast, Amdahl understood the power of compatibility. He also understood that he could poach high-end users with products unconstrained by the requirement of downward compatibility. As a result, his products went right for the top end of the market. Amdahl Corp. remained a viable competitor in the IBM-compatible mainframe business for some twenty-five years until it finally decided to exit the market in 2000.

Although competitors continued to compete with IBM's mainframes at the component and system level, they could never supplant the 360 and its successor machines from its market-leading position; IBM's proprietary technology position was always too strong. Indeed, for many years there was no effective competition whatsoever for one of the 360's most critical components, its operating system, dubbed the OS/360. Though it was delivered months behind schedule and millions over budget, the OS/360 was nevertheless among the first of its breed and gave IBM an unassailable position of control over the 360's architecture. To some degree, IBM benefited from a first-mover advantage (the OS/360 was only the second program actually *named* an operating system; most similar efforts had been dubbed "control programs") and was a truly pioneering effort. The company also benefited from barriers to entry, since the amount of upfront investment needed in programming time alone made the OS/360 virtually impossible to duplicate. As Fred Brooks later remarked, "We spent nearly $400 million on OS/360. That's in 1964 dollars."

It was for many reasons, therefore, that IBM retained enough ownership rights in the key pieces of the 360's architecture to retain their competitive advantage and to turn it into a successful business.

By contrast, the PC no longer has the IBM name attached to it. In some ways, Bill Lowe's architecture for his desktop box wasn't all that different from Amdahl, Blaauw, and Brooks's design. Both architectures were deliberately open and modular. Both took calculated competitive risks. Yet in the case of System/360, IBM was able to capture enough value to justify its massive investment. With the PC, despite its early success, this was clearly not the case. What's the difference between these two architectural tales, then? It's quite simple. The rise and fall of IBM in the PC business can be traced directly to the joint architecture and IP decisions they made in the early days. To get a visual understanding of this, all most of us have to do is simply start our computer.

Using the computer that's recording these keystrokes as an example, four names come up shortly after you press the power key. Three of them, Intel, Microsoft, and Vaio (from Sony), are household names. The fourth name, Phoenix Technologies, however, is more of a mystery. But the role that Phoenix Software Associates (the name they went by in the early 1980s) played in the downfall of IBM's PC business is one of the least appreciated episodes in modern business history. Getting some context on this largely forgotten story requires a quick step back in order to zoom in on the architectural details of Bill Lowe's original design.

The invention of the microprocessor, as we know, made it possible for an individual to have his or her own computer in a box. But the first such machines didn't do much; they were, quite literally, a microprocessor (the Intel 8080 chip) in a box. Computer manufacturers needed to add a number of other components before they had a real PC, things like: user input/output devices (the keyboard and monitor), computer languages (the earliest version was the BASIC written by Bill Gates and Paul Allen for Ed Roberts), and a usable form of memory that enabled someone to store and retrieve files (an IBM engineer named Alan Shugart created the first floppy disk). Once you had the microprocessor and the memory, you then needed an additional program to control the operations of the computer. This component was labeled inconsistently at the start of the PC, though, and while the term "operating system" was more widely used by the mid-1970s, it was still not recognized as the critical component we now understand it to be.

The inventor of the first operating system for microprocessor-based computing was Gary Kildall. In 1973, Kildall, who had consulted for Intel, saw one of Shugart's floppy disks and wrote the first version of CP/M (for Control Program/ Microcomputers) to handle the link between the disk drive and an early computer he was working on. In 1976, he set up a full-time consulting business called Intergalactic Digital Research (he later went more corporate and shortened the company name to Digital Research) and soon found that the rise in demand for floppy disk drives was creating a new demand for his CP/M software.

As that demand grew, driven by a wide variety of machines all using different architectures and specifications, Kildall made a historic design choice. He decided to make his CP/M program "machine independent" and separated his original program into components to make that possible. The two most critical components were the "basic input/output system," BIOS for short, and the "basic disc operating system," which he called BDOS. BDOS was the larger component of the two due to its larger role in the architecture and carried most of the control program workload; BDOS was both the functional and appellative ancestor of the today's PC operating systems. BIOS, by contrast, was a smaller bit of computer code that handled a narrower function; it managed the link between the specific computer hardware and the rest of Kildall's control program. Before long, hundreds of systems relied on BIOS connections to CP/M, including products like the Altair 8800, the IMSAI 8080, the Commodore 128, and the Osborne I.

Interestingly, most histories of the PC, and the fortune that Gates and others made from it, neglect to mention the machine's *architectural* origins, leaving Kildall's key components, the BDOS and BIOS twins, completely out of the story. The BDOS code was the direct ancestor of the MS-DOS, that bit of borrowed code on which the house of Microsoft is built. Few people know however that its sister component, BIOS, played the key role in sealing the fate of IBM's PC business. At the time, though, both components had a bit more evolving to do before their strategic importance became apparent.

By 1975, Digital Research had built a nice little business adapting CP/M for the emerging home computers that followed the Altair. As a result, Kildall and his team were having a bit of trouble keeping up with demand. New hardware developments were always a cause for changes and updates, especially when they involved the microprocessor. When Intel introduced their 8086 microprocessor line, and computer makers raced to get a technology edge based on the new chip, Digital Research found itself with a new surge of demand. When Kildall was slow to update his control program for the 8086, some of his eager customers got impatient and looked for ways to speed the process. In April 1980 one of those customers, Seattle Computer Products, assigned a programmer named Tim Paterson to develop a knockoff version of CP/M so they wouldn't have to wait for Kildall. Paterson completed the project in just four months, working half-time by himself.

Paterson's knockoff program wasn't intended to be a profound innovation. It was simply designed to be completely compatible with Kildall's architecture, with "all the same application-visible elements as CP/M—the function codes, the entry point address, part of the File Control Block layout, etc.," Paterson wrote in 1994. "I used the 1976 *CP/M Interface Guide* for my description of the requirements. I also provided some similar commands from the console—such as DIR, RENAME, ERASE—although any system would have such function, regardless of name chosen."

Paterson initially (and whimsically) named the knockoff QDOS, for "quick and dirty operating system." This is the name that most people remember as the first version of the most valuable software program ever written. Paterson's company soon renamed their commercial version 86-DOS after the Intel chip, and Seattle Computer Products began licensing it later that year. Although Paterson and SCP were able to create a knockoff of CP/M, Kildall and Digital Research were still the market leader. In fact, in the summer of 1980, Kildall was about to have a meeting with the Project Chess team from IBM, and the outcome of that meeting would change the world of computing forever.

Immediately following Bill Lowe's successful meetings in Armonk that set the future of the PC in motion, the Project Chess team was out beating the bushes for suppliers. After all, Lowe had promised IBM's CEO Frank Cary that they would have a product on the market within a year. So Lowe's team was rolling out their plan at breakneck speed. To get to market as fast as possible, they wanted

only off-the-shelf components, placing their bets on reliable and established technologies. Most important, though, and surprisingly, Lowe's team never paused
to patent any part of their original design. According to Lowe, they really had no
plan for anything specific and proprietary that they could put in the box called
"IBM Hardware" in Figure 14 (on page 197). Not only was the PC architecture
open, it was perilously close to being, from an IP standpoint, completely free.

Lowe's plan, out of necessity, was hasty but it was far from philanthropic. His
priority was to get his open-architecture product out into the market. Then once
he was in the game, he could upgrade, differentiate, and eventually protect the
IP covering these new IBM PC components over time. He certainly never planned
on keeping PC-DOS in place forever, for example, as he intended to upgrade
the operating system relatively quickly to what would eventually be known
as OS/2.

In reality, the architecture of the IBM PC wasn't quite as open as it seemed,
and it definitely wasn't free. As part of the original design, IBM included a solitary, yet relatively central component that was completely proprietary, the BIOS
chip (the code was embedded in read-only memory, or ROM, so the chip is most
precisely described as the PC ROM BIOS). This matched the customizable component of Kildall's CP/M architecture, yet was made up of copyright-protected
IBM source code. When IBM eventually bought the exclusive rights to PC-DOS
from Microsoft for a fixed fee of $200,000, it conceded the right to Microsoft to
license their own version of the operating system, MS-DOS, to anyone. While
IBM didn't own an operating system component—not BDOS, QDOS, 86-DOS,
or MS-DOS—in its revolutionary design, the company did ensure that it had clear
ownership rights to one key component, the read-only memory chip that contained the code for the PC ROM BIOS.

From the beginning, Lowe and his team were focused on using their open
architecture to gain industry acceptance. They wanted the IBM PC to have the
most attractive value proposition on the market. To do that, they worked hard to
find ways to promote the PC to software developers, peripheral product designers, and the broader computer industry. One way they did this was to use the PC
ROM BIOS code as a tool to lock in developers. In its *Technical Reference Manual*
for the PC, IBM told the world virtually everything it could possibly want to know
about its BIOS; in addition to detailed specifications, interfaces, and technical
schematics, IBM also published the full source code—all 5,940 lines of code in
an eighty-page appendix, the most proprietary component in the PC design.

Like the design of the architecture itself, publishing the code was a calculated
gamble. IBM knew that any programmer who so much as looked at the BIOS

code would violate the company's copyright if they attempted to write a competing program. At the same time, those source code listings were awfully tempting for any developer looking to connect his program efficiently to the PC hardware. By publishing the source code, therefore, IBM could simultaneously "contaminate" the developer world, reducing the pool of developers who could compete with their BIOS, while also stimulating application development by making it easy to write IBM PC software. This part of the strategy quickly succeeded, as developers flocked to write PC programs, quickly making the PC along with the IBM ROM BIOS a de facto standard. Application developers all over the industry soon adopted the BIOS formats, quirks and all.

There was a flip side to this risky strategy, however. Because it held no patents, (there were no software patents at the time) and chose to give up its trade secret rights through publication, IBM effectively based its entire protection strategy solely on the strength of its BIOS copyright. This was a bit like challenging the hacker world to a duel by saying, Copy this if you dare!

Unlike Paterson's knockoff of Kildall's CP/M design, the stakes this time were clear. As IBM's new product took off in the marketplace, there was ample opportunity for competitors to make products that were *compatible* with the IBM PC, but didn't also require them to purchase any components that were IBM proprietary. IBM-compatible PCs, known as *clones,* began to come out of the woodwork. As a result, the so-called clone wars began. IBM was soon under attack from all sides and a furious (and largely unnoticed) IP battle became the turning point in the competitive struggle.

IBM introduced its PC in August of 1981, and even before the first products shipped, start-up ventures were being launched to offer low-priced clones. The original Compaq clone was conceived in a brainstorming session in a Texas bar in the summer of 1981. Eagle Computer, another aspiring clone, was incorporated in May 1982. Columbia Data Products launched the first clone to get to market in June 1982, and Compaq's announcement followed shortly thereafter with their first clone, the portable PC, in November. By March of 1983, *PC World* listed twenty clones designed around Microsoft's MS-DOS operating system. And by November, a number of larger players like Panasonic, Sperry, and ITT had introduced clones of their own. In relatively short order, therefore, IBM was facing a fundamental challenge to their business.

IBM had been prepared to face off against *some* competition; indeed, they considered companies like Apple, Atari, and Commodore to be tough competitors from the get-go. The company was unprepared for these clones, however, as they hadn't counted on such a determined and systematic attack based on their own architecture. While they had embraced openness to encourage developers to write software, they had underestimated their own power to set a standard for the industry. So while Lowe had hoped for a window of time in which he could first establish position and then upgrade and differentiate the technology, IBM was completely unprepared for the implications of becoming a *standard;* that window was closing much faster than anyone had anticipated. Just two short years after its introduction, the IBM PC was being copied right and left. Whether or not IBM could stop this copying became an urgent issue.

After weighing its options throughout 1983, analyzing the uncertain legal landscape of the BIOS code copiers, IBM finally decided to launch an IP counterattack. Not all clones were the same, however. Some clones were less threatening because their "compatibility" was fairly limited. Others used BIOS versions that were quite obviously copies, and clearly illegal. IBM targeted these pirate machines first. In early 1984, and in relatively quick succession, they sued and shut down Corona Data Products, Eagle Computer, and Handwell (an importer of Taiwanese clones) for violating their copyright on the PC ROM BIOS chip.

But some of the other clones were not as easy to fight off. At the outset, Compaq was the most careful. Working closely with their attorneys, they devised a technique of reverse-engineering the BIOS code that became known as the "clean room" approach. A team of engineers worked with the published specification and source code listings to develop a manual of technical specifications for a cloned BIOS. This "contaminated" team (so named because any code they would write after reading the IBM BIOS listing would be an illegal form of copying) created a document of functional specification, a twenty-page paper of "software interrupts," storage locations, fixed addresses of subroutines, and other "oddball entry points," that they then passed along to a new engineer, allowing them to step out of the process. This new engineer needed to have a special qualification; he must not have ever seen or read the BIOS source code. If he hadn't, he was eligible to become a "virgin author" and could thus use the functional specifications to write a new program that was functionally identical to, but in no way a copy of, the IBM PC BIOS code. The initial line of Compaq portables was built around a BIOS produced by this clean-room technique, and unlike the more careless pirates, they were completely legal. Other clones, like the Columbia Data Products MPC 1600 and the Televideo TS-803, also followed the clean-room technique, and were as a result insulated from IBM's attacks as well.

"Legal" clones, like Compaq, Columbia, Televideo, and others, still faced an uphill battle against IBM, though. Each of these early clones had to design and build a complete computer to compete with IBM's PC. Most important, each had to go through the whole clean-room process on their own. This was a slow, risky, and uncertain business because the legal issues were still quite murky at the time. The CONTU (Commission on New Technological Uses of copyrighted works) legislation of 1978 had made it clear that software was protected under copyright laws, the legality of the reverse-engineering procedures in software had not been fully tested in court, and the general environment for protecting intellectual property rights in applications ranging from semiconductor chip masks to boat hulls was moving against the rights of the copiers/pirates. The clone makers were making a dent in IBM's defenses, but they hadn't yet stormed the gates.

A small company named Phoenix Software Associates (now Phoenix Technologies), though, found itself in a position to turn the tide against IBM once and for all. Phoenix's CEO, Neil Colvin, was a Harvard classmate of Bill Gates and got involved in Microsoft's 1981 roll-out of their new MS-DOS product. While Microsoft focused on the standard DOS component, they contracted with Colvin's company to do the custom work. Colvin would build a BIOS for every new hardware maker that Gates could persuade to use his MS-DOS product in their home or desktop computer designs. Indeed, Colvin and Phoenix were so critical to the success of MS-DOS that Colvin was the only non-Microsoft employee to accompany Gates on selling road shows. These early BIOS programs were not PC BIOS products, though, and therefore not yet clones. Phoenix was instead working entirely on building customized BIOS chips for the *noncompatible* designs of companies like Hewlett-Packard, Texas Instruments, and NCR/AT&T.

When the IBM PC–compatible designs became more popular, however, the Phoenix team saw the opportunity for a bigger business. Lance Hansche, Colvin's head of marketing, made the case for a much riskier play. He argued that there was a huge untapped market potential in a standard design for a PC ROM BIOS clone. Colvin, though, initially resisted. He was nervous about the legal issues; he was more comfortable with the safety of doing custom technical work, tackling one BIOS at a time. But Colvin was also a savvy businessman and he eventually agreed with Hansche that they should fund a new effort. They started to work on their PC BIOS project in the summer of 1983.

Following Compaq's example, Phoenix launched a clean-room effort of its own. A small team of Phoenix insiders developed specifications for the PC BIOS. They then recruited an outside engineer named Ira Perlow to be their virgin author. Perlow met the criteria for a virgin and then some; while he had never seen the BIOS code, he was an experienced hardware engineer, knew the Intel designs well from his work at Raytheon, and had done a lot of work developing BIOS programs for CP/M machines. Over several months in 1984, he developed BIOS clones for the basic IBM PC and then the PC XT and PC AT.

Like Colvin, the potential customers for the Phoenix BIOS were nervous about the legal issues. The Phoenix sales manager then came up with the idea to indemnify their customers against any suits by IBM. They took the insurance company Lloyd's of London through their clean-room procedures and persuaded them to provide an insurance policy against any lawsuits. After that the sales pitch was effortless; Phoenix was on a roll.

That left one little detail, however. What would IBM do? Hansche was confident that IBM could do little to stop them, but he decided not to wait. In a bold move, he reached out directly to IBM instead. Hansche reasoned that he couldn't really establish a new industry standard with a piracy cloud hanging over his head. Besides, IBM was a Phoenix customer on other custom development work. Full disclosure, he reasoned, would simply be good commercial ethics on Phoenix's part. So he and Colvin invited a group of IBM lawyers to come to Boston to review Phoenix's clean-room procedure. The Phoenix leadership and their lawyers walked the IBM visitors through the detail of their methods.

Hansche was right; IBM's lawyers drove away without doing a thing.

It was a pivotal moment in the computer business. "If I had not written this BIOS," Perlow boasted after the fact, "the world would have been so different it's incredible to think about it. It's kind of like that *Star Trek* episode." And he was right. According to Hansche, the customer calls started coming in almost immediately; the floodgates to the full-scale cloning of PCs were opened. Phoenix's first customer for the ROM BIOS, a Massachusetts company named Leading Edge, brought out their Model D in June 1985. They were quickly followed by a host of next-generation clones, including Kaypro, Epson, and even more obscure labels such as Thompson, Harriman & Edward, Computer Dynamics, and American Mitac. The entire PC market, in fact, was overrun with this new breed of clones within just fourteen months. There was no turning back now for this ecosystem spawned by Bill Lowe's open architecture.

As a *Time* magazine article from July 21, 1986, summed it up, the situation in a single headline was this: "Cut-Rate Computers, Get 'Em Here!"

The Trade-Off Between Open and Closed Strategies

If these examples of the interaction between architecture and IP strategies prove anything, it's that simplification strategies aren't always simple to execute. They require nontechnical executives (CEOs and general managers) to engage with issues that many of their peers have historically left to the legal and engineering priesthoods: complex questions of design and component interactions, relationships with technical standards bodies, and a number of complex questions involving the ever-changing rules and practices of IP law. Still, most simplification strategies eventually boil down to making a set of business decisions along two dimensions: (1) how open (i.e., modular) versus how closed (i.e., integral) to make a product's design architecture; and (2) how open (i.e., freely copyable) versus how closed (i.e., proprietary) to make the associated technical standards. The wide range of business choices that are available along each dimension—combined with the flexibility to select different architectural and IP strategies—create a cornucopia of possible business strategies.

These choices often represent the most sophisticated and risky strategies available to companies in today's competitive landscape. As IBM's experience shows, this can be treacherous territory. Not surprisingly perhaps, many companies struggle as they work to realize the economic benefits of simplification while also holding onto their competitive position.

If we zoom out to get a wider perspective on these architecture and IP choices, using the framework of a network helps to guide decisions in three core simplification options: influencing standards, controlling central components, and riding the evolution of the technology stack. When we apply the network lens, we see that standards simplify the ways in which pieces of technology link up together; a clear view of product architecture simplifies the priority setting for IP acquisition; and a clear view of the technology stack simplifies the priority setting for design work in an innovation network.

STANDARDS

The work that a standard does can cover a wide or narrow range of issues. At the highest level, though, standards help ensure compatibility between components in a given area of technology. Any time a group of designers, either explicitly or implicitly, agrees to a technology standard it involves consequential choices between competitors. These choices often determine how profits are distributed between companies with competing designs, and simultaneously constrain the future paths on the technology road map.

The main focus of a standard is to set rules for the interfaces and interdependencies among components in a product design. A standard, therefore, can take as many forms as there are functional specifications in a design. Standards can be protocols for sharing data, like the number of bits in a byte. Or they can be a weight or size specification, like the maximum width of a ship that can pass through the Panama Canal, or even a material property, like octane in gasoline. Standards can also take a physical form, like the plug for an electrical socket or the data ports on a PC. The defining feature all standards share, though, is that they set ground rules, rules that simplify things by reducing the number of choices available to product designers and, as a result, reduce the need for collaboration and customization

Although such rules are often published freely as available product specifications, standards can also be made proprietary. For example, Gillette has a patent (U.S. Patent No. 7,168,173) covering the "deflectable element" that clicks into place when you insert a Fusion razor handle into a Fusion razor cartridge. This patent prevents Fusion clones, whether they be razor handles or cartridges, from breaking into the component market. Similarly, Hewlett-Packard alters the placement of the holes in its ink-jet cartridges to make it harder for refillers to compete with their factory-filled printer cartridges. Architectural patents can also make it more difficult for clones to create a completely compatible product (as in IBM's 360 architecture patent). Or the interface itself can be just the beginning of an important new proprietary component of its own. Just consider how the "disc operating system" began: as a few lines of code to link an external disc drive and a computer's CPU.

Nonproprietary standards also abound in many technology areas, along with the standard bodies and industry groups that have come together to administer them. The World Wide Web, for example, is built on a stack of standards with familiar monikers like "url," "html," and "http," which are governed by a consortium known as W3C (World Wide Web Consortium) that enables the sharing of information between networked computers. Richard Stallman was able to launch his GNU project because the UNIX operating system had a modular architecture and published standards (now called the POSIX standards) that were freely available to him. That standard defined all the relevant component interfaces, and made it possible for Stallman to copy the components' function; GNU was basically a UNIX clone. Modular architectures that allow interoperability thrive on the kind of standards that enable industry participants to use and copy them without restraint or cost. And because of the rise of utilities like Linux and the World Wide Web, the popularity of standards, and aggressively open architectures in particular, is growing.

The penetration of standards is spurring new activity around design specifications for things like automobiles, airplanes, telephones, and household appliances not only in the United States, but around the world. In any industry that involves "component parts flying in close formation," in fact, participating companies have begun to understand the value of clear rules that simplify the coordination problem and the role that those same rules play in distributing profits. The standard-setting process can be mundane and peaceful, contentious and cutthroat, or mysterious and Byzantine, depending on the circumstances. How companies engage within the organizations that make and administer these processes has become increasingly important in the struggle for competitive advantage.

How should companies manage their standards issues as a competitive strategy then? As an initial step, a company needs to decide whether they want to enter the standards game at all, or on the other hand, whether they want to keep their designs as proprietary as possible. Open standards have their benefits, but as IBM's PC story shows, introducing a de facto standard can also be a risky proposition. And lest one get too carried away by the success of open designs, there are numerous cases where closed and integral designs have helped companies to *own a proprietary standard*. Both the Apple Macintosh (versus the PC) and Apple's iTunes format (versus the standard MP3 format) are recent examples of proprietary standards that successfully compete with open standards.

Still, for many full-systems designers and for virtually all component manufacturers, participating in standards discussions is inevitable. These companies will always have an interest in *influencing the discussions so that the standard requires their IP*. This creates a delicate balancing act for companies working on advanced designs; they walk a tightrope between holding ethical and open discussions with potential competitors and licensors while simultaneously sacrificing shareholder investments in proprietary innovation. This, of course, can put companies in some very tricky situations. For one, how much does participation in standards discussions create an obligation to donate technology? There is an emerging (but still murky) body of rules, norms, and law around what constitutes appropriate conduct in this area. Much of it restricts the ability of IP holders to protect confidential information and raises their obligations to make uncompensated disclosures at the same time.

Several companies have actually found themselves involved in legal proceedings subsequent to a standard-setting process that made their patents more valuable. One of the most prominent examples was the fabless semiconductor company Rambus, which withdrew from a semiconductor standards organization in 1995 after it concluded it didn't want to agree to the licensing restrictions that went along with membership. Rambus was subsequently sued for filing (and licensing) patents that its competitors alleged were influenced by the knowledge Rambus gained from the standards discussions prior to their withdrawal. An initial judicial decision that found Rambus liable for fraud was overturned on appeal by the Federal Circuit. In an entirely different venue, Rambus was later penalized over essentially the same issues by the FTC, this time under antitrust law. This kind of double jeopardy speaks volumes about the tension between patent and antitrust law, as well as the difficulty of managing proprietary innovation in the standards process.

For technology companies, the whole situation surrounding Rambus stirred widespread debate about proper conduct, and stoked tensions between fiduciary shareholder obligations and proper competitive behavior. In what some called a "son of Rambus" lawsuit, Qualcomm was accused in 2007 of inadequate disclosure and was stripped of its licensing rights on two of its patents as a result. Another example is Unocal, which was accused of similar transgressions in 1998 regarding its patents on clean-burning gasoline (despite the fact that they merely provided input into a governmental hearings procedure). Unocal then won a court case permitting them to receive 5.75¢ per gallon on reformulated gasoline sales that used their technology (an award potentially worth billions). But when Unocal merged into Chevron in 2005, the FTC insisted that Chevron abandon their licensing efforts in return for getting permission for the merger.

In a less contentious area, many companies have found that IP strategy can be a helpful way to reduce the risk and uncertainty that often results from hotly contested standards battles. The well-known battle between Sony's Betamax and JVC's VHS formats has been portrayed as a major defeat for Sony. But few people realize that after Sony lost the standards battle they did more than simply lick their wounds; they transformed their business strategy from glass house to shark. Sony made huge profits (our sources suggest billions) from licensing its patents to VHS manufacturers, even as their product business faded away. In a similar fashion, Qualcomm has benefited from licensing technology for the European WCDMA standard despite the fact that it has supported the competing CDMA2000 standard. These examples show that, even when standard setting results in a winner-take-all dynamic in the product markets, companies can *use IP to hedge their technology bets* when technology contributions are far less polarized than the standards outcomes turn out to be. As we saw in chapter 3, losing a competitive battle on standards can create new opportunities to generate returns by moving into the position of a shark.

An additional feature of the standards bodies' landscape is that rule-making activity has blurred the boundaries between business and government. As a result, national governments have become increasingly involved as standard setters. The drive for standards affects the law itself, an area where sovereign nations are accustomed to making their own rules. The WTO, however, has set a meta-standard for how member nations' IP laws must conform in order to join the community of trading nations.

Any business that ignores standards rules issued by a government does so at their peril. *Emerging market companies can and have enlisted their governments to assist in rule making,* a move that helps level the competitive playing field. China in particular has begun using its standards-setting power to promote the economic development of its domestic companies. These standards policies go deeper than just technology, though. (See chapter 8 for more on the role of IP in global trade.)

CENTRALITY

As we have demonstrated, analyzing the CDMA, PC, and automotive networks illustrates how many of the world's most successful and profitable companies share a common position in their ecosystem; they are central. We make that point with caution, recognizing the risk of claiming cause where we can only observe effect. Nevertheless, the best strategies in a networked world will be those that *seek and secure central positions* in the critical components and interfaces of a rapidly evolving network of IP.

It's this realistic assessment of the business's prospects of succeeding with open or closed strategies that should guide business decisions rather than a knee-jerk ideological bias toward an open or closed posture for its own sake. Open strategies have the powerful advantage of encouraging others to connect to your position, because the costs, either cash or transactions cost, are lower than the benefits. On the other hand, proprietary standards face a higher bar in terms of attracting connections, but if successful, they can become far more valuable in the process. The story of the IBM PC, in fact, provides a valuable lesson in how delicate these trade-offs can be.

Despite launching one of the most successful product architectures of all time, IBM captured very little value from its extensive investment as its belated efforts to control the PC architecture with a proprietary position in the ROM BIOS ultimately failed. IBM clearly occupied a central position in the PC architecture with its ROM BIOS, as we show in Figure 17, but IBM lost control of the PC business when its IP protection failed to prevent widespread copying of the BIOS. Instead, Phoenix Technologies made millions selling BIOS clones. IBM failed to anticipate their vulnerability and consequently ceded the most important positions to component suppliers that they put in business and could have purchased for

FIGURE 17 Another View of the IBM PC Architecture

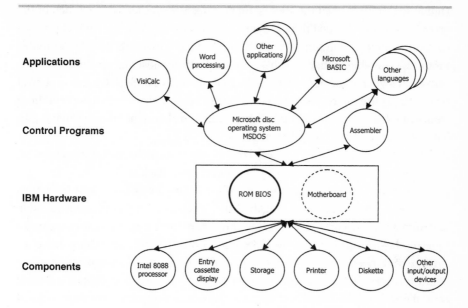

nominal amounts. Today Microsoft and Intel combined are worth nearly three times the market value of all of IBM.

As you can see in Figure 17, the control of the central position in the component network moved up the stack from the "IBM hardware" (and the PC ROM BIOS) to DOS—or more accurately, to MS-DOS. In a comparable miscalculation, IBM paved the path for Microsoft's profits through the terms of their original contract. IBM was so concerned about the unit cost of their PC that they refused to let Microsoft receive license fees for sales of PC DOS, agreeing to pay only a fixed fee of $200,000. In return, Microsoft obtained the right to license MS-DOS independently, which it did, receiving license fees from other computer makers instead. To put it another way, IBM gave Microsoft the incentive to build its own revenue base outside of the IBM PC market, which in turn enabled the creation of PC clones and ultimately destroyed its business.

IBM, though, wasn't the only IP loser as quite a few other players with potentially central roles lost out to Microsoft in the PC architecture battles. MITS, for instance, invented the home computer, but lost their leadership position early on, despite having paid for the development of BASIC for the PC. VisiCalc created the killer application for the office computer and, without a defensible IP position, they lost out first to Lotus 1-2-3 and ultimately to Microsoft's Excel. Digital Research created the successful architecture and (arguably) much of the original code that shaped the PC operating system; yet they lost their clear market leadership position as the result of one bad sales meeting. Seattle Computer Products created the actual code base for MS-DOS, but lost that position too when Microsoft switched its game plan from that of reseller of 86 DOS into a central hub in the entire microcomputer ecosystem. In one way or another, each of these companies lost the game because of their failure to obtain the IP rights that might have secured a clearly central position.

The moral of the story is, *Take good care of your stake in the central component(s).* If you let it get away from you, you may never get it back.

To be sure, centrality is not necessarily valuable in its own right. A central component can lose its value quickly if the function it performs is not valuable and there is strong competition at the component level. One must also be careful to recognize the difference between hub positions that provide a competitive advantage and those that just happen to fall in the middle of a lot of action. (One of our former colleagues is fond of pointing out that the receptionist is the most central position in the hotel business, yet few would argue that manning the front desk is a position that carries much power.) It's easy in retrospect to point to central positions and say your strategy should always be to own the center. Such success, though, often takes a breakthrough in the overall architecture for the positive end result to be achieved.

It's also easy to get confused about thinking of centrality as a goal. Many businesses tend to think about their own profits and positions first and the larger network as a distant second. But a small piece of a large pie is often worth more than a large piece of a small pie. By following this line of thinking, many companies are recognizing that *you shouldn't underestimate the benefits of an open architecture.* Companies have begun supporting open architectures even when the benefits of openness aren't immediately obvious for their bottom line. Companies should realize, however, that their profits depend on their ability to own a stake in a central component that helps them capture value as the overall network prospers. Companies should take care to *avoid putting their best assets at risk* with an idealistic leap to openness. If you aren't paying attention to owning a proprietary and central position, you can be certain that your competitors will.

THE STACK

The value of a central position depends a lot on the way that position figures into the stack of technologies that go into a complex design. The image of a stack (see Figure 14, on page 197, for a view of how the technology elements of the IBM PC can be viewed as a stack) provides a lens to consider not just the snapshot view of centrality, but also the *evolution* of product architecture over time in terms of both the functional relationship of components (see Figures 15, 16, and 17, on pages 200, 201, and 219) and the evolution of the related IP networks. The stack concept also provides a way to consider the decisions and actions that businesses can take to position their proprietary technology in a larger ecosystem, either by controlling their position in a given stack over time or by figuring out when and how the stack is working against their interest. In some cases, it may even make sense to invest in building a competing stack, to effectively blow up an entrenched design that has your company locked on to a disadvantageous development path. Alternatively, when you've found yourself stranded in a losing stack, you can take a sharklike posture toward a competing stack, but only if you've planned ahead and used your IP to hedge your technology bets.

If a network view illustrates connections and component positions at a particular point in time, the perspective of the technology stack gives a more hierarchical view, with layers of technology that build on one another over time. Focusing on the technology stack raises a different set of questions, like which components are foundations of the full architecture, which layers are fragmented or concentrated, and which layers are best positioned to take advantage of innovation and new profit opportunities. If you could animate the evolution of the basic network architecture over time adding in a third dimensions for technology layers, the stack view would simply be one way to view that evolution.

Looking at the IBM PC technology stack, for example, we see that Microsoft and Intel were the big winners. Each company became both central and also quite dominant in their specific layer of the stack. Each company also found their success through a combination of luck (the component position they occupied turned out to be a central hub for new innovation links) and planning (the IP positions they sought out provided a stable foundation for their innovation investments). On the planning front, each company navigated bitter legal conflicts along the way, overcoming contests over ownership rights, accusations of patent infringement, and government intervention based on antitrust concerns. In most cases, the final outcome of these conflicts went their way when it mattered, particularly in the early days. Those outcomes may have been lucky too, and some remain a topic for debate even today. What is certain, however, is that both Microsoft and Intel understood the strategic value of their IP at every stage and fought hard for their proprietary positions. Then, with these IP strengths established, each company has continued to build on their positions, using their central position to continue moving up their respective technology stack.

At Microsoft, MS-DOS's position in the stack led to an entirely new level of user value, the "graphical user interface" that links the user with the Windows operating system. DOS spawned Windows, which in turn enabled Microsoft to capture a dominant position in the application layer of the stack through its "Office" productivity suite (Word, PowerPoint, and Excel). Microsoft also recognized Jim Clark's bid to become the next "asshole in the middle" and moved up the stack again to displace Netscape's position in Internet browsers with its own product, Internet Explorer. In the process, Microsoft took what was initially a modular architecture and extended the operating system in ways that have turned the architectural direction back to a more integral design. This strategy of connecting, developing, and then bundling in new application layers has been called "extend and embrace." It's not much of a technical strategy (while Microsoft defends their approach on economic and technical grounds, many would argue that it makes Windows more cumbersome), but rather an architectural, IP, and pricing strategy rolled into one. Microsoft has recognized better than anyone the strategic value of holding onto a position of centrality in the evolving stack.

Intel has also had similar success in upgrading the features and functions of their standard x86 microprocessor line. Much of this innovation takes place at a lower level of zoom and to visualize it would require a more detailed view of the microprocessor technology stack. From the perspective of the computer user, though, the main benefits of these innovations have been the speed and computing power that go along with the progression of Moore's Law. And despite facing more difficult competition in other areas, Intel has managed to retain its core position in the PC technology stack, driving its product performance forward in compelling ways.

With an awareness of the strategic importance of the stack, you can also identify strategic opportunities beyond simply shooting for the middle of a valuable design. Instead, companies without central positions can look for ownership positions around emerging design standards where the positions are less entrenched. As technology evolves, companies can find strategic opportunities by *owning the new component at the top of the stack*. Alternatively, a more narrow option is to *own the interface in a complex design*, recognizing that even a simple interface like Kildall's link between the disk drive and the microprocessor can, over time, take on added importance and function and may even become an important component in its own right

In short, some of the most powerful and sophisticated strategies in modern business involve the alignment of IP and design strategies behind a new architecture that breaks the compromise between complete *control* and overly complex *collaboration*. These strategies find elegant ways to simplify either the design's front end (customer economics) or the back end (supplier investments) or both. In the process, they force difficult choices that involve the complex interactions of architecture and IP strategies, choices that trade off the dimensions of those strategies that are "open" (and can give huge competitive benefits to even a clunky design) against those that are "closed" (which are required for profitability). As the experience of IBM has shown us, simplification strategies are rarely simple, but any company working in a marketplace where simplification is a big source of value creation has to come to grips with these sophisticated options and hard choices. If you don't, you won't really know what your strategy is.

That said, any discussion of simplification strategies that ignores their limits is incomplete. In the industry-wide, standards-driven, modular architectures that have been the focus of our examples here, the end result of simplification can, of course, end up being not very simple at all. Most simplification efforts focus on imposing order, on rules that limit the creativity and customization options for designers and reduce the range of variables they must deal with. In many cases, these rules can unleash a lot of value. But they can also outlive their usefulness. Almost by definition, these design limitations can create performance losses that are important problems for some customers, either today or in the future. Compounding this effect is that the negotiations that are often required to produce a standard set of rules have a way of turning the stack into a sclerotic and tired mess of inconsistent accommodations: compatibility in all directions, new user needs that strain the old design, old user needs that hold back new design opportunities, and "sow's ears" solutions that make peace in the community of suppliers but add complexity in insidious ways. In short, simplification strategies can lose the war against complexity over time, even in standards that have broad support, open architectures, and modular intent.

Clayton Christensen, author of *The Innovator's Dilemma*, describes a pattern of design strategies that take advantage of this kind of sclerosis by effectively blowing up the stack and starting all over again with entirely new (and often more closed) architectures. These architectures are often built around new technologies that don't fit easily into the old stack or radical rearrangements of components that open up new markets (often at the low end) that were poorly served before. He calls this class of designs *disruptive technologies,* so named because they abandon conventional industry practice, flout the preferences and requirements of the most profitable customer groups, and reject the painstaking consensus outcomes of standards-setting processes. When they do break through, these disruptive technologies can obliterate the delicate balance that often emerges over time, even if open architectures and nonproprietary standards already exist.

Although open-source models like Linux are themselves a form of disruptive technology, disruptive technologists often go the opposite direction of openness. Instead, they frequently reject componentization as they introduce new, and highly integral, designs. Most notably, they often reject convertibility over time (or backward compatibility), a feature that makes them highly threatening to entrenched businesses with large installed bases of users (and related service businesses), since they can throw entire categories of business out of the market.

Strategies like this simplify by rejecting complexity instead of redesigning it. When they succeed, the best IP strategy option is often to exert a new phase of direct control. This move from simplification back to control closes the circle of options we outlined in chapter 4, and it demonstrates how even the most sophisticated strategies can be tossed out the window with a simple return to basics.

SECTION III

IMPLICATIONS FOR NATIONS, MARKETS, AND STRATEGISTS

CHAPTER 8

IP Nations

THE FUTURE OF GLOBAL COMPETITION

Intellectual property is the backbone of America's economy.
—*Carlos Gutierrez, U.S. Commerce Secretary**

[We will] bring about a nation founded on intellectual property.
—*Junichiro Koizumi, Japanese Prime Minister*†

The future world competition will be for intellectual property rights.
—*Wen Jiabao, Chinese Premier*‡

he grainy photograph in the *New York Times* captures an expression on the face of Xerox CEO C. Peter McColough that belies the rosy headline. The date is May 25, 1973, and the headline reads "Xerox Foresees Record Profits in 1973." But the expression of the CEO is not the look of pride and confidence that one might expect. Rather, it is the look of bewilderment, frustration, and anger.

For the previous two decades, Xerox had been on a roll. Xerox was, in fact, the fastest-growing company in the history of the New York Stock Exchange at that time. For context, consider that Xerox had never appeared on the Fortune 500 list of America's largest companies prior to 1963. Just ten years later, the company

*U.S. Department of Commerce Press Release, "United States and European Union Launch Action Strategy for the Enforcement of Intellectual Property Rights," June 20, 2006.

†General Policy Speech by Prime Minister Junichiro Koizumi to the 157th Session of the Diet, September 26, 2003. Prime Minister Koizumi has made similar statements dozens of times, including in virtually every General Policy Speech beginning in 2002.

‡Similar quotations by Premier Jiabao have appeared numerous times, but the earliest identified statement is from a statement during a visit to "model worker Xu Zhenchao" in Shangdong Province, June 20, 2004. www.trade.gov.cn/english2003/php/show.php?id=553.

had leapfrogged into fortieth place on the list of corporate giants. Xerox's growth was so rapid that the late Joseph C. Wilson, founder of Xerox, was often fond of noting during the 1960s that if his company maintained its meteoric growth rate, its sales would soon exceed the U.S. gross national product. And along with the growth, the company generated enormous profits and wealth for its shareholders. Between 1960 and 1970, Xerox delivered the highest growth rate in earnings per share of any company in the Fortune 500, and by 1970, its stock was trading at sixty-six times its 1960 low.

By 1973, that roll was about to end, and CEO McColough knew it.

Xerox was under attack, not by its domestic rivals like IBM and Kodak, or even its future foreign rivals like Canon and Epson, but by a far more powerful adversary: the Federal Trade Commission (FTC) of the United States of America. Just a year earlier, the FTC, responding to pressure by groups like Ralph Nader's Raiders and other consumer activist groups, initiated a regulatory action against Xerox, accusing it of illegally monopolizing the market for plain-paper copiers through an accumulation of patents. The government's action was designed to break up Xerox's monopoly and compel it to license its intellectual property, the unquestioned source of its competitive advantage, to all of its competitors.

The frustration and anger on McColough's face captured by that photo in the *New York Times* showed his bewilderment over the FTC's actions. He said that the government's actions were "almost impossible to understand . . . without concluding that their strategy is not to attack one company but is in fact to attack the fundamental principles on which all companies in this country have grown, prospered and in point of fact contributed in great measure to people all over the world."

Who could blame McColough for his consternation? Xerox had done everything right: rather than being punished for its success, the company should have been celebrated as a model of entrepreneurship and innovation. While that's certainly how the story began, unfortunately it's not how it ended.

The story of Xerox begins with a lone inventor, Chester Carlson, who, ironically, began his career in the patent department of P.R. Mallory & Co. It was his frustration over the time and expense required to copy patents for submission to the U.S. Patent Office that started him on a long and torturous road to find a better way to reproduce documents. A real-life Horatio Alger story, Carlson rose from almost unimaginable poverty (at one point he was forced to sleep outside of the chicken coop that his family was living in to avoid contracting the tuberculosis that his father was dying from) to become one of the richest men in America.

Carlson's xerographic copy machine, like most important inventions, did not simply emerge once the conditions for its discovery were in place. It took him fifteen years of investigation to invent the basic principles of electro photography, and another decade to turn it into a commercial success. Carlson spent years conducting experiments with different materials in the kitchen, bathroom, and coal cellar of his modest newlywed apartment. Eventually, the accumulated flash fires, chemical spills, and minor explosions (along with prodding from his mother-in-law) led him to rent a small room behind a beauty parlor that cost him $10 a month. It was here that Carlson finally succeeded in producing the first electrostatic copy in 1938. And due to his experience as a patent attorney, he wisely used some of his scarce resources to apply for patents all along the way.

It was one thing to solve all the technical problems, and quite another to find a commercial partner willing to back the idea. Over the next six years, Carlson demonstrated his invention and offered to license it to virtually every office machine company in the country (including IBM, GE, Kodak, and others). It wasn't until 1944 that Carlson first struck a deal with the nonprofit research organization called the Battelle Memorial Institute. And what a deal it was. Carlson gave Battelle three-quarters of all future royalties from his invention in exchange for their commitment to spend $3,000 to further develop his idea.

After undergoing some further development at Battelle, Carlson's invention then found its way to the tiny Haloid Corporation of Rochester, New York. Incredibly, Haloid invested about $75 million between 1947 and 1960, far more than the entire earnings of the company during that period, on enhancing Carlson's original idea. To support this investment, Haloid took out loans and sold stock wherever it could and the company's executives took their pay in stock rather than cash. Some of these true believers even loaned the company money from their own personal savings while others went so far as to offer up the mortgages on their homes to help finance the project. All of this sacrifice finally began to pay off when, in 1959, Haloid Xerox (Haloid was dropped from the name in 1961) introduced the "914 copier," a breakthrough that *Fortune* magazine would later call the "most successful product ever marketed in America."

From these humble beginnings, Xerox relied on a commitment to innovation to help it grow into one of the largest and most respected companies in America. Over the years, Xerox developed thousands of inventions both large and small, and created one of the first truly modern corporate research and development programs, the now famous Palo Alto Research Center (PARC). And thanks to Chester Carlson's experience as a patent attorney, Xerox had placed a high priority on protecting its innovations with patents from the very beginning. When the FTC turned its focus to Xerox in the early 1970s, the company already had more than 1,000 patents in its portfolio, and it was adding several hundred more each year.

And therein lies the rub. Normally, when the growth in a new market explodes like it did in the plain-paper copier market, competitors quickly enter the market. The strength of Xerox's patent portfolio was so great however that from 1959 until 1970, no other company in the world was able to produce and sell a plain-paper copier. IBM, for example, reportedly spent millions of dollars trying to work around Xerox's patents. In fact, 25 percent of their R&D budget for xerography was spent on patent counsel. The strength of Xerox's patent portfolio was, apparently, insurmountable.

The company's competitors then sought other means to enter the marketplace. If they couldn't circumvent Xerox's competitive advantage, they turned to the government to help them demolish it. In 1972, the Federal Trade Commission began investigating claims of unfair competition on the part of Xerox. While the FTC leveled a variety of charges of anticompetitive behavior against Xerox, the truth is that their entire case was based on Xerox's use of patents to sustain its market position. Michael Scherer, the FTC's own chief economist, later admitted that the other charges were "fluff. . . . The center of the case was the extension over time of the monopoly through patent accumulation." Scherer and the FTC felt that the advantage that Xerox has sustained for "17 years was enough" and, in a purely arbitrary judgment, applied the life of a single patent to output of a decades-long R&D program, indeed, to an entire new class of products. In Scherer's words, the FTC felt justified in making a "therapeutic intervention" in the name of "social engineering."

Strangely, the FTC's regulatory activism was out of sync with the courts, who consistently upheld the rights of patent holders to accumulate patents through innovation, and to exclude competitors from using them. (Even after the company settled with the FTC, the courts later ruled in favor of Xerox in a patent infringement suit against IBM.) Nevertheless, by 1975 the legal and political pressure was so great that Xerox "voluntarily" accepted a consent decree under which its competitors would be able to use any three Xerox patents royalty free, and could license its entire patent portfolio for a maximum of 1.5 percent of sales.

By Scherer's own admission, the government's case was weak. Which begs the question: why did Xerox accept such an onerous settlement?

For one, the FTC's aggressive antitrust position opened the floodgates to private antitrust suits by Xerox's competitors. With the FTC threatening to disarm Xerox's patents, companies like Addressograph, Litton, and SCM filed private suits, which, in turn, generated tremendous legal costs and distracted Xerox from conducting its business. In this environment, Xerox executives believed they had to settle. In the book *Prophets in the Dark*, David Kearns, a vice president at Xerox at the time who later served as the company's CEO from 1982 to 1990, shed some light on the company's internal thought process at the time of the settlement. Kearns reported that "we . . . realized that if we didn't license people, new competitors would come into the business and infringe our patents anyway. We would sue and they would countersue, claiming antitrust. And the litigation would go on and on. We couldn't conduct a business like that."

Xerox's leaders also gave in to the government because, like many CEOs today, they dramatically underestimated the importance of their intellectual property. "We agreed to forfeit much of our patent protection through licensing arrangements, because McColough [the Xerox chairman at the time of the decision] believed that the erosion of our hold on the market would not be that significant," Kearns writes. "After all, there was our unrivaled sales force to contend with and the two decades of experience building our brand in the marketplace. The patents were simply less important than when Xerox was small and fragile."

McColough could not have been more wrong. Once the government forced Xerox into what's known as a "compulsory license," the situation deteriorated faster than anyone thought possible. Xerox's vaunted sales force, experience, and brand were rendered impotent. Without any patents to impede them, Xerox's competitors rapidly gobbled up market share. In 1972 Xerox owned virtually 100 percent of the market for plain-paper copiers. Just four years later that share had dropped to less than 14 percent. Xerox's unrivaled sales force, its decades of experience, and its brand were powerless to stop the onslaught of new competitors that entered the market once the government handed them the technology on a silver platter.

Yet the FTC economists didn't anticipate what happened next. While the FTC staff was most concerned about Xerox's high share of the American copier market and Xerox executives expected strong competition from domestic rivals like IBM and Kodak, no one anticipated the speed with which competition would emerge from abroad. Within a few short years of the consent decree, Japanese competitors like Canon, Toshiba, Sharp, Panasonic, Konica, and Minolta had each claimed a significant share of the U.S. market. While the FTC's decision ensured lower copier prices for all U.S. businesses, an unexpected side effect of its social engineering in the United States was to adopt a disastrous national industrial policy, one that played out on a global stage: it effectively gift-wrapped an important domestic industry and donated it to the Japanese.

The government's decision to crack down on Xerox continues to have an impact even today. It is well known within the computer industry, for instance, that many of the key elements that make the personal computer so successful were first invented at Xerox's Palo Alto Research Center (PARC). Some of the most significant developments that came from those R&D efforts include the graphical user interface, the mouse, the local area network, the WYSIWYG (What You See Is What You Get) text editor, Ethernet, object-oriented programming, laser printing, and more.

Xerox has been criticized for "fumbling the future" (from the title of a 1999 book) because it failed to profitably exploit these inventions. Few people, though, understand that Xerox was operating under a corporate-wide consent decree that effectively made it impossible for them to protect their innovations from their competitors. When Steve Jobs visited PARC in 1979, for example, he saw the mouse and the graphical user interface for the first time. Jobs then quickly incorporated these features into the Lisa, the forerunner of Apple's Macintosh line of computers. Bill Gates and Microsoft also replicated these features in its Windows operating system, and the rest, as they say, is history. While the "adoption" of these technologies by Apple and Microsoft was later challenged in court, the climate created by the antitrust authorities made it impossible for Xerox to effectively protect its innovations. In many ways, both Apple and Microsoft are offspring of the FTC's so-called social engineering.

And in an ironic twist, when Bill Lowe Left IBM in 1988 on the heels of the collapsing PC strategy, he joined Xerox to head up their advanced product development. One of the first things he did upon joining the company was to file suit against Apple for copyright infringement. And although Lowe proved that he was a quick learner, it was too late for Xerox. The courts dismissed his lawsuit, ruling that Xerox had waited too long to defend its IP rights: the statute of limitations had passed.

The World's Greatest Technology White Sale

If the Xerox story was an isolated incident, it might be little more than an interesting historical footnote. However, the forced licensing of intellectual property from Xerox was just one example in a long string of antitrust actions that systematically stripped IP protection from some of America's greatest companies.

This is the little-known story of how the United States gave away its competitiveness to Japan.

It was a unique moment in time. America had won the war on the battlefields of Europe and Asia in part because of the achievements made by industrialists in their laboratories and factories back home. With victory in hand, the U.S. global preeminence in technology was unquestioned. The United States developed the Marshall Plan to help rebuild the economies of war-torn Europe and, at the same time, provided billions of dollars in aid to assist Japan in its recovery as well. In the 1950s and 1960s, the last concern on the minds of businesspeople and policy makers was international competition. There were simply no serious competitors out there to worry about. In hindsight, it is easy to conclude that this oversight led to some of the greatest business and policy blunders in U.S. history.

Although the Marshall Plan was an intentional act, the international consequences of domestic antitrust activism were of far less concern at the time than the growing power of America's largest companies. Beginning with a case action against the bottle maker Hartford-Empire, antitrust authorities within the government issued compulsory licensing decrees against more than one hundred U.S. companies. Although the facts of each case were slightly different, the effect was the same: to force companies to license their patents for free (or a very small fee) to their competitors. In this way, some 50,000 patents were redistributed to the public.

These patents protected some of the most important technologies of their day, a list that included AT&T's computer and telecommunications patents, IBM's semiconductor and computer patents, and DuPont's patents for nylon and other synthetic fibers. The government's "monopoly busting" policy was designed to increase (mostly domestic) competition, and thereby benefit consumers. Regulators got half of what they wanted, competition in spades, but not from the source they expected it to come from. The toughest competition came not from other U.S. companies, but from Japanese upstarts.

This forced technology transfer on the part of the government has been labeled by one observer as "the largest 'white sale' on technology in history," a bargain that aggressive Japanese companies (with active help from key government ministries) took full advantage of. Between 1950 and 1980, Japanese companies consummated more than 35,000 technology license agreements with foreign, mostly U.S., companies, many of which included the free or low-cost licenses made possible by the numerous consent decrees issued by the U.S. FTC and DOJ.

Quite directly then, the "Japanese Economic Miracle," as economists have called it, was largely a product of the technology imported from the United States. And the Japanese knew how much the imported technology meant to their success. In 1978, a survey of business leaders conducted by the Japanese Ministry of International Trade and Industry (MITI) found that "indigenous technology accounted for only 5 percent of the improvements in Japanese product quality and only 17 percent of the advances made in production processes."

These technology imports got results, and went a long way toward closing the gap with Japan's foreign competition. A second survey, conducted by Japan's Science and Technology Agency, asked 1,000 business leaders about how importing foreign technology had affected their firms. Nearly one-third (32.7 percent) of the interviewees characterized their companies as "overwhelmingly backward" prior to the acquisition of foreign technology, while another half (46 percent) said that their companies were "lagging considerably behind." After acquiring foreign technology, however, those same business leaders felt that their companies had caught up. More than half (56.1 percent) reported that their companies had achieved "roughly the same level" of technology as their Western competitors, and only 3.5 percent felt that their companies were "overwhelmingly backward."

Foreign technology had an overwhelming impact on Japan's economic recovery. Without it, Japan's Economic Miracle would simply not have happened. Absent the vast transfer of technology that occurred, Japanese products and processes would have remained uncompetitive for at least several more decades. Beginning in the 1950s and continuing through the 1970s, Japanese firms spent about $500 million per year on imported technology. Although the cumulative investment added up to many billions of dollars, these technology acquisitions enabled Japan to become competitive in global product markets and generate trillions of dollars of economic growth. According to a study by the "Committee on Japan," which was commissioned to analyze the competitive threat to the United States posed by Japan, the cost of acquiring technology represented:

> . . . a fraction of what it undoubtedly would have cost to develop the technology at home, provided Japanese companies could have achieved the breakthroughs . . . [these] royalty payments represent only a portion of the up-front costs and risks of R&D incurred by foreign patent holders—to say nothing of the uncertainties, false starts, and time required for the processes of invention. For Japanese firms, the benefits of having access to foreign technology far out-weighed the marginal costs.
>
> It would be hard to exaggerate the advantages of being in a position to buy foreign technologies "off the shelf." With modifications, leading-edge technologies could be put to immediate use in manufacturing. For Japanese companies, the immense benefits included crucial time saved, large uncer-

tainties eliminated, promising R&D pathways clarified, rapid movement down technological and commercial learning curves, resources freed to focus on incremental adaptations, and new commercial opportunities opened up.

By the 1970s, as a result of the transfer of all this technology, U.S. corporations found themselves falling behind the fierce new competitors from Japan. At the same time, economists and policy makers were wringing their hands over what seemed like, to them at least, a sudden and unexplained decline in America's competitiveness. As the U.S. recession of the 1970s dragged on, numerous theories were offered for the rise of Japan and the decline of the United States. Some blamed American companies for their laziness, short-term focus, and lack of vision, while others praised the Japanese for their superior culture, stronger work ethic, and visionary long-term planning.

Few analysts, though, understood the dramatic impact that the sale of America's technological wealth had on global competition. The simple truth is that U.S. antitrust policy systematically diminished the value of intellectual property, and created the conditions under which the nation's greatest source of wealth could be transferred to the Japanese at bargain-basement prices.

While only about one hundred U.S. companies were directly forced to license their intellectual property under a consent decree, the antitrust actions sent a clear message to every cutting-edge company. The government would not allow innovators to use their IP rights to create market power. As a result, the very core of intellectual property law defined in Article I of the U.S. Constitution—"to promote the Progress of Science and useful Arts, by securing for limited Times to Authors and Inventors the exclusive Right to their respective Writings and Discoveries"—had been denied to America's most innovative companies.

Under these conditions, several things happened. In a world where every firm lived under the cloud of a potential antitrust suit, it should be no surprise that so many companies were willing to license their intellectual property, and to do so "on the cheap." For example, the Radio Corporation of America, or RCA, the electronics conglomerate based in New York City, agreed to license its patents on radio technology to "all comers" in order to avoid investigation by the Department of Justice. This license paved the way for Japanese companies to later introduce the quintessential Japanese product of the 1970s: the transistor radio.

When other American companies had built a huge technology advantage, they simply failed to protect it. In the automotive industry, General Motors, America's most powerful company by virtue of its 50 percent share of the domestic auto-motive market, lived under constant threat of antitrust action. That meant that even as Japanese automakers blatantly infringed on GM's portfolio of patents, the company made no effort to use the strength of its IP position to stem the ris-ing tide of imported vehicles.

With the returns on their technology investments so reduced, the incentive to invest in innovation declined. Not surprisingly, American companies filed fewer patent applications and a made a lower real investment in R&D as they adjusted to the new realities of the competitive landscape. As we illustrated back in chap-ter 2 with Figures 4 and 5 (pages 67 and 68), U.S. R&D spending began to decline in 1968 and continued on a downward pitch for another decade; patent filings didn't recover fully until the late 1980s. In other words, alongside the competi-tiveness problem, the U.S. economy, with a big assist from its government, en-tered an "innovation crisis" that was of grave concern to everyone from business leaders and consulting firms to economists and politicians. Hearings were held in Congress to determine what could be done to spur a recovery of America's technological advantage.

Beginning in the late 1970s, a rising consensus began to build that the United States needed to strengthen its protection of intellectual property to encourage domestic innovation, and to provide U.S. companies with the tools to defend their domestic market against foreign competition. The U.S. government re-versed its course and began to strengthen IP protection at home and use its in-fluence to encourage stronger IP protection among its trading partners. Table 2 summarizes this shift in the political climate for IP protection within the United States over the past forty years.

This shift resulted not only in stronger domestic IP protection, but in a world-wide adoption of strong IP law as well. IP has now become the single most im-portant trade issue in U.S. industrial policy. This fact was underscored when the world's leading economies joined the United States in its efforts to trade their rights to place quotas and tariffs on textile and apparel imports in exchange for adoption of IP protection laws by their trading partners. This was no small give-away. At the time of the GATT (Global Agreement on Tariffs and Trade) negotia-tions in 1990, where this deal was being negotiated, textiles and apparel represented America's largest manufacturing sector. According to one analyst, more than 1.6 million U.S. jobs and thousands of companies would be traded away in exchange for IP protection. This was, in his words, "an extraordinary proposal."

TABLE 2 Recent Revisions to IP Law/Regulations

Copyright		
Copyright Act of 1976	1976	Copyright extension made automatic; most copyright violations are a federal offense; "fair use" allowed for criticism, commentary, news, teaching, scholarship, and research.
Various copyright infringement actions	1992–1998	Significant copyright infringement made a felony offense; criminalized additional forms of infringement.
Various copyright term extensions	1962–1998	Copyright term extended 11 times from a maximum of 56 years to 70 years beyond the life of the creator.

Patents		
Court of Appeals for the Federal Circuit	1982	Central court established to hear all patent appeal cases.
Hatch Waxman Act	1984	Extended life of pharmaceutical patents to offset FDA approval delays; enabled more rapid entry of generic competition once patent protection ceases.

Border Enforcement		
Trade Act of 1974	1974	Strengthened the ability of the International Trade Commission to enforce IP protection at the U.S. border.

Antitrust		
Agreement on Trade Related Aspects of Intellectual Property Rights (TRIPS)	1994	Provides standards of domestic IP protection for countries participating in world trade.

Government Research		
Bayh Dole Act	1980	Provides patent rights to researchers who receive government funds, but retains "march in" rights for government.

(continued)

Government Research *(continued)*		
Stevenson Wydler Act	1980	Encourages government labs to establish tech transfer offices.
Federal Technology Transfer Act	1986	Encourages collaboration between government agencies and industry by providing patent rights to industry while retaining royalty rights for the government.

International Trade		
Special 301	1984	Established a "watch list" for countries that do not provide appropriate IP protection; enabled tariffs to be used against countries who fail to respect IP rights.
U.S. IP framework in the North American Free Trade Agreement	1993	Mexico and Canada adopt strict U.S. system of IP protection.

IP as Industrial Policy

IP has emerged as one of the most important issues in national industrial policy and the modern economy. Typically when economists talk about intellectual property, they focus exclusively on the microeconomic (company/industry level) impact of intellectual property rights. Few economists, though, have recognized the importance of IP at the macroeconomic (national/international) level.

This is surprising, particularly because IP law from the very beginning was an explicit instrument of industrial policy. It is only recently that policy makers from developed economies have rediscovered this fact. Beginning with the first patent law (created in Venice in 1474—see chapter 1), its purpose has been to create an advantage in the international marketplace. Venice's patent law was created during a long war with the Turks in which it lost the majority of its trading power. Venice recognized that it needed to shift its economy from one built on trade to one built more on innovation and manufacturing. The statute it created was designed to attract inventors and entrepreneurs away from foreign lands and have them settle, invent, and build up the industry in Venice.

Patent laws spread across Europe over the following century, first to Germany, then to Belgium and France, but most notably to England where the first systematic patent system that proved so critical to James Watt's work was created. The British patent system was directly conceived as an instrument of industrial policy under Elizabeth I's chief minister, Lord Burghley, and its objectives included increasing tax revenue to the Crown, increasing employment for the people, and encouraging the creation of domestic enterprise. The most important driver in the creation of the patent system, though, was the desire to substitute domestic production (with its accompanying employment and profits) for imported goods, or what economists call "import substitution," and reduce the outflow of gold.

England, as we know, rode its industrial development and the advances wrought by Watt's steam engine to become the most dominant economic power of its age. Despite the fact that the country lacked both iron ore (which came from Sweden) and cotton (which came initially from India, and later from America) and paid labor rates that were considerably higher than most anywhere else in the world, England nevertheless led the way in creating numerous new industries and captured the lion's share of the world's profits in the process.

But, given its lack of resources, how did Great Britain capture so much? It accomplished it by leveraging its head start in using an IP system to create incentives for innovation. With a system that increased the likelihood of earning a return on an investment, capital flowed to entrepreneurs like Newcomen and Watt; John Kay, who invented the flying shuttle (Patent No. 542-1733 and three others); and Lewis Paul, who first crafted a carding machine (Patent No. 636-1748), and later, working with Richard Arkwright, James Hargreaves, and Samuel Compton, the spinning machine (Patent No. 562-1738, Patent No. 931-1769, Patent No. 962-1770). Together these inventions combined to feed the engine of the Industrial Revolution and in turn increased the productivity of England's labor force to such a degree that the price of cotton cloth fell from thirty-eight shillings per pound in 1786 to less than ten shillings by 1800.

With this kind of industrial power under its control, the English government made every effort to restrict the international spread of its local knowledge and control the export of the key inventions that made its industry so productive. Beginning in the 1780s, the British passed export control laws to ban the export of textile-making technology. Few other countries had patent laws at this time, including the United States, so the British government had a strong incentive to keep many of their inventions a secret or risk losing them altogether. When foreigners attempted to obtain the technology by hiring away skilled workers, the laws were then expanded to make this illegal as well as the export of drawings of production equipment. And to prevent foreign spies from infiltrating key production areas, factories were remade into castles surrounded with fortresslike walls topped with spikes and broken glass. Workers were sworn to secrecy and foreign visitors were brusquely turned away at the door.

Those protections proved futile, however, as the secrets of the Industrial Revolution proved impossible to hide, especially in the face of some Yankee ingenuity.

In 1811 Francis Cabot Lowell, a Boston industrialist, traveled to England to recover, ostensibly, from a bout of poor health. His real mission, though, was to steal the secret to the Cartwright loom, one of the crown jewels of Britain's portfolio of industrial secrets. Upon arriving in England with his family in tow, Lowell did his best to disguise his true intentions. Presenting himself as a wealthy tourist, he traveled in style, staying in the finest hotels and spending money lavishly. But Lowell's plans were all business, and during his stay his most important tours were to meet with various textile manufacturers in the industrial centers of Lancashire and Derbyshire.

Although many of the details of the story are lost to history, Lowell was apparently able to connive his way into factory tours that allowed him to observe the machinery in action. Clearly, he found a way to get around the rules intended to keep foreigners out, perhaps because no one truly believed something like the design of a loom could be stolen just by looking at one. One factory owner, in fact, was quoted as saying, "When machinery is peculiarly complicated you may show it with good effect, I think, because it makes the difficulty of imitation appear greater."

What the factory owners didn't know, however, was that Lowell had a photographic memory, and he was making a careful study of all that he observed on his factory tours. Cabot didn't need a blueprint of the machinery before him when he could essentially take pictures of it with his eyes. Not that he wasn't above suspicion altogether: when he left the country two years later, the British customs officials reportedly searched his bags twice. Of course, they found nothing.

After landing back in Boston, Lowell quickly built a working model of the loom, and subsequently, a series of mills, first in Waltham, Massachusetts, and later in Lowell, the town that was eventually named for him. It didn't take long before Lowell's mills were producing about thirty miles of fabric per day. Lowell later added insult to injury when he successfully lobbied Congress to impose a protective tariff on imported cotton fabric.

Lowell's industrial espionage exemplifies the period's spirit of "Yankee ingenuity": absent mutually agreed-upon patent laws, piracy was the name of the game. The upstart Americans unapologetically copied the best innovations from

Europe, everything from manufacturing equipment to processes and creative work like books and art. The irony, of course, was that even though the U.S. Constitution provided IP rights to U.S. citizens, those rights did not extend to foreigners.

European inventors, artists, and authors like Charles Dickens, whose popular works were widely printed and distributed without his permission in the United States, complained bitterly about the theft of IP by the Americans. A pirated copy of Dickens's *A Christmas Carol*, for instance, sold for as little as 6¢ in America, while in London the authorized copies were selling for the equivalent of $2.50.

Today these same accusations of piracy have now been redirected, of course, toward China and other developing nations. It seems history has a way of repeating itself in this regard. Why not? Developing countries always have an incentive to speed their economic growth by adopting foreign technologies—preferably without having to pay for them. Indeed, any emerging economy can accelerate their growth by using the IP of more developed economies without paying for it, while protecting and profiting from its own innovations at the same time. In the United States, for example, foreigners were unable to apply for patents while American inventors remained free to pursue IP protection overseas. While this might be a good deal if you can get it, getting a free ride in this way is not sustainable; no trading group will allow a member to flout the IP rules of the community for very long.

This was the course the upstart Americans took throughout the nation's formative years as American innovators sought and received patent protection in the United States, Britain, France, and elsewhere, while at the same time U.S. law denied inventors from Europe a reciprocal right. As the fledgling U.S. economy grew and trade became more important, however, the laws were quickly changed to reflect the standards of the trading community in which they operated. By 1836 citizens of any nation were able to obtain patents in the United States.

The United States was not the only nation, though, that tried to circumvent the IP rules of the trading community. The Dutch actually repealed their patent law in 1869 while, as patent laws swept across the rest of Europe, the Swiss resisted instituting patent law altogether. These two small countries became Europe's free riders, using their neighbors' inventions without paying, while at the same time patenting their own inventions in the much larger markets where their products were sold. Although this strategy worked for a time (the Swiss fared better than the Dutch, whose growth rates lagged their neighbors), the pressure brought to bear on these countries by their trading partners eventually brought them back into line.

By the 1800s, the institutions for creating and enforcing international trading rules we know today were still early in their development. Most international disputes were settled bilaterally. A few trade disputes, however, were significant enough to engender large multinational conventions, some of which resulted in multilateral treaties. One such example was the Paris Convention, which formally created the first international standard for the protection of intellectual property rights.

The Paris Convention of 1883 required that all member states afford access to their intellectual property protections to nationals of other member states. This agreement eliminated the ability of a country like the United States to deny patent rights to another country's inventors without running the risk of losing those rights for their own inventors. Interestingly, the rules agreed upon did not require that any particular country adopt a particular kind of intellectual property protection. Both Switzerland and the Netherlands, for example, were signatories in Paris despite the fact that neither country had national patent laws at the time.

That situation, however, did not last long as member states like the United States began to bring pressure on the outliers to bring their IP standards up to the norm.

The United States proposed the first such amendment to the convention's rules, one that would further level the playing field, by ensuring that "any invention that is not patentable in the country of origin, may be excluded from protection in any other Member country that finds it expedient to include it." This proposed change, which was directed at the Swiss and the Dutch since they lacked any patent laws in their own countries, meant that their own inventors would be denied international patents for their inventions if those same inventions could not be protected in their home countries. The Swiss, for instance, were exporting chemicals into Germany without offering German companies the ability to patent their own formulas inside Switzerland. The amendments, once passed, quickly had the desired effect: Switzerland altered its constitution twice, creating a patent statute in 1888 and then expanding it in 1907, while in 1912 the Dutch reinstated the patent laws that they had repealed forty-three years earlier.

Today, as a result of adding the Trade Related Aspects of Intellectual Property Rights (TRIPs) framework into the General Agreement on Tariffs and Trade (GATT), the World Trade Organization (WTO) has effectively become the central enforcement agency for the global intellectual property regime and respecting IP rights has become a condition for participation in the global community of

trading nations. Individual countries now have far less power to flout the standards of the global IP trading community. Developing nations are given a longer
period of time to implement the measure, though there is an ongoing debate
about whether developing countries should have the right to exercise increased
flexibility in their IP laws. As of January 2007, however, all 150 members of the
WTO are required to meet the minimum standards of the community when
it comes to IP protection. This means, of course, that any nation must weigh
the cost of developing its IP laws independently at the cost of exclusion from
the global trading community.

The World Is Spiky

In his widely acclaimed book *The World Is Flat*, Thomas Friedman describes the
increasing openness and connectedness of the world economy. He describes the
forces that have allowed billions of people in countries around the world to participate in the global economy through a series of global, demographic, and technical trends that have leveled the playing field of capitalism.

While it is true that rapid globalization and advances in communications technology have had a "flattening" effect on global trade, it does not imply a level
competitive playing field. The current global IP regime ensures that individuals,
companies, and countries all play by the same rules, but those rules generally
benefit the "IP haves," while forcing the "IP have-nots" to earn their way up the
innovation ladder.

In 2005 Richard Florida, an American economist and urban studies theorist,
wrote a piece for the *Atlantic Monthly* called "The World Is Spiky." In the article,
Florida said:

> By almost any measure the international economic landscape is not at all
> flat. On the contrary, our world is amazingly "spiky." In terms of both sheer
> economic horsepower and cutting-edge innovation, surprisingly few regions
> truly matter in today's global economy. What's more, the tallest peaks—the
> cities and regions that drive the world economy—are growing ever higher,
> while the valleys mostly languish.

The graphs that accompanied Florida's article illustrate this powerful point.
The first (Figure 18, page 244) shows the geographic distribution of patents, while
the second (Figure 19) shows the geographic distribution of scientific publications.

FIGURE 18   "The World Is Spiky"—Patents

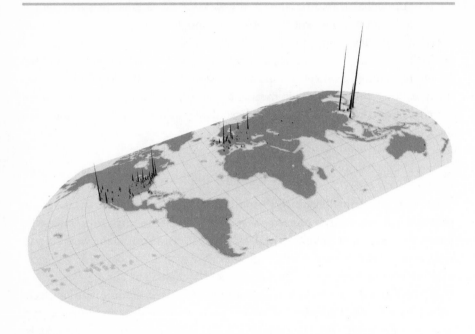

FIGURE 19   "The World Is Spiky"—Scientific Citations

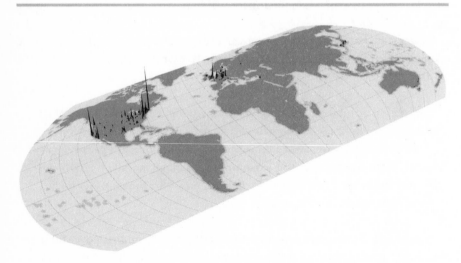

Source: Map by Tim Gulden, University of Maryland. From Richard Florida, "The World Is Spiky," *The Atlantic Monthly,* October 2005.

These striking pictures demonstrate the vast differences between the competitive resources available to countries around the world. Large and rapidly developing economies like Brazil, Russia, India, and China barely even register on the map of global science and innovation. If innovation drives economic growth and IP drives profits, these dramatic differences in the global distribution of innovation and intellectual assets belie Friedman's notion that the world is flat. The truth is far from it.

This geographic spikiness reflects the enormous competitive advantage that has been created by the companies that are based in these innovation hotbeds. The United States, Japan, and Europe, by virtue of their IP portfolios, have a technological advantage over the rest of the world that is measured in decades. This advantage provides incredible leverage for Western companies in their negotiations with competitors from developing nations. In industries where technology is important, and the majority of that technology has been patented, the leading incumbents (mostly U.S., Japanese, and European companies) hold large patent portfolios and powerful global brands.

The strength of their IP position, if used to its fullest advantage, can change the face of global competition in their industry. Strong patent portfolios can be used to exclude competitors from global markets, to force them into the low-value commodity end of the market, or even to extract profits from competitors through licensing. The good news for developing nations, at least, is that the only a select group of managers from the IP-rich developed world have understood how to wield their power effectively.

The technology "white sale" that powered Japan's meteoric economic growth is no longer available to China, India, or the rest of the developing world. Western governments are much less likely to institute policies that will force their leading companies to give away their intellectual property. Western companies are also less likely to cheaply give away their competitive advantage through license agreements with rising competitors from the world's most rapidly developing economies. As one corporate manager said crudely, "After twenty years of selling the Japs technological know-how, other countries are beginning to realize that they've been handing out rods for their own backs and it's going to stop."

The international mechanisms for IP enforcement have also been strengthened in the world's key markets, particularly in the United States and Japan. Consider the numerous reforms in the United States since 1970 listed earlier that have strengthened IP protection within the United States. A similar story could be told about Japan and to a lesser extent Europe.

Not all changes have garnered the attention that TRIPS has, however. One change in particular, the U.S. Trade Act, which became law in 1974, made significant alterations in the functioning of a virtually ignored branch of the government known as the International Trade Commission. The ITC, which was established in 1916, was originally called the International Tariff Commission. Its mission, as its name suggests, was the enforcement of U.S. tariffs placed on products imported into the United States. This all changed in 1974, however, when the ITC became the International Trade Commission. Not only had the organization undergone a name change, it was given more powers to fulfill a new mission: the enforcement of all U.S. policies with regard to imports, most notably on imported products that infringe on U.S. intellectual property rights. The IP rights that the ITC now enforces include utility and design patents, copyright, trademarks, service marks, trade dress, and trade secrets.

Today the ITC is one of the most important and powerful IP enforcement bodies in the world. Any company that does business in the United States (whether a U.S. company or not) can bring a formal complaint to the ITC if it believes that a competitor is importing infringing products. The ITC is responsible for investigating these complaints and, if they are found to be valid, can seize the infringing goods and destroy them.

In a recent case, for example, a Singaporean company called Creative Technology brought a suit against Apple, the all-American icon, in front of the ITC. Creative alleged that the user interface of Apple's ubiquitous iPod infringed on a U.S. patent held by Creative. Though Apple is a U.S. company, the iPod supply network touches various countries around the world and undergoes final assembly in China. Because of that fact, Creative was able to use the powerful lever of the ITC to threaten restrictions on the importation of Apple's main profit engine. With such a threat hanging over its head, Apple agreed to pay $100 million to settle the case and obtain a license for Creative's patents. Apple also agreed to make Creative one of its suppliers by licensing the company some of the IP needed to produce accessories for the iPod.

Not to be outdone by its American counterpart, Japan implemented a similar set of border enforcement procedures in 2003 that may actually be stronger than those available in the U.S. ITC. A company can now file an application in Japan for a preliminary injunction, and customs will immediately block the import of the accused product at the border pending a hearing on the preliminary injunction.

Shortly after this enhanced system was set up, Panasonic used it to stop LG from importing plasma displays into Japan, setting off an international trade dispute. This dispute was later settled with LG taking a license for Panasonic's IP.

By controlling their IP assets, nations gain a nontariff form of protection for their domestic market, and a lever that can be used to open up export markets. In the United States and Europe, it's hard to pick up a newspaper without reading about the loss of the manufacturing jobs to China and other low-wage countries. Politicians and journalists seem to talk endlessly about the difficulty the West will face in maintaining its standard of living if all of its products are produced oversees. What these stories neglect, of course, are the huge IP portfolios that, in one form or another, make up the backbone for a significant amount of the world's most critical technology. That means that, if managed properly, Western companies have an "IP reserve" that gives them a lot more to say about where profits end up than they get credit for.

The Future Competition for IP

For leaders of emerging economies like China, the relative absence of IP reserves has become perhaps their most critical economic policy problem. Recently the chief scientist for China's Academy of Science, Niu Wenyuan, a thoughtful development economist, said that "[intellectual property rights] are the No. 1 strategic reserve in the 21st century and its significance is not inferior to any other strategic reserve, be it food or energy." As Dr. Wenyuan knows well, China's IP deficit is its greatest development challenge, one that it has only recently begun to come to grips with. For a country where the phrase "intellectual property" literally did not exist in the lexicon until 2000, this has required a huge push. "It took Britain 300 years, the U.S. 200 years and Japan 100 years [to establish effective IPR systems]," Tian Lipu, commissioner of China's State Intellectual Property Office, has been quoted as saying, adding that his country still has a long way to go.

In the United States the public angst about the trade deficit with China (and, to a lesser extent, Japan's and Europe's own deficits) hides a very important fact. Although a growing proportion of the world's products are exported from China, the majority of the profits earned from selling those products actually flow back to companies in Japan and the West. A quotation from the *Beijing Review* in 2005 captures the point: "Forty-five percent of the goods [exported by China] were exported in the form of processing trade using foreign brands [in other words, contract manufacturing], and another 45 percent were OEMs (Original Equipment Manufacturers), leaving less than 10 percent using Chinese brands." This trend has only become more extreme in recent years. According to China's Ministry of Commerce, the share of China's exports that were attributable to foreign companies (described as OEMs in the quotation above) by 2006 was approaching 60 percent.

Most Westerners, though, fail to understand this dynamic. In working with Western companies, we regularly hear complaints about "the China price" as companies struggle to figure out how to compete with the low-wage and highly productive Chinese manufacturers. The answer these managers are searching for, of course, is that they need to change the game they're playing from one of cost to one driven by IP.

While some companies lack the necessary IP to compete in this way, many others simply fail to recognize what assets they do own or how to deploy them. Looking ahead, the competitors who play this game well will thrive; those that continue to play the game by the old rules will be soon swept aside. For as Chinese Premier Wen Jiabao has repeatedly said, "The competition of the future world is a competition for intellectual property rights."

The Chinese may be coming from behind, but as the following quotation from China's eleventh Five Year Plan shows, they're working hard to close the gap:

> The new [Five Year] plan stresses the importance of *independent innovation*. In other words, China needs to change from excessive dependence on the input of funds and natural resources, and pressure on the environment, to greater reliance on quality and technological progress. In August this year ... Hu Jintao focused on how to enhance innovative capabilities. He stressed that *independent innovation* was the key to scientific and technological development and the central link to a new model of economic growth.

The Chinese have come to clearly understand the downsides of relying on foreign technology and the challenges that such an imbalance creates for sustaining its rapid economic development. That's why the term "independent innovation" has become a mantra for Chinese policy makers.

The Chinese, however, have a long row to hoe, as they have a vast IP deficit to overcome before they can reach their goals for technological independence. Even under the most optimistic assumptions, it will take Chinese companies in technology-intensive industries at least thirty years to match the strength of their advanced-economy competitors through independent innovation. To make this happen, Chinese companies will need to be able to sustain competitive levels of R&D investments for several decades, despite the fact that most of their trade is low-margin contract manufacturing. Even in the few places where Chinese companies are selling their own branded products, they are forced to pay royalties to their competitors in order to access their technology. These royalties not only depress the profits of Chinese companies, making it harder to build and sustain large R&D investments, but they also directly subsidize the ongoing R&D of the companies they are trying to catch.

While independent innovation is surely the long-run source of global competitiveness, the ability to fund that innovation and build a productive IP reserve remains an enormous hurdle for China, and for every other developing country. In the new world of global IP competition, countries need to think differently about economic development.

The diagram below, borrowed from a report we coauthored, shows the process that developing countries inevitably follow as they move along a path toward IP independence. (The full report is available for download from BCG's Web site at www.bcg.com/publications/files/Beyond_Great_Wall_Jan2007.pdf.)

History has a way of repeating itself when it comes to the IP development process. Although the players and, to some extent, the rules have changed, the path that countries follow in moving from technological dependence to global competitiveness has changed very little. For developing countries and for developed economies that are trying to sustain their competitiveness, the IP development process proceeds through five phases.

FIGURE 20   The IP Development Process

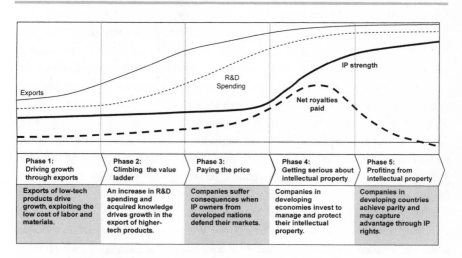

Source: Ralph Eckardt, Mark Blaxill, et al., *Beyond the Great Wall: Intellectual Property Strategies for Chinese Companies,* BCG, January 2007.

Phase 1: Driving Growth Through Exports

Virtually every successful economic development story over several centuries—from Britain in the 1790s to Korea in the 1990s—was built around a surge in exports. Developing economies invariably begin this surge by producing and exporting low-tech, labor-intensive products like clothing, shoes, and toys. Both the products and the production methods are low-tech, as the country and its companies lack the technological sophistication and infrastructure to do otherwise. Since the companies also lack distribution channels, they often act as contract manufacturers for Western companies. This has been the situation in the apparel industry for decades as thousands of small and mostly invisible companies in countries from Azerbaijan to Vietnam toil to produce clothing for the well-known Western brands like Nike and Ralph Lauren. Even the largest of these manufacturers are virtually unknown in the West. For example, four of the largest apparel exporters in India, Gokuldas Exports, Poppys, Orient Craft, and Jyoti Apparels, are virtually unheard of outside of the sourcing departments of the leading apparel brands.

Sometimes the products produced in this phase appear to be relatively high-tech, like some consumer electronics such as DVD players or TVs, but this is almost always an illusion. The truth is that companies from developing nations act almost exclusively as final assemblers. They import the truly high-tech components from abroad, and then export the assembled products.

Phase 2: Climbing the Value Ladder

As a developing economy begins to evolve, its firms grow increasingly dissatisfied with their position at the bottom of the industrial food chain. They begin to understand that their industrial partners are raking in the lion's share of the profits. They recognize their interest in moving up the value ladder to produce more high-tech products and, by mastering modern production methods, begin to produce the higher-value-added components themselves. By doing so, they hope to eliminate the middleman and begin to reap more of the profits for themselves. Among many examples is the Taiwanese company Amtran who for years had exclusively manufactured televisions for foreign-branded OEMs. In 2005, it began to sell its own-branded Vizio flat-panel televisions in the U.S. market, and is now one of the largest LCD-TV brands in North America.

Companies like Amtran learn from their Western partners about how to produce and market the products that they have been assembling. This then fuels their confidence, and they begin to feel capable of sourcing components, assembling products, and selling them under their own brand. Like Amtran's Vizio brand, they often begin by selling low-priced products through large Western discount retail outlets like Walmart, Costco, and Sam's Club. The retailers encourage this behavior and actively develop these low-cost competitors. What they don't understand is that the upstart competitors rarely own the technology that goes into the products they sell. Instead, they have typically copied it from their competitors.

Phase 3: Paying the Price

The copying that takes place as companies move up the value ladder invariably leads to confrontations with IP-rich incumbents. In most industries, it is virtually impossible to produce a competitive product without infringing on someone else's intellectual property. These confrontations take the form of lawsuits, border enforcement actions, and "demand letters" insisting that the company stop producing the infringing product.

This is the point at which these companies truly begin to feel the pain of not owning the technology they are using. They quickly find themselves on the defensive. In some cases, they are excluded from their target market like the United States or Japan through border enforcement or litigation. In others, they are forced to pay onerous licensing fees in order to participate in the market, or they become captive manufacturers for Western companies where they do most of the work, but the globally branded companies capture most of the profits.

Looking back to the matrix we described in chapter 3, these companies become *targets* while their licensors are the sharks, and even the glass houses find they can enter the licensing game. Once again, Amtran and its brand Vizio demonstrate the pattern. Since Amtran has introduced its own brand into the American market, it can no longer rest under the IP umbrella of its Western OEMs. As a result, Amtran and Vizio have been sued multiple times for patent infringement in the United States and are now the subject of an infringement complaint at the U.S. ITC, which could result in having its products seized, destroyed, and excluded from the U.S. market.

This, of course, is where many Chinese companies find themselves today. The vast majority of China's exports come from contract manufacturing or from foreign company–owned operations. It's a trap that Chinese companies in every industry are actively trying to escape from, but they continue to pay a high price in doing so. With their entry into the WTO in 2001, which made the country subject to the international IP rules of trade, Chinese enterprises have paid at least $1 billion to settle IPR disputes related to its exports. But this is only the tip of the iceberg.

For example, U.S. customs agents seized some $150 million worth of knock-offs or IP-infringing products in 2006 alone. The vast majority of those seizures, about 81 percent, were exports from China, a number that rises to 88 percent if you include Hong Kong and Taiwan. In other words, the vast majority of infringing products seized at the U.S. border come from Chinese producers.

Chinese companies have also found themselves hard hit by Western companies in the form of royalties and license fees, which have more than tripled over the past five years. Those fees added up to some $6 billion in 2006 alone. A recent report from China's Ministry of Commerce estimated that the total impact of "technical trade measures"—technology standards and product quality standards where the IP is owned and controlled by Western companies—on the Chinese economy exceeded $75 billion in 2006, up nearly 10 percent from 2005. With these kinds of numbers at stake, it should come as no surprise that the Chinese are working hard to learn how to overcome these barriers.

One case study in particular—the DVD—provides a cautionary tale about the difficulty of overcoming an IP deficit. Prior to 2003, the vast majority of the world's DVD players were made in China. The DVD player is based on a technology standard, though, and not surprisingly the intellectual property required to implement that standard is owned by a group of Western companies that includes Philips, Sony, IBM, and Time Warner. These companies have formed several patent pools, including one with MPEG LA and others called the 3C and the 6C Consortium, made up of the essential patents related to the DVD standard, which they willingly licensed to any manufacturer who wanted to produce DVD players.

Several hundred Chinese companies decided to ignore these patent holders, however, and began producing DVD players, which they sold through "big box" retailers and mass merchants primarily in the United States and Europe. With this influx of competition, the "China price" quickly took hold, and the retail price of DVD players plummeted from about $300 to prices as low as $60.

The patent holders took note, though, and used their IP positions to seek royalties for each DVD player sold. The royalty charge to produce a DVD player has been estimated to be between $14 and $20. This charge is distributed among the various patent holders, including MPEG LA ($2.50); the 3C consortium (Philips, Pioneer, Sony, and now LG—$5); the 6C consortium (Hitachi, IBM, Matsushita, Mitsubishi, Time Warner, Toshiba, Victor—$4); Thomson ($1); as well as other patent holders.

When the patent holders found it difficult to collect royalties from the numerous Chinese manufacturers, they changed their tactics. For example, Philips, among the most sophisticated of the DVD patent holders who manages the licensing for the 3C consortium of companies, was particularly aggressive in cracking down on unlicensed DVD players. Rather than simply going after the manufacturers, however, Philips brought pressure on the European and U.S. retailers who sold the devices.

Philips's novel approach was based on the fact that under patent law, it is illegal to make, sell, import, or use a device that infringes on unlicensed intellectual property. What Philips understood was that everyone in the supply chain—from the manufacturer to the end user—is potentially vulnerable to a patent infringement lawsuit. Philips wisely applied pressure at the point of the supply chain where their impact would be greatest, the Western retailer.

As an aside, it may come as a shock to many retailers that they are liable for selling infringing products in their stores even though they didn't make the products and may be unaware of the infringement. If they aren't careful, deep-pocketed retailers can be left holding the bag for the infringing products that come from their suppliers.

Faced with this potential legal liability, Walmart and other retailers, not surprisingly, changed their purchasing practices. The retailers turned to licensed manufacturers, mostly in Taiwan, to get their DVD players and DVD disks. With nowhere to sell their players, the Chinese manufacturers were hit hard: about 350 of the 500 companies manufacturing DVDs went out of business within a single year.

So why didn't the Chinese manufacturers just pay the royalty like everyone else? The reality was that because the Chinese had forced artificially lower prices, they couldn't afford to pay for the license. The patent royalties had become as much as 30 percent of the selling price of a DVD player, which meant that the potential profit for a Chinese company had fallen from $10 to less than $1 for a DVD player. Not only could companies ill afford to pay licensing fees, they didn't have any IP to trade to help offset them. DVD manufacturers in Taiwan, on the other hand, owned intellectual property that enabled them to cross-license in exchange for the use of the DVD consortium's patents. In effect, their "cost of goods sold" was lower because their cost of technology was lower. When all costs are considered, including IP costs, the low-cost *producer* may not be the low-cost *supplier* after all.

China, in other words, lost the entire DVD industry because it didn't own the intellectual property behind it.

Phase 4: Getting Serious About IP

Once companies have paid the price for their lack of IP, they tend to become far more serious about acquiring more of their own: they recognize the cost of dependence on foreign technology, and they don't like it. The challenge that IP-poor companies face, though, is how to overcome the vast IP gap that exists on their intangible balance sheets.

As the Chinese government has observed, the path to long-term competitiveness is to eliminate overdependence on foreign technology by developing a foundation for independent innovation. For countries like China that face massive IP deficits, though, independent innovation is simply not enough to get them into the game; they simply can't innovate fast enough.

The quickest way most companies can address their IP deficit is through licensing or joint ventures, which means that if you don't own the IP yourself, join forces with someone who does. While this strategy can provide access to the market, most of the value—and profit—in these joint ventures still flows to the party who holds the IP. There are, however, alternative steps that can be taken if business leaders from a developing economy want to break out of their IP trap: acquisition and setting standards.

The fastest way to level the playing field is through the acquisition of IP assets, or even acquisition of entire companies. The most dramatic example of this approach is Japan, which relied on the licensing of technology as the major impetus for its dramatic economic growth during its boom years. But as U.S. policy makers awoke to their mistakes and cut back the supply of cheap IP, Japanese companies came to understand that in order to maintain a sustainable IP position they needed to plan for a future without the bargains that flowed from the American technology white sale, so they turned to a more systematic strategy of IP acquisitions.

Beginning in the mid-1980s, Japanese companies began to acquire technology companies at an extraordinary rate. By one count, Japanese high-tech companies acquired 452 of their U.S. counterparts over the five-year period between October 1988 and May 1994. This new approach had several benefits. By acquiring firms in the United States, the Japanese obtained access to some technologies that were until then not available for license. The strategy also gave the Japanese companies access to existing networks of patent licenses that had been negotiated by the acquired companies. In high-tech industries from computers and semiconductors to telecommunications and biotechnology, Japanese companies acquired dozens or even hundreds of U.S. technology companies. Virtually every major Japanese company in the computer and semiconductor industries acquired one or more U.S. technology companies during the 1980s and 1990s, including Canon, Fuji, Fujitsu, Hitachi, Matsushita, Mitsubishi, Sony, Toshiba, and dozens of others.

This same pattern is repeating itself today in Korea where leading companies have acquired more than fifty foreign technology companies in recent years. For example, the Korean conglomerate LG acquired a controlling interest in Zenith, giving it immediate access to its powerful TV patent portfolio and its brand. These strategic acquisitions provide both the technology and the IP that these companies need to produce leading-edge products, to barter rights with other IP owners, and to have a more direct channel into the world market.

While the Chinese have yet to make the large numbers of technology acquisitions that their predecessors did, they have begun to make some noise recently. The splashiest example so far has been the acquisition of IBM's PC business by Lenovo, a Chinese PC maker, for $2.35 billion.* And while there was some grumblings in the media about why Lenovo would bother plunking down more than $2 billion for a money-losing business unit, you can chalk up virtually the entire purchase price to the value of IBM's IP. Consider this: IBM, the company that set the standard for the personal computer, sold its rights to the ThinkPad brand and, more important, its entire portfolio of PC-related patents to the company that it brought into its supply chain as a contract manufacturer.

Virtually all of Lenovo's self-branded business was inside of China prior to its deal with IBM because if the company had tried to sell its PCs outside of China, it would have run into an IP buzz saw like the DVD manufacturers before them. Lenovo sold only in China because it didn't have any other choice.

But for $2 billion, Lenovo bought itself a ticket to the global game: in fact, it bought an entire section of seats. As the inventor of the PC architecture, IBM, who is also largest patent holder in the world, had negotiated cross-license deals with virtually every other PC-related patent holder in the world over the years. In one fell swoop, Lenovo acquired the right to use every important IP portfolio in the PC industry. Not only did the deal enable Lenovo to overcome its massive IP deficit, its new portfolio reportedly nets it some $30 million a year in licensing revenue.

The Lenovo deal may signal the beginning of a significant trend. China has amassed the largest foreign currency reserve position in the history of the world over the past decade: as of March 2008, China held more than $1.7 trillion in

*The $2.35 billion purchase price equals $1.25 billion in cash, $0.5 billion in assumed debt, and $0.6 billion in Lenovo stock.

foreign reserves. As the impact of China's IP deficit on its economy becomes more acute, the Chinese government has the opportunity to put that money to work by making investments in foreign technology companies. If they do, the flood of outbound M&A activity may be the largest the world has ever seen.

A longer-term strategy for overcoming an IP deficit is for governments to take an active role in the global standards-setting process in ways that benefit their domestic companies.

Companies from developing economies across all technology domains have historically lacked the clout to influence global standards. As a result, these companies have been forced to adopt global standards that were created by foreign companies and built around essential patent portfolios owned by those same companies. Exercising this standards power cements the position of the emerging-market companies as targets for licensing revenue. The end result? They are often forced to pay royalties to foreign patent holders that reach as high as 40 percent of a product's selling price. This is the case today in a wide range of industries, such as DVD players, cell phones, televisions, set-top boxes, RFID, PC communications protocols, and many others.

China, of course, learned this lesson the hard way through experiences like it had in the DVD industry. In an attempt to change the rules of the game, Chinese companies have begun to develop their own national technology standards so that they can reduce or eliminate their dependence on foreign IP holders. In the wireless communications sector, for example, China has developed TD-SCDMA in response to the CDMA and WCDMA standards. In digital video, the Chinese have developed the EVD standard in response to the Blu-ray and HD DVD standards, while in digital television broadcasting, they have developed the DMB standard in response to the ATSC, DVB, and ISDB standards touted by Western companies.

As global standards setters, the Chinese have a significant advantage over many other developing countries: the sheer size of their domestic market. By creating their own domestic standards, they hope to ensure that Western companies who want to serve the largest and fastest-growing consumer market in the world will need to license homegrown Chinese technology in order to do so. This IP helps move the Chinese companies out of the target position and can be used as leverage in obtaining cross-licenses with foreign patent holders for access to the foreign technology (including foreign standards) that has been, until now, off limits (or prohibitively expensive) to them. As these standards are adopted inside China, with their heads well inside the tent, the Chinese will be able to exert a stronger influence over standards around the world.

Putting this practice in place, though, is easier said than done. Consider the challenge of trying to develop a new standard for transmitting cell phone calls without using any foreign technology. Either the Chinese risk pushing inferior technology or, if they are unable to avoid using foreign technology, they face a longer road in reducing their IP deficit. For example, the Chinese have spent years trying to introduce their own third-generation wireless telecommunications standard known as TD-SCDMA. Because they lacked the expertise to do it themselves, they enlisted the help of Siemens, the German manufacturers, to help them develop the needed technology. The strategy, however, has been less than completely successful. In addition to a long series of delays, they have been unable to avoid using foreign technology. A recent report published by the Chinese State Intellectual Property Office (SIPO) found that Chinese companies controlled less than 30 percent of the IP related to the TDD portion of the new standard, and only 51 percent of the SCDMA portion.

China has also been working to develop a proprietary standard for digital television transmission. A recent study by an independent Chinese consulting firm found that Chinese companies (including several Taiwanese firms) held only 7 percent of the 2,000 Chinese patents related to digital television, and that these were mostly design patents rather than patents for the core digital transmission technology.

Phase 5: Profiting from IP
As China's example demonstrates, overcoming an IP deficit is no simple matter. But with success stories like Japan and Korea to learn from, we know that an IP deficit can, in fact, be converted into an IP advantage.

One of the simplest but most telling measures of the competitive strength of a country's global IP reserve is the balance of trade in cross-border royalties and license fees. Using royalties as a proxy, we can see the long process of transition in the Japanese IP reserve. If you trace Japan's IP reserve development starting in 1960, when their exports and economic growth began to take off, you can see that it took more than thirty years before their net royalty payments reached their peak in the early 1990s; it wasn't until 2003 that Japan saw its first net positive inflow of royalties (see Figure 21 on page 258).

Korea, on the other hand, which began its own period of rapid economic development began around 1980, is now nearing its own royalty tipping point (see Figure 22). How then did Korea achieve the same result in almost half the time that it took the Japanese?

FIGURE 21   Royalty Payments and Receipts, Japan

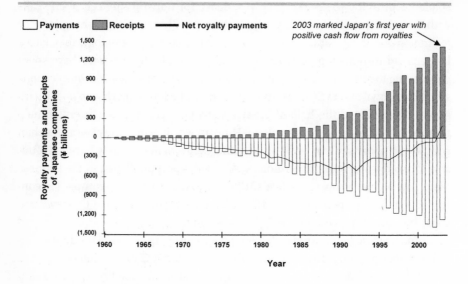

Source: Bank of Japan; author analysis.

FIGURE 22   Royalty Payments and Receipts, South Korea

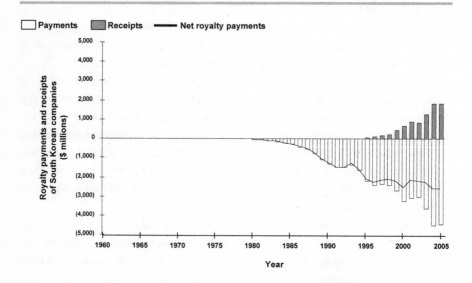

Source: Bank of Korea; Economic Intelligence Unit Country Database; author analysis.

The Korean economy has succeeded by virtue of the success of a few great global companies such as LG, Hyundai, and SK. Each of these is an example of a company that evolved from low-tech contract manufacturers into high-tech global brands. Perhaps South Korea's flagship example, though, is Samsung, one of the largest targets in business history and one of the nine companies forced to settle with Texas Instruments over its semiconductor patents back in the 1990s. While Samsung has in the years since paid billions of dollars in royalty payments to foreign IP holders like TI, Qualcomm, and many others, it has recently begun to wiggle free from its IP deficit. In 1990, for instance, Samsung was granted only sixty U.S. patents, well outside a ranking in the top one hundred U.S. recipients. By 2005, though, Samsung had raced up the list to become the fifth most prolific patent grantee, with 1,641 patents. And in 2007 it exceeded its vice chairman's goal by placing second on the list behind only IBM.

While the overall royalty trade balance provides an economy-wide picture of a country's IP reserve position, in any developing country different companies and different industries can move through the IP development process at different rates. Some race through the development steps quickly and consequently reap the benefits of a strong IP position within a technology niche. One such example is the small but growing Chinese company called Netac.

Deng Guoshun, a former engineer from Royal Philips in Singapore, founded the company in 1999. While cutting his teeth at Philips, Deng learned to appreciate IP. So it was no surprise that when he founded his company, his first two employees were lawyers, a general counsel and a patent attorney. For a small company Netac invested heavily in R&D, and focused its efforts narrowly in the area of flash memory. After earning a flash-memory patent in 2002, Netac sued its largest competitor, Beijing Huaqi, claiming that Huaqi's products infringed on its patents. Netac won some $125,000 in damages and, more important, a court ruling blocking Huaqi's sales of competing products.

With its main competitor blocked from the market, Netac was able to increase its prices by up to 20 percent and capture some of the value of its innovations. The company also filed an IP suit in 2002 against Acer, a rival manufacturer based in Taiwan. The two parties eventually settled out of court, and the resulting deal netted Netac a lucrative manufacturing contract. Through its aggressive defense of its IP rights, Netac has since had ten other rivals, including Samsung, call about getting licenses of their own. Licensing fees, in fact, now account for about 30 percent of Netac's $100 million in revenues in 2005, revenue that has helped the company become the largest flash-memory brand in China.

Netac recently raised its IP profile even higher—this time in the United States.

Not only did Netac file suit against a Chinese plant owned by Sony in 2006, but in 2007 it became the first Chinese company to sue a U.S. company (PNY Technologies in Parsippany, New Jersey) for patent infringement in a U.S. court. This case was recently settled, and although the terms weren't disclosed, Deng has been quoted as saying that "we got all we claimed and were satisfied with the results." Deng also noted, "PNY technologies won't be the last company that we sue." The company has hinted that Apple, SanDisk, and Hewlett-Packard are all in its sights.

While Deng has received some criticism in the Chinese press for following Western business practices, he now recognizes that China's low-cost status is temporary; he understands that Vietnam, India, or Sri Lanka could one day make things more cheaply than even the Chinese can. He wants to build his company around a sustainable advantage like IP instead. And with a portfolio of some 250 patents, including 250 international filings, the company is well on its way.

The Future of Global IP Competition

Assuming that Wen Jiabao is correct and that "the competition of the future world is a competition for intellectual property rights," what does the future look like for the competitive position of nations? Who will be the winners and the losers in the next phase of global competition?

Countries like the United States and Japan are clearly well positioned to reap the rewards of their IP reserves. The United States continues to benefit from a consistent and growing surplus in the royalty trade while Japan has now joined the elite club of net technology exporters. Many developing countries, however, find themselves lacking in the most important strategic asset required for future competition: IP.

It is no fait accompli, though, that the countries who hold an IP advantage today will sustain that advantage. In fact, it seems that some of the countries with the strongest IP positions are actively seeking to destroy the value of their treasure. While the United States, for example, has taken numerous actions to extend and enhance the protection of intellectual property beginning in the early 1980s, there have been a number of recent developments that make the value of IP rights less certain, and perhaps weaker. One central player in these changes has been the U.S. Supreme Court, which has taken a renewed interest in intellectual property law over the past several years. Several cases have been decided that increase the uncertainty about the validity and enforceability of U.S. patents. A bipartisan patent reform bill has also been making its way through the legislative process.

If accepted, the bill will open the window for further challenges to patentability, and new rules for the determination of damages. In doing so, the "reformers" will introduce new measures of uncertainty related to U.S. intellectual property. Even the FTC has begun to renew its activism at the intersection of IP and competition law.

Given the strength of the U.S. IP position, and the importance of technological advantage in a postindustrial economy, it may seem surprising that IP rights might come under attack in the United States. There is, however, a growing zeitgeist of anti-IP sentiment within the academic community and in small pockets of the business world. Perhaps it is time for policy makers to review the lessons of Xerox and other companies from the 1970s.

If U.S. policy makers are showing a tendency to shoot themselves in the foot, then the mind-set among European policy makers verges on suicidal. Despite valiant and long-standing attempts to promote greater policy alignment, IP policy remains highly fragmented within the European Union, and neo-socialist arguments hold sway in some quarters. Europe's disunion has sustained and in many ways worsened a situation in which it lacks some of the basic structures that will enable it to compete in the new IP economy.

For example, despite years of effort Europe still lacks a community patent or a central court to resolve IP disputes, and it does not seem like that will change anytime in the foreseeable future. Europe also lacks the kind of powerful IP border enforcement that exists in both the United States and Japan. Although there has been talk about instituting these measures, there doesn't appear to be sufficient political will to adopt them. Recent challenges by the European Commission against Microsoft and Qualcomm suggest that the Europe may also be moving toward weakening its IP laws in the same way that the U.S. antitrust environment led to a weakening of innovation incentives in the 1960s and 1970s. Anti-IP forces have successfully blocked the extension of patent rights in areas where other countries like the United States have granted them. In a consistent fashion, European policy makers are moving away from the consensus of the more aggressive, innovation-driven IP nations, a move they make at their own peril.

Meanwhile, the leading Asian economies are moving rapidly and forcefully to develop and strengthen their IP systems. Former Japanese Prime Minister Junichiro Koizumi first announced in 2002 "the aim of establishing Japan as a nation built on the platform of intellectual property." In virtually every General Policy Speech (the Japanese equivalent of the State of the Union Address) he gave before he stepped down from his post in 2006, he reiterated the importance of intellectual property to the Japanese nation. Japan has since developed a national

IP strategy, the first of its kind in the history of the world. Few other countries can match the level of attention Japan has given to strengthening its IP system. In overhauling its IP laws, Japan has created a central IP court, improved border enforcement, set up regional offices for training inspectors, developed technology road maps for key industries, and set out a clear plan to further strengthen its national IP system.

Like Japan, China has also begun to rethink its approach to IP. China has, of course, come under constant international criticism for its failure to enforce IP protection within its borders. Those criticisms turned into a formal complaint at the World Trade Organization brought by the United States in 2006, and later joined by Japan and Europe. China also remains at the top of the U.S. annual "Special 301" list of the worst IP violators in the world.

At the same time, China's IP laws have progressed extraordinarily in the short time since they were established in 1984. It is important to remember that British and U.S. patent law goes back more than 200 years, while Chinese patent law is less than 25 years old. In fact, China may be the only country in the world to establish intellectual property protection laws before it created laws to protect private personal property: the first Chinese IP laws were enacted in 1983 (trademark), 1985 (patents), and 1991 (copyrights), whereas the first law explicitly protecting tangible property rights only came into force in March 2007. While China continues to struggle to change the cultural norms that have evolved over thousands of years of the nation's history, it has taken remarkable steps over a short period of time to make itself competitive in the global IP economy. Under the leadership of the powerful Vice Premier Madame Wu Yi, China has established a "Leading Group for National Intellectual Property Strategy Formulation." Composed of high-ranking officials from the various affected ministries within the country, this organization is responsible for developing and implementing an IP strategy that will allow China to achieve its goal of becoming an "innovation based country."

With the increasing importance of IP in global trade, the policy choices made by nations like China, Japan, and the United States will go a long way toward determining which countries will thrive and which will struggle to maintain their standard of living during the next century of global competition. While the incumbents presently hold the upper hand, the academic and policy environments in the United States and Europe create real doubt about the future of IP rights in those countries. Meanwhile, the leading Asian economies are moving ahead at full speed in implementing powerful IP systems for their countries.

The current global trading system is designed to facilitate trade in physical goods. However, an increasing portion of global trade flows are intangible in nature. As the global IP economy develops, trade in IP will come to be just as important as trade in goods. In fact, if goods and their IP content are traded separately, virtually all profits will be derived from the IP content rather than the goods themselves.

This emerging trade in IP assets is an important phenomenon in its own right, and will have a dramatic impact on markets and investing over the next century. The emergence of a tradable IP asset class is the subject we will take up in the next chapter.

CHAPTER 9

A Capital Idea

THE EMERGING MARKET OF INTELLECTUAL CAPITAL

JERRY MAGUIRE: What can I do for you Rod; you just tell me what can I do
for you?

ROD TIDWELL: It's a very personal, very important thing. Hell, it's a family motto.

Are you ready Jerry?

JERRY MAGUIRE: I'm ready.

ROD TIDWELL: Just want to make sure you ready brother.

Here it is. . . . Show me the money.

SHOW! . . . ME! . . . THE! . . . MONEY!

—Jerry Maguire, 1996

f you've accepted even a fraction of what we've argued so far, you've probably
started asking yourself a different set of questions. Whether you're a professional investment manager or simply managing your own finances, you're
wondering about how to apply these insights more directly. In other words,
you want to do more than simply admire the strategy, you want to know how you
can *invest* behind it. After all, if intellectual property is really the most important
source of wealth in the modern economy, and most people don't recognize its
value, shouldn't that mean that there are tremendous opportunities to invest in
undervalued IP assets and not just the companies that own them? We believe
there are. Unfortunately, it has never been very simple to invest in IP, because
the market for these assets hasn't been fully developed. But stick around, because that is about to change.

The Missing Market

For most people, it is a surprising fact that U.S. companies now invest more money in intangible assets than they do in tangible assets. As we illustrated in chapter 2, 2004 marked the first time in history that expenditures on research and development, brand building, software development, and other kinds of intangibles exceeded investment in land, buildings, equipment, inventories, and other tangible assets. U.S. companies, in fact, now invest more than $1.1 trillion per year in intangibles.

Given this extraordinary level of company investment, and the importance of these assets, one might expect to see an active marketplace for the purchase and trade of intangible property, one that would enable both direct investment and greater market liquidity. But where is it?

In the modern world of financial engineering, it seems that virtually every kind of property can be bought and sold in the marketplace. More than 10,000 different stocks and bonds trade on the various stock exchanges around the world. In addition, hundreds of different commodities, including metals (from aluminum to zinc), agricultural goods (from arabica beans to yellow maize), and energy products (from Brent crude oil to Waha natural gas), trade on commodity exchanges daily. Not to mention the trading of dozens of currencies, Exchange Traded Funds, and esoteric securities like carbon credits, and even weather futures.

If IP assets are so important, and we're investing so much money in them, where are they bought and sold? Until recently, they rarely were, and when they were the transactions were mostly hidden from view.

The first market-tradable IP security came from a most unlikely source, a rock star. Most people remember David Bowie as the enigmatic rock star from the 1970s and 1980s who brought us albums like the 1972 classic *The Rise and Fall of Ziggy Stardust and the Spiders from Mars* and songs like "Let's Dance" and "Under Pressure."

In the real world, the surprising intersection of David Bowie and intellectual property took the form of an unusual bond offering in 1997 where he sold bonds backed by the IP rights to his song collection. The innovative transaction created a special entity that would collect royalties from Bowie's songs and distribute them to bond holders. In exchange, Bowie walked away with $55 million in cash, which otherwise he would have had to wait many years to collect. In other words, after Bowie converted his song ideas into property in the 1970s, he later converted that property into capital in the 1990s.

Since then, there have been a number of other significant transactions in which IP assets have been converted into marketable securities, a trend that signals the emergence of the newly tradable asset class of intellectual property. But before we delve into this new marketplace, let's take a step back to understand at a deeper level what is happening here.

From Assets to Property; from Property to Capital

Throughout this book, we have been careful to distinguish between "assets," resources controlled by an individual or organization that can be used to produce a product or service; "property," the legal rights that enable asset owners to maintain exclusive control over their assets; and "capital," the stock of property that can be used to create surplus value in the future. All have specific and distinct meanings yet are often used interchangeably. This, of course, has only added to the confusion about what is what.

Over the past decade, there have been dozens of books and articles that talk about "intellectual capital," including the influential work by Thomas Stewart titled *Intellectual Capital: The New Wealth of Organizations*. In it, Stewart discusses the importance of knowledge as an economic input and the accumulation of knowledge by companies and nations as a critical new source of wealth. This book, and others like it, have created, and perpetuated, an error in the way we talk about intangibles. More than just an exercise in semantics, distinguishing between intellectual capital and intellectual property is critical to understanding the evolving world of intangibles.

Most of the trillions of dollars that companies invest in intangibles every year result in the creation or collection of intangible assets like knowledge. While knowledge assets are important for companies, they are not intellectual property, and they are certainly not capital in the true sense of the word.

The knowledge that companies possess, the ideas stored in the minds of their employees or in knowledge management databases, is not easily traded. Knowledge is not property because the only way to exclude others from using it is to keep it a secret. While most developed countries recognize and protect trade secrets, the lack of exclusive property rights means that that they cannot easily be bought and sold.

Because these intellectual assets have not been turned into property, they cannot be used as capital. They cannot be used as collateral for a loan or packaged and sold as a security. Put another way, *you can't sell shares in knowledge.*

In reality, only a small fraction of intellectual assets are ever converted into property, and an even smaller portion of that is converted into capital. When assets are converted to property, they are more than just know-how; they acquire a legal status that makes it possible to exclude others from using them. These property rights then have the potential to be converted into IP capital, which can be used to produce even more value in the future.

This distinction is critically important because, as economists have recognized for centuries, capital is the engine that powers the market economy. The ability to convert assets into capital may be, in fact, the primary determinant of national wealth.

In his highly influential book *The Mystery of Capital*, Hernando De Soto argues that the major cause of the disparity in wealth between rich nations and poor nations is the failure of capital formation in the developing world. Surprisingly, the difference is not due to a lack of assets. In fact, De Soto shows that "the total value of the real estate held but not legally owned by the poor of the Third World and former communist nations is at least $9.3 trillion." There are plenty of assets; the real problem is the failure to convert those assets into capital.

In De Soto's words:

> [Developing nations] have houses but not titles; crops but not deeds; businesses but not statutes of incorporation. It is the unavailability of these essential representations that explains why people who have adapted every other Western invention, from the paper clip to the nuclear reactor, have not been able to produce sufficient capital to make their domestic capitalism work.

De Soto argues that what the poor nations of the world lack is a fully functional and efficient property system that enables the poor to convert their abundant assets into capital. Access to new capital would then allow them to borrow, invest in improvements, finance new business, and buy, sell, divide, and combine assets. It would also allow for the efficient provisioning of utilities and services, enable insurance, and unleash the economic potential of both the assets and the people themselves.

In other words, it would change the world.

De Soto also describes how the Western nations, particularly the United States, created a property rights system that enabled its citizens and businesspeople to convert real estate assets into the capital that drove the economic boom that has made it such a wealthy country. While De Soto does not formally extend his analysis to intellectual property, there are clear parallels between the process of capital formation in the "real" economy and the present situation in the unseen economy.

The Next New Asset Class

Eight centuries after King John signed the Magna Carta, which granted inviolable property rights to British freemen, economists are finally coming to fully understand the importance of property in economic development. Today it is commonly accepted that property rights are essential to prosperity.

Strangely, though, many economists are reluctant to recognize the even more essential role of intellectual property. Pick up virtually any book on intellectual property, and it will emphasize the fact that patents are negative rights, the right to exclude. In other words, their value comes from stopping somebody from doing something—nothing more, nothing less. This narrow definition, while correct at one level, misses the lion's share of the value. For while all property rights, whether tangible property or intellectual property, do, in fact, give their owner a legal right to exclude others from trespassing, the greatest value of a property right is that it enables us to convert those assets into capital. It was true for James Watt, for example. His ability to use his patents to obtain financing for his business was just as important to him as the ability to exclude others from copying the design of his steam engine. And just as it was during the Industrial Revolution, capital is still the engine that powers the market economy.

Today, more than 150 years after Watt, we find ourselves on the verge of a new capital revolution. Intellectual property rights are becoming fixed in such a way that it is becoming possible to use them as capital. Since the supply of capital in the economy is directly linked to the amount of new investment that can be made, the fact that most intellectual property has not yet been converted into capital implies the potential for an explosion of new investment. In fact, it has the potential to multiply the capital available to drive the world economy, and that would be a revolution indeed.

One of the great economic advantages of the U.S. economy is that it has come further in converting intellectual assets into capital than any other country in the world. For evidence of this, look no further than the level of venture capital financing in the United States, which totaled more than $25 billion in 2006—nearly 75 percent of the world's total VC investment. Most VC-funded companies have few tangible assets, which means that virtually all of this VC financing is backed by intellectual capital. Although VC investment continues to increase around the world (particularly in China), no country or region of the world even comes close to the level of VC investment in the United States.

The $35 billion or so that venture capitalists invest every year is a mere trickle when compared to the trillions of dollars invested annually in intangible assets. But the fact remains that there are few markets for trading these assets.

Today we take it for granted that all kinds of assets can be readily traded, but this was not always the case. Whether we talk about real estate, bonds, stocks, agricultural commodities, or industrial commodities, each class of assets was once untradable yet eventually each one emerged as a tradable asset class. One reason that we take this for granted is that the creation of trading markets for some of these assets is ancient history. The first significant market for government debt appeared in Venice in the thirteenth century. Stock markets trace their history to the formation of the Dutch East India Company in 1602, and the emergence of a market to trade its shares. And although trade in bulk agricultural commodities appeared in ancient and medieval fairs, the first year-round markets for commodity trading appeared in the sixteenth century in Antwerp and Amsterdam.

In more recent times, we have seen the emergence of a wide variety of new asset classes such as Real Estate Investment Trusts (REITs), mortgage-backed securities, and of course "junk bonds." Standard and Poor's designed the first stock index futures in the 1980s, creating the index fund trading business. Other asset categories have emerged more recently, such as pollution credits and catastrophe bonds, along with the securitization of a wide variety of revenue streams, ranging from student loans and credit card fees to insurance settlements and mutual funds. Today intellectual property is largely untraded, but just like these other asset categories, all that is about to change.

The Emergence of New Asset Classes

During the e-commerce boom of the late 1990s, online marketplaces for virtually every kind of transaction appeared virtually overnight. While many of us now frequent consumer-oriented marketplaces like eBay, where one person's trash can truly become another person's treasure, few people know that the e-commerce boom also saw the creation of dozens of business-to-business (B2B) exchanges, markets for the purchase and sale of everything from metals and forest products to automotive parts, airline services, and corporate travel—literally everything that companies buy.

Intellectual property was also swept along in the wave of e-commerce enthusiasm. IP exchanges with names that ranged from the serious (ipmarketplace.com, technologyxchange.com) to the silly (hellobrain.com, brainsupply.com) appeared virtually overnight. By one count there were nearly three dozen online exchanges dedicated to IP transactions. Since that time, though, virtually all of those companies have gone out of business, and the few that remain have radically changed their business model.

Why did these online IP exchanges fail? In large part because they failed to learn the lessons of history.

Financial historian James Grant once noted that "progress is cumulative in science and engineering, but cyclical in finance." When you take a look at the process by which asset markets emerge, an unmistakable pattern emerges. The process is defined by six distinct stages that they all follow on their path to becoming a mainstream market. As we will see, trying to create a marketplace for an asset before its time will likely fail, but understanding how other asset markets have evolved provides insight about the path that IP is on and when that market will emerge.

STAGE 1. IN THE BEGINNING:
ASSETS ARE CLOSELY HELD AND THINLY TRADED.

The first thing you notice about an asset class that hasn't yet emerged is that those assets are held by a small number of owners, most of whom are closely connected with the asset. Agricultural commodities, for example, were once owned exclusively by farmers and food producers. Company stock and debt was once held exclusively by owner-managers; external finance came mostly from investors and bankers who had direct inside knowledge of the business. Mortgages too were once owned exclusively by the savings and loans that operated in the local community and had deep insight into the financial affairs of the borrower.

With this kind of tight ownership in its early stages, few asset transactions can take place. And because there are few transactions to use as benchmarks, owners have difficulties in setting prices for their assets. This, of course, results in an illiquid market where very little property is converted into capital.

This is essentially the situation with IP assets today. Intellectual property is almost exclusively owned by the individuals and corporations who created them. These IP assets are not only bought and sold infrequently, but the transactions involving those assets almost always involve the companies that make the products to which those IP assets relate.

The transactions that do take place are most often barter transactions, where companies trade IP rights for other IP rights. Although there can be many of these transactions, they are almost all private (the details of the transactions are not published) and unpriced (because they are barter transactions, the value of the trade is not defined). As a result, these transactions do not provide visible pricing benchmarks that would facilitate the creation of a liquid market for IP.

STAGE 2. SPECIALISTS EMERGE TO FACILITATE TRANSACTIONS.

In the absence of public pricing benchmarks, specialists with knowledge of the assets must analyze each transaction in great detail. It is not unusual for both parties in these transactions to be represented by agents or for specialized appraisal experts to provide opinions on the transaction.

When we talk about the emergence of IP as an asset class, you might be picturing the modern stock-, bond-, or option-trading markets. You might also think of securities trading where assets are bought and sold at a distance between parties who do not know each other, with lightning speed, and with extremely low transactions costs and buy-sell spreads. While this vision of an efficient IP market may be somewhere in our future, lessons learned from how other asset markets have evolved lead to a very different picture.

Rather than the markets for stocks or commodities, the IP marketplace will eventually look much more like the real estate market.

In real estate, each asset is unique. The value of each property depends on its location relative to the other properties around it, and each property's value can best be determined by examining comparable sales of neighboring properties. In most cases, real estate agents, who know the local community and have a specialist's insight into the prospects of the neighborhood where the property is located, represent both the buyer and seller.

Real estate transactions also involve appraisal experts who keep track of the transactions in the marketplace and can provide advice to the principals in the transaction about the value of the property they are acquiring. Other financial specialists are typically involved in real estate transactions as well. Title insurance companies verify that the title is valid and insure that the seller is legally able to sell the property in question. Mortgage companies provide financing for the asset purchase, and lawyers draft lengthy and complicated contracts that protect the parties against the many contingencies that may arise.

Similarly, an entire ecosystem of IP transaction specialists has emerged to help facilitate IP transactions over the past several years. Although the roles are somewhat different because of the special character of IP, most IP transactions look a lot like a real estate deals.

In the IP ecosystem:

- The government (in this case the USPTO) provides a central registry of property ownership with the specification of each property owner's claim.
- Data providers like Thomson, LexisNexis, PatentCafe, and others gather up and structure information on IP assets and ownership.
- Brokers like Yet2 and PLX Systems provide listings of available assets.
- Licensing companies like IPValue and ThinkFire provide transaction support.
- Reverse-engineering companies like TAEUS and ChipWorks provide product teardowns to determine where the patented technology is being applied.
- IP litigation insurance (both defensive and offensive) is provided by more than a dozen insurers worldwide.
- IP attorneys provide transaction advice, contract drafting, and even contingency litigation services.
- IP merchant banks such as Ocean Tomo provide a full range of IP services to enable complex IP transactions.

Throughout history it has been the existence of transaction specialists like those listed above who have facilitated the emergence of a new asset class. Once an asset becomes widely traded, we can easily forget the role that these specialists played in creating and sustaining the market. The history of every asset market from land and agricultural goods, to stocks and bonds, right up to carbon credits and catastrophe bonds begins with the specialists who first made the transactions possible.

If history is any guide, the fact that so many IP specialists now exist serves as the opening bell for the creation of the IP marketplace. In tracking the emerging IP marketplace, we can see that the number of publicly announced (if not publicly transacted) IP deals has gone from a few dozen per year to hundreds per year over the past few years alone.

STAGE 3. SPECULATORS ENTER THE MARKET.

As the number of transactions around an asset increase, fueled in part by the specialists, speculators are quick to follow. Speculators are, of course, drawn into the market by opportunity. And since IP assets are highly valuable yet poorly priced and thinly traded, that means enormous opportunities.

When assets are held by both investors and producers, it is a sign that a healthy market is beginning to emerge. For anyone with a perspective on financial history, it is both expected and encouraging that IP speculators have entered the market. As we saw in chapter 2, Peter Detkin, then general counsel of Intel, coined the term "patent trolls" for these IP speculators, and the name has stuck. Even this name-calling is no surprise. Detkin is just the most recent in a long line of critics who have hurled invectives at speculators (although it is interesting to note that he no longer uses the term now that he is working at Intellectual Ventures, a major IP investor).

But why are speculators, and more particularly "patent trolls" criticized?

The answer, it appears, is that they are financial investors rather than producers. The U.S. Supreme Court, not known for name-calling, has adopted a more benign moniker for "patent trolls," calling them "non-practicing entities." Members of the Court have expressed "concern" over the fact that "an industry has developed in which firms use patents not as a basis for producing and selling goods but, instead, primarily for obtaining licensing fees." The emergence of this new "industry" should be welcomed with a cheer, but it isn't. And once again this hostile reception should be no surprise.

When we look at the long cycle of financial history, we see that this animosity is a predictable feature of economic life: for as long as their have been markets, nonproducing speculators have been criticized. St. Thomas Aquinas, for example, declared that the exchange "of money for money or of things for money, not to meet the needs of life but to acquire gain . . . is justly criticized." This sort of comment led a financial historian to offer a cutting comeback: "When contemporary politicians rise to condemn the pernicious actions of speculators, they perpetuate unconsciously the Scholastic prejudices of medieval monks."

Speculators through the ages have variously come under fire: from the "illicit practice" of trading government bonds in renaissance Florence, to the commodity speculators of seventeenth-century Holland who were accused of "trading wind" *(windhandel)*. Even the land speculators on the American frontier were criticized for having "contributed nothing to the development of the prairie." At the beginning of the twentieth century, American wheat speculators were decried for their activities. Statements like "the men who own wheat ought to control the sale of it, and not the non-owners or sellers of wind wheat," were typical of the testimonials of the day.

Yet another description of speculators from this era is particularly revealing.

This one is from *Those Fellows with Black Hats: The Speculators,* by John A. Sparks:

> Speculators actually do very little; they do not work for a living in the tradi-
> tional sense. They keep strange hours. They sit staring at stock ticker tapes,
> money market quotations, a company's annual report, or the financial page
> of the newspaper. They operate on the basis of hunches and great doses of
> luck. They are little better than gamblers. Speculators are not producers of
> goods. They do not add to the total wealth. Instead, they merely take a cut
> off the top of what others produce. They are parasitic, enriching themselves
> at the expense of others.

The irony of this long history of criticism against speculators is that the positive role of the speculator in creating liquidity and efficiency in the market is easily overlooked—something we can see within the evolving market for IP.

That the Division of Labour is Limited by the Extent of the Market
—Adam Smith

Economists have understood the value of the division of labor ever since Adam
Smith described the workings of a pin factory in 1776. Similarly, enabling the
separation of the *ownership* of IP as an economic input from its *use* in the production process is no less valuable. As one CEO of a software company put it, "I suppose that it's just as silly to think that a company has to own all of the IP it uses
as it is to think they need to own the building they work in."

The emergence of IP speculators is the surest sign that a new asset class is
emerging. These purely financial investors put their own money at risk on their
belief that an asset is undervalued, and then they seek to prove that they are right.
When they're right, they make a lot of money. If they bet poorly too many times,
they go out of business. The important news is that those assets can now be
bought and sold—and that means opportunity for everyone.

STAGE 4. TRANSACTIONS COSTS DECLINE.

While the market for IP assets is in its nascent stages, the days of a large-scale
online IP exchange remain far in the future. Why? Because transactions costs in
the IP marketplace remain very high.

In chapter 3, we introduced the work of Nobel Prize–winning economist Ronald Coase. The discussion above about the separation of IP ownership from the means of production is reminiscent of his observation about the boundaries of the firm. However, there is another important bit of economics for which Coase is well known. Coase received the Nobel Prize for his observation that property rights will eventually find their way to those who can make the most efficient use of it so long as (1) ownership rights are clearly defined, (2) property can be bought and sold at will, and (3) transactions costs are low.

Historically, these conditions have not been met in the world of intellectual property, but that is changing. This is particularly true when it comes to transactions costs.

One reason that transactions costs for IP remain high is that the boundaries of ownership are unclear. Economists who study property rights call this a "failure of notice." With real property, it is relatively easy to know if you are trespassing on somebody's property. With intellectual property, however, it can be much more difficult to figure out where one piece of property stops and another starts.

If you want to build a house or a factory, for instance, you can go to the local town registry of deeds and find out the entire history of ownership of any piece of property in that town. Because its location can be specified very exactly with only two dimensions, latitude and longitude (the vertical dimension is generally ignored, although there have been some very interesting legal cases that test property rights in the sky and in space), the boundaries of real estate are fairly easy to specify.

The boundaries of IP rights, though, are much trickier to define. Even though the IP records are open and available to the public just like land records, it is no easy matter to determine whether the product you want to build or the process you want to employ is "sitting on" intellectual property that someone else owns.

To help get some sense of where their IP begins and another firm's IP ends, some companies go through what they call a "clearance" process to see whether their new product will infringe on someone else's IP. Oddly, the patent laws actually discourage them from doing so because knowledge of the existence of a patent can lead to a claim of "willful infringement" which, in turn, can lead (in the United States) to "treble damages" if infringement is found. To put it plainly, determining whether a product or process is built on someone's intellectual property can be a surprisingly difficult job.

But "difficult" does not mean the same thing as "impossible." And the times are changing.

Patent data is now readily available and easily searchable. Analytical tools are also available that make it possible to "survey" the boundaries of ownership rights in the IP landscape and the added presence of IP specialists means that companies and investors can more easily assess the value of intellectual property.

In effect, this is what IP speculators do. Through their hard work, they discover IP assets that are valuable because other people have failed to do their homework, and have built their "factories" on other people's property. If speculators can do it, so can companies.

Viewed from this perspective, it should be clear that IP speculators are not the problem; quite the contrary, they show us that a better solution is possible.

When company stocks first started to trade, for example, it was widely believed that they were too esoteric for individuals to own and trade. Conventional wisdom said that unsophisticated individuals couldn't possibly understand all of the complexities required to assess the value creation potential of companies. While there are still rules in the United States that limit the kind of investments that individuals can make, we now know that those early assumptions were off the mark, way off.

Countless individuals today, from the most sophisticated Wall Street analyst to the least sophisticated grandmother (there are lots of financially sophisticated grandmothers, witness The Beardstown Ladies Investment Club, but that would not include our grandmothers), have investments in the stock market.

The system works because the government regulates what is reported, analysts give opinions on what is reported, and a whole industry of information suppliers has sprouted up to help investors understand what a stock is worth. The same structure could just as easily apply to IP. Clearly, IP assets are difficult to understand, but no more so than company stocks. In fact, company stocks are merely a bundle of other assets that includes IP. And if IP assets are too complicated to understand as an investment vehicle, then by definition stocks are even more complicated.

With an increase in the volume of transactions, the increased availability of IP transaction specialists, the improved availability of IP data, and increases in the sophistication of IP analysis, the cost of IP transactions costs is beginning to fall. And as these elements continue to come together, they will inevitably create a virtuous cycle that will speed the emergence of an IP marketplace.

STAGE 5. MARKETPLACES FOR EXCHANGE ARE ESTABLISHED.

One of the seminal moments in the development of the IP marketplace happened on December 4, 2004. About fifty lawyers, technologists, and entrepreneurs gathered at the U.S. Bankruptcy Court for the Northern District of California for the auction of seven technology patents from a defunct e-commerce company called Commerce One.

In its heyday, Commerce One was a major player in the business of B2B exchanges. By 2004, though, the rose was off of the e-commerce bloom, and Commerce One was forced into bankruptcy along with countless other former high-flyers. All that was left from the millions of dollars invested by venture capitalists was a collection of patents that described a standardized method of communications between online exchanges. Invented in the boom of the late 1990s, this technology had been widely adopted among technology companies.

By 2004, as the company's creditors were scrambling to gather the few valuable crumbs of value from the bankrupt company, they were preparing to sell the company to a private-equity firm called Comvest Investment Partners for the meager sum of $4.1 million. Before the sale was completed, however, the bankruptcy trustees were approached by Ocean Tomo, a specialized IP services company based in Chicago, who believed that Commerce One's IP assets were worth more than the proposed purchase price. Ocean Tomo brought along its analysis that showed that Commerce One's patents were of high quality and were widely used. The trustees were intrigued. So they decided to auction off the patents separately from the rest of the company.

By the time of the auction, Ocean Tomo had recruited perspective bidders representing a who's who of the technology and IP world. Although virtually all of the bidders operated anonymously, we now know that the prospective bidders that day included leading technology companies like Novell and LG, as well as IP investment companies like Intellectual Ventures and Thinkfire. Once the bidding opened, it quickly escalated past the original selling price of the bankrupt company. And once the dust settled, those seven patents had sold for a price of $15.5 million, more than three and a half times the value that the creditors had expected in return for the entire company.

Although the Commerce One auction was certainly not the first patent auction, it did serve as an opening bell of a more liquid IP market. Beginning in the spring of 2006, Ocean Tomo began conducting semiannual IP auctions. And each successive auction has seen not only an increase in participation by both buyers and sellers but also significant growth in the number of transactions and the value of the assets auctioned.

IP auctions, though, are just the tip of an iceberg's worth of new activity. Ocean Tomo, for example, is now working to create a physical IP marketplace known as IP Exchange Chicago. The goal of this exchange is to provide a physical location for the trading of IP assets. In the end, Ocean Tomo expects to collaborate and partner with one or more of the world's leading stock, option, and futures exchanges to bring about the world's first financial exchange exclusively dedicated to IP assets.

As the volume of transactions for IP assets reaches a critical threshold, Ocean Tomo's notion that buyers and sellers will benefit from transacting their business in a centralized marketplace starts to make more sense. That marketplace might be a real physical exchange like the floor of the New York Stock Exchange or the Chicago Mercantile Exchange, or it might be a virtual marketplace like the National Association of Securities Dealers Automated Quotations (NASDAQ) electronic trading system. The electronic exchanges of the e-commerce days failed not only because the IP market was not sufficiently developed, but also because they were not capable of handling the complexity of real-world IP transactions. Not all of those online IP exchanges failed however. One of the survivors was Yet2.com. Founded at the peak of the e-commerce boom with investments by Siemens, Bayer, Honeywell, DuPont, Procter & Gamble, Caterpillar, and NTT Leasing, Yet2 was one of the more serious entrants into the IP exchange space.

Like all of the other IP exchanges, Yet2 quickly discovered that merely listing IP assets for sale (or license) and collecting transactions fees was not a viable business model. Unlike the others, however, Yet2 was able to successfully alter their business model to provide the kind of services that make real-world IP transactions possible.

Today Yet2 has more than 100,000 registered users, including more than a dozen Fortune 500 companies and over 10,000 small and medium-size enterprises. Yet2 is able to successfully broker and facilitate IP transactions because it provides a full suite of IP services, everything from technology search and analysis to licensing and transaction support.

The market for IP rights has been growing through private licensing transactions for many years, growing from less than $1 billion in 1970 to an estimated $300 billion today. With this private transaction market as a backdrop, public IP transactions appear set for takeoff.

STAGE 6. DERIVATIVES EMERGE.

As assets become more liquid, trading moves from the asset itself to derivatives like options. In some cases, these derivatives can be more readily traded than the underlying asset. This has been the case with the real estate market, and it is likely that it will be with the IP market as well.

Prior to the 1970s, for example, real estate assets were bought and sold almost

exclusively by principals in the transaction. There were no securities based on
real estate, and the debt associated with these transactions was almost always
held to maturity by the original lender. When more innovative real estate securities made their debut, they quickly became one of the hottest asset categories in
the marketplace. Commercial real estate properties, which were sold as bundles,
were converted into tradable securities known as Real Estate Investment Trusts.
Investors found these extremely attractive, which helped boost the value of these
REITs from about $1 billion in market capitalization to more than $300 billion
in just thirty years.

On the debt side of the equation, residential mortgages were held by the local
savings and loans that originated them. This all changed in the1980s when Sa-
lomon Brothers pioneered the mortgage-backed securities market. Billions of dollars of residential mortgages were purchased from S&Ls, packaged into bondlike
instruments, and then resold to investors. From the original handful of mortgage-
backed securitizations in the 1970s, the market grew explosively to more than
$1.5 trillion of outstanding securities by 1995.

The size and the rapid emergence of the market for real estate–related securities demonstrates the kind of potential that exists for a highly valuable but largely
untraded asset class like intellectual property. So it's no surprise that, even though
the market for IP remains in its early stages, there are already IP-related securities beginning to emerge.

"Bowie Bonds," for example, were those securities created in 1997 backed by
David Bowie's music royalties. And as he did with his music, Bowie established
a trend, as a number of IP-backed securities have been issued based on copyrights
(music and movies royalties), trademarks (franchise fees and brand royalties),
and patents (mostly drug patents).

Most of these securities have been based on a fairly stable set of IP-based royalty streams like the anti-inflammatory drug Remicade, which is used in the
treatment of rheumatoid arthritis, Crohn's disease, and other inflammatory dis-
eases. Other IP-related derivatives are also beginning to emerge. Ocean Tomo,
for example, has launched two IP-based stock indexes and related Exchange
Traded Funds: the Ocean Tomo 300 Patent Index (Amex: OTPAT) and its related
ETF (Amex: OTP) and the Ocean Tomo 300 Patent Growth Index (Amex:
OTPATG) and its ETF (Amex: OTR) are stock indexes of companies with dispro-
portionately valuable patent portfolios. In the future, similar indexes will be created based on brand/trademark and copyright portfolios.

As we look ahead, more varieties of IP-based securities are sure to emerge. One
proposed method of increasing liquidity in the IP market is to pass legislation

that creates Patent Investment Trusts that would look similar to REITs. Another proposed IP derivative is the Tradable Technology Baskets, which are traded financial futures contracts based on the value of a patent portfolio related to a specific technology. Given the value and the variety of IP assets, the potential for financial engineers to create IP-based derivative securities certainly seems promising.

A Search for Value: IP and *Moneyball*

Before IP can fulfill its vast potential as a tradable asset class, there are significant challenges that must be overcome. Because the established economic system in which we all live and operate was designed for an industrial economy, we lack asset valuation methods, and accounting systems that allow us to value, track, and measure the stocks and flows of intellectual capital in our businesses and in the economy. For businesses, economists, and politicians, this is a huge problem. For investors, on the other hand, it presents a huge opportunity.

One of our favorite business books is Michael Lewis's *Moneyball*. While you might find this book in the sports section, it is first and foremost a business book, and a fine one at that. In it Lewis describes the business of baseball. Specifically Lewis illustrates how Billy Beane, the general manager of the Oakland A's, managed to consistently win more games than nearly every other team in the league, despite having the second-lowest payroll. What Beane did was to free his organization from the "unthinking prejudice rooted in baseball's traditions," and completely rethink the game of baseball.

The challenge for Beane was finding a way to compete with teams like the New York Yankees who spent three times as much on player salaries as he could. To compete in that system, Beane realized, he had to become better at finding bargains in the player talent pool than any other team in the league. What Beane discovered was that "baseball scouting was at roughly the same stage of development in the twenty-first century as professional medicine had been in the eighteenth." In other words, baseball's talent valuation system stunk—and for Beane, that smelled like opportunity.

By conducting a "systematic scientific investigation" of his sport, Beane was able to find inefficiencies that allowed him to acquire talented players that other teams didn't want, and to get them at bargain prices. Beane and his cadre of brilliant statisticians broke out of the traditional ways of thinking and made a serious study of what characteristics of a player's performance really contributed to winning. What they found was that traditional baseball "experts" valued the wrong things. By rethinking the value equation in baseball, Beane not only found a way to compete against richer teams, he started a revolution that continues to ripple through the game.

Today the identification of value in intellectual property is at a similar stage of development to that of baseball scouting before Billy Beane, and of eighteenth-century medicine before the germ theory of disease. Like old-time baseball, the traditions of the game of business continue to blind business executives to the value of their IP assets, and this leads to dramatic mispricing of these assets across the entire economy.

Valuing intellectual property, however, is hard. IP valuation experts often come to widely divergent views about the value of a particular piece of intellectual property during licensing or litigation. The alternative methods and assumptions that are brought into play more often lead to conflict rather than consensus. The topic of valuation is so unsettled that even the U.S. Congress has felt the need to weigh in within the context of patent reform. Recently, the International Organization for Standardization (ISO) has proposed to set a standard for patent valuation.

Ultimately, IP assets are worth whatever someone is willing to pay for them. In other words, the market determines the value. As the frequency of IP transactions increases, so too will the number of available benchmarks to help guide valuation. Some leading practitioners in the IP community are even calling for open reporting of IP transactions. Increased transaction volumes, improved valuation methods, and greater transparency will make IP assets easier to value. Meanwhile, a lot of work still needs to be done.

In *Moneyball*, one of the most important observations about valuing baseball players was a seemingly obvious insight: that the objective of the game is to score more runs than your opponent. The value of an offensive player, therefore, should be determined by his ability to produce runs. What Beane and his team did, though, was find new ways to measure the value of offensive production beyond the standard metrics—batting average, home runs, and runs batted in—that had been used for a century. By using a new lens to view player values, the Oakland A's were able to identify highly valuable players that other teams had overlooked.

A similar insight from the world of IP can lead to equally profound results. The objective of the game of business is to generate profits. So an IP asset's value is determined by its contribution to profit generation. By delineating the various ways that IP can contribute to profits, and measuring the performance of the IP asset along those dimensions, it is possible to identify valuable IP assets that others have overlooked. Or at least, it is no more difficult to do this than determine which college baseball player will become the next Alex Rodriguez.

By systematically mapping profits to products, products to technologies, and technologies to IP assets, the most valuable IP assets in any industry can be revealed. And for investors, this ability to identify mispriced assets, acquire them, and place them where they would have the highest value is a formula for tremendous wealth generation.

Although it is often difficult to assess the value of individual patents, brands, and other forms of IP, it is much easier to assess the value of portfolios. In the same way that the volatility of stock portfolios is lower than the volatility of the individual stocks, the same is true of IP portfolios. This fact will affect the way that IP is bought and sold, as well as the kind of financial derivatives that are available to trade.

In the real estate market, for comparison, individual properties or mortgages are difficult to value. An individual property value can rise or fall based on the specific circumstances surrounding that property (the same is true of the relationship between a mortgage and a mortgage holder). If the property down the road is converted into a landfill, the value of a nearby property may decline. If it is instead converted into a golf course, that property's value may rise.

When these assets are bundled together, though, you can eliminate many of the specific risks attached to an individual asset. This not only can provide a more stable return, it makes those assets much easier to value. The same rationale applies in the IP world. While a single patent on a technology may become extremely valuable if that technology is chosen in the marketplace, its value could plummet if an alternative technology wins. By eliminating some of the risks that are unique to a particular patent, the returns from a portfolio of patents can be more stable, and therefore more easy to value.

Put another way, portfolios of patents are more valuable than the sum of their parts.

"You Can Expect What You Inspect"

The world-renowned statistician and consultant W. Edwards Deming, who is best known for his work in Japan after World War II, is often quoted as saying, "You can't manage what you can't measure." In fact, he actually said this belief was wrong and he repeatedly made the point that managers are called on to manage things that are difficult to measure, or can only be measured imprecisely.

What Deming did say, though, is "you can expect what you inspect." Since remarkably few businesses today do much of anything to inspect their intellectual property, it should come as no surprise that they often fail to extract the value out of their IP. The economic and accounting systems that we operate with today were designed to account for industrial companies operating in an industrial age. Investments in intangibles like IP, therefore, do not appear as investments in the financial statements of companies or in the national accounts used by macroeconomists. From an accounting perspective, IP continues to be thought of merely in terms of the expenses its creation generates.

This failure to inspect and properly account for intellectual property leads to awful decision making by companies, managers, and nations. Except for a few special cases, R&D spending and brand-building expenditures like advertising continue to be expensed as incurred. In other words, all of the money that companies spend to create their most valuable assets, their IP assets, never shows up on their books as assets at all.

If a company constructs a piece of equipment, all of the costs associated with that equipment are then tallied and the asset's value gets added to the company's balance sheet. If that equipment is then used in the production of the company's products, a charge for the use of that machine will be included in the cost of producing that product. The discipline of accounting for the use of the company's assets means that managers have a very good reason not to waste these assets— it comes out of their year-end bonus. It also means that the manager's performance in using those assets can be measured and formally reported as return on the assets (ROA).

In contrast, since IP assets don't appear on the company's balance sheet, the cost of using those assets doesn't appear in the "cost of goods sold" of the product. As a result, managers are encouraged to waste the company's most precious assets, it is impossible to calculate an ROA, and the profitability of the products produced is overstated.

Bad accounting creates perverse incentives, and ultimately bad decision making. The currently accepted accounting methods undervalue IP assets and overstate the profitability of production. Worse yet, highly productive IP assets are used to subsidize the low (and often negative) returns of unproductive physical assets. Because the cost of using IP assets is excluded from product accounting, prices are set too low, and many times products that appear to be profitable simply aren't. As a result, numerous companies destroy value by following the conventional strategy of selling, manufacturing, and shipping products (the modern-day version of the River Rouge) when they would actually be worth more if they stopped making things and simply licensed their IP.

The inefficiencies don't stop there, however. As discussed earlier, large companies who do not have all of the IP they need to produce their products often cross-license their IP to other companies in their industries. These are barter transactions where one party's IP rights are exchanged for another's. The value of these transactions is often enormous, but they do not show up in the accounting records. As a result, the companies on both sides of the transaction fail to understand the true return on their innovation activities since they never record the royalty income, while also systematically overestimating the financial performance of their products because the cost of licensing in IP is never subtracted from the products' profit margin.

This means that companies think of their innovation and branding activities as cost centers and their product businesses as profit centers, when, in fact, exactly the opposite is often true. This same error leads to incorrect transfer pricing between business units, wrong decisions in international dumping cases, and a systematic misallocation of resources by companies and nations.

Oddly, there is an exception to the rule of incorrect accounting for IP. When one company acquires another company, then the accounting rules require that the acquiring company place a value on its books for the acquired IP assets. These assets are then expensed as they are used to generate revenue and profits in the future.

While it is a good thing that this small island of precise (but not necessarily accurate) accounting for IP exists, it leads to the strange result that the acquired IP is deemed to be expensive for a product manager while self-developed IP is considered to be free for the taking. Obviously, a rational product manager whose bonus is tied to their product's profitability will do what they can to avoid using acquired IP. Is it any wonder that the "not invented here syndrome" bemoaned by executives continues to persist?

For companies who properly "inspect" their IP assets, there is much that they can "expect." Recognizing the true value of a company's IP assets can change the power structure in the organization as innovation and marketing activities become profit centers. Investment in the creation of IP assets will increase. Both product pricing and make-or-buy decisions will be dramatically altered. It may even lead in some cases to the radical decision *not* to manufacture or market a particular product or product line because marketing the IP is more profitable than marketing the product.

For investors, these horrible methods of accounting for IP create both problems and opportunities. The problem is that the financial statements of the companies whose stocks are publicly traded are misleading in a significant way.

Investors often look to profit margins and cash flows from operations to tell them about the health of a company. But these numbers are skewed and, in some cases, completely false. Companies that appear on the surface to be profitable may, in fact, be destroying value. Other companies, though, that appear unprofitable may be sitting on a gold mine of valuable IP that will (or can) lead to extraordinary future profits.

Either way, the bottom line is that you can't tell by simply looking at the bottom line.

On the flip side, mispriced assets mean opportunities for investors who know how to spot them. The news gets even better once you realize the wealth of public information that is available about a company's IP assets. Patent and trademark databases around the world record company ownership of critical IP assets. By examining the IP holdings of companies, and adjusting the financial statements to reflect their true strength, a much more accurate picture of company value can be assembled. To demonstrate how different the real economics of IP are, consider the story of Sears.

In November 2004, the cover of *Business Week* posed the question: is Eddie Lampert "The Next Warren Buffett"? Lampert, a hedge fund operator of growing fame, acquired a controlling interest in Kmart for about $1 billion. At the time, many people questioned the wisdom of acquiring the retailer, which was struggling to compete with Walmart and Target. Lampert, though, knew that his investment was a safe bet.

What did Lampert know that everyone else was missing? Lampert recognized that Kmart owned assets that were worth much more than what he paid for them, a fact he quickly proved. Shortly after Kmart emerged from bankruptcy, Lampert sold off sixty-eight stores to competitors Sears and Home Depot for some $850 million. In just a few short months, Lampert had recovered almost the entire purchase price by selling less than a mere 5 percent of Kmart's 1,500 store locations. Shareholders have been richly rewarded, as the stock price increased tenfold between the time it exited bankruptcy in May 2003 and the summer of 2005. Since that time, Kmart has continued to maintain that lofty valuation.

But Lampert wasn't done. He used the cash from asset sales and the improved operations of Kmart to acquire the much larger (but also struggling) Sears for $11 billion. Like Kmart, Lampert saw that Sears also had unrealized asset value. Some of that value is in real estate, but some of it is also in IP.

In May 2006, Sears Holdings packaged up its three most valuable brands, Kenmore, Craftsman, and DieHard, into a separate (but wholly owned) subsidiary called KCD IP. This new entity then issued $1.8 billion in bonds backed by the value of its IP. The parent company, Sears Holdings, now pays royalties for the use of these three brands just like it would if it was licensing them from another company (even though, in reality, Sears still owns them).

To date, Sears continues to retain ownership of all of these bonds. Nevertheless, holding them gives the company many options. For example, Sears could sell the bonds to investors. Or it could exchange them for some other asset like the stock or debt of a competitor that it might want to acquire. By realizing the value of an off-balance-sheet asset, Sears has created a source of financing which it can use to funds its operations, or as a source of cash to fund further acquisitions.

In the Kmart deal, Lampert recognized that the value of the real estate holdings on the books (recorded at their original purchase price) was nowhere near their real economic value. But at least they were on the balance sheet: Sears's highly valuable brands were not on the balance sheet at all.

This bit of financial engineering, although relatively new in the IP world, is not particularly novel. Companies often borrow money against assets like inventories, and receivables. What's new is the creation, for the first time, of asset-backed securities out of intangible assets. Perhaps even more significant, however, is the impact that securitizing its brands can have on the company's operations.

Now that Sears has placed a price on its brands and its product managers are forced to pay royalties for their use, you can be sure that the cost of using them will now be included in the cost of sales of its products. By making the value of its IP explicit, the cost of advertising can be seen for the investment that it is. Product prices will also need to be adjusted to reflect the cost of using the brand, and perhaps, Sears may discover that some of its products are not profitable at all.

Now imagine if all companies were to place an explicit value on their IP assets, and charge themselves (and others) a market rate for their use. The implications would be staggering. The availability of capital could suddenly multiply. Product profitability would be radically altered. Transfer pricing between divisions would change dramatically. And cross-licenses would cease to be barter transactions, but would have to reflect actual market prices. In short, the business world would change forever.

For an investor like Eddie Lampert, unrecognized value is the name of the game. In the modern economy, there is no greater pool of unrecognized assets than the IP that is hidden inside corporations. The opportunity to convert IP assets into capital in this way has the potential to unlock trillions of dollars of value for reinvestment into the economy. If the accounting is right, investors and managers will also understand that investing in innovation, the creation of new IP assets, is the highest-return investment that they could make.

While many companies are hesitant to venture into the unseen economy, they will eventually be forced to change, whether they like it or not. The fact is that other companies are illegally using the property of many of the world's most innovative companies, both large and small, and the managers are either unaware or unwilling to make them stop.

If competitors or customers were illegally using the company's factories, or if the sales force was moonlighting by selling competitors' products, you can bet that management would intervene immediately. But this is essentially what happens when companies fail to enforce their intellectual property.

Practices like this cannot go on forever. In the near future, we fully expect to see more frequent shareholder litigation against managers who waste valuable intellectual assets (shareholder activists have recently forced strategy shifts at companies like Mosaid and Transmeta). Patents, of course, are available for anyone to read. All it takes is for an individual shareholder to read a patent, discover an unprosecuted infringement by a competitor, and bring a shareholder suit against management for failure to enforce its property rights. When that happens, managers will suddenly discover the incentive to "inspect" and manage their most valuable assets.

Eventually, decision rights will be taken away from managers who fail to exercise their responsibility to utilize and defend their intellectual property.

The creation of a marketplace for IP assets has the potential to be the greatest financial revolution of our lifetimes. We are at the beginning of a self-reinforcing cycle in which increased transaction volumes provide improved valuation benchmarks. Improved valuation will then encourage companies to recognize the value of their IP assets on their books and in their product costs. And when this happens, enormous amounts of capital will be created, and investments in innovation will be revealed as the most profitable investments available. This in turn will lead to increased investment in new innovation and a race to create the next generation of IP assets.

For smart investors, this signals tremendous opportunities for wealth creation. For corporate executives, it means radically altering the way they do business. But for the rest of us, this virtuous cycle has the potential to fuel an increase in the rate of economic growth not seen since the Industrial Revolution.

Now, that really is a capital idea.

CHAPTER 10

Strategy Reloaded

INVISIBLE ADVANTAGE FOR THE PRACTICING STRATEGIST

Welcome to the real world.
—*Morpheus to Neo*, The Matrix, 1999

O
n July 7, 2006, Peter Johnston, a student who had recently finished his freshman year at Yale, was home in Hinsdale, Illinois, for the summer. Little did he know that, as an early riser, he would soon find himself at the center of a race that would speed, ever so slightly, the emergence of what we now call Web 2.0. One of the rapidly emerging types of intangible asset–driven companies that deserve to be called a company of ideas, the businesses that are part of the Web 2.0 revolution are driven by a wave of powerfully innovative new Internet-based tools like blogs, wikis, mashups, and other forms of social software that are changing how humans interact with each other. But when it comes to celebrating the profit potential of the interactive, networked world of Web 2.0 businesses, many stories about Web 2.0—specifically those written about the exploding phenomenon of online social networking—tend to focus on the wrong thing. When such stories tout the free and open nature of these new technologies, or simply the age of those who use these new tools, they miss out on the fact that there is a race to control the key intangible assets—the IP—underlying these emerging technologies. It is no surprise that the competition is fierce, since the winner will potentially gain vast influence over the future of how business is conducted. In other words, there's a lot of money at stake. As

in any race, strategy plays a pivotal role. But what form does strategy take when it comes to Web 2.0? That's where Peter's story comes into play.

Back in the summer of 2006, Facebook.com, the now seemingly ubiquitous online hangout founded in 2004, was available only to students like Peter. Facebook was also divided into many small networks, where each network was based around a single college or university. While students like Peter used the site to organize online groups to convene everything from late-night study sessions to discussions about the Harry Potter books, the groups could only be as large as the number of users in a specific network. (Yale's network, for instance, had about 5,000 users.) While that limitation may have thrown some cold water on the potential for intercollegiate dating, it did give the site an air of exclusivity.

But that all changed on July 7 when Facebook introduced something it called Global Groups. With this new feature, users would be able to form groups with users that belonged to any other Facebook network. Whether Facebook's founders realized it or not, they had just offered up a prize in a contest many a college student would covet: bragging rights for whoever could create the biggest group Facebook had ever seen. As one prescient blogger, a Middlebury College student named Ryan Kellett, wrote that morning, "Now, the hard part begins. Students across the country will compete on recreating their favorite groups on the universal scale (luckily, you can't join another school's existing local groups). Individuals will now possibly belong to a local and national version of the same group. But with so many students entering the fray, which groups will win out?"

College students on summer break are not typically known to be early risers, so even in the Central Time Zone, Peter was one of the first Facebook users to see the posting that announced the creation of Global Groups. And he was certainly among the first to grasp and act upon their potential. Whatever the reason that propels innovators forward—The thrill of competition? A desire for fame? The lure of a cool problem?—he decided to enter the competition at full throttle. Leaving aside any pretense at subtlety, he declared his intentions right from the start. As he sat at his computer that morning, he decided to create a Global Group with the goal of attracting more than 1 million members and to name it "The Largest Facebook Group Ever." Beginning with a few e-mails to his brother and some friends, the race was on. And it truly was a race; Peter's group soon faced several competitors vying to claim the prize as the world's largest Facebook group.

For Peter, competing in the race became an all-consuming passion as well as an adventure filled with enough twists and turns to fill a novel. There were technical and operational obstacles to overcome, like solving Facebook's limitations on how the group could virally extend invitations to potential members (Peter solved that one in part by creating "feeder" groups and even coined a term, "admin me," an act that temporarily gave a group member administrative powers to add members, a term that has since made its way into the online "Urban Dictionary"). There were also online battles to be fought and won with evil-minded trespassers (Peter had to fight of a group of collegiate hackers who staged a coup d'etat of sorts by electronically removing Peter from leadership of the group he founded). Peter even had to wage a battle against Facebook itself after administrators used their power of eminent domain to take over possession of the group's management (Peter ultimately won back authority after Facebook programmers sided with him in a dispute with both the hackers and renegade members of the group who complained about his censorship of profane postings on the group's message board). To keep his followers motivated during these setbacks, Peter exhorted them with inspirational messages. On groupwide postings, he sent out notes inspired by sources ranging from Plato's *Republic* to Lincoln's Gettysburg Address:

> We hit a hard cap for admins (not anymore), were taken over and shut down, slowed facebook itself, began to disappear, faced a crisis on the board, and suffered the tyranny of eminent domain (twice!) . . . yet still we rumble on. This group was dedicated to an idea. In the pursuit of this idea we have given our toil, our hopes, and our dreams. Shall we now, in the face of adversity, give up on the group and thereby let the idea perish? Or shall we wholly consecrate ourselves to the idea, rising to fight all the powers arrayed against us? Arise and go forth! UNITE and INVITE!

But right from the outset "The Largest Facebook Group Ever" lived up to its name. Within hours of launching the group, it was placed firmly near the top of the rankings with 10,000 members. By the end of the week he had passed 50,000. During the second week, things really took off. Peter's group moved into first place among all groups as it reached the 400,000 point, a group size so unexpectedly large that Facebook took the group off the server for a few hours to avoid having the system shut down. After that, although the growth slowed down a bit, over the next few weeks the membership rolls surged ahead like a juggernaut. Over the rest of the summer, he passed every 100,000 marker comfortably ahead of any other group. By the end of August, group membership stood at over 900,000 (a full 10 percent of Facebook's 9 million registered users) but by then the growth rate was leveling off. But with his goal of 1 million members firmly in sight, it was time to go back to school. Like the serious student he was, Peter decided to put his summer hijinks behind him and move on to other things. Still,

"The Largest Facebook Group Ever" lived on, and remained the number one group for over a year, hovering between 900,000 and 950,000 members for most of the 2006–7 school year.

Things picked back up after the school year ended and, some fourteen months after beginning his project, on August 16, 2007, Peter finally did achieve his goal of attracting 1 million members. His only disappointment was that he wasn't the first to cross that threshold. The prize for that achievement went to a nostalgia group called "If you remember this, you grew up in the 90s," although Peter did edge out another group founded in support of Stephen Colbert, the Comedy Central news host, and his whimsical quest to become U.S. president. In the end, while Peter had lost the gold medal, he won a kind of moral victory anyway as he set the pace all the way to the finish line. Not only that, he gained some modest fame—he says that, more than once, people have asked him, "are you *the* Peter Johnston?"—and along the way he learned some particularly valuable lessons in how to motivate and organize people.

But Peter's story points to more than just another college kid's lark: it highlights, in fact, a bit of opportunistic collaborative strategy on the part of Facebook itself. Consider the valuable knowledge Facebook learned from the thousands of hours that Peter's friends and competitors logged in their race. Perhaps without realizing it, or because of his passion for competition, Peter launched a system-wide quality assurance test on the scalability of the network tools, helping expose flaws and weaknesses at no cost to the company. He also gave Facebook's administrators direct feedback on the way members like him were using the system at peak times and potentially what new features they could add to make the network even more sticky to its users—user-driven features that Facebook could potentially patent and own. And that was only the beginning.

Global Groups was a prelude to a more aggressive shift in its network structure. On September 11, 2006, Facebook abandoned its focus on student networks, and opened its network to anyone over thirteen years of age. Since then, Facebook has continued to roll out hundreds of new features and applications to its growing user base. More than 50 million men, women, and children currently visit the site to check for updates on their personal or professional networks while another 150,000 or so sign up every single day to join them. In a little more than four years, the site has become the sixth-most-visited site on the entire Internet. Thanks to the passion of users like Peter, and a strategy that embraces innovation and massive collaboration, Facebook has become the face of Web 2.0 today—and consequently the early leader with the potential to change the face of how business is done tomorrow.

"Why do my eyes hurt?" "You've never used them before."

The race for advantage in Web 2.0 technology is one of the most dramatic struggles in the world of business today. While some folks mistakenly see the advent of Web 2.0 as a return to the truly free roots of the Internet, or simply the realm of youthful hijinks, they miss the fact that there is a significant story of IP competition just under the surface. Sure, there are plenty of business plans that call for giving away pieces of software or free membership aimed at attracting eyeballs. But recall our story from chapter 6 about the open-source movement and the development of so-called freeware like the Linux operation system. When we use an IP lens to focus in on Web 2.0 like we did with Linux, we begin to see the themes of this book take shape as we also observe the evolution of the technology that continues to change our lives. If any single cluster of technologies emerges as the dominant standard of how we interact with each other, and a company manages to own that distinction, we could see a shift in power not unlike that which occurred when Microsoft Windows became the de facto standard for a computer's user interface.

As its name implies, Web 2.0 applications are made possible by dozens, perhaps thousands, of breakthroughs that preceded it. The foundation for the Internet itself, which has its roots in the U.S. military's ARPANET, is built upon the technology breakthroughs in the areas of computing power, affordable memory, and user interfaces that helped turn computers into household appliances. The idea that this network of computers could do more than just store data, that it could come alive with photos, music, and virtual representations of ourselves called avatars, also required a mental leap on the part of the users themselves. To give credit to any one individual or team for "inventing" the Internet (sorry, Al Gore)—let alone the more recent Web 2.0 phenomenon of social networking—would clearly be a disservice to all those who contributed to the base technologies that made this a reality. But what does this all mean for Facebook?

Wunderkind Mark Zuckerberg, then twenty years old, founded Facebook back in February 2004 while he was attending Harvard (he dropped out a year later to run his company full-time—one of many parallels, in fact, between he and Bill Gates). And it was also Zuckerberg who famously rejected several bids to sell his company—including a reported $1 billion offer from Yahoo—because he wanted, as he put it later on, "to build things." When Microsoft agreed to pay a reported $240 million for a 1.6 percent slice of Zuckerberg's company in October of 2007, it meant that Facebook was worth an estimated $15 billion and that Zuckerberg's 20 percent stake in his venture was worth a cool $3 billion. In March 2008, Zuck-

erberg made the *Forbes* annual billionaires list. At twenty-three years of age, coming in at number 785 out of more than 1,100, he was the youngest self-made
billionaire ever.

The more important question, though, is why would Microsoft value Facebook
so highly? (And why would a bright young person like Peter Johnston spend so
much time on it?) After all, Facebook was far from the first social networking site
to take the Web by storm (consider Friendster or even Usenet). And while it may
be the fastest-growing site these days, growing by about 3 percent a month, its
user base remains about half that of Rupert Murdoch's Myspace.com. To com-
plicate things even further, Zuckerberg and Facebook have become something
of a magnet for lawsuits. For one, Zuckerberg has been accused of stealing both
the idea of Facebook and some original source code from former Harvard class-
mates. At the same time, Facebook has been named in at least two lawsuits that
claim that the site's underlying technology infringes on existing patents. So again,
why in the world would a software titan like Microsoft make that kind of investment in a fledgling site like Facebook that just might prove to be the next spectacular dot-com flameout? What does Microsoft see that others don't?

For one, just as James Watt built upon the mostly failed efforts of those who
preceded him, Mark Zuckerberg and his Facebook team had a lot of existing technology to study and learn from before launching their business. Facebook clearly
had predecessors, as we can see by the growing number of patent infringement
lawsuits initiated by early innovators like Six Degrees, an early social network
that appeared in the late 1990s, and Friendster, an early but now fading Web 2.0
star. While pioneers like Jonathan Abrams, Friendster's founder, laid the foundation for the modern social networking application, they also failed to solve all the
technical and business design problems that came with implementing a functional, large-scale social circle. Friendster's servers, for example, couldn't keep
up with demand during peak networking hours, and users quickly tired of wait-
ing for their profile pages to load. MySpace, on the other hand, has inspired fear
among parents because it embraces anonymity and allows users to post false
identities. (There have been multiple reports about online predators prospecting
within MySpace, and also the well-known story of a girl who, at the end of 2007,
committed suicide after a neighbor used a false profile to ridicule her.)

Zuckerberg, though, learned from both the promise and the mistakes of these
early efforts. For one, Facebook's users serve as volunteer editors, making sure
that profiles represent real people. He also moved to take advantage of new opportunities these earlier sites failed to capitalize on, like opening up the Facebook
programming environment to outside developers and listening to his user base

to see how he could integrate advertising into their social networks (though the example of Beacon, a controversial purchase notification feature that automatically broadcast a user's online activities to everyone in their network, shows that Zuckerberg has also moved too far for his users' tastes at times).

While many folks under the age of thirty admire Zuckerberg's achievements, not everyone in America is apparently as aware of or enamored with him: the *60 Minutes* episode that featured him on January 11, 2007, drew a season-low number of viewers, only 9.6 million compared to its normal 14.4 million. While some of this could be written off to a football game between the New York Giants and the Dallas Cowboys that aired at the same time, some of this disappointing response could clearly be credited to the fact that young people simply don't watch *60 Minutes*—it's their parents and even grandparents who would have been tuning in. On one hand it's certainly true that the baby boomers and the generations that preceded them simply aren't interested in this thing the "kids" in Silicon Valley are calling Web 2.0. But is it possible, in fact, that the lack of mainstream interest in Facebook is a sign that Facebook may be just another fad? After all, the kids in what we call Gen-Y or the Obama Generation have no respect for things like making money let alone something like IP. They expect to get content like music, videos, and software for free, right? "How could someone as young as Zuckerberg ever create a successful business if he gives away everything?" the naysayers will ask.

The truth is that Zuckerberg does understand the business value of IP, at least intuitively, and that Facebook is actually an intriguing IP strategy story—if you know how to look.

"I can only show you the door. You're the one that has to walk through it."

While there is no question that Facebook has a long road ahead of it before it earns a spot in the same league as IBM, P&G, or even Microsoft, the company looks, when you don this new lens we've given you, a bit different from the one you think you know. It also happens to be a great case study of how the lessons of this book look when applied to a Web 2.0 business—an industry where IP supposedly doesn't matter. The important question then becomes, what does Facebook teach us about what *you* should do differently on Monday morning? If we would make one point above all others, it's that in the real world you have to *do your homework*. Throughout our journey together we've worked hard to convey our lessons through an entertaining collection of stories and morals, so instead of delivering the homework assignment through a tedious list of bullets and tendentious exhortation, we'll use Facebook's story to illustrate how this leading Web 2.0 company is learning to leverage the three key IP strategies we've described in Section II: Control, Collaborate, and Simplify. Your homework assignment, should you choose to accept it, is to apply these lessons to your own business.

CONTROL IN ACTION

One of the more interesting aspects of the battles being fought in the social networking space is the question of who owns what. While there is no question that sites like MySpace and Friendster preceded Facebook, it is less clear that any of them did an effective job at establishing any kind of meaningful ownership over the technology besides a few patents related to finding dates online. This may be because it wasn't until Rupert Murdoch bought MySpace for $580 million in 2005 that anyone fully understood the kind of value social networking sites would someday have. That is, besides Mark Zuckerberg.

As Facebook has prospered and Zuckerberg has become wealthy, he has emerged as a somewhat controversial figure. While many in the media celebrate his youth and precocious business acumen (he filed his first patent application—not related to Facebook—as a Harvard freshman), the claims made by his past business associates paint a far less rosy picture. Cameron and Tyler Winkelvoss, two brothers who reportedly hired Zuckerberg to work on their Harvard-based social networking site—ConnectU—back in 2002, have sued Zuckerberg, claiming he stole their idea. Aaron Greenspan, another Harvard classmate of Zuckerberg's, has said that Zuckerberg literally stole the name Facebook from him: Greenspan had written a program called houseSYSTEM that contained a section of code called "The Face Book."

While it would be foolish to discount these stories altogether, and at press time the cases against Zuckerberg were still pending, the question embedded in these conflicts is not whether Mark Zuckerberg stole ideas from his friends, but whether they actually *owned* anything in the first place. The key point is that Zuckerberg understood the importance of *owning* the intangible assets that were crucial to making his investments in building Facebook worth something. He demonstrated this by working to aggressively secure his ownership from the very beginning. While Greenspan may have named his code, Zuckerberg purchased the domain name: thefacebook.com (he also later spent $200,000 to purchase the domain facebook.com in 2005 to coincide with a rebranding of the site). After launching his site, Zuckerberg also moved aggressively to secure patents on its technology. As of press time, Zuckerberg and his Facebook colleagues had eight pending patent applications on topics such as "social mapping" and "social timelines," which he filed starting in December 2005—less than two years after start-up and just seven months after receiving his first round of financing. (MySpace, on the other hand, has not yet applied for a patent as far as we can tell.) We would submit that one reason Microsoft moved so aggressively to invest in Facebook is because of Zuckerberg's foresight in establishing ownership over key intellectual property assets related to the social networking sector as a whole. This, of course, is another parallel between Zuckerberg and his new partner Gates. Just like Zuckerberg, Gates's acquisition of the code behind DOS, the operating system that launched the PC, involved controversies over ownership as well.

The key lesson, therefore, is that ownership matters. Just as we saw in the examples of companies like NTP and Qualcomm, companies with a strong IP ownership position are, in fact, the most valuable. And as we discussed in chapter 9, businesses now need to think globally when they consider the reach of their IP position. Facebook, to that point, expanded globally in the first year of it existence, enrolling students throughout the United States, Canada, Mexico, the United Kingdom, Australia, New Zealand, and Ireland. That means that Facebook not only has extended its user base globally but also has increased its number of application developers and advertising partnerships. The next lesson for Zuckerberg and his team, then, may be to ensure that they obtain and enforce their global property rights wherever possible. If imitation is the sincerest form of flattery, Facebook should certainly feel flattered, as there has been an explosion in the number of social networking clones and competitors around the world since it has come to prominence. The list of imitation sites includes Europe's StudiVZ, Australia's studentface.com.au, China's xiaonei.com, and Russia's vkontakte.ru. Interestingly, Friendster may be making a comeback based on its strong member base in the Philippines, which just might prove that Friendster and its IP could still prove to be a buying opportunity for someone armed with the right kind of lens.

But what can you learn from how Zuckerberg and Facebook have aggressively pursued ownership over key IP assets in the social networking sector? Practicing strategists should consider the following action agenda in order to ensure that they don't unintentionally become philanthropists:

1. **Own your distinction.** Whether it's your name, your software code, your inventions, or a Web address, you're not really in business unless you own the intangible assets that your customers value and that give you an edge over your competitors. As we've seen with Facebook, Mark Zuckerberg saw the opportunity

in social networking and he set out to own the assets he needed to profit from the opportunity, even though he may have left some of his college buddies behind in the process.

2. **Think global, act local.** We've been surprised at how frequently even well-educated executives don't grasp the local nature of the property rights associated with intangible assets. Only copyright protection extends globally, so if you want to protect your brands and inventions in global markets, you need to obtain exclusive rights to them in every country where you want protection. As Facebook has become more global, it has extended its IP ownership around the world as well. For example, Facebook has filed six of its eight patent applications with the World Intellectual Property Organization.

3. **Protect the company jewels.** As we've seen, intangible assets vary widely in value, which means that the lion's share of your current profits often depend on a small portfolio of assets. Zuckerberg has recognized the need to protect these key assets and filed for patents on his core technology, including Facebook's killer app, the feature that provides a regular social news feed to users.

4. **Own your future.** Strategists constantly make business decisions in the face of an uncertain future. Committing tangible resources to cover multiple bets about the future can get expensive. But IP investment can be a less expensive way to acquire options on multiple futures at the same time. To date, virtually all of Facebook's investment has been in developing its offering for consumers, but what happens if social networking jumps the divide between consumer application and corporate application? Have Zuckerberg and his team considered how they might develop their IP portfolio to give them a strong position in the corporate world?

5. **Balance market share growth with IP share growth.** Companies like MySpace and Facebook that break through in a new market always risk infringing on competitor technologies and paying a hefty price when a low-market-share shark comes calling. Facebook (with at least eight pending patent applications) is far better positioned than MySpace (with none yet published) to avoid becoming a target. And if they find that social networking providers as a group are becoming more dependent on using technology developed by others, they'll have a competitive advantage when it comes to buying in the technology that pure-play IP licensors have to sell.

6. **When you can't beat 'em, host 'em.** The companies who try to keep up with an intense pace of innovation on multiple fronts usually fall behind. Unlike MySpace and Friendster, who developed their own (and unremarkable) social software application suites, Zuckerberg decided early on not to try to control the

applications business. Instead, he encouraged developers to post their applications on Facebook and has done his best to turn Facebook into a friendly
host for the small companies who were betting their futures in Facebook.

7. **If you didn't make it, buy it.** Businesses who shed the "not invented here" syndrome
and embrace the idea of paying fair value for the inventions of others have a
huge advantage in a fast-changing markeplace. Facebook hasn't shifted much
into acquisition mode yet, but in July 2007 they did make their first acquisition, a software company named Parakey that, interestingly enough, was
started by former heads of the Mozilla Firefox project, Blake Ross and Joe
Hewitt. In light of the rapid expansion of patent estates in social networks, we
expect to see more IP-related acquisition, as either individual patent purchases
or entire company portfolios, in the near future. Has Zuckerberg considered
acquiring the IP of some of the other failing social networking competitors?
If he hasn't, he may find himself facing a few sharks down the road.

COLLABORATION IN ACTION

Needless to say, social networks like Facebook provide eloquent testimony to the
power of the network lens that we brought up in chapter 4. Zuckerberg's singu-
lar accomplishment may lie in his demonstrated ability to tap into powerful social
drives that no other business had yet served. Zuckerberg realized that most people didn't want a formal dating service à la Friendster; they wanted a place to hang
out with their friends from college instead. Now his network has grown and
evolved to include friends of all kinds. Girls in particular found their killer application in Facebook. Unlike virtually any other major Internet site, Facebook
has more females aged seventeen to twenty-five visiting the site than males. (After all, who wouldn't want a social timeline that could give you the latest news
feeds on their BFFs'* relationship status? Duhhh!!)

But why did Facebook succeed in tapping this audience when early movers
like Friendster failed? Friendster's growth, for one, stalled largely for technical
reasons right at the time it began to face stiff competition from upstarts like Facebook. Friendster users reported that page downloads would routinely grind to a
halt, largely because the system was poorly designed to keep up with large
amounts of traffic. In particular, a user's home page included statistics on the
number of network connections they had, a particularly onerous statistic to calculate given the limited server resources Friendster had at its disposal. Despite

*For those without a teenage daughter, "BFF" means "Best Friend Forever."

a number of active users who were raising warning flags, Abrams, a former software engineer with a prickly personality, thought the answer was to add more functionality rather than speed. The result was that, as we know, Friendster's following wasted away.

Could Friendster have flourished if it embraced its users and their needs in a different way? Looking back, it is clear that Abrams tried to control too much as he lost sight of the unpredictable nature of network interactions and how they grow. As a young single man, he assumed incorrectly that the main value of social networking was bringing two people together for relatively strong connections: in Friendster's case mostly dating. What Abrams missed entirely was the larger swarm of interactions for which less intense friends and even casual acquaintances have an appetite. If Abrams had taken a less restrictive view of networking, he might have seen that incentives to collaborate, as we saw in the case of Peter Johnston, don't always take the shape of one-on-one connections.

Zuckerberg and Facebook have also worked hard to embrace collaboration by establishing close relationships with application developers outside the organization. When Facebook first opened up their programming interface in 2006, it set off a tidal wave of innovative new applications that rapidly made their way into the Facebook community. At press time, there were more than 5,000 applications and widgets available—everything from photo-, music-, and video-sharing utilities to games of every conceivable theme. While not all of the applications reached a tipping point for users, massively popular games like "Pirates vs. Ninjas" and "FoodFight," both of which have been downloaded several million times, have meant significant popularity—along with some moderate financial success—for their developers. In fact, SocialMedia, a two-year-old software development company in Northern California, is an example of a company that now makes Facebook apps exclusively, gambling that by partnering with advertisers, it can build a successful business while renting its software to Facebook's 50 million users for free. TouchGraph, the software company whose technology underlies the network charts in this book, also has developed a Facebook app, which has been ranked among the top twenty-five Facebook applications. (In the wake of its rival's success in drawing new applications and developers, MySpace also has opened its doors to developers—but with much less fanfare, and results.)

There are also unfortunate examples of popular Facebook apps like Scrabulous, an online version of the ageless board game Scrabble, that have run into IP infringement problems. Hasbro and Mattel, the two companies who own the rights to the Scrabble trademark around the world, have pushed to have Facebook remove the application from the site.

Since Facebook, like Toyota, works closely with its own supplier network, it does find itself at risk if its suppliers go astray. However, these risks are clearly outweighed by the benefits of their innovation *keiretsu*. As more and more applications become successful, they will attract new developers, and users, to the community. And as the community draws new users, Facebook and its suppliers will share the spoils together, in the form of either advertising dollars or nominal access fees some application developers charge. Facebook's success, though, isn't tied to any one developer, which means that it can afford to experiment and fail with new technologies without risking a major hit. An agnostic approach to applications also means that Facebook can in theory team up with developers around the world.

Facebook has gone beyond simply making its social software environment open to developers: it has taken steps to ensure that there are funding sources available for them. The company launched its FBFund in September 2007, a $10 million fund backed by Facebook investors Accel Partners and the Founders Fund, that will supply $25,000 to $250,000 grants to qualified developers. Interestingly, other venture capital firms have set up their own funds targeted at Facebook developers, namely the Altura 1 Facebook Investment Fund and the AppFactory backed by Bay Partners. This kind of trend only serves to reinforce the legitimacy of Facebook's innovation network since a generation of new start-ups like SocialMedia has emerged to serve Facebook's community.

So what else can you learn from how Zuckerberg and Facebook have embraced collaboration in their business model? Practicing strategists should consider the following action ideas to avoid overplaying their hands and getting trapped in games of mutually assured destruction:

1. **Keep potential IP enemies close.** Underneath the covers of many prominent alliance announcements lies an agreement for an IP nonaggression pact. For example, when Facebook and Microsoft signed their partnership agreement in October 2007, most of the business press treated the deal like the dating game, one where Microsoft beat out Google for Facebook's affections. But both sides in this deal have an IP agenda. Certainly, when Facebook looks at Microsoft one of the things they see is their patent position: Microsoft is among the top patent applicants in the domain of social networking, way ahead of Facebook, in fact. They also have other IP that could prove critical to opening up new markets for Facebook, such as corporate accounts. By allying with Microsoft, Facebook is covering a vulnerable IP flank while also opening up new opportunities.

2. **Use IP to induce partnership.** On the other side, established players who face market limits in monetizing their innovations may find, as we saw with P&G, that licensing can be a profitable way to reach markets they could never hope to capture through conventional means. Microsoft may have this perspective when looking at Facebook. Imagine Microsoft trying to make a move to dominate yet another layer of the technology stack: they would likely fail for many reasons ranging from negative marketing buzz to antitrust enforcement. But by nurturing an alliance with Facebook (using their IP as both a carrot and a potential stick), they can sell their technology and solutions to Facebook while acquiring an insider's stake in the success of what might turn out to be the operating system for social interaction. We don't know whether Microsoft used its IP in this particular instance, but IP opportunities and threats often play a role in inducing partnership.

3. **Build an advantaged innovation network.** Developing more complex collaborations between companies requires an investment, often by the network leader, in building a set of alliances to support (and in some cases enforce) collaborative activity. It's hard to argue here that Facebook has built much of a *keiretsu* so far, but as an emerging company its alliance with Microsoft signals its choice to enter Microsoft's network rather than Google's. Microsoft has made over a hundred investments in promising companies over the last decade, from DreamWorks to Expedia.com, and it's likely to be Microsoft's *keiretsu* that will benefit the most from the addition of its newest member.

4. **Unleash user innovation.** Like eBay, Yahoo, and Wikipedia, the bulk of the content on Facebook is generated by volunteers who provide valuable work to their hosts without getting paid. As Facebook was building its system to grow and accommodate Global Groups, Peter Johnston's army of volunteers—an army that reached 1.2 million group members at its peak—and the whimsical wars in which they engaged provided tremendous value to Facebook by demonstrating scalability, pressure-testing security provisions, identifying technical bottlenecks, and fine-tuning administrative routines for large-scale operations. For Peter, when a pretty girl learns his name and asks, "Are you *the* Peter Johnston?" financial compensation is beside the point; for Facebook, Peter's participation is a key part of the engine that makes its business go.

5. **Support innovation with trust.** Facebook has made relatively few missteps in their short history, but during the launch of the controversial "Beacon" project they learned a lesson about the constraints that network participants place on even their most central players. When, in late 2007, Facebook introduced a feature that sent purchase information to a user's friends as part of a news feed, they

crossed a sensitive line—and apparently spoiled a lot of Christmas surprises as well. Their move prompted an outcry from users over a violation of their privacy expectations (even the political advocacy group Moveon.org inserted themselves into the mix). Despite initially taking some heat from users, bloggers, and the media, Facebook quickly recovered. They engaged in a public dialogue (on the site) with the most vocal critics, quickly modified the feature to address user concern, and Zuckerberg publicly apologized—admitting that Facebook "made a lot of mistakes" and "did a bad job" with the release. By responding quickly and with integrity, Facebook avoided a potential user revolt and enhanced one of its most valuable assets, its ability to innovate with the support and participation of its users.

6. **Welcome joint investments.** Every stable, large-scale collaborative effort needs an ownership environment that encourages effectively sharing in IP benefits while also promoting joint investment. Unlike the jointly owned patents of Toyota's innovation *keiretsu*, Facebook's investments have largely been side by side so far: Facebook invests in the network while the developers invest in the applications. As the new venture funds evolve, we may see more direct co-investment if Facebook ever decides to make investments directly.

7. **Pool IP to compete.** When Facebook and Microsoft signed their partnership deal in October 2007, leaving Google the odd man out, Google responded by orchestrating a competing social network alliance called OpenSocial. Google recruited competitors like MySpace, Friendster, LinkedIn, and Plaxo, and launched an open-source project called Shindig, which pooled their (copyright-protected) software code. Shindig is essentially a copyright pool (as opposed to a patent pool) that licenses its code under the "Apache license" (a less restrictive variant of Richard Stallman's GPL). Unable to compete effectively with Facebook as individuals, these companies are hoping to build on the copyrighted code of multiple partners to produce a competitively viable alternative.

SIMPLIFICATION IN ACTION

Mark Zuckerberg doesn't call Facebook a new-media company; he calls it a "technology company" and has defined its product as an "operating system" rather than a software application. Literally, he and his team call their architectural model the "Facebook Platform"—one that sets a standard for how user-generated content and behavioral targeting intersect. From the beginning, Zuckerberg designed Facebook with a different architecture than his competitors. While both

Friendster and MySpace were tightly controlled software environments, Facebook was always more open and certainly never defined by any proprietary applications. Zuckerberg's open posture toward developers encouraged them to write software for the Facebook Platform rather than its competitors. Just as Bill Lowe set out to achieve in the architecture of the IBM PC, Zuckerberg soon found himself way ahead of the competition, not because of the superiority of his own technology, but because of the huge amount of value that his application developers could bring to his users.

Bill Gates has seen this movie before. You can bet that it is the promise of this platform that led Microsoft, the king of the desktop platform, to come calling with such a big check—and why there were so many rumors of an IPO before that. Facebook, in other words, while not a "shark" in the mold of NTP, is still quickly evolving into the kind of company that focuses on building upon only the assets that they own and that distinguish them from the competition. Since Zuckerberg and Facebook have been aggressive about filing patents related to its platform, it stands to reason that they will also be aggressive about enforcing them should those patents be approved. After all, even if the Facebook Platform is an open one, they still understand the importance of owning their distinction. The keys will be in the next steps: Will Facebook's openness cause it to lose its position at the center of the architecture that it created (like IBM did with the PC)? Or will it be able to balance openness and control in a way that will enable it to expand its ecosystem, and maintain ownership over the platform?

For Facebook, control of that platform doesn't just apply to traditional PC-based Web browsers either. In February 2007, Facebook announced the launch of its "Facebook for Mobile Operators platform," which makes it easy for Facebook to run on mobile devices like cell phones and PDAs. By adopting the standard, users will be able to send photos and videos to their Facebook profile via their cell phones. Vodafone, a leading mobile phone provider in Europe, has already adopted the new standard and announced plans to develop the platform in the UK, Germany, Greece, Italy, Spain, Ireland, and Portugal.

This move into the mobile world only reinforces Facebook's early decisions to open up its platform to third-party developers. They recognized that an open-architecture approach secured by a proprietary platform would provide a critical source of advantage in attracting both users and application developers: not unlike Richard Stallman's GNU open-source movement that we learned about in chapter 6. Like Stallman, Zuckerberg's team made the philosophical commitment early on that they wanted their system to be open, yet protected by strong IP at the same time. Facebook has also avoided getting into the applications business and they don't try to force applications on their users or guess what they may want. Rather, by focusing on the platform, Facebook's model gives users lots of choice over which applications they want to download, something they can do for free. Friendster and MySpace, on the other hand, employed closed systems and, until recently, developed and supplied all the gadgets for their users as well. Clearly, if growth rates are any measure, Facebook is winning the race to own the platform that will support the next software generation.

When it comes to thinking about how your company can compete by using simplification strategies, consider the following actions:

1. **Link strategy to architecture.** In its May 2007 launch, Facebook formalized its architectural approach, while also branding it in capital letters, the Facebook Platform (interestingly, while Zuckerberg has trademarked Facebook and related terms like Facebook Beacon, he has been slower to register these service marks and hasn't yet registered Facebook Platform). By linking several themes—their highly collaborative developer strategy, their desire to focus on the core technology, and their ambition to become a powerful and Independent Internet hub—the Facebook Platform has become the most prominent statement of their strategy to date.

2. **Attack complexity for users and suppliers.** Users who compare Facebook with MySpace routinely note that "in contrast to MySpace, Facebook is clean and clutter-free." Similarly, we've learned from our software partner at TouchGraph how simple Facebook has made the connection with application developers, in part because of the Facebook Platform commitment, but also because of the care and attention to a clean operational interface. This attack on complexity has been a big reason for Facebook's success.

3. **Embrace open architecture.** Zuckerberg has suggested that Facebook's motto might be "Make the world more open" and his architectural commitments certainly embrace openness, to a point. Outsiders have described Facebook's open architecture as the "anti-MySpace," noting, "While MySpace frets over third party widgets, alternatively shutting them down or acquiring them, Facebook [opens] up its core functions to all outside developers." Facebook has made significant investments to make the Facebook Platform *really* open to their developers, including deep integration of developer and Facebook operations, channels for mass distribution of developer content to Facebook users, and meaningful support for commercial transactions and advertising from within the Facebook architecture.

4. **Own your central component.** Unlike Bill Lowe's emergent plan for owning components of the IBM PC, Mark Zuckerberg had a clear plan for control of the central components of his business model. The choice of the word *platform* reflects a clear strategic intent: to stake out a proprietary position in the center of an otherwise open architecture, even while he actively conceded IP rights to applications that his competitors attempted to claim in their own designs. In that choice he has been criticized for owning too much of his architecture, and not really operating in the full spirit of Web 2.0. But until users see an advantage in logging onto less proprietary competitors, Facebook's architecture seems well positioned for success.

5. **Migrate to the middle.** Any time you can influence the evolution of a market, it pays to position yourself centrally as the associated technology stack evolves. In Facebook's case, a combination of good fortune and good strategy has placed them squarely in the middle of the interactive heart of Web 2.0. In their early days as just another software application with a target audience of college campuses, they operated more like a "River Rouge," building the full suite of functions—like "the Wall," "Pokes," and "Photos"—that set them apart from other social networking sites. Like Qualcomm building the CDMA business, Facebook needed to provide a complete experience that users found compelling. But over time, just as Qualcomm pulled back from making handsets and switching equipment as CDMA took off, Facebook pulled back from controlling its users' interactions (like Friendster) and its application developers (like MySpace) as it found itself moving toward the middle of a rapidly growing ecosystem. Facebook is now well positioned to become one of just a handful of connecting points between a generation of computer users and the technology that shapes their interaction with Web 2.0.

6. **Play the standards game hard.** Standards are serious business and executives consign them to the technical periphery at their company's peril. Google's OpenSocial alliance has played out in practical terms as a standards development group, with Google trying to mobilize a larger group of social network sites around a set of open standards for developers, so that applications developed, say, for MySpace can work on Orkut (Google's social network site). If successful, OpenSocial could provide a counterbalance to Facebook's leading position among developers. This strategic move sets up a standards battle between Facebook's proprietary platform and the OpenSocial collaboration. The outcome of this standards competition will likely determine how the future of social software will develop—in this game, Facebook had better play hard.

7. **Beware of disruptive attacks from below.** Time and again, users have made the point that the simplicity of Facebook is what draws them there, in contrast to the laborious page downloads of Friendster and the cluttered home pages of MySpace. But is there a disruptive technology (possibly handset based) that will blow all of these other sites out of the water? Often the most dangerous attacks come from below—the simple technology that initially appeals only to the "low end" user. Those bare-bones, poorly featured solutions have a way of migrating upward into the core of your customer base and eating away at your business from underneath. Whether Facebook is vulnerable to this kind of attack has yet to be seen, but there are a number of companies you've never heard of, such as Mocospace, ZYB, and Mig33, that are working on the problem!

We think you will agree that after examining how Facebook is using Control, Collaboration, and Simplification strategies to build its business, the IP story that emerges is quite different from most of the stories that feature the company and its wunderkind founder. It should also make you wonder how many other similar stories are out there and perhaps your eyes have been opened so that you can see them for what they are. Maybe one such story is your own company. If so, you have a new opportunity before you—and maybe a lot of hard work to get your team to see it in the same light.

We find Facebook a fascinating business, in part because it's a business that embodies our network-oriented lens as part of its core value proposition, in part because the competitive race in which Facebook is running in Web 2.0 places it at the leading edge of modern business practices, and in part because they have created so much market value so quickly. We also find that in many ways Mark Zuckerberg's strategic choices are in line with the lessons we're teaching here; certainly, anyone who can claim the title of "world's youngest self-made billionaire" has done a few things right. Still, despite the $15 billion valuation placed on the four-year-old company in the Microsoft deal, in early 2008 Zuckerberg projected company revenues of only $300 million to $350 million. Clearly, Facebook has a long way to go before Zuckerberg earns his permanent place in the history book of great business successes.

The Facebook story also highlights the challenges faced by practicing strategists: namely, when, where, and how do you commit to a particular strategy or strike a balance between them? Zuckerberg needs to own something that people can't copy, and at the same time develop an environment where others can innovate and where he can rely on their innovation. He needs to generate advertising revenue streams without compromising the trust of his users over privacy concerns. He also needs to set a standard for interaction that will allow the community to grow and thrive. If he strikes the wrong balance on any of these choices, the whole thing might come apart. If he grabs for too much control, for instance, he could chase away his innovators. On the other hand, if he opens up his platform too much, he'll have nothing left to defend. Certainly, we can't credit Zuckerberg with consciously trying to strike a balance between Control, Collaboration, and Simplification—but Facebook has, so far, been effective in playing all three cards. What happens as the game continues to change—and more players enter it—remains to be seen. What we do know is that IP is playing a central role in the development of Web 2.0 and will continue to play a critical role in the future of business, and we'll be watching to see how it plays out.

"I didn't say it would be easy, Neo. I just said it would be the truth."

We've taken you on a journey, one that started on the 18th hole at Augusta and continued on to trace the origins of economic growth and the core innovations that drove the Industrial and Information Revolutions. We learned that IP is the engine that drives economic growth and that it's the most important—and often most overlooked—source of competitive advantage. We learned that most business profits in the advanced economies of the world come from IP and that as markets for trading in it become more open and more liquid, this will only increase.

We have shown you how strategies built around IP are different because the competitive economics are different. IP competition is tough. But if you want to succeed in the modern knowledge economy, you have to wake up and see the new realities. You must learn how to compete using a new set of strategies. If you don't, you risk getting left behind.

In the process, we've tried to make the invisible assets that shape these strategies more visible to you by sharing stories with you from a wide range of businesses that included both high-tech—mobile phones—and low-tech—fabric softeners. We focused not on exotic niches but rather on companies at the core of the economy that surrounds us every day. We've guided you to familiar places, from the morning shave and the daily commute to the computer staring at you on your desk, and have shown you things you may not have seen there before. Once you learn to focus on this unseen world of business competition, we predict you will see new things everywhere you look. We hope we've equipped you with ways to formulate new strategies for your familiar business activities and, if you're like us, you won't think about them quite the same way again.

ACKNOWLEDGMENTS

This book has its intellectual origins in Boston and San Francisco. As two dwarves, we had the privilege of standing on the shoulders of giants on two coasts. We've accumulated a lot of frequent-flyer mileage in the process.

From the Boston side, our earliest inspiration came from Bruce Henderson, the founder of The Boston Consulting Group. Bruce was the pioneer of the idea that business strategy was the same thing as competitive strategy: a red pill of its own that inspired a generation of business executives. Bruce was always provocative, relentlessly inquisitive, occasionally wrong, but never dull. At his core, Bruce's ideas and perspectives on competitive strategy were revolutionary. Their power is demonstrated by what we take for granted today. His ideas have been extended and enriched by the academic and consulting community in Boston, most notably by Harvard Business School Professor Michael Porter, on one hand, and our former colleagues at BCG on another. We have had the good fortune not only to learn from their ideas but also to work with them personally for many years: Bruce used to host lunch meetings with the new BCG analysts fresh out of college; Michael Porter has been a teacher, a client, a collaborator, and a friend. On the other side of the river, Professor Jay Forrester pioneered the disciplines of systems dynamics at the MIT Sloan School that not only influenced Bruce

Henderson's perspectives on strategy; he inspired us personally in the classroom and through his writings as well. Among our early BCG colleagues, Thomas Hout, with his unique charm and relentless curiosity (about Japan, China, and what makes things really work on the front lines of business competition), deserves special mention. Tom made the opportunity to focus on strategy consulting a compelling career choice.

From the innovation hotbeds of Silicon Valley, Kevin Rivette helped us build the bridge between East and West that allowed us to make sense of competitive strategy in a completely new way. Kevin is one of those people whose journey through life has been one of those happy accidents where talent meets opportunity in a completely novel way. Son of a serial entrepreneur, Kevin went to law school (for reasons that baffle us), then went into patent law after growing bored with antitrust and corporate litigation. He recognized that writing patents was fun, at least for part of the time! And it allowed him to immerse himself in cutting-edge technologies every day. After experiencing firsthand the difficulties of obtaining patent information in a timely way, he went on to the main work of his life, becoming the first to solve the information access problems in the U.S. Patent Office, the first to build a software company to make patent analysis possible, and the first to write a *business* book about IP, *Rembrandts in the Attic*, one that remains an influential best-seller. Kevin's personal influence on our book is impossible to calculate; indeed, this is a book that Kevin could have written himself (although we have no doubt he would have written it differently!).

More directly, the path to this book began with our work in BCG's Strategy Practice Initiative (SPI). We owe a great debt of gratitude to BCG's former CEO, Carl Stern, who set us on this journey and provided resources, encouragement, and shelter along the way. Kevin Rivette joined us for several years as a critical member of this team before he went on to IBM to become the head of IP Strategy there (Kevin has since become our partner at 3LP Advisors). We also extend thanks to Mike Deimler, Mark's successor as head of the Strategy Practice, who suggested we undertake the book project in the first place, and to Philippe Guy, who supported the SPI investments and our teams during his tenure as head of the practice areas. Finally, we want to thank the longest-tenured BCG CEO, John Clarkeson, for his friendship, intellectual interest, and moral support at many stages of our work.

We also want to thank the extended SPI team for their many contributions. Wendi Backler has been a great thought partner, terrific analyst, and continues to be a valued codevelopment partner. Karim Lakhani brought his deep interest in open-source software to the project early on and continued to provide help and camaraderie on many fronts, from helping us with library access to academic papers to arranging seminars with his students and HBS faculty colleagues. Philip Evans and Bob Wolf helped us sharpen our views: both where we shared views and passions and also in the places where we disagreed. Yves Morieux brought a completely different perspective to the issues we explored together and encouraged us to apply a critical perspective to the network lens. Many other colleagues contributed to the work and investigations along the way, including Vladik Boutenko, David Morland, Ajan Reginald, David Michael, Collins Qian, Axel Heinemann, Mark Hoffman, Greg Gottlieb, Gregor Elbel, Nicholas Kachaner, Valery Panier, Michael Yeh, Christopher Kaufmann, Howard Davis, Matthew Lamiaux, Mark Freedman, Mark Lubkeman, Simon Goodall, Ian Frost, Rob Lachenauer, Andy Blackburn, Raj Varadarajan, Mel Wolfgang, Bart Kalkstein, Jason Sydow, Matt Stack, Alison Sander, Rodrigo Martinez, Mary Ellen McCabe, Emily Case, Thomas Roehm, Vikas Taneja, Antonio Riera, Simon Kennedy, Julie Urda, Antonio Rodriguez, Carlos Bhola, Erol "KC" Munuz, and George Stalk.

Alex Shapiro built the visualization engine that powers the social network graphs in the book. Alex's company TouchGraph LLC has the coolest SNA applications available for a range of applications, including Amazon, Google, and Facebook. He has been a helpful partner and collaborator from the moment we stumbled across the visualization software in his Google browser. We've also enjoyed working with Andy Gibb from PatentCafe, who has built one of the best patent data businesses around and also helped us get a list of the world's most highly cited patents, one of the first of its kind.

A number of trusted colleagues read and provided valuable comments on the entire manuscript or significant parts. Scott Stephenson worked together with Mark in one of his most satisfying client service collaborations ever and has been a close friend through thick and thin. His perspective as both thought partner and as senior executive of a major information services firm was inspiring to us. John Weber has been a classmate, a serial client, and a great colleague to both of us; he is probably one of the smartest "industrial slugs" one could ever hope to call a friend. Ian Harvey has shared our passion for the subject, one to which he brings a career's worth of experience and wisdom; his input and insights have made this a better book, and we look forward to even deeper collaboration with Ian in the years ahead. Geoff Hyatt literally gave us the space to write the book and also provided a uniquely valuable perspective based on his combination of consulting and entrepreneurial experiences. Victoria Wang provided the opportunity for us to see the world from the perspective of the Chinese economic miracle; she is an extraordinary talent. Bill Mattasoni, the best professional-services marketer in the business, contributed to the project in so many ways it's hard to count them all; his enthusiasm for the ideas was infectious. John Clarkeson, the perfectionist's perfectionist, made our year when he read an early draft of the manuscript and admitted "I'd buy it"—strong validation from a man that we both admire and respect.

We have many other friends, clients, teachers, and colleagues to thank, people with whom we have had helpful and extended conversations based on a wide range of perspectives and experiences; they all influenced our thinking in the many years that it took for these ideas to come together. These include John Dudas, John Dillon, David Oskin, George O'Brien, Gerry Marterer, Marianne Parrs, Pankaj Ghemawat, Jay Lorsch, Bob Gibbons, Rebecca Henderson, Eric von Hippel, Rob Cross, Ruud Peters, Takashi Iseyama, Damon Mateo, Marshall Phelps, Steve Goldby, Val Rahmani, Don Weinstein, Jim Liang, Scott Radtke, Orin Herskowitz, Paul DiGiammarino, Jason Sydow, Rob Kasdin, Larry Sorrel, Hugh Simons, Mike Eisenson, Mark Nunnelly, Rob Schwartz, and Paul Maeder.

With regard to specific companies in the book, we are grateful to the business and technology leaders who shared their time to give us greater insight into the companies that we chose as lead examples, including Bob Trotta, Carol Johnson, Fred Brooks, Bill Lowe, Neil Colvin, Lance Hansche, Tom Jennings, Ira Perlow, Dave Mock, Steve David, Jeff Weedman, and Richard Stallman.

We want to give special thanks to the young people who gave us the user perspective on Web 2.0, especially: to our face of Facebook, Peter Johnston, who has great things ahead of him, and greater legacies than "the biggest Facebook group ever"; and to Sydney Blaxill for her daily insights as she introduced her dad to the central role of Facebook in her life as we moved through a series of hotel rooms in Florence, Venice, and Rome. Sydney was a patient and generous guide (as she waited in line for her turn at her dad's computer), and she also recruited to her dad's tutorial her friend Kacey Buderi, who gave us a visceral sense of the user passion surrounding Facebook. In a discussion of an IP conflict facing Facebook, one where the (remote) prospect of an injunction had been raised, Kacey burst out, "If they shut down Facebook, I'll just die!" And Sophia, Katie, and Lexi Eckardt (ages seven, five, and three as of this writing) who deeply understand the "Control" strategy (Mine!) and who constantly remind their daddy of the need for the more sophisticated strategies of Collaboration and Simplification both in IP and in life.

We'd also like to thank several academic researchers who provided us with support for selected data analyses. Marvin Lieberman was gracious in his willingness to share source data on automotive productivity performance. Gavin Clarkson helped us understand the dimensions of MPEG LA. Karim Lakhani put us in contact with Carliss Baldwin, Alan MacCormack, and John Rusnak, who in turn shared the call graph data that made the Mozilla analysis possible; they also encouraged us with respect to the value of the network lens as applied to architecture analysis. Christine McLeod provided insight on the data sources surrounding patents during the Industrial Revolution in England. Carol Corrado shared her insights on the challenges of "measuring capital in the new economy." And to Tim Gulden, a special thanks for allowing us to use his fabulous "The World Is Spiky" charts.

To our agents, Esmond Harmsworth and Todd Shuster, we owe enormous thanks for their sure-handed guidance and marketing judgment. They embraced the project from the very beginning and never let go. Darren Dahl was our "collaborative editor" and deserves enormous credit for giving us the strength to "drown our puppies" and to help us beat the draft into shape. Darren shared our passion for sports, for business, and for all things cool, and made the polishing process—including arbitrating our own creative differences—as painless as it could be. Ned Scharff was a great help in the early stages of the project. Adrienne Schultz, our editor at Portfolio, was a true pleasure to work with, always supportive, nuanced, and parsimonious in her suggestions. Adrian Zackheim, who has managed a number of book projects that we admire greatly, saw the promise of the book and believed in us.

We would be remiss without acknowledging our debts to our parents. Sidney Blaxill introduced Mark to the world of international business: he helped open the Tokyo office of Morgan Stanley, encouraged an interest in Asia and the Japanese miracle, and inspired Mark to follow in his footsteps. He died too young and he's been missed for a long time. Marjorie Blaxill instilled the love of ideas and encouraged in Mark the intellectual curiosity to think deeply about important issues. Ralph's parents, Dr. Ralph and Joyce Eckardt, instilled in him the value of persistence and hard work (although it required a large measure of both to do so), opened his eyes to the wider world of possibility, and taught him to see that world through the eyes of both the powerful and the powerless. Their constancy, compassion, and curiosity have left an indelible imprint on their son.

Our deepest gratitude goes to our wives, Elise and Melody. They've put up with the disruption, travel, and emotions that surrounded this project and have never wavered in their support for the mission. Most important, they've believed in us and gave us the confidence to make this the best book we could write.

NOTES

INTRODUCTION

1   *O'Meara's children:* "Out of the Woods: Young Lions and Tiger and a Golden Bear—Mark O'Meara Slipped Past a Menagerie of Rivals to Win the Masters," *Sports Illustrated*, Wednesday, April 15, 1998, sportsillustrated.cnn.com/augusta/stories/042098/si/masters.html (accessed March 27, 2008).

1   *"ape spit with happiness":* Ibid.

1   *years of rank-and-file anonymity:* Barker Davis, "1998: The Year of the Putt," October 12, 1998, findarticles.com/p/articles/mi_m1571/is_n37_v14/ai_21212832 (accessed March 27, 2008).

3   *For almost a century:* "Callaway Golf Company's Opposition to Acushnet's Rule 50(b) and 59 Post-Trial Motions to Reverse or Vacate the Jury's Verdict," *Callaway Golf Company, Plaintiff, v. Acushnet Company, Defendant,* C.A. No 06-91 (SLR), February 5, 2008, 3.

5   *Tiger Woods officially announced:* Bob Harig, "Woods Gets Industry's Attention with Ball Switch to Nike," *St. Petersburg Times,* June 8, 2000, www.texnews.com/tiger/ball0608.html (accessed May 12, 2008).

5   *"the greatest performance in golf history":* John Garrity "Open and Shut," *Sports Illustrated,* June 26, 2000, sportsillustrated.cnn.com/2005/golf/specials/tiger/2005/06/09/tiger.2000 usopen/index.html (accessed August 15, 2007).

5   *60 percent of the players on the PGA Tour: Darrell Survey Golf Equipment Almanac 2002,* Darrell Survey Company, 2002.

5   *threatened to terminate his contract with Titleist:* "Callaway Golf's Proffer Regarding the Rebuttal Testimony of Phil Mickelson," in the United States District Court for the District of Delaware, *Callaway Golf Company, Plaintiff, v. Acushnet Company, Defendant,* C.A. No. 06-91 (SLR).

6   *it wasn't a great surprise:* Adam Schupak, *Golf Week,* February 19, 2007.

6   *"a fad or a legitimate innovation":* Ibid.

6   *"the value previously did not exist": HK Pro Golf,* hkprogolf.com/double_covers.html (accessed March 14, 2008).

6   *Titleist introduced its new multilayer ball:* Statistics on Pro V1 market share come from *Darrell Survey Golf Equipment Almanac,* Darrell Survey Company, 2000, 2001, 2002.

6   *forty-seven professional golfers:* E. Michael Johnson, "Mortally Wound-ed? Hot, New Solid-Core Balls Have Nearly KO'd Their Wound-ball Rivals—Popularity of New Solid-Core Multilayer Golf Balls," *Golf Digest,* June 2001, findarticles.com/p/articles/mi_moHFI/is_6_52/ai_75622953/print (accessed October 9, 2007).

6   *"massive switch":* Ibid.

6   *average driving distances:* Jaime Diaz, "Special Report: The Growing Gap, Driving Distances Are Skyrocketing on the PGA Tour," *Golf Digest,* May 2003.

7   *8 percent almost overnight: Darrell Survey Golf Equipment Almanac 2002,* Darrell Survey Company, 2002.

7   *the most successful ball in the history of golf:* "Callaway Golf Company's Opposition to Acushnet's Rule 50(b) and 59 Post-Trial Motions to Reverse or Vacate the Jury's Verdict," *Callaway Golf Company, Plaintiff, v. Acushnet Company, Defendant,* C.A. No 06-91 (SLR), February 5, 2008, 20–21.

7   *more than $1.5 billion worth of Pro V1s:* "Callaway Golf Company's Opposition to Acushnet's Rule 50(b) and 59 Post-Trial Motions to Reverse or Vacate the Jury's Verdict," *Callaway Golf Company, Plaintiff, v. Acushnet Company, Defendant,* C.A. No 06-91 (SLR), February 5, 2008, 20.

7   *"saved the company":* "Callaway Golf Company's Opposition to Acushnet's Rule 50(b) and 59 Post-Trial Motions to Reverse or Vacate the Jury's Verdict," *Callaway Golf Company, Plaintiff, v. Acushnet Company, Defendant,* C.A. No 06-91 (SLR), February 5, 2008, 21.

10   *his influential book* Rembrandts in the Attic: Kevin G. Rivette and David Kline, *Rembrandts in the Attic: Unlocking the Hidden Value of Patents* (New York: Harvard Business School Press, 2000).

15   *"a competition for Intellectual Property Rights":* Similar quotations by Premier Jiabao have appeared numerous times but the earliest identified statement was during a visit to "model worker Xu Zhenchao" in Shangdong Province, June 20, 2004, www.trade.gov.cn/english2003/php/show.php?id=553 (accessed June 11, 2008).

16   *they left the innovators no choice but to go to court:* For information on the patent disputes in the golf industry, an indispensable resource is www.golf-patents.com.

16   *around $150 million:* "Callaway Comes Out Swinging," Philip Brooks' Patent Infringement Updates, February 14, 2006, infringement.blogs.com/philip_brooks_patent_infr/2006/02/callaway_comes_.html (accessed August 8, 2008).

CHAPTER 1 Fueling the Fire

22   *"preserve my journal book":* Andrew Carnegie, *James Watt* (New York: Cosmo Classics, 2005), 80.

22   *"more foolish than inventing":* Robert H. Thurston, *A History of the Growth of the Steam Engine* (London: Kegan Paul, Trench & Co., 1883), 92.

25   *"steam which entered it":* Eric Robinson and A. E. Musson, *James Watt and the Steam Revolution: A Documentary History.* (London: Adams and Dart, 1969), 60.

25   *"cooling the cylinder":* Carnegie, 53.

26   *whims of royalty:* Christine MacLeod, *Inventing the Industrial Revolution: The English Patent System, 1660–1800* (London: Cambridge University Press, 1988), 59.

27   *coining money:* Jennifer Tann and M. J. Breckin, "The International Diffusion of the Watt Engine, 1777–1825," *Economic History Review* 31 (1978): 541–64.

28   *power textile mills:* Thomas H. Marshall, *James Watt* (Edinburgh: Leonard Parsons Ltd., 1925), accessed on July 16, 2006, at http://www.history.rochester.edu/steam/marshall/chapter8.html.

28   *François Arago penned:* François Arago, *Historical Eloge of James Watt* (London: John Murray, 1839).

30   *"nasty, brutish, and short":* William J. Bernstein, *The Birth of Plenty* (New York: McGraw-Hill, 2004), 80.

30   *"it previously possessed":* Karl Marx, *Wage Labour and Capital* (Whitefich, MT: Kessinger Publishing, 2004), 21.

31   *stock of physical capital:* Robert Solow, "Technical Change and the Aggregate Production Func-
      tion," *Review of Economics and Statistics* 39 (1957): 312–20.
32   *a few years earlier:* Jacob Schmookler, "The Changing Efficiency of the American Economy,"
      Review of Economics and Statistics, 34 (1952).
32   *Moses Abramovitz calculated:* Moses Abramovitz, "Resource and Output Trends in the US Since
      1870," *American Economic Review* 46 (1956): 5–23.
32   "measure of our ignorance": Ibid.
33   *three basic premises:* Paul Romer, "Endogenous Technological Change," *Journal of Political Econ-
      omy* 98 (1990): S71–102.
34   *increased agricultural productivity:* A thirty-five-fold increase in agricultural productivity is a
      conservative estimate. The actual number is higher due to an increase in food exports by the
      United States. Labor statistics from U.S. Bureau of the Census, Employment and Earning,
      U.S. Department of Labor.
34   *one hundred years of innovation:* The Model T was first produced one hundred years ago in
      1908. Wikipedia, en.wikipedia.org/wiki/Ford_Model_T (accessed August 8, 2008).
34   *three government economists:* Carol Corrado et al., "Intangible Capital and Economic Growth,"
      NBER Working Paper Series 11948 (2006).
36   "recommend abolishing it": Fritz Machlup, "An Economic Review of the Patent System," Study
      No. 15 of Committee on Judiciary, Subcommittee on Patents, Trademarks, and Copyrights,
      85th Congress, 2d Session (1958).
37   "the printing press": Bernstein, 93.
37   *the Industrial Revolution:* Angus Maddison, *Growth and Interaction in the World Economy: The
      Roots of Modernity* (Washington, DC: The AEI Press, 2005), 6–12.
37   "love the ancients": William P. Alford, *To Steal a Book Is an Elegant Offense: Intellectual Property
      Law in Chinese Civilization* (Stanford, CA: Stanford University Press, 1995), 25.
37   "utterly incapable of it": Karl R. Popper, *The Open Society and Its Enemies. Volume I: The Spell of
      Plato* (Princeton, NJ: Princeton University Press, 1966), 7.
37   *in the guild system:* Pamela Long, *Openness, Secrecy, Authorship: Technical Arts and the Culture
      of Knowledge from Antiquity to the Renaissance* (Baltimore: Johns Hopkins University Press,
      2001), 7.
38   *his annual salary:* Frank Prager, "Brunelleschi's Patent," *Journal of the Patent Office Society* 28
      (1946): 109–35.
39   "our commonwealth": Frank Prager, trans., "Venetian Patents (1450–1550) by Giulio Mandich,"
      Journal of the Patent Office Society 30 (1948): 166–224.
39   *pro-competitive policy:* Frank Prager, "A History of Intellectual Property from 1545 to 1787,"
      Journal of the Patent Office Society 26 (1944): 711–60.
39   *all glassmaking patents:* Maximilian Frumkin, *Early History of Patents for Invention.* Paper pre-
      sented at the Chartered Institute of Patent Agents, London, November 12, 1947 (London: The
      Newcomen Society, 2004).
40   "a marked upward trend": MacLeod, 5.
41   "new and useful things": Abraham Lincoln, "Discoveries and Inventions," April 6, 1858.
42   "the productivity statistics": Robert Solow, *New York Times Book Review,* July 12, 1987, 36.

CHAPTER 2 Monopoly Money

45   *remained relatively flat:* Leonard Nakamura, Federal Reserve Bank of Philadelphia, "The Rise
      of US Intellectual Capital: A Trillion Dollars of Intangible Investment Annually." Paper pre-
      sented at World Bank Institute Conference, Intellectual Capital for Communities in the Knowl-
      edge Economy, Paris, France, June 29–30, 2006.
47   *His short essay:* Gordon Moore, "Cramming More Components onto Integrated Circuits," *Elec-
      tronics* 38 (1965).
48   "at least 10 years": Ibid.
49   *the ratio of intellectual capital:* Keith Cardoza et al., "The Power of Intangible Assets An Analy-
      sis of the S&P 500," Ocean Tomo white paper, January 2006, http://www.icknowledgecenter
      .com/WhitePapers/OceanTomoS&P500.pdf (accessed July 21, 2008).
49   *these studies all find:* Bronwyn Hall, "Innovation and Market Value," *NBER Working Paper* 6984

(1999); Bronwyn Hall et al., "Market Value and Patent Citations," *Rand Journal of Economics* (2005); Bronwyn Hall et al., "The Market Value of Patents and R&D: Evidence from European firms," Draft Working Paper, October 2006; Sadao Nagaoka, "Patent Quality, Cumulative Innovation and Market Value: Evidence from Japanese Firm Level Panel Data," Hitotsubashi University, Institute for Innovation Research Working Paper 05-06 (2005).

50   *Fortune 500 put together:* Marcia Angell, *The Truth About the Drug Companies* (New York: Random House, 2004), 11.

51   *rises to 33 percent:* Google Finance, Intel page (accessed March 28, 2008).

51   *fallen by 85 percent:* Edward Tuttle et al., "Your Patent Is About to Expire: What Now?" *Pharmaceutical Executive,* November 2004.

54   *"in the antitrust context":* United States Department of Justice and the Federal Trade Commission, "Antitrust Guidelines for the Licensing of Intellectual Property" (April 6, 1995).

55   *direct competitive rivalry:* Michael Porter, *Competitive Strategy* (New York: Free Press, 1980).

59   *"become very rich":* Brenda Sandburg, "You May Not Have a Choice: Trolling for Dollars," *The Recorder,* July 30, 2001.

63   *"patent troll on steroids":* Interview with Peter Detkin, "Has the Enemy of Patent Trolls Become One?" *CIO Insight,* December 5, 2005.

66   *"worldwide decline in patenting":* Zvi Griliches, ed., *R&D, Patents and Productivity* (Chicago: University of Chicago Press, 1984), 15.

CHAPTER 3 The Company You Keep

71   *built a modest licensing stream:* Rich Tehrani, VoIP Blogger, "Rates Technology Inc.," April 19, 2005, http://blog.tmcnet.com/blog/rich-tehrani/voip/rates-technology-inc.html (accessed January 4, 2007).

71   *JPEG digital image format:* Matt Slagle, "Forgent Networks Settles JPEG Patent Case for $8 Million," Associated Press, November 3, 2006.

71   *digital image compression technology:* Spencer E. Ante, "How Ampex Squeezes Out Cash," *BusinessWeek,* April 18, 2005; Daniel Gross, "The Profits in the Attic," *Slate,* March 29, 2005.

72   *NTP for short:* Kim Isaac Eisler, "BlackBerry Blues," *Washingtonian Magazine,* September 2005; Showwei Chu, "Inventor at Centre of RIM Patent Fight," *Globe and Mail,* December 10, 2002.

72   *operator based in Canada:* Answers.com, "Encyclopedia of Company Histories," http://www.answers.com/topic/research-in-motion-ltd-usa (accessed January 8, 2007).

74   *"not a close case":* Eisler.

76   *strategy innovation around:* Fred Warshofsky, *Patent Wars* (New York: John Wiley & Sons, 1994), 111–28.

76   *pipeline for new drugs:* Peter Tollman et al., *Rising to the Productivity Challenge,* The Boston Consulting Group (2004).

78   *the workers inside:* Joseph P. Cabadas, *River Rouge: Ford's Industrial Colossus* (St. Paul, MN: Motorbooks International, 2004), 160–63.

81   *their transactions costs:* Ronald H. Coase, "The Nature of the Firm," in Ronald. H. Coase, *The Firm, the Market and the Law* (Chicago: University of Chicago Press, 1988), 33–55.

81   *the memo's author argued:* Robert Berner, "P&G: New and Improved," *BusinessWeek,* July 7, 2003.

82   *Palmisano saw the future:* Steven Hamm, "Beyond Blue," *BusinessWeek,* April 18, 2005.

82   *"Technology is forever":* Martin Veitch, "Top Five Women in Tech: In Memory of Hedy Lamarr," *The Inquirer,* August 24, 2007, http://www.theinquirer.net/en/inquirer/news/2007/08/24/the-inquirer-top-five-women-in-tech (accessed July 22, 2008).

86   *"let others do the manufacturing":* Russ Arensman, "Meet the New Qualcomm," *Electronic Business,* March 1, 2000.

87   *counted the number of patents:* David J. Goodman and Robert A. Myers, "Analysis of Intellectual Property for Third Generation Cellular Technology." Paper presented at IEEE WirelessCom, June 13, 2005. For a criticism of this paper, see Donald L. Martin and Carl De Meyer, "Patent Counting, a Misleading Index of Patent Value: A Critique of Goodman and Myers and Its Uses," December 4, 2006 (see http://ssrn.com/abstract=949439).

88   *the standard was finalized:* Rudi Bekkers and Joel West, "The Rules, Norms and Standards on Knowledge Exchange," DIME Working Papers on Intellectual Property Rights, March 2006.

91   *$50 per handset:* David Pringle, "Dial Time: Hidden Asset Could Let Nokia Capitalize On Boom for 3G Phones," *Wall Street Journal*, March 10, 2005, C1.

92   *$40 billion in research:* National Science Foundation, "U.S. Research and Development Expenditures, by Performing Sector and Source of Funds: 1994–2004," http://www.nsf.gov/statistics/nsf06327/tables.htm (accessed January 23, 2007).

95   *holds up well today:* Jacob Schmookler, *Invention and Economic Growth* (Cambridge, MA: Harvard University Press, 1966).

CHAPTER 4 Advantaged Innovation Networks

98   *what exactly was going on over at P&G:* A number of news and journal articles provided background for the shifts involving Durk Jager and A. G. Lafley at Procter & Gamble. *Business Week* articles included: "What's Driving P&G's Executive Spin Cycle?," June 8, 2000; "Warm and Fuzzy Won't Save Procter & Gamble," June 26, 2000; "P&G, New and Improved," July 7, 2003. *Fortune* articles included: "Can Procter & Gamble Change Its Culture, Protect Its Market Share, and Find the Next Tide?," April 26, 1999; "Plugging the Leaks at P&G," February 21, 2000; and "The Un-CEO," September 16, 2002. Local Cincinnati newspaper articles include: "P&G Scrubs Stodgy Image," *Enquirer*, November 21, 2004; "P&G Back on Old Course, Core Brand Focus Boosts Stock Price," *Cincinnati Post*, March 7, 2001; and "Procter Still a 'show-me' Despite Top Executive Changes," *Business Courier*, June 16, 2000. National news articles from the *New York Times* included: "Hemorrhage in P.& G. Share Price Drags Down the Market," March 8, 2000; "Procter & Gamble Shake-Up Follows Poor Profit Outlook," June 8, 2000; and "Hot Seat Awaits New Chief at P.& G.," June 18, 2000.

102   *"available to others":* Ron Lieber interview with Jeff Weedman, "P&G's Not-So-Secret Agent," *Fast Company*, July 2001.

102   *outside the company:* Larry Huston and Nabil Sakkab, "Connect and Develop: Inside Procter & Gamble's New Model for Innovation," *Harvard Business Review*, March 2006.

104   *"could potentially use":* Ibid.

105   *a factor of two:* Ibid.

105   *leverage your intellectual property:* Lieber.

105   *orange juice king, instead:* Ibid.

110   *advantage relative to competitors:* Michael Porter, *Competitive Strategy* (New York: Free Press, 1980), 29.

111   *hype their products:* Malcolm Gladwell, *The Tipping Point: How Little Things Can Make a Big Difference* (Boston: Little, Brown and Co. 2000).

111   *find the right path:* Stanley Milgram, "The Small World Problem," *Psychology Today* 1 (1967), 61–67.

113   *"One asshole in the middle":* Michael Lewis, *The New New Thing: A Silicon Valley Story* (New York: W. W. Norton and Co., 2000), 170.

113   *"access to holes":* Ronald Burt, *Structural Holes: The Social Structure of Competition* (Cambridge, MA: Harvard University Press, 1992), 2.

115   *"cheek by jowl":* Ibid., 4.

116   *"focal inventions":* Joel Podolny and Toby E. Stuart, "A Role-Based Ecology of Technological Change," *American Journal of Sociology* 100 (1995): 1224–60.

CHAPTER 5 Control

125   *"worked on it get paid?"* Bill Gates, "Open Letter to Hobbyists," *Homebrew Computer Club Newsletter* 2 (February 3, 1976).

125   *the history of the USPTO:* Kevin Maney, "Search for the Most Prolific Inventors Is a Patent Struggle," *USA Today*, December 6, 2005.

126   *a powerful patent portfolio:* Gary S. Vasilash, "A Disruptive Approach to Strip Steel," *Automotive Design and Production*, January 2003.

126   *a software company envious:* Christopher Lawton, "H-P Chemists Hunt Violators of Ink Patents," *Wall Street Journal*, August 29, 2006.

127   *eleven weighty patent applications:* A number of books, news articles, journal articles, and case studies provided background for the Gillette account. Two book-length treatments are by Gordon McKibben, *Cutting Edge* (Boston: Harvard Business School Press, 1998), and Russell Adams, *King C. Gillette: The Man and His Wonderful Shaving Device* (Boston: Little, Brown & Co, 1978). A feature-length article was by James Surowiecki, "The Billion Dollar Blade," *The New Yorker*, June 15, 1998. Business school case studies included: Benjamin Esty and Pankaj Ghemawat, "Gillette's Launch of the Sensor," Harvard Business School: 9-792-028 (1997); Rosabeth Moss Kanter and James Weber, "Gillette Company: Pressure for Change," Harvard Business School: 9-303-032 (2005); Jay W. Lorsch and Ashley C. Robertson, "The P&G Acquisition of Gillette," Harvard Business School: 9-405-082 (2005); Frank C. Schultz and Michael McCune, "Gillette's Energy Drain: The Acquisition of Duracell," Ivey: 905M26 (2004); and Schultz and McCune, "Gillette's Energy Drain: Energizer's Acquisition of Schick," Ivey: 905M27 (2004). Articles in the *New York Times* include: Claudia Deutsch, "For Mighty Gillette, These Are the Faces of War," October 12, 2003; Deutsch, "Gillette Is Betting That Men Want an Even Closer Shave," September 15, 2005. *BusinessWeek* articles include: William C. Symonds, "Gillette's Edge: The Secret of an Innovation Machine? Never Relax," January 19, 1998; William C. Symonds and Robert Berner, "In a Lather Over the Gillette Deal: Critics of Its Merger with P&G Say Conflicted Investment Banks Pushed the Move and Execs Put Their Own Hefty Gain Above Investors," June 16, 2005. Articles from the *Boston Globe* include: Naomi Aoki, "The War of the Razors: Gillette-Schick Fight over Patent Shows the Cutthroat World of Consumer Products," August 31, 2003; Aoki, "Gillette Creates a Little Buzz with Its New Razor: Latest Mach3 Offering Features Pulsating Action, Higher Price," January 16, 2004; Jenn Abelson, "And Then There Were Five: Gillette Unveils Fusion, Taking Back Bragging Rights from Schick," September 15, 2005.

127   *"metrosexual nirvana":* Deutsch, September 15, 2005.

128   *"back to the designers":* Deutsch, October 12, 2003.

129   *"General Motors of shaving":* Surowiecki, June 15, 1998.

129   *reach that milestone:* Procter & Gamble Q4 2007 Earnings Conference Call Transcript, http://seekingalpha.com/article/74961-procter-gamble-company-f3q08-qtr-end-3-31-08-earnings-call-transcript (accessed July 22, 2008).

130   *more than 70 percent:* Ibid.

136   *Consumer Reports taste test:* Janet Adamy, "McDonald's Takes On a Weakened Starbucks," *Wall Street Journal*, January 7, 2008, A1.

137   *"company that makes it":* Mark Pendergrast, *For God, Country and Coca-Cola: The Unauthorized History of the Great American Soft Drink and the Company That Makes It* (New York: Collier Books, 1993).

138   *"violated software copyrights":* Nathan Myhrvold, "Perspectives on Patents: Post-Grant Review Procedures and Other Litigation Reforms." A hearing before the Subcommittee on Intellectual Property, Committee on the Judiciary, United States Senate, May 23, 2006.

142   *$50,000 or more:* Michael S. Malone, "The Smother of Invention," *Forbes*, June 24, 2002.

142   *$5 price level:* Kanter and Weber, 1.

144   *"corporate version of CSI":* Lawton, August 29, 2006.

149   *pocketed some $150 million:* Lorsch and Robertson, 5.

CHAPTER 6 Collaborate

154   *as many as 70 percent:* Stefano Comino et al., "Joint Ventures vs. Contractual Agreements: An Empirical Investigation," *Spanish Economic Review* 9 (2007): 159–75.

155   *"flying together in close formation":* Don Tapscott and Anthony D. Williams, *Wikinomics: How Mass Collaboration Changes Everything* (New York: Portfolio, 2006), 224.

159   *the most world's most valuable auto company:* For the Toyota account, we relied on a number of books and academic articles. Books include: Jeffrey H. Dyer, *Collaborative Advantage: Winning Through Extended Enterprise Supplier Networks* (Oxford: Oxford University Press, 2000); Jeffrey K. Liker, *The Toyota Way: 14 Management Principles from the World's Greatest Manufac-*

turer (New York: McGraw-Hill, 2004); James P. Womack, Daniel T. Jones, and Daniel Roos, *The Machine That Changed the World: The Story of Lean Production* (New York, Rawson Associates, 1990); Hideshi Itazaki, *The Prius That Shook the World: How Toyota Developed the World's First Mass Production Hybrid Vehicle,* trans. Albert Yamada and Masako Ishikawa (Tokyo: Nikkan Kogyo Shimbun, 1999). Articles include: Jeffrey K. Liker and Thomas Y. Choi, "Building Deep Supplier Relationships," *Harvard Business Review,* December 2004; Jeffrey Dyer and Kentaro Nobeoka, "Creating and Managing a High-Performance Knowledge-Sharing Network: The Toyota Case," *Strategic Management Journal* 21 (2000): 345–67; Jeffrey H. Dyer and Wujin Chu, "The Economic Value of Trust in Supplier-Buyer Relations," IMVP Working Paper #w-0145a; Marvin B. Lieberman and Shigeru Asaba, "Inventory Reduction and Productivity Growth: A Comparison of the Japanese and U.S. Automotive Sectors," *Managerial and Decision Economics* 18 (1997): 73–85; Marvin B. Lieberman and Lieven Demeester, "Inventory Reduction and Productivity Growth: Linkages in the Japanese Automotive Industry," *Management Science* 45 (1999); Marvin B. Lieberman and Rajeev Dhawan, "Assessing the Resource Base of Japanese and U.S. Auto Producers: A Stochastic Frontier Production Function Approach," *Management Science* 51 (2005), 1060–75.

159 *most admired company:* "Global Most Admired Companies: 2006," *Fortune,* http://money.cnn.com/magazines/fortune/globalmostadmired/top50/index.html (accessed May 31, 2007).

161 *a number of managerial mechanisms:* Dyer and Nobeoka, 345–67.

163 "rather than firm, level": Ibid., 358.

169 *allocated to administrative costs:* Joel I. Klein, "Cross-Licensing and Antitrust Law." Address Before the American Intellectual Property Law Association, May 2, 1997.

169 *through the 1990s:* Josh Lerner and Jean Tirole, "Public Policy Toward Patent Pools," NBER Conference Working Paper, Innovation Policy and the Economy, March 23, 2007.

169 *way to do business:* Carl Shapiro, "Navigating the Patent Thicket: Cross Licenses, Patent Pools, and Standard-Setting," Competition Policy Center, CPC00-011 (2000).

170 *MPEG LA continued to branch out:* Alan Cohen, "Patent Pools' Big Splash," *IP Law & Business,* February 16, 2005.

171 *size and profitability:* Gavin Clarkson, "Objective Identification of Patent Thickets: A Network Analytic Approach" (PhD thesis, Harvard Business School, 2004).

172 *slow the pace of innovation:* Gavin Clarkson and David DeKorte, "The Problem of Patent Thickets in Convergent Technologies," *Annals of the New York Academy of Sciences* 1093 (2006): 180–200.

172 *using prizes to stimulate innovation:* Alan Boyle, "How Prizes Push Progress," MSNBC, June 16, 2004, http://www.msnbc.msn.com/id/5191763/ (accessed May 15, 2007).

173 *Red Lake, Ontario, mine:* Tapscott and Williams, 7–9, 97–99.

174 *all the utopian socialists:* For the Linux and open-source software account, we have relied on several books. These include: Eric S. Raymond, *The Cathedral and the Bazaar: Musings on Linux and Open Source by an Accidental Revolutionary* (Sebastopol, CA: O'Reilly Media, 2001); Linus Torvalds and David Diamond, *Just for Fun: The Story of an Accidental Revolutionary* (New York: Collins, 2002); Glyn Moody, *Rebel Code: Linux and the Open Source Revolution* (New York: Perseus Books Group, 2002); Sam Williams. *Free as in Freedom: Richard Stallman's Crusade for Free Software* (Sebastopol, CA: O'Reilly Media, 2002); Steven Levy, *Hackers: Heroes of the Computer Revolution* (New York: Penguin Books, 1994); and Steven Weber, *The Success of Open Source* (Cambridge, MA: Harvard University Press, 2005).

174 *"money to pay for them":* Tim Blangger, "Free Software Foundation's Richard Stallman: 'Live Cheaply,'" *Linux Insider,* April 4, 2007, http://www.linuxinsider.com/ (accessed June 14, 2007).

177 *"use your code":* Torvalds and Diamond, 77–90.

CHAPTER 7 Simplify

185 *shortly after its launch:* Bryan Chaffin, "iPod Claims 82% HD-Based Retail Market Share," *Macobserver,* October 11, 2004, http://www.macobserver.com/article/2004/10/11.11.shtml (accessed July 22, 2008).

187 *Developing an architecture:* We found a number of books on architecture informative. These

include: Carliss Y. Baldwin and Kim B. Clark, *Design Rules: The Power of Modularity*, vol. 1 (Cambridge, MA: MIT Press, 2000); Gerrit A. Blaauw and Frederick P. Brooks Jr., *Computer Architecture: Concept and Evolution* (Boston: Addison-Wesley, 1997); and Frederick P Brooks Jr., *The Mythical Man-Month: Essays on Software Engineering* (Boston: Addison-Wesley, 1995). There were also several academic articles we found helpful, including: Rebecca M. Henderson and Kim B. Clark, "Architectural Innovation: The Reconfiguration of Existing Product Technologies and the Failure of Established Firms," *Administrative Science Quarterly* 35 (1990): 9–30; Manuel E. Sosa et al., "The Misalignment of Product Architecture and Organizational Structure in Complex Product Development," *Management Science* 50 (2004): 1674–89; and David Sharman and Ali Yassine, "Characterizing Complex Product Architectures," *Systems Engineering Journal* 7 (2004).

188   *moving away from vacuum tubes:* For the IBM 360 account, we relied on the following sources: Emerson W. Pugh et al., *IBM's 360 and Early 370 Systems* (Cambridge, MA: MIT Press, 1991); Bob O. Evans, "Introduction to the SPREAD Report," *IEEE Annals of the History of Computing* 5 (1983): 4–5; J. W. Haanstra et al., "Processor Products—Final Report of the SPREAD Task Group, December 28, 1961," *IEEE Annals of the History of Computing* 5 (1983): 6–26; J. D. Aron et al., "Discussion of the SPREAD Report, June 23, 1982," *IEEE Annals of the History of Computing* 5 (1983): 27–44; Gene M. Amdahl, Gerrit A. Blaauw, and Frederick P. Brooks Jr., "Architecture of the IBM System/360," *IBM Journal of Research and Development* 8 (1964) (reprinted in *IBM Journal of Research and Development* 44 [2000]: 21–36); Blaauw and Brooks, "The Structure of System/360: Part I—Outline of the Logical Structure," *IBM Systems Journal* 3 (1964): 119–35; James E. Strothman, "The Ancient History of System/360," *Invention and Technology Magazine* 5 (1990).

189   *"more chaos than we have today":* Pugh et al., 119.

191   *"blood all over the floor":* T. A. Wise, "IBM's $5,000,000,000 Gamble," *Fortune*, September 1966, 118.

192   *six-, seven- and twelve-bit alternatives:* Amdahl et al., 25.

192   *"performance range factor of 50":* Ibid., 21.

192   *"support efforts":* Haanstra et al., 18.

193   *third day of the meeting:* Interview with Brooks, August 29, 2007.

193   *IBM found itself:* For the IBM PC account, we relied on interviews, books, DVDs, and some academic articles. Interviews included: Bill Lowe, the original IBM PC architect; Neil Colvin, Lance Hansche, and Tom Jennings of what was then Phoenix Software Associates; and Ira Perlow of Computer Systems Design & Associates. Books include: Paul Freiberger and Michael Swaine, *Fire in the Valley: The Making of the Personal Computer* (New York: McGraw-Hill, 1984); James Chposky and Ted Leonsis, *Blue Magic: The People, Power and Politics Behind the IBM Personal Computer* (New York: Facts on File, 1988); and Robert X. Cringely, *Accidental Empires: How the Boys of Silicon Valley Make Their Millions, Battle Foreign Competition and Still Can't Get a Date* (Boston: Addison-Wesley, 1992); as well as Cringely's documentary, *Triumph of the Nerds: An Irreverent History of the PC Industry* (New York: Ambrose Video Publishing, 1996), and IBM Personal Computer Hardware Reference Library, *Technical Reference*, rev. ed., 6025008, July 1982. Important articles include: Richard N. Langlois, "External Economies and Economic Progress: The Case of the Microcomputer Industry," *Business History Review* 66 (1992): 1–50; and Tim Paterson, "The Origins of DOS," *Microprocessor Report* 8 (1994): 1–3

194   *"We have a BASIC":* Freiburger and Swaine, 53.

196   *layout, symbols, and all:* Triumph of the Nerds, vol. 2.

199   *project called Mozilla:* Alan MacCormack, John Rusnak, and Carliss Y. Baldwin, "Exploring the Structure of Complex Software Designs: An Empirical Study of Open Source and Proprietary Code," *Management Science* 52 (2006): 1015–30.

199   *Into the breach:* Interview with Brendan Eich, October 2005.

206   *"in 1964 dollars":* Interview with Brooks, August 29, 2007.

208   *"regardless of name chosen":* Paterson, 1.

209   *far from philanthropic:* Interview with Lowe, August 29, 2007.

210   PC World *listed twenty clones:* Andrew Pollack, "Technology; Compatible Computers," *New York Times*, March 3, 1983.

210 *clones of their own:* Pollack, "Panasonic Introduces Computer," *New York Times,* November 29, 1983.

211 *Taiwanese clones:* David E. Sanger, "I.B.M. Sues Rivals On Chip Copyright," *New York Times,* February 1, 1984.

211 *"oddball entry points":* Interview with Tom Jennings, September 2007.

211 *the clean-room technique:* Interview with Kevin Rivette, August 2007.

212 *customized BIOS chips:* Interview with Neil Colvin, September 12, 2007.

213 *it was a pivotal moment:* Interview with Ira Perlow, August 30, 2007.

213 *"Cut-Rate Computers":* Gordon Henry, "Cut-Rate Computers, Get 'Em Here!," *Time,* July 21, 1986.

216 *prior to their withdrawal:* "FTC Ruling May Hit Rambus Royalties," AFX International, August 2, 2006.

217 *"son of Rambus" lawsuit:* "Federal Court Convicts Qualcomm in a 'Son of Rambus' Lawsuit," *Lawfuel,* April 14, 2007.

217 *accused of similar transgressions:* Andrew Pollack, "Jury Tells Six Competitors to Pay Unocal," *New York Times,* November 4, 1997.

224 disruptive technologies: Clayton M. Christenson, *The Innovator's Dilemma: When New Technologies Cause Great Firms to Fail* (Boston: Harvard Business School Press, 1997).

CHAPTER 8 IP Nations

227 *"Xerox Foresees Record Profits":* "Xerox Foresees Record Profits in 1973," *New York Times,* May 25, 1973.

227 *fastest-growing company:* Reflections from the Frontiers (Explorations for the Future: Gordon Research Conferences 1931–2006)—Reflections by Charles Duke, Xerox Innovation Group, www.frontiersofscience.org/reflections.aspx?category=1&essay=21 (accessed April 3, 2007).

228 *fortieth place on the list of corporate giants:* Calculated by authors based on data from the Fortune 500 archive at money.cnn.com/magazines/fortune/fortune500_archive/snapshots/2005/1589 .html.

228 *soon exceed the U.S. gross national product:* "A Lull at Xerox," *Time,* April 12, 1976.

228 *any company in the Fortune 500:* Calculated by authors based on data from the Fortune 500 archive at money.cnn.com/magazines/fortune/fortune500_archive/snapshots/2005/1589 .html.

228 *sixty-six times its 1960 low:* David T. Kearns and David A. Nadler, *Prophets in the Dark* (New York: HarperBusiness, 1992), 4.

228 *Ralph Nader's Raiders:* F. M. Scherer, "Technological Innovation and Monopolization," March 2006 Draft, 29.

228 *"almost impossible to understand":* "Xerox Foresees Record Profits in 1973," *New York Times,* May 25, 1973.

228 *The story of Xerox begins with a lone inventor:* On the life of Chester Carlson: David Owen, *Copies in Seconds: How a Lone Inventor and an Unknown Company Created the Biggest Communication Breakthrough since Gutenberg—Chester Carlson and the Birth of the Xerox Machine* (New York: Simon & Schuster, 2004), and Xerox Corporation, "The Story of Xerography" (1989), www.xerox.com/downloads/usa/en/s/Storyofxerography.pdf.

229 *It took him fifteen years:* "Chester Carlson," Wikipedia, en.wikipedia.org/wiki/Chester_ Carlson (accessed August 8, 2008).

229 *and another decade:* Ibid.

230 *the other charges were "fluff":* Willard K. Tom, "The 1975 Xerox Consent Decree: Ancient Artifacts and Current Tensions," *Antitrust Law Journal,* American Bar Association (2001); 979, citing "Roundtable Discussion on Competition Policy, Intellectual Property and Innovation Markets," Anderson & Gallini, supra note 16, at 448–49 (remarks of Professor F. M. Scherer, chief economist at the Federal Trade Commission from 1974 to 1976).

230 *"17 years was enough":* Ibid.

230 *"therapeutic intervention":* Ibid.

230 *"social engineering":* Ibid.

230 *out of sync with the courts:* U.S. Supreme Court, *Automatic Radio Co. v. Hazeltine,* 339 U.S. 827

(1950)—"The mere accumulation of patents, no matter how many, is not in and of itself illegal."

231   *"We couldn't conduct a business like that"*: David T. Kearns and David A. Nadler, *Prophets in the Dark: How Xerox Reinvented Itself and Beat Back the Japanese* (New York: HarperBusiness, 1992), 65.

231   *"The patents were simply less important"*: Ibid. 64.

231   *dropped to less than 14 percent*: Timothy F. Bresnahan, "Post-Entry Competition in the Plain Paper Copier Market," *American Economic Review* 75, no. 2, Papers and Proceedings of the Ninety-Seventh Annual Meeting of the American Economic Association (May 1985): 15–19.

232   *in an ironic twist*: "Xerox vs. Apple: Standard 'Dashboard' Is at Issue," *New York Times*, December 20, 1989.

233   *50,000 patents were redistributed to the public*: Marcus A. Hollabaugh and Robert Wright, "Compulsory Licensing under Antitrust Judgments" (staff report of the Subcommittee on Patents, Trademarks and Copyrights, Senate Committee on the Judiciary, Washington, DC, 1960), 2–5.

233   *some of the most important technologies of their day*: F. M. Scherer, "The Political Economy of Patent Policy Reform in the United States," working paper, Harvard University, August 2006, www.researchoninnovation.org/scherer/patpolic.pdf (accessed August 8, 2008).

233   *"largest 'white sale' "*: Robert J. Girouard, U.S. Trade Policy and the Japanese Patent System," working paper no. 89, August 1996, 14, brie.berkeley.edu/publications/WP%2089.pdf (accessed August 8, 2008), quoting the president of the American Chamber of Commerce–Japan.

233   *more than 35,000 technology license agreements*: James C. Abegglen and George Stalk Jr., *Kaisha: The Japanese Corporation* (New York: Basic Books, 1985), 126–27.

233   *"indigenous technology accounted for only 5 percent"*: Ministry of International Trade and Industry, *1982 Japan Science and Technology Outlook* (Tokyo: Fuji Corporation).

234   *A second survey*: Science and Technology Agency, 1972 White Paper on Science and Technology—English Summary, 229; footnote taken from *Asia's New Giant*, 537–38, footnote 19.

234   *"a fraction of what it undoubtedly would have cost"*: U.S.-Japan Strategic Alliances in the Semiconductor Industry: Technology Transfer, Competition, and Public Policy, Committee on Japan, Office of Japan Affairs, Office of International Affairs, National Research Council, (Washington, DC: National Academy Press, 1992), 3–4. Available online at: www.nap.edu/catalog.php?record_id=2021.

235   *the Radio Corporation of America*: Pat Choate, *Hot Property: The Stealing of Ideas in an Age of Globalization* (New York: Knopf, 2005), 157.

236   *Hearings were held*: F. M. Scherer, "The Political Economy of Patent Policy Reform in the United States," working paper, Harvard University, August 2006, www.researchoninnovation.org/scherer/patpolic.pdf (accessed August 8, 2008).

236   *"an extraordinary proposal"*: Pat Choate, *Hot Property: The Stealing of Ideas in an Age of Globalization* (New York: Knopf, 2005), 231.

238   *Venice recognized that it needed to shift its economy*: Ladas and Parry LLP, *A Brief History of the Patent Law of the United States*, www.ladas.com/Patents/USPatentHistory.html (accessed August 8, 2008).

239   *The British patent system was directly conceived*: Christine MacLeod, *Inventing the Industrial Revolution: The English Patent System, 1660–1800* (London: Cambridge University Press, 1988), 11.

239   *England nevertheless led the way*: William Bernstein, *The Birth of Plenty: How the Prosperity of the Modern World Was Created* (New York: McGraw-Hill, 2004), 290.

239   *the price of cotton fell*: Ibid., 219.

240   *In 1811 Francis Cabot Lowell*: John J. Fialka, *War by Other Means: Economic Espionage in America* (New York: Norton Paperbacks, 1999), pp. xi–xvi.

241   *A pirated copy of Dickens's*: Choate, 42.

241   *The United States was not the only nation*: Eric Shiff, *Industrialization Without National Patents: The Netherlands, 1869–1912, Switzerland, 1850–1907* (Princeton, NJ: Princeton University Press, 1971).

242 *The Swiss, for instance:* Dominique S. Ritter, "Switzerland's Patent Law History," *Fordham Intellectual Property, Media, & Entertainment Law Journal* vol. 14, (2004): 463.

243 The World Is Flat: Thomas L. Friedman, *The World Is Flat: A Brief History of the Twenty-First Century* (New York: Picador, 2007).

243 *"The World Is Spiky":* Richard Florida, "The World Is Spiky: Globalization Has Changed the Economic Playing Field, but Hasn't Leveled It," *Atlantic Monthly,* October 2005, 48.

245 *"After twenty years of selling":* P. B. Stone, *Japan Surges Ahead* (New York: Praeger, 1969), 137.

246 *In a recent case:* Ellen Lee, "Apple to Pay $100 Million in iPod Patent Disputes," *San Francisco Chronicle,* August 24, 2006.

246 *Not to be outdone:* As reported in the *Japan Times,* December 8, 2004.

246 *A company can now file an application:* Japan's Intellectual Property Strategic Program 2004, May 27, 2004, www.kantei.go.jp/foreign/policy/titeki/kettei/040527_e.html#68 (accessed August 8, 2008).

247 *"No. 1 strategic reserve":* "Focus of IPR Strategy to Be Broadened," *China Daily,* March 28, 2007, us2.mofcom.gov.cn/aarticle/chinanews/200704/20070404525475.html (accessed August 8, 2008).

247 *"It took Britain 300 years":* Sun Shangwu, "National Strategy on IPR Coming Soon," *China Daily,* October 19, 2007, www.chinadaily.com.cn/china/2007-10/19/content_6189007.htm (accessed August 8, 2008).

247 *"Forty-five percent of the goods":* Lan Xinzhen, "Getting Recognized: There Is Still a Long Way to go for Chinese Brands to Become World-Famous," *Beijing Review,* 2005, www.bjreview.cn/EN/En-2005/05-42-e/bus-1.htm (accessed August 8, 2008).

248 *approaching 60 percent:* China Statistical Yearbook, Ministry of Commerce.

248 *"The new [Five Year] plan":* Yongnian Zheng, China Policy Institute—Briefing Series—Issue 1: *The New Policy Initiatives—China's 11th 5 Year Plan,* www.nottingham.ac.uk/china-policy-institute/publications/documents/Yongnian_China11th5-YearPlan.pdf.

250 *four of the largest apparel exporters:* Profiles of Four Leading Indian Apparel Exporters: Gokuldas Exports, Poppys, Orient Craft, and Jyoti Apparels, *Textiles Intelligence,* May 1, 2004, www.marketresearch.com/product/display.asp?productid=988939&xs=r&SID=35595295-401046487-368598984&curr=USD&kw=%22production+volume%22&view=abs (accessed August 8, 2008).

250 *one of the largest LCD-TV brands:* "AmTRAN's Vizio-Brand LCD TVs Tap into Wal-Mart," *Taiwan Headlines,* english.www.gov.tw/TaiwanHeadlines/index.jsp?categid=9&recordid=93623 (accessed November 28, 2007).

251 *at least $1 billion:* "China Pays US$1 Billion Compensation IPR Disputes," *China Daily,* May 15, 2006, 05.

252 *the vast majority of infringing products:* U.S. Customs and Border Protection and U.S. Immigration and Customs Enforcement—FY 2006 Top Trading Partners for IPR Seizures, www.cbp.gov/linkhandler/cgov/import/commercial_enforcement/ipr/seizure/trading/fy06_ipr_stat.ctt/fy06_ipr_stat.pdf (accessed November 30, 2007).

252 *Those fees added up:* China's Balance of Payments—Royalties and License Fees (Line 2.8b), State Administration of Foreign Exchange, www.safe.gov.cn/model_safe_en/tjsj_en/tjsj_list_en.jsp?ID=30304000000000000&id=3 (accessed August 8, 2008).

252 *"technical trade measures":* "Impact of Foreign Technical Trade Measures," Department of Information Technology, July 12, 2007, bb2.mofcom.gov.cn/aarticle/chinanews/200707/20070704883344.html (accessed August 8, 2008).

252 *One case study in particular:* As reported in various Chinese news outlets, including info.news.hc360.com/html/001/002/003/013/55606.htm (accessed August 8, 2008).

254 *Japanese high-tech companies acquired:* Linda M. Spencer, *Foreign Acquisitions of U.S. High Technology Companies Database Report, October 1988–December 1993* (Washington, DC: Economic Strategy Institute, March 1994).

254 *Virtually every major Japanese company:* Ibid.

255 *a Chinese PC maker, for $2.35 billion:* Purchase price equals $1.25 billion in cash, $0.5 billion in assumed debt, and $0.6 billion in Lenovo stock.

255 *$1.7 trillion in foreign reserves:* State Administration of Foreign Exchange, People's Republic of China. www.safe.gov.cn/model_safe_en/index.jsp (accessed August 8, 2008).

257   *A recent report:* Lin Sun, "TD-SCDMA Poised for Centre Stage: China's Homegrown 3G Standard Threatens to Overshadow WCDMA and CDMA 1xEV-DO," *Telecommunications Online,* November 28, 2006, www.telecommagazine.com/newsglobe/article.asp?HH_ID=AR_2603 (accessed August 8, 2008).

257   *A recent study:* Pei Hong, "Digital Television: Do Not Walk the DVD Old Route," *China Intellectual Property Rights Newspaper,* www.sipo.gov.cn/sipo/zscqb/yaowen/t20040818_32681.htm (accessed January 29, 2007).

259   *Deng Guoshun, a former engineer:* "Chinese Flash-Memory Producer Reaches Settlement in U.S. Patent Case," *China View,* March 26, 2008, www.chinaview.cn.

CHAPTER 9 A Capital Idea

265   *$1.1 trillion per year:* Leonard I. Nakamura, "What Is the US Gross Investment in Intangibles? (at Least) One Trillion Dollars a Year!" working paper no. 01-15, Federal Reserve Bank of Philadelphia, October 2001, 5.

265   *intersection of David Bowie and intellectual property:* "Bowie Bonds—Pioneer Deal Uses Copyright to Raise Capital," *New York Law Journal,* May 15, 1997.

266   Intellectual Capital: Thomas A. Stewart, *Intellectual Capital: The New Wealth of Organizations* (New York: Broadway Books, 1998).

267   The Mystery of Capital: Hernando De Soto, *The Mystery of Capital: Why Capitalism Triumphs in the West and Fails Everywhere Else* (New York: Basic Books, 2003).

267   *In De Soto's words:* Ibid., 7.

268   *venture capital financing:* "Acceleration: Global Venture Capital Insights Report 2007," Ernst & Young, 2007, 10.

269   *The $35 billion:* Ibid., 1.

269   *market for government debt:* William N. Goetzmann and K. Geert Rouwenhorst, eds., *Origins of Value: A Document History of Finance* (New York: Oxford University Press, 2005), 146, 154–55.

269   *market to trade its shares:* Ibid., 165.

269   *Antwerp and Amsterdam:* Ibid., 192–93.

270   *By one count:* The authors maintain a personal list of IP marketplaces that have started, and typically folded.

270   *"progress is cumulative":* James Grant, *Minding Mr. Market: Ten Years on Wall Street with Grant's Interest Rate Observer* (New York: Farrar, Straus & Giroux, 1993), 7.

273   The U.S. Supreme Court: *MercExchange, L.L.C. v. eBay, Inc.,* 275 F.Supp.2d 695 (E.D. Va. 2003), aff'd, 401 F.3d 1323 (Fed. Cir. 2005), vacated and remanded, 547 U.S. 388, 78 U.S.P.Q.2d (BNA) 1577 (2006), on remand, 500 F.Supp.2d 556, 83 U.S.P.Q.2d (BNA) 1688 (E.D. Va. 2007).

273   *Members of the Court:* Ibid., see Justice Kennedy's concurring opinion.

273   *"of money for money":* A. E. Monroe, "Early Economic Thought," London, 1934, 15.

273   *"When contemporary politicians rise":* Edward Chancellor, *Devil Take the Hindmost: A History of Financial Speculation* (New York: Tarcher, 1998), 7.

273   *"illicit practice":* Goetzmann and Rouwenhorst, 159.

273   *"trading wind":* Neil De Marchi and Mary S. Morgan, eds., *Higgling: Transactors and Their Markets in the History of Economics* (New York: Duke University Press, 1994), 6, 51.

273   *"contributed nothing":* Paul Wallace Gates, Jon Gjerde, " 'Roots of Maladjustment' in the Land," *Reviews in American History* 19, no. 1 (March 1991), 142–53.

273   *"the men who own wheat":* Testimony of John Whittaker in *Report of the Industrial Commission on Agriculture and on Taxation in Various States,* Vol. XI (Washington, DC: U.S. Government Printing Office, 1901), 12.

274   *"Speculators actually do very little":* John A. Sparks, "Those Fellows with Black Hats: The Speculators," *The Freeman: Ideas on Liberty* 24 no. 8 (August 1974), 1.

274   *"That the Division of Labour":* Adam Smith, *An Inquiry into the Nature and Causes of the Wealth of Nations* (London: Methuen and Co., Ltd., 1904), ed. Edwin Cannan, Library of Economics and Liberty, title to Book I, Chapter III, www.econlib.org/LIBRARY/Smith/smWN1.html (accessed August 13, 2008).

274   *"I suppose that it's just as silly"*: Conversation with Geoffrey Hyatt, founder and former CEO of the software company Contact Networks, now part of Thomson.

275   *property rights will eventually find their way*: Ronald H. Coase, "The Problem of Social Cost," *Journal of Law and Economics* (October 1960).

276   *One of the seminal moments*: The story of the Commerce One patent auction can be found, along with numerous links to related resources, at the "Cover Pages" Web site called "CommerceNet Proposes Collecting Contributions to Purchase Key Web Services Patents," which can be found at xml.coverpages.org/ni2004-11-24-a.html (accessed August 8, 2008).

279   *from about $1 billion in market capitalization*: February 2008 NAREIT Media Update, National Association of Real Estate Investment Trusts, available online at www.reit.com/portals/0/PDF/Feb08NMU_2.pdf (accessed August 8, 2008).

279   *like the anti-inflammatory drug Remicade*: Information on the securitization of royalty streams from Remicade and other drugs can be obtained from Royalty Pharma at www.royaltypharma.com.

279   *Ocean Tomo, for example*: Information about Ocean Tomo and its auctions, Exchange Traded Funds, and other activities can be found on their Web site at www.oceantomo.com.

280   *Patent Investment Trusts*: Elizabeth D. Ferrill, "Patent Investment Trusts: Let's Build a PIT to Catch the Patent Trolls," *North Carolina Journal of Law & Technology* 6, no. 2 (Spring 2005).

280   *Tradable Technology Baskets*: You can read about "TTBs" at www.ipxi.com/products.html.

280   *One of our favorite business books*: Michael Lewis, *Moneyball: The Art of Winning an Unfair Game* (Boston: Norton, 2003).

281   *a standard for patent valuation*: Joff Wild, "ISO Moves to Establish a Global Standard for Patent Valuation," *Intellectual Asset Management Magazine* blog, at www.iam-magazine.com/blog/detail.aspx?g=04c39ef2-5788-41e7-b772-7db5d103bb5d.

282   *he actually said this belief was wrong*: Deming actually said that "it is wrong to suppose that if you can't measure it, you can't manage it—a costly myth," W. Edwards Deming, *The New Economics for Industry, Government and Education* (New York: MIT Press, 2000), 35.

282   *"expect what you inspect"*: Deming, *The Reference Encyclopedia* online, at www.reference encyclopedia.com/?title=W._Edwards_Deming (accessed February 26, 2008).

285   *is Eddie Lampert*: "The Next Warren Buffett?," *BusinessWeek*, cover story, November 22, 2004.

285   *sold off sixty-eight stores*: Andy Serwer, "A Marriage of Inconvenience," *Fortune* online, December 13, 2004, money.cnn.com/magazines/fortune/fortune_archive/2004/12/13/8214235/index.htm (accessed August 8, 2008).

285   *issued $1.8 billion*: "The New Alchemy at Sears," *BusinessWeek* online, April 16, 2007, www.brandsavants.com/pdfs/TheNewAlchemyatSears.pdf (accessed August 8, 2008).

287   *shareholder activists*: Loeb Partners and Riley Investment Management put pressure on Mosaid and Transmeta to reorganize their companies to take full advantage of their IP holdings. See: Mark LaPedus, "Firm Seeks to Acquire Transmeta," *EE Times* online, January 31, 2008, at www.eetimes.com/news/semi/showArticle.jhtml?articleID=206101360 (accessed August 8, 2008); and "Loeb Partners Calls for Sale of MOSAID Technologies," *TechFinance.ca News Service*, August 15, 2006, at www.techfinance.ca/modules/topnews/news.php?tnid=1064&tnd=20060815 (accessed August 8, 2008).

CHAPTER 10   Strategy Reloaded

289   *"which groups will win out?"*: Ryan Kellett, "Facebook Groups Go Global," ryankellett.com, July 7, 2006, http://ryankellett.com/blog/?p=532 (accessed March 6, 2008).

290   *9 million registered users*: Katharine Q. Seelye, "Microsoft to Provide and Sell Ads on Facebook, the Web Site," *New York Times*, August 23, 2006.

292   *"You've never used them before"*: Neo and Morpheus, *The Matrix*, 1999.

292   *wunderkind Mark Zuckerberg*: For the Facebook account, we have relied on a large number of newspaper and magazine articles, too numerous to list here. Some of the most helpful include: Luke O'Brien, "Poking Facebook," *02138*, November/December 2007, http://www.02138mag.com/magazine/article/1724.html (accessed July 22, 2008); Jeremy Kirk, "Facebook Links Up with Vodafone on Mobile Platform," *New York Times*, February 7, 2008; Louise Story,

"Apologetic, Facebook Changes Ad Program," *New York Times*, December 6, 2007; Saul Hansell, "Facebook to Turn Users into Endorsers," *New York Times*, November 6, 2007; and Michelle Slatalla, "Cyberfamilias," *New York Times*, November 8, 2007.

294   *"You're the one that has to walk through it"*: Morpheus, *The Matrix*, 1999.

304   *"Facebook is clean and clutter-free"*: Tessa Wegert, "Could Facebook Become the New MySpace?," ClickZ, April 12, 2007, http://www.clickz.com/showPage.html?page=3625544 (accessed March 28, 2008).

304   *"Make the world more open"*: Vauhina Vara, "Facebook Opens Its Pages as a Way to Fuel Growth," *Wall Street Journal*, May 21, 2007.

304   *the "anti-MySpace"*: Michael Arrington, "Facebook Launches Facebook Platform; They Are the Anti-MySpace," TechCrunch, May 24, 2007, http://www.techcrunch.com/2007/05/24/facebook-launches-facebook-platform-they-are-the-anti-myspace/ (accessed March 28, 2008).

307   *"I just said it would be the truth"*: Morpheus to Neo, *The Matrix*, 1999.

INDEX